M000201752

SERMONS

OF THE CONSPIRACY OF THE GOWRIES,

.AND OF

THE GUNPOWDER TREASON.

NINETY-SIX SERMONS

BY THE

RIGHT HONOURABLE AND REVEREND FATHER IN GOD,

LANCELOT ANDREWES,

SOMETIME LORD BISHOP OF WINCHESTER.

PUBLISHED BY HIS MAJESTY'S SPECIAL COMMAND.

VOL. IV.

NEW EDITION.

WIPF & STOCK · Eugene, Oregon

Wipf and Stock Publishers
199 W 8th Ave, Suite 3
Eugene, OR 97401

Ninety-Six Sermons by the Right Honourable and Reverend Father in God,
Lancelot Andrewes, Sometime Lord Bishop of Winchester, Vol. IV
By Andrewes, Lancelot
ISBN 13: 978-1-60608-122-8
Publication date 3/03/2009
Previously published by James Parker and Co., 1871

EDITOR'S PREFACE.

This volume contains two separate and entire series of Sermons: the one, upon the Conspiracy of the Gowries, preached upon the fifth of August, consisting of eight Sermons; the other, upon the Gunpowder Treason, preached upon the fifth of November, consisting of ten.

The Sermons in the first series were delivered at intervals between the years 1607 and 1622, both inclusive, before King James I. at Rumsey, Holdenby, Burleigh near Oakham, in the Cathedral Church of Salisbury, and at Windsor. The last Sermon, for 1623, was only prepared to be preached, but was never actually delivered. The whole may be considered as exhibiting in a clear and distinct light, the original source and subsequent derivation of kingly power; the sacredness of the persons of princes, as the anointed of the Lord; the protection afforded them from above, in the discharge of their royal functions; the extreme and desperate wickedness of those who presume, on any pretence whatever, to rise up in rebellion against their authority; and the certainty of drawing down the Divine vengeance upon their heads, and upon their posterity, if they attempt to do so. The arguments in support of these views, are for the most part drawn from Holy Scripture, supported by the authority of Catholic Fathers, and the decrees of Councils.

The Sermons in the second series were all delivered at Whitehall, before King James I., between the years 1606 and 1618, both inclusive. They are in some respects similar to the preceding, particularly as regards the rights of Kings; and are mainly occupied in the consideration of God's infinite mercy in preserving the King and Parliament from the atrocious designs of traitorous conspirators, and of the necessity of keeping up a thankful remembrance of this great deliverance; of the lesson to be learned from the rebuke given to the disciples, who would have called down fire from Heaven upon the Samaritans; of the divine commission with which Kings are entrusted by the King of Kings; of the duty of fearing God and the King, and avoiding the seditious; of the causes to which the failure of the conspiracy in question is attributable, and of the various duties, both public and private, consequent upon the experience of this signal act of mercy.

Such is a brief outline of these discourses; and as they are conversant with principles of scriptural and therefore unchanging truth, they are not of mere temporary interest, referring to past generations with which we have no connection; but are calculated for the instruction of all who are willing to submit to the divine guidance, in their public and social, as well as in their individual relations.

The variations between the texts at the commencement of the Sermons, and the same in the Genevan Bible, are given as before in a note below [a].

[a] The variations are in italics—

CONSPIRACY OF THE GOWRIES.
Serm. I. II. III. No variation.
Serm. IV. Ps. lxxxix. 20—23. Ver. 21. *Therefore* Mine hand shall be *established with him.* ... Ver. 22. The enemy shall not *oppress* him, *neither shall the wicked* hurt him. Ver. 23. But I will destroy. . . .
Serm. V. Ps. xxi. 1—4. Ver. 1. . . . *yea how greatly shall he rejoice in.* . . . Ver. 2. Thou hast *given* him . . . Ver. 3. *For* Thou *didst prevent* him with *liberal* blessings, and *didst* set . . . Ver. 4. *even* is omitted.
Serm. VI. Esther ii. 21—23. Ver. 21. Bigthan and Teresh, *which kept the door,* were wroth . . . .
Serm. VII. and VIII. No variation.

GUNPOWDER TREASON.
Serm. I. Ps. cxviii. 23, 24. Ver. 23. This *was* . . .
Serm. II. III. IV. V. No variation.
Serm. VI. Prov. xxiv. 21—23. Ver. 21. . . . and meddle not with them that are *seditious.* Ver. 22. . . . and who knoweth the *ruin* of . . . Ver. 23. *Also* those things *pertain* to . . .
Serm. VII. No variation.
Serm. VIII. Isaiah xxxvii. 3. . . . *no* strength . . . .
Serm. IX. Luke i. 74, 75. Ver. 74. . . . *out of* the hands . . . *should* serve Him . . . Ver. 75. The order is changed. *All the days of our life, in holiness and righteousness before Him.*
Serm. X. No variation.

The Editor has to acknowledge his obligations to the Rev. C. Seager, M.A., formerly Scholar of Worcester College, and also to the Rev. J. B. Morris, M.A., Fellow of Exeter College, for revising the Hebrew quotations which have occurred in the course of this volume.

J. P. W.

Magdalene College,
All Saints' Day,
1841.

CONTENTS.

SERMONS OF THE CONSPIRACY OF THE GOWRIES.

PREACHED UPON THE FIFTH OF AUGUST.

SERMON I.

(Page 3.)

Preached before the King's Majesty at Rumsey, on the Fifth of August,
A.D. MDCVII.

2 SAMUEL xviii. 32.

And Cushi answered, The enemies of my Lord the King, and all that rise against thee to do thee hurt, be as that young man is.

SERMON II.

(Page 24.)

Preached before the King's Majesty at Holdenby, on the Fifth of August,
A.D. MDCVIII.

1 SAMUEL xxvi. 8, 9.

Then said Abishai to David, God hath closed thine enemy into thine hand this day : now therefore, I pray thee, let me smite him once with a spear to the earth, and I will not smite him again.
And David said to Abishai, Destroy him not : for who can lay his hand on the Lord's anointed, and be guiltless ?

SERMON III.

(Page 43.)

Preached before the King's Majesty at Holdenby, on the Fifth of August,
A.D. MDCX.

1 CHRONICLES xvi. 22.

Touch not Mine Anointed.

SERMON IV.

(Page 77.)

Preached before the King's Majesty at Burleigh, near Oakham, on the Fifth
of August, A.D. MDCXIV.

PSALM lxxxix. 20—23.

I have found David My servant; with My holy oil have I
anointed him.
My hand shall hold him fast (or, stablish him;) and Mine arm
shall strengthen him.
The enemy shall not be able to do him violence; the son of
wickedness shall not hurt him.
But I will smite down his foes before his face, and plague them
that hate him.

SERMON V.

(Page 103.)

Preached before the King's Majesty in the Cathedral Church at Salisbury,
on the Fifth of August, A.D. MDCXV.

PSALM xxi. 1—4.

The King shall rejoice in Thy strength, O Lord; exceeding
glad shall he be of Thy salvation.
Thou hast granted him his heart's desire, and hast not denied
him the request of his lips.   Selah.
Thou hast prevented him with the blessings of goodness; and
hast set a crown of pure gold upon his head.
He asked life of Thee, and Thou gavest him a long life, even
for ever and ever.

SERMON VI.

(Page 128.)

Preached before the King's Majesty at Burleigh, near Oakham, on the Fifth
of August, A.D. MDCXVI.

ESTHER ii. 21—23.

*In those days, when Mordecai sat in the King's gate, two of the
King's eunuchs, Bigthan and Teresh, were wroth, and sought
to lay hands on the King Ahasuerus.*

*And the thing was known to Mordecai, and he told it unto
Queen Esther, and Esther certified the King thereof, in
Mordecai's name.*

*And when inquisition was made, it was found so; therefore
they were both hanged on a tree: and it was written in the
book of the chronicles before the King.*

SERMON VII.

(Page 155.)

Preached before the King's Majesty at Windsor, on the Fifth of August,
A.D. MDCXXII.

1 SAMUEL xxiv. 5—8.

*And the men of David said unto him, See the day is come
whereof the Lord said unto thee, Behold, I will deliver thine
enemy into thine hand, and thou shalt do to him as it shall
seem good to thee.   Then David arose, and cut off the lap of
Saul's garment privily.*

*And afterward, David was touched in his heart, because he had
cut off the lap which was on Saul's garment.*

*And he said unto his men, The Lord keep me from doing that
thing unto my master the Lord's anointed, to lay my hand
upon him, for he is the anointed of the Lord.*

*So David overcame his servants with these words, and suffered
them not to rise against Saul.   So Saul rose up out of the
cave, and went away.*

SERMON VIII.

(Page 185.)

Prepared to be preached on the Fifth of August, A.D. MDCXXIII.

GENESIS xlix. 5—7.

Simeon and Levi, brethren in evil; the instruments of cruelty are in their habitations.

Into their secret let not my soul come; my glory, be not thou joined with their assembly: for in their wrath they slew a man, and in their self-will (or fury) *they digged down a wall.*

Cursed be their wrath, for it was fierce; and their rage, for it was cruel: I will divide them in Jacob, and scatter them in Israel.

SERMONS OF THE GUNPOWDER TREASON,

PREACHED UPON THE FIFTH OF NOVEMBER.

SERMON I.

(Page 205.)

Preached before the King's Majesty at Whitehall, on the Fifth of November, A.D. MDCVI.

PSALM cxviii. 23, 24.

This is the Lord's doing, and it is marvellous in our eyes.

This is the day which the Lord hath made; let us rejoice and be glad in it.

SERMON II.

(Page 225.)

Preached before the King's Majesty at Whitehall, on the Fifth of November,
A.D. MDCVII.

PSALM cxxvi. 1—4.

*When the Lord brought again the captivity of Sion, we were
like them that dream.*

*Then was our mouth filled with laughter, and our tongue with
joy ; then said they among the heathen, The Lord hath done
great things for them.*

The Lord hath done great things for us, whereof we rejoice.

O Lord, bring again our captivity, as the rivers in the South.

SERMON III.

(Page 243.)

Preached before the King's Majesty at Whitehall, on the Fifth of November,
A.D. MDCIX.

LUKE ix. 54—56.

*And when His disciples James and John saw it, they said,
Lord, wilt Thou that we command that fire come down from
Heaven, and consume them, even as Elias did?*

*But Jesus turned about and rebuked them, and said, Ye know
not of what spirit ye are.*

*For the Son of man is not come to destroy men's lives, but to
save them.*

SERMON IV.

(Page 263.)

Preached before the King's Majesty at Whitehall, on the Fifth of November,
A.D. MDCXII.

LAMENTATIONS iii. 22.

*It is the Lord's mercies that we are not consumed, because His
compassions fail not.*

SERMON V.

(Page 279.)

Preached before the King's Majesty at Whitehall, on the Fifth of November,
A.D. MDCXIII.

PROVERBS viii. 15.

By Me Kings reign.

SERMON VI.

(Page 298.)

Preached before the King's Majesty at Whitehall, on the Fifth of November,
A.D. MDCXIV.

PROVERBS xxiv. 21—23.

*My son, fear thou the Lord, and the King; and meddle not
with them that are given to change.
For their destruction shall rise suddenly; and who knoweth the
destruction of them both?
These things also belong to the wise.*

SERMON VII.

(Page 320.)

Preached before the King's Majesty at Whitehall, on the Fifth of November,
A.D. MDCXV.

PSALM cxlv. 9.

*The Lord is good to all, and His mercies are over all His
works.*

SERMON VIII.

(Page 344.)

Preached before the King's Majesty at Whitehall, on the Fifth of November,
A.D. MDCXVI.

ISAIAH xxxvii. 3.

*The children are come to the birth, and there is not strength
to bring forth.*

SERMON IX.

(Page 365.)

Preached before the King's Majesty at Whitehall, on the Fifth of November,
A.D. MDCXVII.

LUKE i. 74, 75.—7th and 8th verses of BENEDICTUS.

That we being delivered from the hands of our enemies might serve Him without fear,
In holiness and righteousness before Him, all the days of our life.

SERMON X.

(Page 389.)

Preached before the King's Majesty at Whitehall, on the Fifth of November,
A.D. MDCXVIII.

ESTHER ix. 31.

To confirm these days of Purim according to their seasons; as Mordecai the Jew, and Esther the Queen had appointed them, and as they had promised for themselves, and for their seed, with fasting and prayer. .

SERMONS

PREACHED UPON THE FIFTH OF AUGUST.

A SERMON

PREACHED BEFORE

THE KING'S MAJESTY AT RUMSEY,

ON THE FIFTH OF AUGUST, A.D. MDCVII.

---

2 SAMUEL xviii. 32.

*And Cushi answered, The enemies of my Lord the King, and
all that rise against thee to do thee hurt, be as that young
man is.*

[*Cui respondens Chusi, Fiant, inquit, sicut puer, inimici domini mei
Regis, et universi qui consurgunt adversus eum in malum.* Lat.
Vulg.]

[*And Cushi answered, The enemies of my Lord the King, and all that
rise against thee to do thee hurt, be as that young man is.* Eng.
Trans.]

THAT young man was Absalom. And he was now hanging
upon an oak, with three darts through him. Like him doth
Cushi wish all may be, that do as he did : that is, be the
King's enemies, and rise up against him. For I find in the
text a dangerous treason plotted against King David : plotted,
but defeated ; and Absalom, the author of it, brought to a
wretched end. Good news thereof brought by Cushi that
saw it. And that good news here concluded with this wish,
That all the King's enemies may speed no better, no otherwise than he sped. For all the world, like glad tidings doth
this day afford us, in a like memorable example of God's just
proceeding against a couple of like treacherous wretches.
A barbarous and bloody treason they imagined against our

B 2

S E R M. sovereign[a]. God brought their mischief upon their own
I. heads, *Et facti sunt sicut Absalom.* And we are here now

[a] [The following account of this re-
markable conspiracy from Arch-
bishop Spotswood may not be un-
acceptable to the reader :
" It was in August this year (1600)
that the conspiracy of Gowry fell forth ;
a conspiracy plotted by him alone, and
only communicated to Mr. Alexander,
his brother; two youths of great hope,
at whose hands no man could have ex-
pected such an attempt. Their father
had been taken away by form of justice
in the year 1584, whilst the King was
yet a minor, and forced he was unto
it, as unto many other things that
agreed not with his mind. But the
care he took of the nobleman's children,
and kindness wherewith he used them,
did shew how much he disliked that
proceeding ; for he restored the eldest
to his father's honour and living, his
brother Alexander he made one of his
bed-chamber, a sister of theirs he preferred to be chief maid about his
Queen, and had a purpose to advance
the Earl himself to a principal office of
the kingdom. Such and so great benefits might have endeared the most barbarous and hard-hearted. But benefits
are no benefits to the malicious, and
those that are set for revenge. The
device was, to allure the King to the
Earl's house at Perth, and there to kill
him. The King was then remaining
in Falkland, and one day early in the
morning (it was the fifth of August), as
he was going to take his sport in the
park, Alexander meets him and telleth
that his brother had intercepted a man,
a Jesuit as he supposed, with a great
quantity of gold, and that he kept the
man fast in his house at Perth, and
sent him with the news, praying the
King to make haste, for that he doubted
not he should learn things worthy of
his travail. The King, moving some
questions touching the man's station
and habit, and the place where he was
taken, received no other answer, but
that his brother would satisfy all those
things at his coming ; which put him
on a suspicion that the gentleman was
distracted, for he observed in him some
perturbation : yet because of the instance he made he yielded to go, willing him to ride back, and shew that
he would be with his brother before
dinner.

" After a short chase, and a buck
killed, the King made towards Perth,
accompanied with the Duke of Lennox,
the Earl of Mar, and a few gentlemen, all in their hunting coats. By
the way the King did ask the Duke of
Lennox, if he had known Mr. Alexander (for the Duke had married his
sister) at any time troubled or distem-
pered in his wits. The Duke answering that he had never known any such
thing in him, the King insisted no farther. Being come to the town, the
Earl did meet him, and was noted by
all the company to be in some trouble
of mind, the very imagination of the
fact he went about perplexing his
thoughts. But he coloured all with the
want of entertainment, saying that he did
not expect the King, and that his dinner was not prepared. The King wishing him not to trouble himself with
those thoughts, because a little thing
would content him, and for the noble-
men a part of his dinner would suffice
them, they discoursed of hunting and
other common matters till meat was
dressed. How soon the King had
taken a little refreshment, and the
Lords were placed at a table in another room, Mr. Alexander did sound
in the King's ear, that the time was fit,
whilst the Lords were at dinner, to go
and examine the stranger. At which
word the King arose, and went up
stairs, Mr. Alexander going before him.
The King did call Sir Thomas Erskine,
afterwards Earl of Kelly, to follow
him ; but Mr. Alexander turning at
the door, after the King was entered,
said that the King willed him to stay
below, whereupon Sir Thomas went
back. Thus the door was shut, and
Mr. Alexander guiding him to an inner
room, the King did perceive a man
standing alone, whereupon he asked if
that was the man. 'Nay,' said Mr. Alexander, 'there is another business in
hand ;' and with that word covering his
head, 'You remember,' said he, 'how
you used my father, and now must
answer for it.' 'Your father?' answered
the King, 'I was not the cause of his
death ; it was done in my minority by
form of justice. But is this your purpose, and have you trained me hither
to murder me? Did you learn this
lesson of Mr. Robert Rollock your

to renew with joy the memory of these glad tidings: and withal, to pray Cushi's prayer, and all to say Amen to it, That

master? or think you, when you have done your will, to go unpunished?' Mr. Alexander, stricken with the speeches, and the man who was placed there to assist him trembled for fear, desired the King to be quiet, and make no noise, for that he would go speak with his brother, and pacify him. This said, he went down a back way, as it seemed, to the court below.

"Whether he did meet with his brother at that time or not is unknown, but his stay was short, and when he returned, he said to the King, 'There is no remedy, you must die.' Then making as though he would tie the King's hands, they fell a-wrestling, and the King drawing him by force to a window in the corner that looked toward the street, as he espied the Earl of Mar, cried 'Help Earl of Mar, help!' The voice and words were discerned by all the Lords and Gentlemen, who thereupon ran to seek the King by the way that went up; but the doors being shut, there was no entry that way till the same was broke by force, which took up a large time. Upon the first cry, Sir Thomas Erskine, suspecting treason, did flee upon Gowry, and taking him by the gorge said, 'Thou art the traitor;' but they were quickly sundered by his servants that stood by. The first that came to the King was a page called John Ramsey, who falling upon a back passage by which the traitors, after the deed committed, had purposed to escape, found the King and Mr. Alexander struggling. The King calling to him and bidding him strike the traitor, he gave Mr. Alexander two or three wounds with his dagger, and so parted him from the King. The man who was placed there to assist Mr. Alexander did steal away secretly; and he himself, perceiving that the treason was discovered, made down the stairs, where being encountered by Sir Thomas Erskine, and asked how the King was, because he gave no direct answer, and only said, that he took God to witness that he was not in the fault, he thrust him through the body with his sword, and killed him outright.

"Sir Thomas was followed by Hugh Hereise, Doctor of Medicine, and a foot-boy named Wilson, who seeing the King safe were not a little joyed, and placing him in a little room, and shut-ting the door, they prepared to defend the entry. Gowry, accompanied with three or four servants, breaketh presently into the chamber, and with his two swords, one in each hand, puts them all to their shift, and had undoubtedly overthrown them, but that one of the company crying, 'You have killed the King our master, and will you also take our lives?' he became astonished, and setting the points of his two swords to the earth, as if he minded to cease from any more fight, he was instantly stricken by the page with a rapier which pierced the heart, so as he fell down dead. The servants, seeing him fall, made away; only Mr. Thomas Cranston being sore wounded, and not able to shift for himself, was apprehended. In this fight Sir Thomas Erskine and Doctor Hereise were both hurt, but nothing dangerously.

"By this time the doors of the other passage being made open, the Lords and a number with them entered into the room, who hearing what happened went all to their knees, and the King himself, conceiving a prayer, gave thanks to God for his deliverance, and that the device of those wicked brothers was turned upon their own heads. The danger that ensued was not much less, for the people of the town taking up arms did environ the house, crying to give them out their Provost, otherwise they should blow them all up with powder. The rage of the multitude was great, (for they loved the Earl, as being their Provost, beyond all measure,) and with great difficulty were they kept back from using violence. At last the bailies and certain of the citizens being admitted to enter and brought to the King, when they were informed of the truth of things, returned and pacified the people. After which the King took horse and returned to Falkland, where he was welcomed (the rumour of the danger having prevented his coming) with great acclamations of joy.

* * * *

"The 15th of November, a Parliament was held at Edinburgh, wherein sentence of forfeiture was pronounced against Gowry and Mr. Alexander his brother, their posterity disinherited, and in detestation of the parricide attempted, the whole surname of Ruthven abolished. But this last was afterwards

SERM.   the like end may ever come to the like attempts. Last year
I.
———   we changed but one word; David into James: we change no
more now, but the number; one into two. The enemies of
my lord be as that young man, saith Cushi. Say we, The
enemies of our lord be as those two young men were: those
Gen. 49, 5. two "brethren" in mischief. I will not do them that honour,
to name them; no more than Cushi did him here.

The words we read, as a prayer; they may also be read as
a prophecy. Either, Let them be; or, They shall be as that
young man is (for the verb is the future tense). They have
no other way, in Hebrew, to express their optative but so:
that hard it is, many times, to say whether it be a prayer
or a prediction, that so runs in the future. And for aught I
know, it must be left to the discretion of the translator, to
[Ps. 21. 1.] take which he will, since it may be both. As Psalm the
twenty-first, either, "The King shall rejoice," by way of
foretelling: or, "Let the King rejoice," by way of wishing.
The sure way is, to take it both ways: so, we shall be sure
not to miss Cushi's meaning. And so will we do, (for so we
may do,) even take it both ways: for it is both: both a good
prayer, and a true prophecy. And prayer and prophecy
sort well together. ῞Ο τις βούλεται τοῦτο καὶ οἴεται, saith
the philosopher. *Affectiones facile faciunt opiniones,* saith
the Schoolman. Our wishes we would always have ominous,
and our prayer turn into the nature of a prediction. What
we pray for rightly, we would gladly persuade ourselves
shall be certainly.

The di-   Of this prophetical prayer then. I. As a prayer, first;
vision.
1.   II. then, as a prophecy. Prayer is of two sorts: 1. for, or
2. against. As 1. for good, so 2. against evil; both things
and persons. This is against, a kind of prayer; indeed, an

dispensed with, and such of that name
as were known to be innocent tolerated
by the King's clemency to enjoy their
surnames and titles as in former times.
The bodies of the two brothers, being
brought to the Parliament-house were,
after sentence given, hanged upon a gibbet in the public street, and then dis-
membered, their heads cut off and af-
fixed upon the top of the prison-house.
This done, the Estates, in acknowledgment of the favours and grace they all
had received of God, by the miraculous,

and extraordinary preservation of his
Majesty from that treasonable attempt,
did ordain, 'That in all times and ages
to come, the fifth of August should be
solemnly kept with prayers, preachings,
and thanksgivings for that benefit, dis-
charging all work, labour, and other
occupations upon the said day, which
might distract the people in any sort
from those pious exercises.' "—Spotswood's History of the Church of Scotland, Book 6. Anno 1600.]

imprecation. Two things give forth themselves in the prayer: 1. The parties, against whom it is; 2. and the wish itself, what it is. The parties are, 1. first, the King's enemies: 2. then, those that rise up against him, that is, the King's rebels. Two diverse kinds : neither superfluous. For there be no tautologies in Scripture: no doubling the point there, but with some advantage ever.

The wish is, that they may be as Absalom. And two things are in that wish (if we mark them well): 1. Be as he: that is, not perish only (that is not all); 2. but perish, and so perish, as he did. How was that? *Vidi Absalom pendentem,* 2 Sam. 18. and so hanging yet alive, thrust through with three darts. 10. As he, in his end : as he, in the manner of his end. That the heads that contrive may hang as high as his; and the hearts that effect, be thrust through as his was: thrice through, though once would serve.

And when we have done with it, as a prayer; then will we II. begin with it, as a prophecy. That, so he wished; and that, as he wished, so he foretold; and as he foretold, so it came to pass. All that rose after fell as fast as they rose; *et facti sunt sicut puer iste.*

Last of all, that this prayer or prophecy is not pent or shut III. up in David's days: not to end with him. It reacheth unto these of ours. Hath his force and vigour still : hath, and shall have, unto the world's end. God heard him praying, and inspired him prophesying. As it came to pass in Absalom, so did it in those that rose after him : that rose against David, that rose against many others since David, and namely, against ours. So it hath been hitherto ; and so ever may it be ! Cushi, not only a Priest, to pray that so they be ; but a Prophet, to foretell that so they shall be.

Fiant sicut Absalom, is a prayer, and, which more is, an im- I. precation. Before we pray it, it will not be amiss, to enquire Of the text whether we may lawfully pray any such, or no. I move it, as a prayer against, or because of some so tender-hearted men, that they can by no cursing. means brook or endure any imprecation ; to wish any so evil, as to pray they may come to an evil end. It is nothing fit- ting, (as well saith St. James,) that with the tongue we should Jas. 3. 9. bless God; and with the same wish evil to man. It is Ba- laam's office, *veni et maledic;* and who would succeed him in Nu. 22. 6.

SERM. his office? It is Shimei's practice; and who would be like
I. him? And this is Cushi's prayer, like himself: some would
2 Sam. 16. have him an Ethiopian; but some black swart fellow, as his
13. name giveth.

Again, these were Jews all; we are Christians. We have a
charge given us by St. Paul not to do it: not to them that
Rom. 12. do us hurt. "Bless them that persecute you : bless," I say,
14. "and curse not." We have a pattern set us by St. Peter, of
1 Pet. 2.23. Him, *Qui cum malediceretur non, &c.* That wished not their
evil, that both wished, and did Him all the evil they could,
both in deed and in word.

And this I know : yet is not all this so peremptory, but
that notwithstanding even all this, against some, in some
cases, such prayer hath been, and may be used. May be?
nay, ought to be otherwhile. For such may the persons be,
2 Pet.2.14. as St. Peter called some, *maledictionis filii :* and their facts so
Deu.27.13. execrable, as God Himself commanded Moses to go up into
the mount Ebal, and there, against twelve sundry sorts of
such, pronounce *maledictus.* Even as we see, the serpent's
Gen. 3. 14. sin was so exorbitant, as it drew a *maledictus*, even from God's
own blessed mouth. It is not good then, to be nice or tender
in this point; nor I would not wish men to be more tender
or pitiful than God ; whose doing of it sheweth us it ought to
be done. For to begin with the last (of Christians). He that
Acts 13. 10. gave us the charge, (St. Paul,) for all his charge given, we
know what he did to Elymas. And he that set us the pat-
tern, (St. Peter,) for all his pattern set, we know he used it
Acts 8. 20. against Simon Magus. And for the other: it is not Balaam
Nu. 12. 3. only; but even Moses, as mild a man as ever the earth bare, you
Nu. 16. 15. may read that he came to it though. Neither was it Shimei
only, but David too: (though a gracious and gentle prince,
may Shimei well say ; yet) what a Psalm of imprecations hath
he penned! I mean the one hundred and ninth Psalm. It
was thought by our fathers, that there was not a more heavy
or bitter curse could be wished to any, than to say *Deus
laudum* upon him, which is the beginning of that Psalm.
Neither was it Cushi with his swart colour only, but an Angel
as bright as the sun, even the Angel of the Lord, that curseth
Jud. 5. 23. (himself), and giveth an express warrant to curse the inhabit-
ants of Meroz. But what speak we of Saints, or Angels?

Christ Himself doth it in the Gospel, as appeareth by His Lu. 11. 43, many *Væs.* Yea, God Himself, we see, against the serpent, &c. Gen. 3. 14. and his whole brood. What the Saints, Angels, God Himself, have done, may be done, I trust. It may be done then, *licet;* and ought to be done sometimes, *oportet :* and in this very case, it ought and must : a necessity lieth upon us, we cannot choose but do it. For pray we must for the King's safety : Cushi, and all good subjects; but for his safety we cannot pray, but we must (withal) for the overthrow of his underminers. *Pro* includeth *contra :* if for him, then against his foes. If wish him to rise, and stand upright; then them to fall, and become his "footstool." So that, if all be well Ps. 110. 1. weighed, it is not voluntary, it is even wrung from us.

And that indeed is the only caveat, that it be not voluntary : that we be drawn to it hardly, and use it not upon every slight and trifling occasion, against every thing that crosseth our humour ; but when the foulness of the fact seems to exact it : and that caveat is not amiss. I like well of the Hebrew proverb : (Gerizim is the mount where they blessed ; Ebal, where they gave the curse :) they say, We must creep into Ebal, and leap into Gerizim : that is, be swift to one, and slow to the other. We are then not to forswear going into mount Ebal utterly ; but to be well advised, ere we go into it. To do it, but not to do it, where God blesseth : which Balaam Nu. 22. was still itching to do. The cause it is, which maketh the [19, &c.] curse fall; otherwise, if it be causeless, it will not light, but fly over as a bird. Therefore, to know well, both men and matter, against whom we let it fly. And we cannot better know them, than if we take our light from God : if we do it, but where, and when, and for what, God doth it, we need not be scrupulous : never fear to follow, where He goeth before us. And, by the grace of God, we will be well aware, not to wish aught to any, in this point, but such as shall have warrant even from God's own mouth.

The special point of advice thus being, to know the parties 1. well, against whom we send it forth; it will concern us, (and The parties cursed. our next point it must be,) to take perfect notice of these men. They offer themselves to us, in two terms : 1. "The enemies Ps. 3. 1. of the King;" 2. They that "rise against" him : joined here, Ps. 59. 1. Ps. 44. 5. and as here, so in sundry other places.

SERM.   The word "enemy" is by David himself glossed, Psalm the
I.   fifty-fifth. "It was not an enemy did it to me:" meaning

1. The
enemies   a known, open, professed enemy ; "for then," saith he, "I
of the   could have been provided for him :" so may we take it.
king.
Ps. 55. 12. The other of "rising against," the phrase is first used of

2. Those Cain (and lightly the first phrase is the key of the rest) ; when
that rise
against   Abel and he were in the field together walking, it is said,
him.   "Cain rose up against him," and knocked him on the head: so
Gen. 4. 8.
          is meant of such as keep their malice secret, to do one a mis-
          chief suddenly. And the next time it is used, is of Korah,

Nu. 16. 2. and his complices : of them it is said, "They rose up against
          Moses." In the former of Cain, it is treachery; in this latter of
          Korah, it is plain rebellion. In a word, all that " rise against"
          are "enemies ;" but not backward. For enemies may be such
          as stand on even ground ; as one King, or state, with another.
          Rising, in propriety of speech, is of such as are of inferior
          place, and yet lift themselves up against their lawful superiors.
          In the end, both prove enemies, and do the part of enemies ;
          but the former have many times no bond of allegiance ; the
          latter ever have.

1 Pet. 4.12. We may not ξενίζεσθαι, (to use St. Peter's own phrase,)
          "think it strange," that both these sorts, Kings have them :
          yea, though they be good Kings, (as was David,) yet that they

Ps. 3. 1. have them. Hear David himself speak : " How are mine ene-
          mies increased? many are they that rise against me." Nei-
          ther the place of a King, nor the virtue of a good King, could
          quit him, but he had both. He had " enemies :" Ishbosheth,
          Hanun, Hadadezer, the States of the Philistines. He had
          those that "rose against" him : Absalom, Ahithophel, Amasa,
          here; Sheba, Adonijah, Joab, afterward; he had both. And
          let us not ξενίζεσθαι " think this strange ;" since Christ Him-

Ps. 92. 9. self, yea, since God Himself hath them too. " For, lo Thine
          enemies, O Lord, lo Thine enemies," and those that rise up
          against Thee (it is the ninety-second Psalm). That we may
          cease to marvel that Kings have them ; or think it is because
          it is not as it should be. Be they never so as they should;

1 Sam. 13. be they as David, "according to God's own heart ;" nay, be
14.
          they as Christ, as God Himself; both these they shall have.
          Let not this make us stumble, but that we may go forward.
          Of these two then, if we shall fit ourselves to the present,

we shall not need to speak of the one sort, of "enemies." The
King hath none: no King, nor state, profess themselves for
such; nor never may do. The latter, it shall not be amiss to
stay a little, and look better on, who they be. This day's peril
was, all his peril, both in August and November, is from
them that (like Cain,) rise up against him. A King by nature
is *Rex Alkum,* saith Solomon; one, against whom there is no Prov. 30,
rising: so God would have it. Subjects, saith the Apostle, אַל־קוּם
to lie down before them: rising up against is clean contrary Heb. 13, 17.
to that; and so, contrary to God's will. He would have no
rising. The thought to rise (*voluerunt insurgere in Regem*) is
said of Bigthan and Teresh, two of Ahasuerus' chamber,
(mark that *voluerunt insurgere*) was enough to attaint them: Esther 2.
the rising but of the will, to bring them to the gallows. Nor 21.
the tongue is not to rise, or lift up itself. Korah did but gain-
say: his tongue was but up, and he, and all that took his part,
perished in their gainsaying, "the gainsaying of Korah." But Jude 11.
chiefly none, either, with Judas, to "lift up his heel" to betray; Joh. 13. 18.
or, with Cain, to lift up the hand to do violence. No party,
no part of any party, to rise against the King. Yet, rise they
will, and do: both the thought swell, and *exsurgent e vobis,* Acts 20. 30.
saith the Apostle, *perversa loquentes,* yea, and *perversa fa-
cientes:* lewd speech used; and, worse than speech, presump-
tuous deeds too.

Now of these that thus rise, two sorts there be. For either they rise against the very state itself of Kings, the very
authority they exercise: that is, would have no Kings at all;
saying with them, *Quis est Dominus noster,* "Who is Lord Ps. 12. 4.
over us?" as much to say as, by their good will, none; or
such as only rise against their persons, as he in the twentieth
chapter, that said, "We have no part in David;" and they 2 Sam.
in the Gospel, that say, *Nolumus hunc,* "We will not have 20. 1.
this man." Rule they would not have quite taken away; but Lu. 19. 14.
not this person to rule over them.

Of the first sort of these risers, are the Anabaptists of our
age, by whom all secular jurisdiction is denied. No law-
makers they, but the Evangelists: no courts, but Presbyteries:
no punishments, but Church-censures. These rise against
the very estate of Kings: and that should they find and feel,
if they were once grown enough to make a party.

SERM.
I.
A second sort there be, that are but bustling themselves to rise: not yet risen; at least not to this step: but in a forwardness they be; proffer at it, that they do. They that seek to bring parity, not into the Commonwealth, by no means; but only into the Church. All parishes alike, every one absolute, entire of itself. No dependency, or superiority, or subordination. But, this once being had, do we not know their second position? Have they not broached it long since? The Church is the house; the Commonwealth but the hangings. The hangings must be made fit to the house, that is, the Commonwealth fashioned to the Church; not the house to the hangings: no, take heed of that. And when they were taken with it, and charged with it, how slightly in their answer do they slip it over. These, when they are got thus far, may rise one step higher; and as Aaron now must not, so (perhaps) neither must Moses, then, exalt himself above Nu. 16. 3. the congregation, seeing that all God's people are "holy," no less than he.

These two rise against their states. Against their persons, two other sorts of persons, both discontented. 1. But the 2 Sam. 15. 2—6. one was, of ambition: as Absalom here, that thought it was wonderful great pity, that all causes were not brought before him, considering how able a man he was for it, and the King being negligent in looking to his subjects' grief. But when 2 Sam. 16. 22. he spread a tent aloft, and did you know what, not to be told, and that in the sight of all Israel; sure, he that could commit that villanous act in the eyes of all Israel, he that 2 Sam. 16. 17. could charge Hushai, as with a foul fault, for forsaking his friend, himself, then being in armour against his own father, was not so very fit a man to do justice. No matter: so he took himself; that was enough, to rise. 2. The other, out of revenge (the case of Bigthan and Teresh: and of our two, as is thought). They were angry at somewhat, it is not said Esther 2. 21. what, nor it skills not what, but *voluerunt insurgere*, rise they would for it, that they would. These did not wish government quite taken away; only the King's person they heaved at. Him, for some purpose, they must needs have out of the way.

By this time we know the parties reasonable well. Be these they whom God, Angels, and Saints, hold for execrable? They, whom Cushi may pray against, and we with him? These be they. It was Korah, one of the crew, against whom Moses prayed, they might be visited with a strange visitation, and not die the common death of other Nu. 16. 29. men. No more he did. It was Ahithophel, another of them, against whom David penned the Psalm of bitter imprecations. They of Meroz, whom the Angel giveth warrant, and charge both, to curse: wherefore was it? Because "they came not [Jud. 5. to help the Lord," that is, Deborah, the Lord's lieutenant, 23.] against the forces of Midian. If to be cursed, because they laid not their hand to help him, much more, I trow, if they would seek to lay their hands on him, to mischief and make him away. It was Judas, he was one of these, against whom Mar. 14. 21. Christ cried, *Væ per quem.* And it was the serpent whom Gen. 3. 14. God cursed; and why, what was his fault? What, but that he sought to withdraw our parents from their due subjection; to rise against God, to be gods themselves, and never acknowledge Him, or any, for their superior. These be they, certainly, against whom (God, Angels, and Saints, approving it,) we may say Cushi's prayer, every syllable of it. May? nay, ought; are even bound to it. Yet, to give full satisfaction; that there be no striving, but that all may say Amen to it, it shall not be amiss, if I may, with your good favour, lay before you some reasons, and those so enforcing, that we shall hold ourselves so bound, as that we cannot avoid but yield to it. I care not much, if I keep the number of Absalom's darts: they are three.

First, I hold it for clear, if we knew any were God's ene- The reamies, we would none of us make any question, but say, (with sons of this Cushi, we need not: it is set down to our hands:) "So 1. perish all Thine enemies, O Lord." So: how? Even as Sis- Because era. Little difference, in effect, between him and Absalom. mies of Sisera perished with a nail driven into his head: Absalom, Jud. 5. 31. with a dart thrust through his heart. To the enemies of God, you see, we have warrant. But they that rise against the King are God's enemies; for God and the King are so in a league, such a knot, so straight between them, as one cannot be enemy to the one, but he must be to the other. This is the knot. They are, by God, of or from God, for or instead of God. Moses' rod, God's: Gideon's sword, God's: Ex. 4. 20. Jud. 7. 20.

SERM.
I.

1 Chron.
29. 23.

Ps. 82. 6.

David's throne, God's. In His place they sit: His Person they represent : they are taken into the fellowship of the same name. *Ego dixi*, He hath said it, and we may be bold to say it after him, They are gods : and what would we more? Then must their enemies be God's enemies. Let their enemies know then, they have to deal with God, not with them ; it is His cause, rather than theirs : they, but His agents. It standeth Him in hand, it toucheth Him in honour. He can no less, than maintain them, than hold their enemies for His

Rom.13.2.

own. St. Paul is plain, "He that resisteth them, resisteth God:" he that the regal power, the divine ordinance.

1 Kings
21. 13.

The indictment was rightly framed, (in judgment of all writers,) though it were misapplied, *Naboth maledixit Deo et Regi.* Naboth did neither, therefore it was evil applied. But, if he had done the one, he had done the other; and so it was truly framed. Even as he in the New Testament framed

Lu. 15. 18.

his confession aright, "I have sinned against Heaven and against thee." For no man can trespass against a lawful superior, but withal he must do it against Heaven first; and so he must confess, if ever he have His pardon for it.

But, there is no more pregnant reason to prove, God's enemies they be, these that rise against Kings, than this : ye shall observe still they are called the sons of Belial, Belial

2 Sam. 20.

God's professed enemy. Sheba is so called in express terms, in the next chapter save one, that rose up against David. And indeed, what was the drift of the first tentation, but only to have made Adam and Eve the adopted children of Belial, that is, to be under no yoke? not God's ; much less man's : to brook no superior. They are all his by adoption, that carry such minds. It cannot otherwise be. And if it were

1 Chron.
12. 18.

the Spirit of God that fell on Amasa, when he said, "Thine are we O David, and on thy side thou son of Jesse ;" what spirit could it be but of Belial, or whose son Sheba but his,

[2 Sam.
20. 1.]

that cried, "We have no part in David, nor any portion in the son of Jesse ?" If it were the finger of God that touched their hearts that went after Saul, their lawful liege lord ; whose claw must it be, the print whereof was in theirs who

2 Cor.6.15.

rose and went against him ? Whose but Belial's ? *Et quæ conventio Christi et Belial?* Christ and Belial, so out, so at odds, that no hope of ever agreeing them. Now then being the sons of Belial; and they, and Belial their father, God's enemies; make we any doubt, but we may say after the Holy Ghost, "So perish all Thine enemies, O Lord?"

The one might be enough. But there were three darts in Absalom's heart: one would have served the turn: so this one would suffice; but I would cast yet a second and third at them. If then, secondly, we knew any that were not only *hostis Dei,* but *hostis humani generis,* would we yet doubt to pray he might be as Absalom? I trust not: especially seeing we should therein but follow God's own example. He curseth the serpent, even for this cause, that he was "enemy to the woman and all her seed," and sought the utter ruin of both. Those that are such, well may all men pray against them; for at all men's hands they well deserve it. Now thus reasoneth St. Paul. Rulers not only come from God, but they come from Him in particular; *tibi in bonum,* "for thy good," whosoever thou art. "Thy good," thou nobleman, thou gentleman, thou churchman, thou merchant, thou husbandman, thou tradesman. "Thy good:" that is, for our good they come, and are sent for all our good, for the general good of us all. Us all; nay, even of all mankind. Mankind should be as a forest, (saith Moses,) the strong beasts would devour the weak; as a fish-pool, (saith Habakkuk,) the great fish devour the small, were it not for these. Without these, mankind could not continue. They then, that are enemies to them, mankind's enemies: and so of the serpent's seed certainly, to be cursed with the serpent's curse, *conteratur caput eorum.*

Now then, of this great monarchy of mankind, of the whole world, the several monarchies of the world are eminent parts. What the estate of Kings is, in the whole; that, is the person of every particular prince, in his several sovereignty: David, in his of Jewry; ours, in his of Great Britain; the health and safety of the kingdom, fast linked with the King's health and safety. "The head of the tribes" (so is David called); "The light of Israel;" *Tu pasces,* "the shepherd of the flock;" "The corner-stone" of the building. I will content me with these. If the "head" be deadly hurt, I would fain know, what shall become of the body? If "the light" be put out, is aught but darkness to be looked for in Israel? "Smite the shepherd," must not the flock be in peril? If "the corner-stone" be

2.
The enemies of mankind.

Gen. 3. 14, 15.

Rom. 13. 4.

Gen. 10. 9.
Hab. 1. 14.

1 Sam. 15.
17.
2 Sam. 21.
17.
2 Sam. 5. 2.
Ps. 118. 22.

[Zech. 13. 7.]

SERM.
I.

shaken, will not both the walls feel a wrack? Verily, all our weal and woe dependeth on their welfare or decay. Therefore bless we them; and they that bless them, be blessed; and they that set themselves against them, accursed, even with the capital curse, the serpent's, all our enemy; as the first of all, so the chief of all, as from God's own mouth.

3.
The enemies of the Church.
Ps. 129. 5.
Gal. 5. 12.

    To these two I add yet one more, and that by good warrant, both of the Old and New Testament. "Let them be confounded and turned backward," (saith the Prophet,) "so many as have evil will at Sion." *Utinam abscindantur,* (saith the Apostle,) *qui vos conturbant.* Against them well may we pray, that malign the peace and prosperity of the Church, in which, and for which, we and all the world to pray, as that, for which, all, world and all was made, and is still upholden: for were the Church once gathered, the world dissolves straight. God is too high, as for any our good, so for any our evil or enmity, to come near Him. He reckoneth of no enemies but His Church's. They that persecute her persecute Him; they that touch her touch the apple of His eye. Now they that are enemies to David are enemies to Sion: so near neighbourhood between David and Sion, the King and the Church, as there is between his palace and the temple; both stand upon two tops of one and the same hill. The

Isa. 49. 23.

King is *nutritius Ecclesiæ :* if enemies to the nurse, then to the child; it cannot otherwise be. Experience teacheth it daily, when the child hath a good nurse, to take such a one away is but to expose the child to the evident danger of starving or pining away. I know not, men may entertain what speculations they will; but, sure, *in praxi,* how much the Church's welfare hath gone by the good and blessed inclina-

[Lib. v.
Proœm.]

tion of Kings, it is but too plain. Socrates long since truly observed it, in the beginning of the fifth book of his story. Consider me in the commonwealth of the Jews, these four Kings, immediately succeeding each the other, Jotham, Ahaz, Hezekiah, and Manasseh. Consider these four emperors in the primitive Church, likewise in succession, Constantine, Constantius, Julian, and Jovinian. Consider me here at home the four last princes before his Majesty, and the waxing and waning, the alteration and alternation of religion, under them: forward and backward, backward and forward again;

and tell me, whether the King and the Church have not reference, as I said; and whether the Church have any greater enemies than such as alien the minds of Kings, and make them heavy friends to her welfare and well-doing. Of such then, safely may we say, " Be they confounded, be they Ps.129.5,6. as the grass upon the house-top," which withereth before hay-time : that is, let them come to untimely ends, let them be as Absalom ; or, (as another Psalm wisheth such kind of people,) like them that "perished at Endor, and became like dung upon Ps. 83. 10. the earth." So then, being God's 1. enemies, 2. mankind's, and the 3. Church's; against the enemies of any one of these the prayer were warrantable : how much more against them, that are enemies to all three? One nail served Sisera, in his head ; so would one spear Absalom, in his heart ; but he had three : not without a meaning. A moral allusion they make of it : three were the faults he made, three the parties he highly offended, 1. God, 2. the State, 3. the Church. Enemy to all three : for every one, a dart. Each, deadly alone; but he had them all, to shew he deserved them all ; and so they do, that sin Absalom's sin. The prayer, sure, is good: Cushi prayed well : all are bound to say Amen to it.

But, besides that, it is a prayer, Let them be ; it is a prophecy too, They shall be. The tenor of the prayer we have heard; let us see the success of the prophecy, what became of it : whether Cushi were a true Prophet, or no. So true, as, from Moses to Malachi, never any of the Prophets more true in his foretelling, than he in this. All the enemies, all that rose against him, *erant sicut,* were even so indeed. II. Of the text, as a prophecy.

Pity it is, but that a good prayer should be heard, and (as we said,) turn into the nature of a prophecy. They were three good prayers, we heard ; there is none of all the three, but hath a prophecy, that so it should be, answering to the prayer, that so it might be. Against God's enemies, the prayer, "So perish," &c. The prophecy, "For lo Thine enemies, Judges 5. O Lord, lo Thine enemies shall perish ;" as if he saw it with 31. Ps. 92. 9. his eyes, called others to see it with him, pointed at it with his finger, lo, twice, once and again, (one lo not serve,) so sure he is, that so it shall be. 2. Against the enemies of mankind, the wish, "Cursed be thou above every beast of the Gen. 3. 14, earth," the prophecy followeth in the neck of it, *Ipse conteret* 15.

SERM. *caput,* One there is "shall bruise his head" all to pieces.
I.
——— 3. Against the maligners of Sion, " Let them be confounded,"
Ps. 129. 5.
&c. that is the prayer: the kingdom or nation that shall
malign Sion shall perish, and utterly be destroyed, there is
the prophecy. Now that that is prophetical, in each of
those, is no less verified in the King's enemies, in whom
they all meet.

Do but, after this prophecy, enquire what became of them :
ask but the question. The King doth here in the forepart
of the verse. " Is Absalom safe," how doth he ? He doth, as he
deserveth to do. Ask, how the rest, that after rose against
him. Within a chapter after, Sheba riseth ; how did he ?
2 Sam. 20. Before the end of the chapter, his head came over the wall.
22.
1 Kings 1.5. After him, Adonijah was up, and spake even broadly, *Regnabo.*
1 Kings 2. What became of him ? His end in blood. And, (that which is
25.
strange,) with him rose Joab, he that took off Sheba's head.
he that threw these darts ; and he that was the true man here,
how sped he ? He was even drawn from the altar, (that is no
1 Kings 2. sanctuary for traitors,) and executed by Benaiah. Could not
34.
take heed by Absalom's example, but came to Absalom's end.
They all that sought, that rose to pluck him down, whom
Ps. 62. 3. God had exalted, they were " slain, all the sort of them ;"
were all " as a tottering wall, or as a broken hedge," which
every man runs over.

But this judgment of God was in none more conspicuous
than Absalom. A straight charge was given by the King
himself, to have him saved : it would not serve, he was slain
for all that. And slain by Joab: one, before, that had highly
favoured him, and been a special means to restore him to
grace ; even by him was he slain, notwithstanding the King's
charge ; and then slain, when he made full account of the
victory. For, else he would have been better horsed. He
2 Sam. 18. 9. was on his mule, now he never doubted the event, and yet
was slain. Sure God's hand was in it, to rid the world of
a traitor.

III.   Neither was this a peculiar prophecy to King David alone.
The
prophecy   The prayer is said, and the prophecy taketh hold of other, as
perpetual. well before, as since. Ask of Korah, he rose against Moses :
Nu. 16. 2, 3,
&c.   how sped he ? he went to hell quick for it. Ask of Baanah
2 Sam. 4. 12. and Rechab, that rose against their lord : look over the pool

of Hebron; there stand their quarters on poles. Ask of
Bigthan and Teresh: what of them? Fairly hanged at the Esther 2.
court-gate. Time will not serve, to enquire of all. The short 23.
is: all that were as Absalom came to his end. Some hanged,
and their heart opened, being yet alive, (so was Absalom:) and
their bowels plucked out, to make them like Judas. Some, Acts 1. 18.
their heads strucken off (so was Sheba). Some quartered, 2 Sam. 20. 22.
and their hands, feet, and head, set up on poles, that the ravens 2Sam.4.12.
might pluck out their eyes, as Baanah and Rechab: that
upon them might come all the punishments due to them
that rise with Absalom. For all the punishments of traitors,
as now they are in use with us, may seem to have been col-
lected and drawn together from those several examples that
stand in the book of God.

All to shew, that a King is *Alkum*, no rising against him: Prov. 30.
or, if any rise, he had better sit still. For, no sooner rise they אלקום 31.
up, but our Prophet straight crieth, "Rise up, rise up, and put Isa. 51. 9.
on strength, thou arm of the Lord; rise up, as in old time, in
the generations of the world." Art not thou the same that
didst smite Absalom by Joab? and art not thou the same that
didst smite Joab by Benaiah? that settest thyself still to bring [1 Kings
them down, that rise up against *Alkum*, against whom there 2. 34.]
is no rising?

For, Kings being from God, (saith Gamaliel,) we cannot set Acts 5. 39.
ourselves against them, but we must be found even θεομαχεῖν
"to fight against God." Being "ordained of God," (saith
Gamaliel's scholar, St. Paul,) to resist them is to resist "the Rom.13.2.
ordinance of God;" and as good put ourselves in the face of
all the ordnance in the Tower of London, as withstand God's
ordinance. None might better say it, than he: it was told
him from Heaven, when he was about such another business;
persecuting Christ in His Church, (and Christ is persecuted
in His chief members, as well as His inferior;) he was told
plainly, in so doing, he did but "kick against the prick." Acts 9. 5.
His heels might ache and run of blood; the prick not remove,
but stand where it did still. Therefore, as here Cushi, in the
Old, so St. Paul, in the New, falleth to prophesy. "They that Rom.13.2.
resist shall receive to themselves damnation," is St. Paul's
prophecy. And a true prophecy, even as was Moses' of Korah, Nu. 16. 29.
That they should not "die the death of other men," but be

c 2

SERM.
I.

And
reacheth
to our
times.

The appli-
cation to
the day.

Deu. 27.
16.
Prov. 30.
17.

1 Kings
15. 1.
אבים
Judges 5.7.

Gen. 9. 25.

2 Kings 5.
27.

visited with some strange extraordinary visitation; but have their end in blood. All, as Cushi prayed they might, and prophesied they should. And his prayer was heard, his prophecy came to pass, not a word of either fell to the ground.

Having now dealt with it as a prayer first; and then, as a prophecy; let us now see' how it suited with the business in hand, and whether the force and vigour of these have reached to us and our times.

It is with God no new thing, this, to reward such as rise up against Kings. Of that which is with Him no new, but old, (as old as David, nay as Moses,) He giveth us new examples every otherwhile, to shew, His ear is still open to this prayer; and that His arm is stretched out to reach them still. Yea, I dare be bold to say, there is no one of His promises hath so many seals hanging at it, by way of confirmation of it, as this hath: no one, so many judgments upon record, as it. In every story of every land, there is still standing some gibbet or other, and their quarters hanging on it there still, to put us in mind of the truth of Cushi's prophecy.

This very day yieldeth us one of fresh memory, (but seven years since,) wherein in our Sovereign God hath given a memorable example of the hearing Cushi's prayer, and the accomplishing his prediction, not in one, but in a couple of Absaloms. A couple of Absaloms I may well term them: in many other points like him, but namely in these two: 1. like, in their rising; and 2. like, in their fall. For, that Absalom was a son, and these but subjects, it altereth not the case much. Sons and subjects are both under one commandment, as *Pater* and *Rex* both in one name, Abimelech, the name of the first Kings of Canaan. If under one, then under one curse. If they do but speak evil, under Moses' curse, in mount Ebal; if but look upon them with a scornful eye, under Solomon's curse, that the ravens pick those eyes out. The same, against a father, to reach much more to Abijam, *Pater populi* (so did Solomon name his nephew): Abijam, a father of Judah; even as Deborah was "a mother in Israel." In a word, what Noah might wish to a bad son, (Ham,) and Elisha wish to a bad servant (Gehazi); no cause in the world, but Cushi might wish the same to a bad subject. All is one case. This then breeds no unlikeliness; and in all the rest, exceeding like.

" As that young man" (to keep the words of the text). 1. For those were young men too. Their years, not many. Not many : nay, so few, so green, as it may well seem strange, that there could such inveterate malice and mischief be hatched in so young years. " As he," in that, first.

As in years, so in malice; bloody-minded both. Said not 2. Absalom to his assassins, " When I give you a sign, see you 2 Sam. 13. smite, kill him, fear not : have not I commanded you?" Said 28. not they the same to him, whom, to that end, they had armed, and placed to do that wicked act? In that like, second.

As in this malicious bloody mind, so in raking it up, and 3. keeping it close, divers years together. Not only, (as Absalom in this,) to say neither good nor bad; but in this too, to entreat the King, and all his company to their house : to entertain and feast him, and besides, promise and pretend I know not what, and all to cover and conceal their devilish intent. In this like, thirdly : this young man, and these.

And not in this kind only of outward dissembling; but in 4. a worse kind of religious hypocrisy. He made a religious vow; 2 Sam. 15. it lay on his conscience, he could not be quiet, till he had 8. got leave to go pay it; and then, even then, went he about all his villany. And was it not so here? He, so holy, as to a sermon he must needs; to God's word; no remedy, he might not be from it in any wise : and that, when he trusted the deadly blow should have been given. In this, like.

And yet fifthly, the same man, like Absalom, when he was 5. in Geshur. Absalom in Geshur, and this in Italy, as devout at his masses then, as he was here zealous for his exercise of the word. Alike at both, as they served his turn. Like in this too.

And last of all, in this too : that for all this goodly mask of 6. religion, when he saw his treachery was discovered, as Absalom blew his trumpet, so he was content to uncase himself, 2 Sam. 15. and to rush forth, and appear for such as he was. In which 10. act, he perished, as Absalom ; got in his heart that Absalom got in his : only that was a dart, and this was a dagger.

For (sure) being thus like in their conditions, and in so 7. many circumstances besides, pity but they should be like in

SERM.   their ends too: and they were.   And, that so they were, is
  I.
———   the matter of public gratulation of this day, of the day of
the week all the year long: of this, the day itself, specially
above all: that the prayer and prophecy of Cushi took place;
his prayer heard, his prophecy fulfilled, no less in these young
men, than in that; no less in the enemies of our King James,
than in his lord King David.

In the treasons, little difference or none: in the delivery
some difference; but all for the better.   For first, in far
greater peril was His Majesty, far greater than ever was
David.   1. David was but pursued; but he was even caught,
and within (I know not how many) locks and doors.   2. David
was all the while without the reach of any blow: how near
the blow was to his breast, it is able to make any man chill,
but to think.   3. David had his worthies still about him; the

Isa. 63. 3.   King was *in torculari solus,* " in the very press alone," *et vir de*
gentibus, " and not one of his people" to stand by or assist
him.   4. That David was delivered, it must be ascribed to
the providence of God; but, in that it was a fought field, his
army must take part of the praise.   It was another manner of
providence, that was shewed here; of a more near regard, of
a more strange operation.   I dare confidently affirm it, (I may
well, I am sure,) God's hand was much more eminent in this,
than in that: praised be His name for it.   5. And last of
all, David (here) heard of his delivery by Cushi.   Ours saw it
himself: and yet (I cannot tell well what to say), the danger
was so great, and the fear must needs be accordingly, whether
it had not been to be wished, that some Cushi had rather
brought tidings of it, than he seen it himself.   But since it
pleased God, so from Heaven to shew Himself in it, (if ever
He did in any,) and though with such fear, yet without any
harm, *dulcis laborum præteritorum memoria.*

[Horat.   David heard his, *segnius irritant;* ours saw his, *oculis sub-*
Epist. ad
Pison.   *jecta fidelibus:* the impression of joy was the greater, and did
180—1.]   work both the stronger and the longer.   The stronger, in
a votive thanksgiving then undertaken: the longer, in the
continual renewing it, not only from year to year, but from
week to week all the year long.

And what shall we say then?   What but as Ahimaaz
before, at the twenty-eighth verse, " Blessed be the Lord his

God, That hath this day given sentence for him, upon those that rose up against him." And then, secondly, with Cushi, So be it to all the rest, as it was with these. Though it be to go into mount Ebal, let us not fear, God goeth before us, and saith it before us; let us not make danger, to go after, and to say after Him. 1. They be His enemies, so proved: say we boldly, " So perish all Thine enemies, O Lord." 2. They be enemies of mankind, in being enemies to them, by whom order and peace is kept in mankind, and without whom there would in mankind be nought but confusion: the serpent's curse be upon them, and let their heads be trod to pieces. 3. They be Sion's malignant enemies: let them be " as grass upon the house-top," as " those that perished at Endor, and became dung for the earth." Let them be as stubble scattered, as wax melted, as smoke driven, no man can tell whither. Let them perish; perish, as Sisera, and Oreb, as Absalom. Jael's hammer on their heads: Gideon's axe on their necks: Joab's dart in their hearts. One, nay three: one, for the enemies of God: another, for the enemies of mankind: a third, for the enemies of Sion. Let Cushi be both Priest and Prophet: this his prayer never return empty, this his prophecy never want success. And, " Let the King Ps. 21. 1. ever rejoice in Thy strength, O Lord; let him be exceeding glad of Thy salvation." Ever thrust Thou back his enemies, and tread them down that rise up against him. Let their swords go through their own hearts, and their mischief [Ps. 37. light upon their own heads. Let his ear still hear his desire 15.] upon his enemies, and his eye still see the fall of the wicked that rise up against him. Be he as David; we as Cushi; they as Absalom. God, by Whom this prayer was allowed, receive and grant it! God, by Whom this prophecy was inspired, make it good, and fulfil it, as this day, so for ever! Even for ever and ever, for His Christ's sake.

A SERMON

THE KING'S MAJESTY AT HOLDENBY,

ON THE FIFTH OF AUGUST, A.D. MDCVIII.

————

1 SAM. xxvi. 8, 9.

Then said Abishai to David, God hath closed thine enemy into
thine hand this day : now therefore, I pray thee, let me smite
him once with a spear to the earth, and I will not smite him
again.
And David said to Abishai, Destroy him not ; for who can lay
his hand on the Lord's anointed, and be guiltless ?

[*Dixitque Abisai ad David, Conclusit Deus inimicum tuum hodie in*
manus tuas : nunc ergo perfodiam eum lanceâ in terrâ semel, et
secundo opus non erit.
Et dixit David ad Abisai, Ne interficias eum, quis enim extendet
manum suam in christum Domini, et innocens erit ? Latin Vulg.]

[*Then said Abishai to David, God hath delivered thine enemy into*
thine hand this day : now therefore let me smite him, I pray thee,
with the spear even to the earth at once, and I will not smite him
the second time.
And David said to Abishai, Destroy him not : for who can stretch
forth his hand against the Lord's anointed, and be guiltless ?
Engl. Trans.]

SERM.
II.
————
The sum.
THERE is somebody here, in this text, in danger to be de-
stroyed; and the party is "the Lord's anointed," King Saul.
The matter is come to hard hold : "Destroy him," and
"Destroy him not." Abishai would have it done : David at
no hand; he cries, *Ne perdas.* But the end was, Saul was
saved. Thus lieth the case here in the text.

And was not the very same the case of this day ? There
was somebody in as great danger to be destroyed, this day.
It was *Christus Domini,* "God's anointed," here before us. The
case was come to the very same plunge : *Perdas, ne perdas ;*
a king, or no king. Some were of Abishai's mind. God was
fain to supply David's ; there was none else. But blessed be
God, all ended in *Ne perdas.* And again, blessed be God,
Who then also verified the latter part of the verse, that none
shall seek to lay hands on "the Lord's anointed," but they
shall be found, and handled as guilty persons. For so they
were ; and their blood was upon their own heads. Both cases
suiting so well, this text might well serve for this day.

There is, in the former verse, a motion made by Abishai The di-
for a blow at Saul, thus : "See," &c. There be three perilous vision.
motives in it : 1. *Inimicum,* he is your enemy ; 2. *Conclusit,* I.
here is an opportunity ; 3. *Sine me,* the act shall not be
yours, let me alone, I will take it upon me.

There is, in the latter, David's utter dislike of the motion, II.
thus : "Destroy not," &c. Wherein, first there is a double
charge to the contrary : 1. One *ad oculum,* "Destroy him
not ;" 2. The other rising out of the reason, yet plain enough.
He had said, "Destroy him not." Not that ; *Quis enim mis it
manum ?* for, a less matter than that you may not do, not
lay your hands, not so much : which is (as it were) a sur-
charge to the former ; or (if I may so say,) a second edition
of *Ne perdas.* No talk of destroying : so far from that, as
no stirring the hand toward it.

1. Then upon this double charge, followeth a double
reason ; two retentives (as it were) against the first motion.
1. He is "the Lord's anointed :" that may stay you, if you
be a good subject.

2. Be you good subject or no, if that will not, this must ;
You shall not be "guiltless." If not "guiltless," then guilty :
and what becomes of them that be guilty, we all know. That
is, Do it not ; if you do, it shall bring you to Guilty or not
guilty. If you lay your hand, you shall hold up your hand
for it : it is as much as your life is worth.

3. Thirdly, it is not indeed, *Non eris insons.* For, if it had
been so, it might have been thought to have reached to
Abishai, to this particular, and no further. But he chose

rather to utter it by *Quis?* For by asking, *Quis?* "Who"
shall? he plainly implieth *Ne quis unquam*, that none ever
may: not he, not Abishai; nay, not any. So there is a
double charge: 1. "Destroy not," 2. "lay not your hand."
A double retentive: 1. He is "God's anointed;" 2. You
shall not be "guiltless;" 3. and a *Quis* upon all, to bind all,
and to shew, the charge is general without exception.

1. In all which, there is a protection for Saul the first
King, and all after him, not only from *perditio*, 'destroying,'
giving of the blow; but from *missio manús*, 'stirring of the
hand.'

2. There is a neck-verse for Abishai, and all undertakers
in that kind: they are all cast, they are all found guilty ere
they come to the bar; they are attainted, every one.

3. There is an *Euge* for David, who sheweth himself
through all. 1. In his charge, "Destroy not," a good subject;
2. in his reason, He is "God's anointed," a good Divine;
3. in his sentence, *Non eris insons*, a good judge: 4. in his
challenge, *Quis mittet?* a stout champion, to any that shall
maintain the contrary.

4. But for that, besides this reason in the text, of *inimicum
tuum*, there have been other reasons framed in our days, to
the same end; and all of them in Saul, the party in the
text: we will take them in too, to rule this case once for
all. For Saul's case will be found to have in it all that can
be alleged, why any king should be, if any king might be
touched. All, I say, will be found in him. But he, for all
them, may not be touched: therefore none may.

5. And this done, we will come, as the duty of the day
requireth, to lay these cases case to case; ours of the day,
to this in the text. Where we shall see, that we have as
great cause: nay, of the twain, the greater cause of gratulation, for the happy *Ne perdas* of this day.

I.
Abishai's
motion. This is Abishai's motion. There be three motives in it:
1. The party is your enemy; 2. God hath sent you opportunity; 3. I will take it upon me. Enmity makes us willing
to take revenge; opportunity, able; and if another will do
the act, the rather for that; for then we shall bear no blame.
Three shrewd motives, where they meet: and here they meet
all in one. Let us weigh them: which I do the more will-

ingly, because all three meet also in this day's attempt.
1. Enmity, that was the colour, an old wrong: so, there
were in both the same pretence. 2. And the same advantage in both. For the King was shut up indeed, and that
literally. 3. And he that was at Church, he should not
have done it, not he. Abishai should have done it, he in
the chamber. Of these motives then.

He is an enemy. But not every enemy is to be destroyed,
but they that would destroy us. All enmity is not deadly
feud. Saul's was; nothing would serve him but David's life;
and many ways he sought it indirectly. 1. By matching him
with his own daughter, and laying on him, for a dowry, so
many foreskins of the Philistines, so he might fall by their
hands. 2. That would not do: he went to it directly: 1. at
three several times cast his javelin at him, to have nailed
him to the wall. 2. When he escaped him so, then gave
he express charge openly to all men to kill him, wherever
they met him. 3. When that would not be, sent to his
house for him: when word came, he was sick in his bed,
bade bring him, bed and all, that he might see him slain in
his own presence. Was there ever the like? who would
not have been quit of such an enemy? *1. The first motive. Inimicum tuum. 1. A deadly enemy. 1 Sam. 18. 25. 1 Sam. 18. 11. 1 Sam. 19. 10. 1 Sam. 19. 1. 1 Sam. 19. 15.*

It may be, there was cause why, and then it holds not.
Nay, no cause. To God he protests, Saul "without any
cause" was his enemy. For no cause he gave him to be
his enemy; he never hurt him: but great cause to have
been his good lord; he had many ways done him good service. Not to speak of his harp, wherewith he had rid him
of many a furious fit of melancholy, or a worse matter: with
his sling, it cannot be denied, he did him and the whole
realm good service, in the overthrow of Goliath; and took
away the rebuke from Israel. Yea many times after, "put
his soul in his hands," as Jonathan pleaded for him, that is,
ventured his life to do him service in his wars, and ever
with good success; and yet for all this, sought his life.
And who would save the life of such an enemy? *2. An enemy without cause. Ps. 7. 4. 1 Sam. 16. 23. 1 Sam. 17. 49. 1 Sam. 19. 5.*

Yes, there may be hope to win an enemy, and in that case
he would not be destroyed. Nay, no hope of ever winning
Saul. He was an enemy out of envy, and they will never be
won more. From the time the fond women made that foolish *3. An enemy not to be won, as out of envy. 1 Sam. 18. 6, 7.*

S E R M.
II. rhyme of a thousand and ten thousand, he could never abide to look right on him. Envy was the matter : that is the dangerous enmity, that never will be pacified. Well saith Prov. 27. 4. Solomon, " Anger is fierce, and hatred is cruel, but who shall stand before envy ? " As who should say, There be means to satisfy both those ; but the enemy from envy, no appeasing him, no hope ever to do it. If aught would, when 1 Sam. 24. 18, 20. he saved his life at the cave, and shewed, by cutting a shred from his mantle, he might have gone further, if he would : Saul himself confessed it was a great favour ; yet that would not win him ; he sought his life still. And even after this here, yet he sought it still. There was no hope to appease him. And who then would not make sure of such an enemy ? Verily if any enmity might have served, here it was.

4. An enemy to his rising.
1 Sam. 16. 12. But there is yet a worse enmity than all these. Saul was not only an enemy to David ; but Saul's life an enemy to David's rising. David was in reversion, we know ; so Saul stood in his way. There was not only the sting of revenge ; but the edge of ambition, to help this motion forward. It Mat. 21. 38. was but, *Occidamus eum ;* here he is, " kill him, and the inheritance is ours," all is ours. Any other enemies spare, and spare not ; but these that stand in our light, away with Jud. 9. 5.
2 Sam. 15. 1, &c.
2 Kings 11. 1. them. It made Abimelech not to spare his own brethren ; nor Absalom, his father ; nor Athaliah, her children. Sure, he that weighs it well, that at one blow he might have rid himself of such an enemy, and withal have gained the crown, will wonder he let not the blow proceed. Now, lay them together : 1. An enemy, such an one, so deadly ; 2. so without cause ; 3. so without all hope of appeasing ; 4. such a stop to his fortunes : who would have stayed Abishai's hand ?

2.
The second motive.
Conclusit Deus. This is enough to give his appetite an edge : but we lack opportunity to do it ; and want of opportunity saves many an enemy's life. Men must deal wisely, and forbear, till they find him handsomely, at some good advantage. Nay, it is now grown to be good divinity, *rebus sic stantibus,* to be as gentle as David ; and *Ne perdas* is good doctrine. But as soon as time serves, and strength, if we get him once within locks, penned up, and in our power, then do as we see cause, destroy him and spare not. So that, upon *conclusit eum* ever stayeth our conclusion. Why here now, *conclusit eum.* It

was night. Saul lay all weary asleep, in a dead sleep, he and all about him. David and Abishai came and went; said what they would; took what they would; none waked or knew of it. It might have been done safely, there was none to resist them; and been carried closely, none to descry them. An opportunity it was, and a fair one. 1. It was night, a fair opportunity.

And (as it might seem) of God's own sending. It was perilously put in (that) of Abishai, *conclusit Deus;* that it was God's doing, sure: it was the sleep of God was fallen on them: none awake; all asleep; watch and all. They might stay all the days of their life, and God never send the like again. What now? 2. Of God's sending, as it might seem.

Though David wanted no courage to be revenged on an enemy, nor wisdom to discern this opportunity; yet, for his reputation, he must not soil his hands: but possibly, if some other would take it upon him, he would not be much against it. Why, it was undertaken by Abishai, that too: he shall go his way, and do nothing to it. *Sine me,* you shall bear no blame, let that be upon me; you shall go to Church and sing Psalms, and hear the sermon, and never appear in it. What now? I know not what can be required more. Thus you see the motives: now, what saith David? 3. The third motive. *Sine me.*

Nay first, what saith Saul? Can we have a better judge than him in this case? *Et inimici nostri sint judices,* an enemy to be judge in his own cause? If you will know what he saith; he it is, that (in the twenty-fourth chapter and the nineteenth verse) saith thus. " Who shall find his enemy at such an advantage, and let him go free?" As much to say, Not any; sure, not he. But if he, or many another had found David, as David did him, in the cave, he would have cut his skirts so close as he would have made him have bled in the reins of his back; or, if he had taken him (as he did Saul here) asleep, he would have set him out of that sleep into another, a perpetual sleep, and made him sure enough for ever waking more. This is Saul's doom, from his own mouth. And indeed, *hæc est via hominis:* with flesh and blood these motives would have wrought. They did not with David: what saith he? these motives move him not. II. David's dislike.

For all this, all this notwithstanding, *Ne perdas,* saith he. And first, mark; he denieth none of his three motives; I. The first charge: *Ne perdas.*

1. that Saul was his enemy; 2. or that the time served fitly; 3. or that the colour was good : but granting all these, for all our enmity, for all this opportunity, for all your colourable offer to save mine honesty ; for all this, Destroy him not.

Secondly, mark, it is not *negando*, a bare denial, *Non est faciendum ;* but with an imperative, with authority, *Ne feceris :* straightly charging and commanding him not to be so hardy as to do it. *Et est efficacior vetandi ratio quam negandi ;* by *ne* than by *non :* the imperative negative is most effectual.

And thirdly, that this is not the first time: once before, he had done the like : and *iteratio præsupponit deliberationem.* And indeed, there is a mystery in this same, *Sine me,* of Abishai. They had had him once before at like advantage, in the cave ; and will you but observe how it went then? it is well worthy your observing. Then, they were at David, to have done it himself, Destroy him you. What was his answer? Who ? I ? God forbid. Never move it, I will never do it. Now then, here at this, Abishai, knowing by the former, it was in vain to move him to do it, he offers to be the doer : it shall be none of your act; *Sine me.* What answer now ? No, nor you ; see you do it not. *Perdas,* saith Abishai before: *Non perdam,* saith David. *Perdam,* saith Abishai, now : *Ne perdas,* saith David. So, he will neither do it himself, nor suffer it to be done. The short is : neither waking, as at first ; nor sleeping, as now : neither by day, as in that ; nor by night, as in this : neither by himself, nor by other, will David endure to do it, or to have it done. But, in the one and the other, first and last, still and ever, *Ne perdas,* saith David : Saul must not be destroyed.

4. Yea, so far was he after this, from forethinking this speech, or wishing it unsaid, that he pleased himself in this *Ne perdas* so, that, not content to have said it, he made [Ps. 57.] a Psalm of it, to sing himself, and all Israel with him ; and by singing it, to sing their duty, in this point, into all their minds and memories. A sign, the words were good, he would bestow a ditty and tune upon them, as if he gloried in them. Yea, to make them the more memorable, that they might never be lost, he hath framed divers other Psalms to the same tune. You may turn to the fifty-eighth, fifty-ninth, and seventy-fifth. You shall find all their titles, to

the tune of *Ne perdas;* that so, all that then were, and all
that were to come, might know how good a speech he took
it to be, how meet to be said, and sung, of all ages.

5. And what would ye more? Not these two only, said,
and sung; but in the verse following, takes his oath, and
swears to it. "As the Lord liveth," saith he, "God's hand [1 Sam. 26.
may, but mine shall never be upon him: and his day may ¹⁰·]
come;" but not a day sooner for me. So that, he said no
more in this, than he meant to swear to.

But now, to come to look into the reason: we shall find 2.
he goeth further than so, than not destroying. For being The rea-
to give a reason of *Ne perdas,* keeping the rule, he should second
now have gone on with it, as he begun, and said, *Quis enim* charge:
perdidit? 'For who ever destroyed' a king? He doth not so. *Ne manum mittas.*
That, as it seemeth, would not serve his turn: he changeth
his verb now, and saith, *Quis enim manum misit?* "Who hath
but put forth his hand?" As if he had given too much scope,
in saying no more, but Destroy not. Indeed, it was well
spied; it must be stopped, before it come to destroying. If
it come to the deed once, we are all undone; *Ne perdas* is
not enough. Much mischief may be; at least much fear
and fright, as this day there was, and yet no destruction.

To make sure work then, so far is he from *perdas,* as he
will not allow *manum mittas.* By which denying the latter,
the former is put past all doubt. If the hand be stayed, no
blow can be given: if order be taken for one, the other will
follow of itself. You may not destroy, for you may not stir
your hand, is a good consequent.

And sure, God's care, in this point, is worthy all observation; it descendeth to such minutes. Here in this place we
have two restraints together: 1. "Destroy not;" 2. and,
which is more, "Lay no hand." In another place, he goeth Ps.105,15.
yet further, "Touch not Mine Anointed:" there needs no
hand to that, the finger will serve. And yet further, in
another place, *Ne surgas,* 'Rise not out of your place;' or, Prov. 30.
as the Psalm expresseth it, Lift not up your heel: that is, 31.
Stir not hand nor foot, to any such end. Men may stir Ps. 41. 9.
their foot, and not rise; and rise, and not touch; and touch,
but lay no hands; and lay the hands on, and not destroy.
But God's meaning is, from the first to the last, to restrain

[¹ *i. e.*
stirring.
Bailey.]

1.
The first
reten-
tive :
*Christum
Domini.*

Hag. 2. 13.

2 Sam. 1.
21.

[² should]

Ps. 82. 6.

all : to have all so far from destroying, as not to lay your hand; nay, not touch with your finger; nay, not so much as rise, or stir the foot; but keep every joint quiet from any the least quetching ¹, in this matter of *Ne perdas.* To go about to do it, is as much as to do it.

We hear his charge : but all this while we see not the retentive, that holds him so, that all Abishai's motives could not move him. He tells us now what it was : *Christus Domini.* In which word is the solution of Abishai's argument, thus : That his military maxim (destroying an enemy), which he and many one else in the world take to be universal, is not so. It admits exceptions divers; but among the rest, and above the rest, this : if the party be *Christus Domini,* it holds not. There is more retentive force in *Christus Domini,* to keep him alive, than there is motive in *inimicus tuus,* to destroy him. This is his answer. And it is, under one, both a solution of Abishai's argument, and a new one propounded by David, to conclude his part, thus : "The Lord's Anointed" is not to be touched (God's own express words, "Touch not Mine Anointed") ; but Saul, what terms soever he stand in of amity or enmity, "God's Anointed" he is; therefore, no touching him. And I observe this, that he maketh choice of *Christus Domini,* for his *medius terminus,* rather than *Dominus Rex,* or any other : rather of "God's Anointed," than of his liege lord the King. (Yet there is force in them too; but nothing such as in this.) To the Sanctuary he goeth, as to the surest place, and from thence fetcheth this term of "the Lord's Anointed," and so makes the matter surer, as he thinketh. For, when all is done, from that place it cometh, that maketh both their callings and persons sacred and holy : therefore, not without sacrilege to be violated ; nay, not to be touched. For such is the nature of holy things, not to be touched; I say, not by any enemy; no, not in war. For, so we see, David is dis-pleased with the Philistines, for so dealing with Saul, " as if he had not been anointed with oil;" as who ² say, it was their duties to have spared him, even in that respect.

And sure, a high term it is, and not slightly to be passed over. In another place he calleth them "gods;" here, *Christos Domini.* So they participate with the name of God, and with the name of Christ, Anointed; and if they be anointed, it is "with the Holy Ghost and power" from Acts 10.38. above. Which all shew a near alliance between God and them, Christ and them, the Holy Ghost and them, so as they are not to be harmed, the least way, if God, or Christ, or the Holy Ghost, can keep them from it.

And this retentive is strong enough, where there is any sense of religion. But, it is to be doubted, Abishai, and some besides him, have no great feeling that way, and so not capable of this. What care they for Samuel or his horn of oil? It must not come out of the Sanctuary; it must come from the bar and the bench, that must prevail with them. Tell them of *Non eris insons,* guilty or not guilty, and then you say something. We said before, there is no more effectual way to deny than to forbid; and, it is true, *Nec efficacior vetandi ratio, quam pœnâ propositâ,* 'no way of more force to forbid, than set a penalty on it;' specially, the great penalty of all, death. And yet, death a soldier careth not so much for neither, except it be *mors sontica,* 'a male-factor's death,' and the chief malefactor's, the traitor's death, to be drawn and dragged from his place, as Joab; hanged, as Bigthan; his bowels pulled out, to suit him to Judas, whose gushed out of themselves; to have his heart opened, yet being alive, as Absalom; his head chopped off, as Sheba; and it and his quarters hanged up, as Baanah and Rechab's were. To have their lands and livelihoods seized on, and given to strangers; their issue miserable for their sakes; to be *damnatæ memoriæ,* their name and memory as a curse: which three are set down in the hundred and ninth Psalm, the Psalm against treachery. Tell Abishai of this, and this may perhaps stay him.

2.
The second
retentive:
Non erit in-
sons.

1 Kings
2. 28—34.
Esther 2.
23.
Acts 1. 18.
2 Sam. 18.
14.
2 Sam. 20.
22.
2 Sam. 4.
12.
Ps. 109.
11—15.

And to say truth, this was no more than needful: without it, all that was said might have been thought to have had but *rationem consilii et non præcepti;* to have been spoken by way of good honest advice, but to have been no penal or capital law. Gently said of David, *Ne perdas;* and well done of Abishai, to forbear; but no necessity in it. Therefore he tells them, These words, *Ne perdas,* are a binding precept: and that so, as if they be transgressed, they will bear an action; yea, an indictment; that whoso breaketh them, *Non erit insons.* And, *Non erit insons* are judicial words, and this they import:

S E R M.   That not only they may be arraigned; but that no quest can
   II.   acquit them, or find them not guilty; that by no book, they
can; that by this book, they cannot be saved.   But if they
stretch forth their hands against "the Lord's Anointed," their
necks must stretch for it; and being found guilty, they must
be dealt with as those that are so found; and upon them
must come all that is written in this book, which erewhile
we recounted.

And yet, *Non erit insons* goeth further.   For suppose some
of them should happen not to be brought to the bar, it shall
not serve; for all that, *Non erit insons*, still.   God will not
hold them guiltless; He will not so leave them; but, rather
than there should not be holden, hold an assize Himself, and
bring them to the end of guilty persons, all the sort of them.

Ps. 144. 6.   Heaven shall do it by lightning, as in Psalm one hundred
Nu. 16. 32.   and forty-four; or the earth do it by swallowing up, as Korah;
2 Sam. 18.
14.   or their own friend shall do it, as Joab; or their own beast,
2 Sam. 18.
9.   as Absalom; or their ownselves hang themselves, as Ahitho-
2 Sam. 17.   phel; or burn themselves, as Zimri.   If they will not say
23.
1 Kings   *Ne perdas* to *Christus Domini, Christus Domini* shall say
16. 18.   *perdas* to them, and send them all to their own place, the
pit of perdition, so many as will not say *Ne perdas* to "the
Lord's Anointed."   It was not for nought, that David said
2 Sam. 1.   to him, (2 Sam. 1,) "How wast thou not afraid to do it?"
14.   There is (sure) matter of fear in it, every way, to stay them:
fear of God, in *Christus Domini*, to move David; fear of the
gallows, in *Non eris insons*, to move Abishai.

3. Abi-   But upon all this, would it not do well, if we had Abishai's
shai's own
confession.   own confession given in evidence against himself?   That, I
2 Sam. 16.   suppose, would take up the matter quite.   We have it 2 Sam.
9.   16.   There, in a case only of looseness in the tongue, where
Shimei let go certain railing speeches against David, could
Abishai say, What, shall this foul-mouthed cur thus be suffered to speak against the Lord's Anointed? and no remedy,
he would needs have gone, and fetched his tongue, and head,
and all.   Yea, after this return in peace, when King David
had, upon Shimei's submission, given him his pardon, Abishai
pleaded hard to have it called back, and would needs have
him die for it; and well worthy he was.   And all was but
for *misit linguam:* and Abishai himself is here laying hands,

violent hands, on "the Lord's Anointed:" a worse matter by
far. So that, upon the matter, Abishai is judged out of his
own mouth, and David justified by him, in his *Non eris insons.* There are your two retentives: 1. the first for good
subjects, 2. the latter for whomsoever.

Now, lest any might conceive, this is but a case of instance; holds in this particular, but extends not to all:
somebody, in some case, may do it for all this, therefore is
it, he carrieth it along through all, with his *Quis?* to tell us
his meaning is, that not only Abishai, but that *Ne quis perdat, Ne quis manum mittat,* 'that none at all destroy, none
lay hands at all:' that his *Ne* is general, without exception
of any.

3.
The gene-
rality of the
charge:
*Quis erit
insons?*

And in this, even his manner of denying, his *figura dic-
tionis,* the tenor of his speech is such, as I dare make a note
of it. There be divers ways of denying, one more full and
forcible than another; but of all, the way by interrogative is
holden the fullest, and most of force. To have said, None
did ever attempt it, which was not guilty: this had been
a denial, but a calm one. But to say, Who ever went about
it, but he was found guilty? there is more life and vigour in
it, by a great deal. Indeed, of all negatives, the strongest,
the most peremptory, is by *Quis?* For it is not a bare negative; but a negative with a challenge: sending a challenge
to any, if he can for his life, to shew one that was holden
innocent in that case. They call it the triumphant negative;
as bearing itself confident, that none can rise up against it.
Who? that is, Shew if ever any such had peace, if ever any
were reputed innocent; as much to say as, Never was there
any, never. If there were, name him, bring him forth; but
that you cannot. Therefore, *Quis fuit insons?* maketh the
case clear, and past all question. So you see, David told us of
Christus Domini, as it were in his Ephod, as a Prophet. Then
went he into his long robe, and told us, *Non erit insons,* as
a judge. And now he is in his armour, as a challenger, with
Quis unquam? to challenge any that holdeth the contrary.

And his challenge will be taken; and there be, that hold
the contrary, in our age; and that dare step forth, and make
a question of it for all this; or rather, make no question at
all of it, but can tell David, both who may lay his hand on,

SERM. to destroy God's Anointed; and who shall acquit, absolve,
II.
—— and make them innocent, that so do.

Who shall? *Quis?* marry *quisquis*, 'any whosoever,' being
warranted. And who shall warrant him? That shall the
High Priest, by his last censure.

These fellows would not stick to tell Abishai a clean contrary tale to that of David's. "Destroy not," saith he. Go
to, say David what he will, or what he can, we say, Destroy
him. What, if he be; yea, though he be "the Lord's
Anointed?" You shall be guilty then certainly, saith David.
What say they? Say they thus, You shall not be guilty, you
may do it, we will absolve you? that were too much. No;
but you shall merit by it, you ought to do it, we will saint
you for so doing. This is not matter of talk, we know it
hath been done.

Quis, "who?" A Jacobin lay his hand: yea, hand and
knife, and thrust it into the body of God's Anointed [1]. Yea,
anointed with the oil that came down from Heaven, (as
they tell us,) sent purposely to anoint the French Kings, and
make them God's Anointed, κατ' ἐξοχήν. What, and not
guilty? Not guilty: yea, and hardly scaped from being a
saint, if the Cardinals' faith had failed as well as the Pope's
did, and if they had not kept St. Peter's successor from
erring. Be not we fallen into strange times, wherein David
must be driven to recant, and Abishai prove the Prophet?
and in which, (as if there were no such verse as this in the
Bible,) the illusion of error is grown so strong with some,
as they will rather themselves be destroyed, than say, "the
Lord's Anointed" is not to be destroyed?

I will do them no wrong. They will say, This text is
enough to condemn this day's attempt, it cometh full home
to that case. It was upon *inimicum tuum;* in which case of
private revenge, themselves hold it clear, *quod non*, as well as
we. But, when they dispense with *Ne perdas*, it is upon other
grounds: upon misgovernment, or, (to speak as they do,) tyranny; upon usurping power in matters ecclesiastical; upon
bloody persecution, and that of God's Priests: and these are
not in the text. Yes: they are in him in the text, concerning
whom this *Ne perdas* was given, every one: and yet *Ne perdas* stands, for all that. And this I say, howsoever Abishai did

[1 Henry III. of France, assassinated by Clement, a Dominican, August, 1589.]

Saul's case a ruling case for *Ne perdas.*

look upon Saul, but with a soldier's eye, and saw nothing in him but an enemy, to move him to destroy him ; if some of these quick and sharp-sighted Abishais had had the looking into him, they would have spied in him other manner of matter, to have resolved him meet to be made away : they would have found him, not David's enemy only, but an enemy to God, and all goodness ; and return him culpable of all those faults, which they use to insist on, when they write their books to that end.

And I verily think, God, in this first example, of His first King over His own people, hath purposely suffered them all to fall out, and to be found in him ; even all that should fall out in any King after him, to enforce their position ; that so we might find them answered to our hands.

To touch them in order. They would easily have quarreled at Saul's misgovernment. Not at the first : he then was a mild and a gracious Prince. Never came there from any prince's mouth a more princely speech, than the first speech he is recorded to have spoken, *Quid populo quod flet ?* "What ails the people to complain?" A speech worthy everlasting .memory, so they complain not without cause. But within a while, he grew so stern and fierce, as no man might speak to him. Upon every light occasion, nay upon no occasion at all, his javelin went straight to nail men to the wall: not David only, but Jonathan his son and heir apparent, and no cause why. In the thirteenth chapter it is said, Saul had then been King a year, and reigned two years in Israel: yet it is well known his reign was forty years. Their own writers resolve it thus: how long soever he reigned, he was a King but two years. All the time after, he was somewhat else, or somewhat more than a King. And they let not to tell what : applying to Saul that of the Psalm, "Tyrants that have not God before their eyes seek after my soul." And that, "Under Thy wings shall be my refuge, till this tyranny be overpast." Yet for all this tyranny, *Ne perdas,* saith David.

Yet for all this, he fell not into the sin of all sins, which they stand so much on, Usurping power in things spiritual. Yes : and that would they have found too. Why ? did he call himself Head of the Church ? Indeed no : Samuel did

Notwith-standing his mis-government and tyranny.

1 Sam. 11. 5.

1 Sam. 20' 33.

1 Sam. 13 1.

Ps. 54. 3.

Ps. 57. 1.

2. Usurp-ing the priest's office.

SERM.
II.
1 Sam. 15.
17.
[2 Chron.
26.16—
21.]
1 Sam. 13.
9. that for him : he it was that said, " When thou wert little
in thine own eyes, the Lord made thee head of the tribes of
Israel" (of which the tribe of Levi was one) : for that,
Samuel must answer.   But Saul went further a great deal;
yea, further than Uzziah : for he took upon him to sacrifice
in person himself; to offer burnt offerings upon the very
altar, the highest part of all the Priest's office : that is,
usurped further than ever did any.   And all this David
knew ; yet it kept him not from saying, *Ne perdas*.

3. Shed-
ding the
priests'
blood.
1 Sam. 22.
18. They never had done with persecuting and shedding
Priests' blood : was Saul's finger in that too ?   In that he
passed : he put the High Priest himself, and eighty-four
more, all in one day, to the sword : and all but upon the
single accusation but of Doeg, all protesting their innocence
in the fact ; and all, loyalty to him : and all but for a dozen
of bread given to David.   This could not but grieve David
exceedingly : it was for his sake ; yet he saith *Ne perdas*
though, for all that.

4. Being
possessed
with " an
evil spirit."
1 Sam. 16.
14. And one case more I give in for advantage.   It is well
known, he was a demoniac, one actually possessed with " an
evil spirit ;" which is a case beyond all other cases : yet,
Destroy him not, Abishai, though. , So that if Abishai, instead of *inimicum tuum*, had said, God hath shut up 1. this
tyrant, 2. this usurper, 3. this persecutor, 4. this possessed
party, this what you will ; David would have said no other
than he did, *Ne perdas*, still.   I would fain know, which of
all their destructive cases is here wanting.   They be all
here : all in Saul ; all in him, at the time of this motion ;
yet all alter not the case ; David saith still, as he said.   If
then all be in Saul, all incident, all eminent in him ; nay, if
his case be beyond all ; said it must be, that David here
saith.   Though he be any of these, though he be all these,
Destroy him not ; or, Destroy him and be destroyed ; destroy
him, and be the child of perdition.

5. There
was an
High
Priest,
Abiathar. I would be loth to deceive you : there may seem yet to
want one thing.   Here was no High Priest to excommunicate
him, or give warrant to do it.   Yes, that there was too.   For
Abiathar escaped that great massacre of Priests by Saul ;
and now, he was lawful High Priest.   Now he fled to David
1 Sam. 22.
23. thence, and brought the ephod with him.   So as by good

hap, the High Priest was with David now in the camp, and
the ephod too. There wanted no just cause, you see, to pro- 1 Sam. 23.
ceed against Saul. There wanted no lawful authority: the 6.
High Priest we have. There wanted no good will in Abiathar, ye may be sure; his father and brethren having been
murdered by Saul. So here was all, or might have been, for
a word speaking. All would not serve ; David is still where
he was ; saith still, *Ne perdas :* knew no such power in the
High Priest's censure ; was not willing to abuse it; cannot
see *Quis ?* any person to do it, nor any cause for which it is
to be done. Enough to make a ruled case of it for ever :
that Abishai may not do it, nor Abiathar give warrant to it.
His charge is honest, *Ne perdas :* his reason good, *Christus
Domini :* his sentence just, *Non erit insons :* his challenge
unanswerable, *Quis mittet manum ?*

And, this being cleared, come we now to the principal The text
cause of our coming. Which is, in this public manner, to and day
compared.
render our yearly solemn thanks to *Christus Dominus,* for
the deliverance of our *Christus Domini,* this day (a deliverance like this in the text) ; even for His *Ne perdas,* at Perth.
For it, and for both points in it. 1. That His Anointed was
not destroyed. 2. That they, that put forth their hand to
do it, carried it not away, but found the reward due to
guilty persons. The two cases, 1. this in the text; 2. and
that of this day, are both like in the main : if in circumstances dislike ; this of ours hath the advantage. The fact
more foul, the deliverance more famous.

To speak then of *malitia diei hujus,* ' the malicious practice of this day.' Had the King been an enemy : yea, such
an enemy as Saul, it had been no warrant. But he was no
enemy : no, but many ways, a gracious prince to them both.
I know, pretence there was of a wrong. Say it had been
one ; what was done was done by others, in the King's
minority. And though done by others, yet justly done :
and no wrong was it at all, but wrongfully so called.

Secondly, the King was shut up it is true; but not as in
the text, by God ; but by wicked men, who found him not
casually, as Saul was ; but trained him guilefully to the
place, and there shut him up treacherously. It was not
sudden, it was a long plot : the malice the more ; the fact

the fouler. And there he was *conclusus et derelictus* both ; shut up by Abishai, forsaken of David.

Thirdly, and it was not night, nor the King asleep, that he might have passed away without any fright or terror.

Ps. 91. 6. No: it was *dæmon meridianus* this, " a noon-day devil." He was broad awake, and the fear of death, (worse than death itself,) I know not how oft and many times, before his eyes.

Fourthly, and as beyond it in these; so, in the principal beyond it too. Both of them lift up, Abishai his spear, this his dagger, to have given the fatal blow. Abishai, but once; this, twice. And certainly, nearer it came to the King, than David would suffer it come to Saul. So, the danger nearer, and the delivery greater. And yet, there was a *Ne perdas* in this too; and that a strange one. Not by David, no. Judge, if it may not seem a miracle, that God then shewed. When there was none to say, "Destroy not," else; God opened his mouth, that was there set, himself to be the destroyer, to say once and again, 'O destroy him not, destroy not the King.' The voice was David's; the hands Abishai's. It calls to my mind, what long since I read in Herodotus; that at the taking of Sardis, when one ran at Crœsus the King, to have slain him, that a little boy born dumb, that had never spoken word in all his life, with the fright and horror of the sight, his tongue loosed, and he broke forth

[Herodot.
Clio. 85.]
and cried, Ὤνθρωπε, &c. 'O man, destroy not the King,' and so saved his life. So writeth he, as of a wonder : and see, if this were not like it. But so we see, if there were nobody else to say it, they that are born dumb shall say it; yea, the destroyer himself shall say it, rather than *Ne perdas* shall not be said. This would not serve, though it did to Abishai; but they were worse than Abishai, that were here. That God therefore might have the honour of the day, he passed over to the latter part of the verse; and when there was none else to do it, he took the matter into his own hands; himself held the assize, found him guilty, gave order for his execution, sent up one to do it; and one that formerly had been his special friend, and (if I be not deceived) sworn brother, as Joab, to bring Absalom to his end ; that destroyed him, for not hearing " Destroy not."

And yet the goodness of God stayed not here neither; but,

where in the text, in Saul's case, there was but one blow, one danger, one delivery ; in this, there were no less than three, one after another. First came Abishai ; he and his armed man : God delivered him. Then came the other, the master of the mischief, then betrayed, and (as one betrayed,) desperately set : God again delivered him. Then last of all, (and that was worst of all,) came the popular tumult, whose rage knows no reason, who, as they (Numb. [Numb. 16. 41.] 16.) called Korah and Dathan "the people of the Lord ;" so these, little better : and even then also did God by His mighty providence turn away the destruction. This in the text was soon done : a few words, and away. This of the day, it was long first, and much ado, ere it was done : the longer, and the more, the more is God to be magnified for it.

And when all was done there, he that was saved was but Saul ; but here, (envy flatters not, but) if envy itself should speak, it would say, *major Saule hîc,* ' a greater than Saul ' any : (for the territory of the least of your kingdoms was greater than that of his :) and *melior Saule hîc,* ' a better than Saul' was here saved ; better, without all comparison. So, the beginning was, (as they made account,) *conclusit Deus inimicum nostrum :* the end was, as it proved, *conclusit Deus inimicos Domini Regis,* God made a conclusion of their wicked premises and their wretched persons all at once. So, the conclusion was *Ne perdas* to the king, and *Non insons* to the children of perdition.

Now, to that God, That, when you were shut up, forsook you not, but delivered you *a malitiâ diei hujus et a dæmone meridiano ;* That, in the depth of all your danger, when there was no tongue on earth could say *Ne perdas,* said it from heaven, and said it thrice over : for that His three-fold delivery render we three-fold thanks and praise : thrice blessed be His holy Name for it. And He grant, that this lesson of David's may take deep root in all our hearts, that there may never be a *Quis* in Israel to lift up his hand to the like action : all may be quit, none found guilty ever of so foul a crime. None, on Abishai's side, to make any such motion : all of David's mind, to mislike it, to say *Ne perdas : Ne perdas,* though it be Saul. But for David, *Ne perdas* is

SERM.
II.
not enough.   To him, and such as he is, let us with one voice cry Hosannah; not only, "Not destroy," but Hosannah, "Lord save," Lord prosper, Lord add days to his days, that his years may be as many ages.   And as this day Thou didst, so still and still prepare Thy loving mercy and truth, that they may preserve him, even for ever and ever.

A SERMON

PREACHED BEFORE

THE KING'S MAJESTY, AT HOLDENBY,

ON THE FIFTH OF AUGUST, A.D. MDCX.

---

1 CHRON. xvi. 22.

Touch not Mine Anointed.

[*Nolite tangere Christos Meos.*]

[*Touch not Mine Anointed.* Eng. Trans.]

HERE is a speech; but we know not whose, nor to whom, nor yet (well) concerning whom; only concerning certain persons, whom the speaker (whosoever he is) calleth his "anointed." It behoveth us to know these three, who they be.

The Person, Whose the speech is, *Persona loquens*, He 1. That saith *Meos*, Him we find at the fourteenth verse. *Ipse* [Ps. 95.7.] *est Dominus Deus noster*, "He is the Lord our God:" God it is, That speaketh here: He That challengeth them for His, by calling them "Mine."

The persons to whom. In the verse before, *non reliquit* 2. *hominem*, "He leaveth not a man." So, it is to all, in general; but specially to some, more quick of touch than the rest, whose fingers are never well, till, some way or other, they be touching whom God would not have touched.

The persons concerning whom (whom He styleth His 3. "Anointed") will fall out to prove the princes of the earth. We must not say it, but prove it: say it now, prove it anon.

Now, as if somebody were about to offer them some wrong; here cometh a voice from heaven, staying their hands, and saying, See you touch them not. *Quos Deus unxit, homo ne tangat*, "Whom God hath anointed, let no man presume to touch."

SERM.
III.
[Ps. 95. 7,
8.]
Of which it may well be said, as the Psalmist saith to us every day, *Hodie si vocem,* "To-day, if ye will hear His voice, harden not your hearts," and ye may; for as this day, (now ten years,) from the same person, and the same place, a like voice there came, concerning His "Anointed," in whose presence we stand. That God would not have His "Anointed" touched, this text is a witness, and this day is a witness: the text, *dixit;* the day, *factum est.*

Referred
unto the
text next
before,
1 Sam.
26. 9.
Touching the same point, when time was, in this place you heard, *Ne perdas:* you shall hear it again now, but from a higher person, under a straighter charge, and with a larger compass.

1. The person higher; for that was David: *sed ecce major Davide hic,* 'but behold a greater than David is here.' This is no voice on earth, (neither of Prophet nor Apostle,) we now hear. *Audivi vocem de cœlo,* we hear a voice from heaven: and thence, neither of saint nor angel, but of God Himself. To shew His care of them, (His "Anointed,") He would have none give the charge about them but Himself; Himself in person, *non alienæ vocis organo, sed oraculo suæ,* from none other, but from His own mouth.

2. The charge stricter: for there it was, "Destroy not," the worst that could be. Here it is, "Touch not," the least that may be; and so, even that way, amended much.

3. The compass larger. That was to Abishai, but one man; and it was concerning Saul, one King only; and therefore it was in the singular, *Ne perdas.* This is, *Nolite,* and *Christos:* the number altered, of a larger extent far, even to all men, concerning all His "Anointed." *Nolite* in the plural, that is, none of you: *Christos* in the plural, that is, none of them. Them, not touched, not any of them: you, not touch, not any of you. *Non reliquit hominem,* "He leaveth not a man," but forbiddeth all. Now, out of this plural you may deduce any singular; out of *christos,* any king; out of *nolite,* any party; out of *tangere,* any hurt; and so, not any man to do any hurt to any His "Anointed."

This text,
"the first
and great
command-
ment" con-
cerning
this point.
A commandment it is, and I may safely say, *primum et magnum mandatum,* "the first and great commandment," touching the safeguard of Princes.

"The first:" for, (as the verses before shew,) it was the

first given in this kind, and that before all other, in the Patriarchs' time, long before Moses, under the law of nature.

"The greatest:" not only because it is of the greatest in
heaven, and concerning the greatest in earth; but for that
it is the original main precept, touching Princes and their
safety, or (as the phrase is) the fundamental law, upon the
which all the rest are grounded, unto the which all the rest
reduced, and from the which all the rest derived. David's
"Destroy not" is but an abstract of this "Touch not." Ask
him what text he had for his *Ne perdas*, hither he must come,
this must be it, and none other. This *Nolite tangere* is the
main wing of protection : *Ne perdas*, or any other particular,
is but a feather of it.

To see the parts of it. A precept it is, and negative; and
the negative precept is of the nature of a fence, and the fence
leadeth us to the thing fenced. First of all then, we take it
in sunder, in the midst: *Meos*, whose the fence is; and then
Nolite tangere, as it were a circle or fence round about them.
The di-
vision.

Christos Meos hath in it two things : not only the par-
ties, whom they should not; but the reason why they should
not touch them. Not "touch?" Whom "not touch?" His
"Anointed." And why "not touch?" Even because His
"Anointed."
I.

In *Christos Meos* taken together, are the parties *non
tangendæ*. Again, in *Christos Meos*, taken in sunder and
weighed apart, are two reasons couched, *de non tangendo*.

Why not touched? first, they be His. And secondly, what
of His? His "Anointed." These two be two several : His
"Anointed" is more than His; for all that be His be not
anointed.

1. His alone were enough; that they be His, they pertain to Him, and so, He to see them safe.

2. But then besides, they be the very choice and chief of
His, His "Anointed;" and so, a more special care of them
than the rest.

3. And then, from the nature of the word, not only His
"Anointed," *Uncti Ejus*, but *Christi Ejus*, His "Christs,"
which is the highest degree of His "Anointed:" for higher
than that ye cannot go.

And last, what that is, that maketh them thus, His

S E R M.
III.

"Anointed:" to know whether they may be stripped of it, or no.

II. Then come we to the circle or fence, and that we may di-
1. vide too: for *Nolite tangere* is a double fence; 1. from the
2. act, 2. and from the will. "Touch not" (so we read), where the touch, the act is forbidden. *Nolite tangere* (so read the Fathers), where the will to touch is forbidden likewise. *Nolite*, that is, Have ye not the will, not so much as an inclination to do it. So, both the act and will of touching is restrained: the act, in *tangere*; the will, in *Nolite*.

In the former, we are to take the extent of *tangere* and *Christos*: 1. to what matters *tangere* will reach; 2. in how many points to *Christos*. And in the latter, to what persons, in *Nolite*.

And so see we the sum of the text, which is sufficient enough to keep Kings from touching, if itself might be kept untouched: but as the times are, the text itself is touched, there needs a second *Nolite tangere* for it. To that end then, to see the text safe and well kept, the three persons in it, all to join together: Kings, touching whom; and subjects, to whom; and God Himself, by Whom it is given in charge. And if the two former do their parts, God will not fail in His.

Let me add one thing more. That this text, besides that it is a commandment, it is also a thanksgiving; but both have but one errand, the King's safety.

A commandment, it is from God: the very style, the mood, *Nolite*, giveth it for no less.

And a thanksgiving, it is to God; for it is a verse of a Psalm, of a Hallelujah Psalm, of the first Hallelujah Psalm. (There be twenty of them in all, this is the first of them all.)

A commandment it is; for it is proclaimed with sound of trumpet, and that by Benaiah and his company. And a thanksgiving it is; for it is sung with solemn music by Asaph and the quire, at the sixth and seventh verses before. It is both, and both ways we to have use of it.

First, as of a commandment from God, to teach us this duty towards God's "Anointed." I trust, we will perform better duties to them than this; but whatsoever we do besides, what good we do them, *ne noceat*, not to touch them, to do them no hurt.

And, never so much need of this doctrine as now, when by a late heavy accident, we see, wretches there are dare attempt it: and other, (and they the more wretches of the twain,) that did dare to avow it. Did dare, I say; for now, they would seem to disavow it; but so poorly and faintly, as all they say may hold, and yet another like act be done to-morrow.

And then secondly, as a thanksgiving to God, Who hath set the print of this commandment upon this day, in cutting short this day two wicked imps, that went about to break it, by touching, and more than touching, the Lord's Anointed.

And never were we so much bound to do it, as this year: for that, this year, upon this fresh occasion, truly we may say, He hath dealt thus with us, *Non taliter fecit omni nationi,* Ps.147.20. "He hath not so dealt with all nations," nor hath every King[1] found Him so gracious. Others have not, in theirs; I speak it with compassion: we have, in ours; I speak it to our comfort, and to the praise of God. Both these ways.

Christos Meos. An honourable title to begin with: and begin with it we must: the very grammar-rules lead us to it. "Anointed" is but an adjective, we are to seek the substantive for it. But besides, we are to find who they be, whom we are not to "touch," lest we "touch" them unawares. And as well, that we may know the right, and do them their right; as that we may discern them from the wrong; for wrong there be, that call themselves *Christos Domini,* whom the Holy Ghost never christened by that name.

As, of Christ Himself, many come and say, *Ecce, hic est* Mark 13. *Christus, ecce illic,* "here is Christ, and there is Christ," and [21.] deceive many; so of these Christs here likewise: See, here is *Christus Domini,* and there he is, and no such matter. Our first point then is to know who they be.

These, in the text here, were the Patriarchs, it cannot be Patriarchs, denied. They be set down by their names, Abraham, Isaac, Domini. Jacob, touching whom *primâ intentione,* this charge is given, that they be not touched.

And let not this seem strange: for in the first world, the Patriarchs were principal persons, and as I may safely say, princes in their generations, and for such holden and reputed by those with whom they lived. I may safely say it: for of

[1 Henry IV. of France was murdered in May this year.]

Christos Meos, who they be.

Patriarchs, Christi Domini.

S E R M.
III.
Gen. 23. 6.
Gen. 14.
14—16.
Gen. 26. 28.
Gen. 48. 22.
Abraham it is in express terms said by the Hethites, *Audi domine, Princeps Dei es inter nos,* "Thou art a Prince of God," that is, a mighty Prince, here among us.   As indeed, a Prince he shewed himself, when he gave battle and over-throw to four kings at once.   Of Isaac no less may be said, who grew so mighty, as the King of Palestine was glad to entreat him to remove further off, and not dwell so near him; and then, to go after him in person, and sue to him, there might be a league of amity between them.   And the like of Jacob, who by "his sword and bow" conquered from the Amorite (the mightiest of all the nations in Canaan) that country which by will he gave to Joseph for his possession. It was near to Sychar, well known; you have mention of it John the fourth, and the fifth verse.

Great men they were certainly, greater than most con-ceive; but be their greatness what it will, this is sure, they were all the rulers the people of God then had; and besides them, rulers had they none.   And that is it we seek : *pater* was in them, and ἀρχή too, fatherhood and government: In Ps. 140.
[4 Tom.
887. *Ben.*
Edit.] and these two made them patriarchs, *et unctos ante unctionem,* saith St. Augustine, 'anointed before there was any material anointing at all.'

Princes,
Christi
Domini. In them then this term began, and in them it held so long as they had the government in them.   But Patriarchs were not always to govern God's people; but Kings, in ages following, were to succeed in their places.   And so did succeed them : succeed them in the word *pater,* and in the word ἀρχή both; both in the right of their fatherhood, and the rule of their government, as fathers of their countries, and governors of their commonwealths.   Where the patri-archal rule expired, the regal was to take place, being both one in effect.   For, Abraham the Patriarch is termed "a Prince" (Gen. 23. 6) : and to make even, David the Prince is termed "a Patriarch."   "Let me speak boldly unto you of the Patriarch David," saith St. Peter (Acts 2. 29).   So that two things we gain here : 1. That *jus regium* cometh out of *jus patrium,* 'the King's right' from ' the father's,' and both hold by one commandment.   Then 2. that this text bindeth, as a law of nature, being given for such to the old world, long before the Law came in any Tables.

Now, that as in other things, so in this term of *Christi* 1 Sam. 12.
Domini, Kings do succeed the Patriarchs, we have, first, our 3, 4.
2 Sam. 19.
warrant from the Holy Ghost, applying this term here, after, 21.
to Saul, to David, to Solomon, to Hezekiah, to Josiah, to 2 Chron.
6. 42.
Cyrus : Kings all. Secondly, from the Councils : the third Hab. 3. 13.
Lam. 4. 20.
general Council of Ephesus ; the great Council of Toledo, the Isa. 45. 1.
fourth ; the great western Council of Frankfort. Thirdly, Append.
ad tom. 4.
from the consent of Fathers. To dispatch them at once : vol. 1.
so saith the Council of Frankfort, *B. Hieronymus, et cæteri* p. 1097.
Can. 74.
S. Scripturæ tractatores, &c. ' St. Hierom and the rest of the Con. Tol. iv.
vol. 3. 76.
writers on Scripture,' all understand it not of others, but of Synod.
Kings. Yea, lastly, from their own writers, Cajetan and Ge- Franc.
vol. 3.
nebrard, who themselves so apply it, upon this very place. p. 649.
Nay, Kings they will grant (they can neither will nor Editio
Venet.
choose): but then, they would hem in others likewise, to 1585.
enter-common in the title ; as the Pope, as the Cardinals, Princes
only in
and as any else, save them that be indeed. But that they Scripture
have the
must do then without book : for, in this book, warrant have title of
they none. For this term, *Christi Domini,* here, originally Christi
Domini.
ascribed to the Patriarchs, is ever afterward, without variation, continually appropriate to Kings, and to Kings only,
all the Bible through. The question is, whether we will
speak as the Holy Ghost doth, or no. If we will, then upon
a just survey taken of all the places, where the word *Christus
Domini* is to be found in Scripture, three and thirty they be
in number. Of which one only is in the New, and that is Lu. 2. 26.
of our Saviour Himself; the rest, all in the Old. Four
times by God, " Mine Anointed ;" six times to God, " Thine
Anointed ;" ten times of God, " His Anointed ;" twelve
times in terms terminant, " God's Anointed." Of which,
twice it is said of the Patriarchs ; here, and in the hundred Ps. 105. 15.
and fifth Psalm (which two places are indeed but one). All
the rest are said either of Christ, or of Kings, all ; and never
applied to any other, but to them only. And here we join
issue : if to any other the Scripture apply *Christos Domini,*
we yield ; if to none but them, we carry it. For, what reason
have we, if the Scripture appropriate it to them, and none
but them ; to take it from them, and give it to others, to
whom the Holy Ghost never gave it ?
Yet have I no meaning to deny, but that others, not only

Though
other
persons
" anoint-
ed," yet
none call-
ed " the
Lord's
anointed."

[2 Mac.
1. 10.]

persons, but (if they will) even things too, were anointed under the Law. Persons, as Priests and Prophets; things, as the tabernacle, and all the vessels of it, even to the very fire-forks, ash-pans, and snuffers. But though they were so, yet none of the things, nay, nor any of the persons, have ever the name given them of *Christus Domini.* No Prophet, of all the fellowship of the Prophets; no Priest, no not the High Priest himself, ever so called. It may be anointed, but not " the Lord's Anointed :" it may be *uncti,* not *Christi ;* or, in a corner of one chapter of the Maccabees, *christi* once, but not with his full Christendom, not *Christi Domini.* Still they fall short; and *Christus Domini* follows the King, and him only.

Yea, this ye shall observe in their own old translator : that the same word in Hebrew and Greek, when he speaketh of the Priest, he ever turneth it *unctus ;* when of the King, *Christus* ever : as if, of purpose, he meant by this word, to make a partition between them. Any will think, there was surely meant them some special prerogative more than the rest; that from the rest it is given them, and ever to them, and to none of the rest.

We may well conclude this point then, with the Apostle : 'They are made so much the more excellent than the rest, by how much they have obtained a more excellent name than the rest. For unto which of all the rest at any time said He,

Heb.1.4,5. Thou art Mine Anointed ?' Enough to settle this term upon Kings. The Holy Ghost attributes it to them, and none but them. We to understand it of them, and none but them. It is, and so let it be, their own due style, their proper denomination. " Touch not Mine Anointed." Who be they ? If we go by the book, Princes : why then, Touch not Princes.

Meos,
the claim
whose
they be.

Christos Meos, who they be, we see. But in these words, we said, there are not only the parties, whom they should not; but the reason, why they should not "touch" them. And not one reason ; but two at the least. Now then, let us take the words in sunder, and weigh either by itself; seeing either word is a reason *de non tangendo.* First, whose they be : His, *Meos.* Then, what of His : His " Anointed." And His " Anointed" is *Christi Ejus :* which, it may be, will amount to two reasons more. *Meos,* is his claim; *Christos,* His character or special mark.

Meos, His claim : which word is not slightly to be passed Lay no
by. It is to the purpose. To claim is to touch. He that title to them.
saith *Meos*, He that claims them, toucheth them : toucheth
their freehold, as we say. He that saith, Touch them not,
saith, Claim them not. Some question there is grown,
whose they be. Two claims there are put in, and laid to
them, besides. *Meos*, saith the Pope ; and *meos*, say some
for the people ; but neither say true. God, He saith *Christos
Meos*, and He only hath the right to say.

Meos, saith the Pope. For he, or some by his commission, 1.
used to anoint the Emperors, and because he was master of *Meos*, the Pope's
the ceremony, he would be master of the substance too : claim.
and his they were. The Pope, he was God's ; and they
were his anointed, and of him had their dependence, and
he to depose them, and to dispose of them, and to do with his
own what he list. And this claim is not yet given over.
For, he that shall mark the Pope's faintness, when some
Kings are sought to be touched ; nay, are touched indeed,
out of his *meos;* will easily think, he is well enough content
they be touched, though they be God's " Anointed," if they
be not his too. Touch not his : not his ; as for others, it
skilleth not, touch them who will.

But this claim by the ceremony is clean marred by this
text ; for when these words here were spoken, there was no
such ceremony instituted, it was *non ens*, no such thing *in
rerum naturâ*. That came not up, till Moses. Now these
here in the text were in their graves long before Moses was
born. No *Meos* then ; no claim by the ceremony.

And after it came up, no Priest went out of Jewry to Per- 2.
sia, to carry the ceremony to Cyrus ; yet of him saith Esay, Isa. 45. 1.
Hæc dicit Dominus Cyro Christo Meo, " Thus saith the Lord
to Cyrus Mine anointed," and yet never came there any oil
upon his head. So that even after it was taken up, yet the
ceremony, and the claim by it, would not hold. The truth
is, the ceremony doth not any thing ; only declareth what is
done. The party was before, as much as he is after it ; only
by it is declared to be, that he was before, and that which
he should have been still, though he had never so been declared. The truth may and doth subsist, as with the ceremony, so without it. It may be retained, as with some it is,

SERM. III.

and with us it is: and it may be spared, as it is with others.
Spared or retained, all is one; no claim groweth that way.

3.

But last of all, where it was used, as by Samuel to Saul, by Zadoc to Solomon; yet they claimed nothing in the parties they anointed, but called them still God's, and never their own "anointed." They knew no claim lay by it: nay, if it had been a Sacrament, as it was but a ceremony; he that ministereth the Sacrament hath no interest in the party by it, but God alone; and then much less he, that performeth but a ceremony, is to plead any *meos.* So that every way this claim vanisheth, of *christi pontificis.*

Meos, the people's claim.

Bellar-mine.

Now then, a second claim, another *meos,* hath of late begun to be buzzed of, as if they were *christi populi,* and held of them. And whatsoever the matter is, the Cardinal himself waxeth very earnest for it: (I think, because he seeth the Pope's arm groweth short, and loth he is but that there should be still some hands to touch them:) he will not so much as give God leave to appoint Saul or David of Himself, but he taketh upon him to suspend them both, until the people with their suffrage come in, and ratify God's doing.

But this claim likewise falleth to the ground, even by this verse: then must we go mend our text here. For if so; God was properly to have said, *Nolite tangere christos vestros,* 'Touch not your anointed;' for to the people He speaketh. Of all others, *Meos* cannot be theirs, unless we will gloss it thus, *Meos, id est, non Meos;* "Mine," that is, 'none of Mine,' but your own. And then sure, He should have done them some wrong, to have forbid them to touch that, which was their own. The Pope saith, he can make *Christum Dominum,* 'Christ the Lord Himself.' If he could so do indeed, it were not altogether unlike, he might make *Christum Domini.* But God help, if the people fall to make gods, or make christs, if they shall take God's verse from Him, and

Ps. 82. 6.

John 19. 11.

say, *Nos diximus, dii estis,* 'We have said, ye are gods;' yea, and christs too; and change it, "Thou shouldest have no power unless it were" *data desuper,* "given from above," saith he; they, unless it were *data de subter,* 'unless it were given you hence from beneath:' then must we go change all our texts that sound that way. Enough to let you see, they both claim that is none of theirs, but God's.

To give in evidence now, for God's right ; that His *Meos* is the only true claim, that His only they be. Three times over, it is told us by Daniel in one chapter, that "the Kingdoms be God's," and that "He giveth them to whom He will," as having the sole property of them. And it is said there, that this is *sententia vigilum, et sermo sanctorum.* And if it be *sententia vigilum,* they are scarce well awake, that think otherwise : and if it be *sermo sanctorum,* they talk profanely, that speak otherwise. And this verily was the divinity of the primitive Church concerning Kings, which, of all, had least cause to favour them. *Cujus jussu nascuntur homines, ejus jussu constituuntur Principes,* ' By whose appointment they be born men, (and that is, neither by people's, nor by Pope's,) by His appointment, and no other, are they made Princes,' saith old Irenæus. *Inde illis potestas, unde spiritus,* ' Thence have they their power, whence they have their breath,' saith Tertullian : and that is from neither, I am sure, but from God alone.

His they be : for His their crown, *Diadema Regis in manu Dei,* Esay the sixty-second. And as if he saw a hand come from Heaven with a crown in it, so speaketh he in the twenty-first Psalm. *Tu posuisti,* "Thou hast set a crown of pure gold upon His head." His, their sceptre, or rod : *Virga Dei in manibus ejus,* " God's rod in His hand," of Moses. His their throne : *Sedebat Salomon in throno Dei,* " Solomon sat upon God's throne." Nay, long before, in the law of nature, saith Job, *Reges in solio collocat in perpetuum,* He takes them by the hand, and " placeth them in the throne," and that *in perpetuum,* there to sit, in themselves, and their succession, " for ever." His, their anointing : *Oleo sancto Meo,* " with Mine holy oil." The anointing His, therefore the " Anointed." And if all these, their crown, their sceptre, their throne, their anointing His ; then His they be, *Christi Domini.* And of *Christi Domini* we shall shew twelve fair evidences in express terms, " God's Anointed." And ten more we shall bring forth with an *Ejus,* a plain reference to Him, " His Anointed." *Christi Pontificis,* Samuel's or Zadoc's anointed ; *Christi populi,* Judah's or Israel's anointed, *non legitur,* ' we shall not find.' His they be then.

Marginal notes:

3.

Meos, God's claim. Dan. 4. 17, 25, 32.

Lib. 5. [cap. 24. Lut. Par. 1675.]

Apolog. p. 6. [27. Rigalt. c. 30.]

Isa. 62. 3.

Ps. 21. 3.

Exod. 17. 9.

1 Chron. 29. 23. Job 36. 7.

Ps. 89. 20.

Now infer. His; therefore hand off, what have you to do with that is none of yours? what to claim or to touch that is His? *Nolite tangere Meos.* This only, and no more but this, in very equity were enough, "Touch not Mine." This for *Meos;* now to *Unctos.*

"Anointed,"
Uncti.
His then; but not as all are by a general tenure; but His, as His "Anointed," by a more special and peculiar kind of interest. His "Anointed" is more than His, for all His are not "anointed;" for if all were "anointed," there should be none left to "touch" them: we might strike out this verse, the charge were in vain, there were none to receive it. If all be *Uncti,* where should be *tangentes?* We must then needs leave a difference between *Christiani* and *Christi.* For,

Numb.
16. 3.
holding all that are Christians, all God's people "anointed" and "holy" alike; it will follow, why should Moses then, or any, take upon him to be their superior? And so we fall

Jude 11.
into the old "contradiction of Korah:" which is all one with the new parity and confusion of the Anabaptists, or those that prick fast towards them.

But the very ceremony itself serveth to shew, somewhat is added to them, by which they be His, after a more peculiar manner than the rest, to whom that is not added. Oil itself designeth sovereignty. Pour together water, wine, vinegar, what liquor you will, oil will be uppermost. And that is added by their anointing. Besides then this general claim "Mine," here is His special signature "Anointed," whereby they are severed from the rest. His hand hath touched them with His anointing, that no other hand might "touch" them. Things anointed of ourselves we forbear to touch; but specially, if the anointing have the nature of a mark, that we wrong it not. And this hath so, these are so marked, that we might forbear them. And yet more specially, if we have a caveat, not to do it, as here we have. *Nolite tangere Unctos,* "Touch not them that I have anointed."

" Anointed," yet not *uncti,* but *christi,* which is more.
This were all, if it were but "Anointed;" but there is yet a further matter than all this. For it is not *Unctos,* but *Christos Meos.* We read it, "Mine Anointed:" in the Hebrew, Greek and Latin, it is more full. In Hebrew, "My Messiahs;" in Greek and Latin, *Christos Meos,* that is, "My Christs," which is far more forcible. Somewhat (we may be

sure) was in it, that all the old writers uniformly forbore to turn it *unctos,* which is enough for " anointed," and all have agreed to turn it *christos,* that is, " christs," which is a great deal more. It seems they meant not to take a grain from this charge, but to give it his full weight. And it cannot but weigh much with all that shall weigh this one point well, that Princes are taken into the society of God's Name in the Psalm before; and here now into the society of Ps. 82. 6. Christ's Name in this: and so made *synonymi,* both with God and with Christ: specially, since God Himself it is That so styleth them; for He flatters not, we are sure. God Himself is a King, " King of all the earth," and Christ Ps. 47. 7. is His Heir of all, as appeareth by His " many crowns on Rev.19.12. His head." Those whom God and Christ vouchsafe to take into the charge of any of their Kingdoms, them they vouchsafe their own names of God and of Christ. They two, the first Kings; to these other the after Kings, ruling under them, and in their names.

A third gradual reason then there riseth here. All " Anoint- anointed are not *christi;* for all anointing is not chrism. ed," not with every Chrism is not every common, but an holy anointing, a sacred ointment, signature. *Oleo sancto Meo,* " with Mine holy oil have I but with "holy," anointed them." *Meo* to make them His; *sancto* to make and so, them sacred. He might have taken this oil out of the apo- Ps. 89. 20. thecary's shop, or the merchant's warehouse. He did not, but from the Sanctuary itself, to shew their calling is sacred, sacred as any, even the best of them all. From whence the Priests have theirs; thence, and from no other place, the King hath his: from the Sanctuary, both. The anointing is one and the same. All to shew, that sacred is the office where- unto they designed, sacred the power wherewith they endued, sacred the persons whereto it applied. And for such were they held, all the primitive Church through. Their writ, *sacri apices:* their word, *divalis jussio:* their presence, *sacra vestigia* (the usual style of the Councils, when they spake of them.) And when they ceased to know themselves for His, (That here saith *Meos,*) and to hold of Him, then lost they their holiness. He that took from them the one, took to Himself the other. Now then, will ye infer: Holy they be, their anointing hallowed; therefore *Nolite tangere sacros,*

S E R M.
III.
——————
Exod. 19.
12, 13.
Heb. 12.
20.
1 Chron.
13. 10.
" Anoint-
ed," not
with every
" holy oil,"
but with a
special
above
the rest,
and so
christi.
Ps. 45. 7.

"Touch not Mine holy ones." No more touch Moses, than the holy Mount, which neither man nor beast might touch upon pain of death : no more touch David, than the holy Ark. It is not good, touching of holy things. In the thirteenth chapter before, Uzzah so found it.

And yet still methinks we fall short : for it is not *sanctos* neither : it is more than *sanctos*, it is *Christos;* in which word, there is more than in *commune sanctorum. Omnes Sancti non sunt Christi, at Reges Christi ;* ' We cannot say of all Saints they be Christs, of Kings we may.' Verily, every degree of holiness will not make a synonym with Christ. He was " anointed," saith the Psalm, *oleo exultationis supra socios,* " with a holy oil or chrism above His fellows." To hold this name then of *Christos Domini,* it is not every ordinary holiness will serve, but a special and extraordinary degree of it above the rest, which they are to participate ; and so do, from Christ, whose name they bear, eminent above others, that carry not that Name ; as if they did in some kind of measure partake *chrisma Christi,* even ' such a chrism as wherewith Christ is anointed.' And the inference of this point, and the meaning of this style of *Dii* and *Christi,* is, as if He would have us, with a kind of analogy, as careful in a manner to forbear touching them, as we would be to touch God, or the Son of God, Christ Himself. It is not then *Meos,* nor *Unctos Meos,* nor *Sanctos Meos* only, but it is *Christos Meos,* " Mine," and that " Anointed," " anointed with holy oil :" so " anointed," and with oil so " holy," as it raiseth them to the honour of the denomination of the Holy of Holies, Christ Himself. These four degrees, and from them these four several reasons, are in *Christos Meos.*

What this
anointing
is.

One thing more of *Christos Meos :* for I should do you wrong certainly, if I should slip by it, and not tell you what this anointing is, and leave a point loose, that needeth most of all to be touched. Upon misconceiving of this point, some have fallen into a fancy, His " Anointed " may forfeit their tenure, and so cease to be His, and their anointing dry up, or be wiped off, and so Kings be un-christed, cease to be *Christi Domini ;* and then, who that will may touch them.

They that have been scribbling about King's matters of

late, and touching them with their pens, have been foully
mistaken in this point. Because, anointing, in Scripture,
doth otherwhile betoken some spiritual grace, they pitch upon
that, upon that taking of the word; and then anointing,
it must needs be some grace: some *gratia gratum faciens*,
making them religious and good Catholics; or some *gratia
gratis data*, making them able or apt for to govern. So that
if he will not hear a mass, no Catholic, no " Anointed." If
after he is " anointed" he grow defective, (to speak their own
language,) prove a tyrant, fall to favour heretics, his anointing may be wiped off, or scraped off; and then you may
write a book *De justâ abdicatione*, make a holy league, touch
him, or blow him up, as ye list. This hath cost Christendom
dear : it is a dangerous sore, a *Noli me tangere;* take heed
of it, touch it not.

Before I tell you what it is, I may safely tell you, that this
it is not. It is not religion, nor virtue, nor any spiritual
grace, this royal anointing. *Christos Domini* is said not
only of Josiah, a King truly religious, by Jeremy; but of
Cyrus, a mere heathen, by Esay: not only of David a good
King, but of Saul a tyrant, even then when he was at the
worst. Religion then is not it, for then Cyrus had not
been; nor virtue is not it, (especially the virtue of clemency,) for then Saul had not been God's " Anointed."
If it were religion, if that made kings, then had there been
of old no kings but those of Judah ; and now, no kings, but
those that be Christian. But by Cyrus's case we see, one
may be *Christus Domini*, and yet no Christian.

[marginal notes: It is no spiritual grace. Lam. 4. 20. Isa. 45. 1. 2 Sam. 19. 21. 1 Sam. 26. 9.]

Among Christen, if the orthodox truth were it, Constantius, Valens, Valentinian the younger, Anastasius, Justinian,
Heraclius, I know not how many, had been no emperors;
yet all so acknowledged by the Christians of their times.

Then, if religion make them not, heresy will not unmake
them. What speak I of heresy ? Harder is the case of
apostasy, yea hardest of all : yet when Julian from a Christian fell away to be a flat pagan, his anointing held; no
Christian ever sought, no bishop ever taught to " touch" him.
And it was not *quia deerant vires*, that their hand was too
short : it is well known, far the greater part of his army were
Christians, and could have done it, as appeared instantly

SERM. upon his death, by their acclamations to Jovian his suc-
III. cessor, *Christiani sumus.*

Will ye see it in the Patriarchs? These in the Psalm
Gen. 49. here were holy and good men. But twelve Patriarchs there
5, 6, 7; were presently after, of whom Simeon and Levi were two
35. 22; very [tyrants; Reuben, scarce honest; nor Judah, no better
38. 16; than he should; Issachar, by his blessing, should seem none
49. 14. of the wisest (as it might be Rehoboam) : yet were they
numbered with the twelve, and were Patriarchs still, no less
than the other.

And after the Patriarchs, Saul the first King (that there
might be no mistaking), with his anointing, there came no
grace to him. "The Spirit of God came" indeed "upon
1 Sam. 10. him;" but he was anointed, and gone from Samuel first:
9, 10. and the same Spirit, as It came, so It went, and left him
1 Sam. 16. afterward: and God's "Anointed" he was, before It came,
14. and God's "Anointed" he remained, after It was gone
again, and that no less than before, and is so termed by
David ten times at the least.

It is *jus*   *Unxit in Regem,* Royal unction gives no grace, but a just
regnandi. title only, *in Regem,* 'to be king:' that is all, and no more.
It is the administration to govern, not the gift to govern
well : the right of ruling, not the ruling right. It includes
nothing but a due title ; it excludes nothing but usurpation.
Who is anointed? On whom the right rests. Who is
Gen. 10. 9. *inunctus?* He that hath it not. Suppose Nimrod, who
cared for no anointing, thrust himself in, and by violence
usurped the throne: came in rather like one steeped in
vinegar, than anointed with oil: rather as a ranger over
a forest, than a father over a family. He was no anointed,
nor any that so cometh in. But on the other side; David,
or he that first beginneth a royal race, is as the head; on
him is that right of ruling first shed; from him it runs
down to the next, and so still, even to the lowest borders
Job 36. 7. of his lawful issue. Remember Job, *Reges in solio collocat
in perpetuum.* It is for ever. God's claim never forfeits :
His character never to be wiped out, or scraped out, nor
Kings lose their right, no more than Patriarchs did their
fatherhood.

Not but that it were to be wished, both anointings might

go together, and that there might go, as there doth, a fragrant odour from the precious ointment which is shed upon them, at their crowning; so like a scent from their virtues, and they no less venerable for their qualities, than for their callings; and happy the people, *qui currunt in odore un-* Cant. 1. 3. *guentorum Principis sui,* "that can trace their Prince by such a savour." This we are to wish for, and pray for daily, and use all good means, it may be. But, if it be not; ever hold this: allegiance is not due to him, because he is virtuous, religious, or wise; but because he is *Christus Domini.* Let this be still in your mind: God saith not, Touch him not, he is a good Catholic, or endued with this virtue or that; Touch him not, he deserveth well, or at least doth no harm. No; these would fail, he saw; or be said to fail, though they failed not: we should never then have done, never have been quiet. But this He saith, He is "Mine Anointed." Mark that well, God giveth no other reason here, nor David after, in as evil a Prince as might be. That is the true reason then, and we to rest in it, and let other fancies go.

Now, by whose appointment they be set, by His com- II. mandment they be fenced: fenced from touching, and that *Tangere,* the act is the lightest and least; consequently from whatsoever is forbidden. greater or worse. What talk you of *Non occides,* or *Ne perdas?* I tell you, *Ne tangas,* "Touch them not."

Yet are we not so sillily to understand it, as if one might not "touch" them at all, not for their good; for how can they be "anointed," but they must be touched? No, the verse before telleth us, it is for their hurt, this touch is forbidden. *Non permisit nocere,* "He suffereth no man to do them hurt;" to that end saying, "Touch them not." Yea, the very word itself, without any gloss, giveth as much, which is נגע, properly *plaga,* and that is *tactus noxius,* "a hurtful touch," that leaveth a mark behind it, *qui tangit et angit,* as the verse is. For, it is good ye understand, this phrase is taken from the devil: and good reason; and whosoever the fingers be, his the touch is, when God's "anointed" are touched. He calleth it but touching Job; Job 1. 11, but touching, when he did him all the mischief he could and 2. 5. devise. And his nature, and the nature of hurtful things,

is well set out by it.   Few things are so good, *ut in transitu
prosint,* 'as they only touch, and do good :' evil is far more
operative, if it but touch and away, if it but blow or breathe
upon any, it is found to do mischief enough.

The extent
of *tan-
gere :* how
many ways
" touch."
To speak then of this touching, and the extent of it.
Where the Scripture distinguisheth not, neither do we ; but
let the word have its full latitude.   *Nolite tangere* is general, no kind is limited ; then, not to " touch" any manner
of way.

1.   There is none so simple, as to imagine there is no touch,
but that with the finger's end, immediate.   The mediate,
with a knife or with a pistol, that is a touch : if we touch
that whereby they are touched, it is all one.

Again, be the touch so as we feel it, or be it by means
unsensible, as of poison, or sorcery, it is a touch still, and
these no less guilty.   No less ? nay, a great deal more, as
the more dangerous of the twain.   One shall be touched,
and know not how, when, or by whom.   " Cursed be he
that smiteth his neighbour secretly," saith the Law.   His
neighbour ? much more his Prince, between which two there
is as great a distance, as between *Non occides* and *Non tanges.*
In a word, as it is the lightest, so it is the largest term He
could choose.   For, *Non est actio nisi per contactum,* saith
the philosopher, ' Nothing can be done but a touch there is :'
some touch, superficial or virtual, immediate or mediate,
cominus or *eminus,* open or privy ; and all come under *tangere.*   For it is not, *Nolite sic tangere,* " Touch not this way
or that ;" but, *Nolite tangere,* " Touch not any way at all :"
let nothing be done at all, to do them hurt.

Deut. 27.
24.

2.   And is there no touch, but that of the violent hand ?   The
virulent tongue, doth not that touch too ? and the pestilent
pen, as ill as both ?   *Venite, percutiamus eum linguá,* say
they in Jeremy, " Come, let us smite him with the tongue."
If " smite him," then " touch" him, I am sure.   " There
is," saith Solomon, " that speaketh" (and is not there also
that writeth ?) " words, like the pricking of a sword."   *Et
qui quos Deus ungit, eos pungit,* cometh not he within the
compass of this charge ?   Yes, they be Satan's weapons,
both tongues and pens ; have their points and their edges :
their points, and prick like a sword ; their edges, and cut

Jer. 18. 18.

Prov. 12.
18.

like a razor; both touch, and with the worst touch that is,
tactus dolore cordis; therefore the worst, because of the best
part. These it is God's meaning to restrain : you may see
it by the verse before, *Non dimisit hominem calumniari,*
saying, *Nolite tangere.* So that even *calumnia* is a touch.
You may see it exemplarily in the Patriarchs. One of
God's *nolite tangere*s was touching Laban to Jacob, and this
it was : *Vide ne quid loquare durius,* "See you give him no
ill language," no foul words ; for they touch too. Touch
him not so. As well to Shimei's tongue, as to Jacob's
hand, is this *nolite tangere* spoken.

Gen. 31.
24.

Is this all? What say you to the touch with the foot?
the foot of pride upon the necks or crowns of emperors
(though no crick or bodily pain ensued) ? Will not *Nolite
tangere* reach to *Nolite calcare?* Yes, certainly : this *Nolite
tangere* was a stronger text against it, than *Super aspidem
et basiliscum* was a text for it.

3.

[Ps. 91.
13.]

Yea, I go further. By an undecent and over-familiar
touch, void of the reverence that is due to them, *læditur
pietas,* 'duty taketh hurt,' and wrong is offered to His
"Anointed." Mary Magdalene was not about to have done
our Saviour any harm, when after His resurrection she
offered to touch Him; only because she did it as to one
mortal (where the case was altered now), and not with the
high reverence pertaining to His glorified estate, she heard,
and heard justly, *Noli Me tangere.* The touch which any
way impeacheth the high honour of their anointing, *Nolite
tangere* takes hold of that too.

4.

"Touch them not;" not them. And when we say, not
them, mean we their persons only, and not their states?
Are not they touched, when those are wronged? They that
"touch" their crown and dignity, their regalia, shall we say
they "touch" them not? Yes, no less ; nay rather, more.
For then the "anointed" are properly touched, when their
anointing is, and that is their state and crown, as dear every
way, and as precious to them, as their life. Indeed "touch"
one, and "touch" both. If their state hold not holy, no
more will their persons. It hath ever been found, if their
crown once go, their life tarrieth not long after. And even
in this point also, it may safely be said, that the loose and

1.
The extent
of *christos,*
how many
ways they
touched.

licentious touching their state, with Mary Magdalene's touch, without the regard due to it, as if it were a light matter, that might be lifted with every finger, falleth within the reach of this *Nolite.* I list not dilate it, it would be looked to. These light and loose touchings are but the beginnings of greater evils.

2. Again, not them. Satan's motion was twofold : 1. One, that he might "touch" that was Job's; 2. the other, that "touch" himself : and in either of these, he reckoned that he should "touch" him home. They are touched, when that is touched, that is theirs. It was so here directly. Pharaoh, one of them to whom originally, nay the very first of all, to whom this *Nolite* was spoken, touched not Abraham himself; it was Sarah was wronged : in Sarah was Abraham touched. So God esteemed it, and gave his first *Nolite tangere* in that point. So, even unto her wrong, doth this touch extend : take in her too, as being the one half, yea, one and the same person with "the Lord's Anointed."

3. Not them. One more yet : for two kinds of "anointed" I find in Scripture : Saul's and David's : the one *in esse*, the other *in fore;* one 'in being,' the other 'to be.' If David had been touched (Saul yet living), though but "anointed" to succeed, I make no doubt this commandment had been broken : for we are bound by it, to preserve the anointing, not only upon the head, but even in the streams running down from it : that with the King himself, the whole race royal is folded up in this word, every one of them in their order, that not one of them is to be touched neither.

Nolite :
The will
forbidden.
This bar then is set to the touch every way, and to the touch of them, and every of theirs, every way. But there is a further matter yet. For, (if we mark it well,) it is not *Ne tangite,* but *Nolite tangere : Nolite,* that is, " Have not so much as the will," once to go about it. So that, not only *tactus,* 'the touch' is forbidden, but *voluntas tangendi,* 'the very will to do it ;' for that will is *tactus animæ,* 'the soul's touch :' the soul can touch no way but that. And God's meaning is absolute : neither body nor soul should touch ; neither the body by deed, nor the soul by will.

And *Nolite* standeth first, beginneth the text ; for indeed with that, is the right beginning. The devil toucheth the

will, before the hand ever touch God's "Anointed:" he
doth *mittere in cor,* 'put a will in the heart,' before any do
mittere manum, 'put forth their hand to do it.' Therefore,
even *velle tangere* was to be made a crime, and that a capital
crime. And so it is: for in the attainder of the two
eunuchs, (Esth. 2.) there was no more in the indictment but Est. 2. 21.
voluerunt, "they would" have done it, they would have
touched Ahasuerus. That being proved was enough: they
died, and died justly for the will, though no touch followed.
Pity it should be otherwise. He toucheth not always, that
hath a will to touch: hath a will to touch the throat, toucheth but a tooth. What though? To break *Nolite, voluit* is
enough; and *voluit* he would have touched, at another place.

They that laid the powder ready, and lighted the match,
it was but *voluerunt,* (as God would,) it touched not any;
but righteous and just was their execution. To teach them,
or others by them, *Ne tangite* is not it: *Nolite tangere* is the
charge; and if you break *Nolite* only, it is enough, though
tangere and it never hap to meet.

Of which *Nolite,* I hold it very pertinent to touch the The extent
extent also, as I did even now of *tangere,* the touch itself, of *Nolite,*
to whom it
and of the persons to whom it may reach; that we may see reacheth.
it, it is true in the verse before, *Non reliquit hominem,* "He
leaves not out a man," he exempts not any from it. I will 1.
not once speak of subjects, no question of them: over whom
they are "anointed," them it toucheth nearest, and bindeth 2.
them fast. But this I say, that even foreigners, born out
of their allegiance, are within it. The Amalekite was a 2 Sam. 1.
stranger, none of Saul's lieges, born out of his dominions; 10, 13.
yet died for saying he had touched Saul: and that sheweth,
that even aliens here *sortiuntur forum ratione delicti,* and
that they are intended, within this *Nolite.*

Yea, even such aliens as are in open hostility, even at 3.
that time they are in camp and in arms against a King,
they are barred by this *nolite,* and are to spare him. So 2 Sam.
saith David in his mourning-song for Saul's death: he 1. 21.
blames there the Philistines, as if they had done more than
they might, in so touching Saul, considering he was a King
with "holy oil anointed," as if they ought, even in that
respect, to have spared him. So that this *Nolite* is a law

of nations, making their persons so sacred, as even in the battle they are to be forborne, and their lives saved.

4. Yea, if we look to the words next before, it is given even to Kings, this "Touch not." The parties were Pharaoh King of Egypt, and the two Abimelechs Kings of Gerar, and even they in particular charged not to "touch" (for Pharaoh did touch): not "to will to touch" (for Abimelech went no further). Kings not to "touch them," none but God to "touch" them. As if it were another law of nations, not one King to "touch another; but, by virtue of this *Nolite*, each to spare, and to save the other's life.

5. And the difference in religion maketh here no let: for, these being Egyptians and Philistines, to whom it was given, there can be no greater difference, than between them and the Patriarchs, in the worship of God: for all that, not to 1 Cor. 6. 5. "touch" them though. Which is *ad erubescentiam nostram* "to our shame," that heathen men, and idolaters, were kept from it by this charge: and now, I will not say Christians, but holy religious men, Friars, and Priests, yea, and Martyrs forsooth, will not be held in by it, but they will be touching.

6. And last of all, this restraint of will and deed, it is not in the singular *Noli*, to this or that private man: it is in the plural, *Nolite*, and so reacheth to whole multitudes. *Nolite* will serve even people and countries, to restrain them also. I wonder at it: it is God's manner, to give His precepts in the singular: witness the whole Law, and all the Ten Commandments in it. How happeneth it, the number is here changed? Somewhat there is in that. He saw, multitudes might assay it, as well as single men, and take liberty to themselves, thinking to be privileged by their number. To make sure, He putteth it in a number that encloseth them too. For, be they many or be they few, *Nolite* will take them in, all. So, neither subject, nor alien, nor enemy, nor King, nor people; nor one religion, nor other; nor one, nor many; *non reliquit hominem*, none left, none exempt, not any to "touch" them, not any "to will to touch" them. For, with *Nolite*, God toucheth the heart: and so many as God toucheth their hearts, will have *idem velle et nolle*, 'make His will their will,' and will obey it. This is the sum of the charge: here is the double fence I spoke of. "Touch not," by which he raiseth (as it

were) a high wall about them, that none may reach over to them. And then, with *Nolite*, diggeth deep even *in profundum cordis*, 'the very depth of the heart;' casteth a trench there: and so they be double fenced. Or you may (if you will) call them the Cherubim's two wings spread over His "Anointed," to protect them: "Touch not," one wing; *Nolite*, the other, reaching, as the Cherubim's wings did, from one wall to the other, covering them from all, that none may come any way to do them hurt. And by this we see the full of this text. We see it; but we are to feel it also, and see whether the text be whole, whether it will be well kept, and have taken no hurt.

The charge is short, ye see; a hemistichion, but half a verse; "Touch not Mine anointed:" four words only, and but six syllables. One would think, it might well be carried away, and well be kept. But, as short as it is, we see it is not though; for, the very text is touched and broken. And I speak not of inferior touchings, that every tongue is walking, and every pen busy, to touch them and their rights, which they are to have, and their duties which they are to do; and if they do not, then I know not what, nor themselves neither. This is too much, but I would it were but this.

Hands have been busy of late, and that in another more dangerous manner. Two fearful examples we have, in two[1] great Kings. One, no very long time since; the other, very lately made away: not so far from us, but that they may, and, I trust, do "touch" us. What shall I say? I would this were the worst.

Yea, I would this were the worst: for this hath happened in former times too. This Psalm, he that indited and set it (David), he living, Ishbosheth, his neighbour King, was slain upon his bed. The like hath happened then; broken it hath been, in former ages. But then, upon revenge, or ambition, or hope of reward, or some other sinister respect; never, upon conscience and religion, till now. *Nolite tangere* was still good divinity, till now. The text itself never touched, never taken by the throat before, and the contradictory of it given in charge: Touched they may be, Touch them notwithstanding: never books written, to make men willing to

Marginal notes:
How this text is observed.

[1 Henry III. and Henry IV. of France.]

The text itself touched, and a *Nolite* given to it.

S E R M.
III. God's *Nolite*, before. Baanah, he, upon hope of reward, slew
Ishbosheth: Bigthan, upon revenge, would have done the
like to his liege-lord. Zimri, upon ambition, slew his master.
But religion came never forth with the knife in her hand,
till now: a King's life was never a sacrifice to expiate sin,
before.

1. And will ye but consider the great odds betwixt those
touchers, and these of late? They, ever, ere they went
about it, cast how to escape; and, when they had done it,
fled and hid themselves, as guilty to themselves of evil they
had done: these stir not an inch, as if they had done that,
2. they might well stand to. Those formerly grew ever con-
trite, at their end detesting the act, and crying God mercy:
these now rejoice in it, as if by it they had done God a piece
3. of good service. Then yet it was ever a crime, and a grievous
crime, and they that did it were generally, upon the first
1. report, ever condemned by all men, none to defend them:
Mariana.
page 5 t. now it is, *multis laudantibus* (you know the book): ' it find-
eth many to justify, nay to praise it,' *et immortalitate dignum
judicantibus,* ' and think them worthy immortality,' for their
2. worthy act. Yea, write they not further? *Præclare cum*
Page 60. *rebus humanis ageretur, si multi,* ' It were a merry world,
if there would many so exercise their fingers,' to keep them
in ure. And to Kings themselves, God's " Anointed," dare
3. they not to say, This is *salutaris cogitatio,* ' a wholesome
Page 61.
[De Rege
et Regis
Instit. Lib.
1. c. 6.] meditation' for them, next their heart, to think *se eâ con-
ditione vivere,* ' they live in that case or condition,' *ut non
solum jure,* ' that they may not only be slain lawfully,'
sed cum laude, et gloriâ perimi possint, ' but to the praise
and glory of them that shall do it?' How now ! What
is become of our text, of *Nolite tangere,* with these ? Are
we not fallen into strange times, that men dare thus print
and publish, yea, even *prædicare peccatum suum,* ' preach
and proclaim their sins,' even these sinful and shameful po-
sitions, to the eyes and ears of the whole world ? Whereby,
God's " Anointed" are endangered, men's souls are poisoned,
Christian religion is blasphemed, as a murderer of her own
Kings, God in His charge is openly contradicted, and men
made believe, they shall go to Heaven, for breaking God's
commandments.

But now, we have all great cause to rejoice: the book is The cen-
condemned, if we may believe it. Whether condemned or sure upon Mariana
no, that we know not: this is too sure, eleven years ago set idle.
out it was, and that authorized, and so went eight whole
years, by their own confession; and even the whole eleven,
for aught that we know. How went it forth so allowed at
the first? How went it so long uncontrolled; without an
Index expurgatorius at least?

But now lately we have news, that some few years since,
it was censured in a privy Provincial Council. But that was
as strange a censure, as ever was heard of, a censure *sub
silentio,* kept close, and none knew of it but themselves:
fast or loose, censure or no censure, as they pleased. If
any such censure were, why made they it not as public as
their approbation? The approbation the world seeth; their
censure we but hear of, and peradventure it is but a tale,
neither. Why came it never to light till the deed was done,
and it was too late? Why heard we not Jacob's voice, till
we had felt Esau's hands? But this is all they have to say
for themselves: after so great a loss, this we must be fain to
take for payment.

But, I ask, is it condemned? indeed no; but the matter
so faintly carried, as all they say standing for good, he that
will give the like attempt again, may. For, what say they?
An usurper may be deposed: so they all agree. And is it
not in the power of Rome, to make an usurper when it
will? If he have no right, he is an usurper: if he be lawfully deposed, his right is gone: if he but favour heretics;
nay, though he favour them not, the Pope may depose him,
Non hoc tempore, sed cum judicabit expedire: and that done,
he hath no right, then is he an usurper, and ye may touch
him, or do with him what ye will.

What say they then further? A private man may not do
it, by his own authority. Not by his own; but may he, by
some other? Belike, some other then there is, whereby he
may. Authority then there is, and it may be given, and
when it is given him, he may do it. And so we are where
we were before. And this is their condemning: indeed the
condemnation of the world, if they love darkness so well as
to be deluded by it.

SERM.   First, they will do it. Will do it? Have done it, touched,
III.
——— touched in the highest degree, against *tangere*. It may be
against their wills; nay voluntary, have done it wittingly,
and willingly, against *Nolite*. But, it may be, repent themselves. Nor that : for they give a charge against this charge,
willing men, and making men willing, to do flat against it,
to touch even the text, and break it, and spare not; by holding, They may be touched for all it.

The text   What is then to be done of us? The more busy they, to
itself to be
preserved, suggest the devil's motion, *Mitte manum, et tange ;* the more
and kept   earnest we, to call on God's charge here, *Nolite tangere*
untouchen.
Christos Ejus. The more resolute they, to be touching ; the
more careful we, to look to their fingers. The more they
endeavour to break down this double fence; the more we
labour to strengthen it. How will that be? Ourselves not
to touch them? I will not speak of that, for shame. I
trust, God hath so touched all our hearts, as we detest the
least thought that way. Never was any truly partaker of the
inward anointing of a Christian man, but he was ever fast
and firm to the royal anointing. That we will do: and
that is not all ; (I trust) we will do more than so, even
provide a *Nolite tangere* for the text too, keep that from
touching, and that will keep God's Anointed untouched :
keep one, keep both.

By the   Three persons there be in the text : 1. God's "Anointed"
three per-
sons in the themselves, touching whom it is given. 2. We all, *Non reli-*
text.   *quit hominem,* not leaving a man of us out, to whom it is
given. 3. And He That saith *Meos,* God That giveth it.
The two first, to do their parts toward it, we to look to ours ;
and God will come in at His turn, and not fail with His
part, we may be sure.

1.   Let me begin with *Christos Domini,* whom it toucheth :
God's "an-
ointed."   that they would be touched with it, and not lay themselves
open to this touch, nor carelessly go where they may be
within the reach ; or fall into such fingers, as tickle to be
touching them : not to put it upon, What shall be, shall be.

[Tertull.de *Non est bonæ et solidæ fidei, sic omnia ad voluntatem Dei*
Exhort.
Cast. Cap. *referre, et ita adulari, ad unumquemque dicendo, Nihil fieri*
2.]   *sine jussione Ejus, ut non intelligamus aliquid esse in nobis*
ipsis. It is Tertullian : and most true it is that 'it is

neither good nor sound divinity, in these cases, to put all upon the will of God, and every one to flatter himself or others, saying, Nothing can be done without God's will, but to conceive aright, that withal there is somewhat that belongs to our part.' Therefore subordinately to serve God's providence with our own circumspect foresight and care, knowing that His providence doth not always work by miracle. This day it did: every day it will not do so. That He "gives Ps. 91. 11. His Angels charge over them that tempt Him not," that do not *mittere se deorsum*, "cast themselves wilfully into dan- Matt. 4. 6. ger." That Belshazzar's "days were numbered," when he Dan. 5. 26. forgat his duty, not before. That He hath indeed promised to "save His Anointed;" but He promised St. Paul also Ps. 20. 6. "his life, and all theirs with him in the ship," and that by Ac·s 27. "an Angel:" for all that, Paul would not let the mariners 23, 24, 30, go away with the boat, but cut the rope, and said, "If these tarry not in the ship, we cannot be saved," for all the Angel's promise. Let His "Anointed" say and do the like: keep your "mariners" about you in the name of God, keep yourselves with that state and guard that is meet for the Majesty of Princes; and think God saith to you, *Christi Mei, nolite tangi*, 'Be you willing to keep yourselves from being touched,' and I, for my part, will not be behind.

This way only is now left them. Another way there was, Exod. 19. that God's "Anointed" might not be touched: to set lists 12. about them, as about the holy mount, that is, laws: whereby, that desperate wretches might not touch God's "Anointed," God's "Anointed" might touch them first. I find Abime- Gen. 26. lech made a law to strengthen this law of God, made a list 11. about this very *Nolite*, a law upon pain of *morte morietur*. And this was wont to keep them from approaching. But, if that which should give strength to the law, and make it a law to the conscience, Divinity, if that be corrupted, if it be a matter of the will, as appeareth by *Nolite*, and the will be made wilful (a horrible sin, being now become a heroical and holy act): these lists will not hold them, the law cometh too late. For, if men grow wilful, it is well known, *Vitæ alienæ* [Seneca, *dominus est, quisquis contemptor est suæ*. And who would Ep. 4.] not be *contemptor suæ*, if he may be sure to be *comprehensor æternæ*? Then do but once persuade them, that for their

SERM.   touching they shall straight go to Heaven, and no " anoint-
III.   ed " shall ever stand before them.   *Nolite* is gone then : take
order for *tangere* how we can.

2.   Our part then is (and to us it is spoken, and to us properly
The
subject.   doth *Nolite* belong), every man in his place to do нiѕ best.
They that are His Priests, by bowing their knees daily, and
lifting up their hands to God.   They that in the place of
Council, by all the ways of wisdom.   They that in the seat
of justice, by just and due execution.   All, by all the means
[Virg. Æn. they can, *hanc talem terris avertere pestem*, to devise and
3, 620.]   procure, if it may be, *ne velint*, that evil-disposed hands
' would not :' but howsoever, *ne possint*, ' that they may not
be able,' if they would, to " touch" His " Anointed."   It
must be in part, by carrying a continual eye, and keeping
a continual watch over them ; or a shorter way, by removing them far enough off, that are in any likelihood to
do it : and those be such as hold God's " Anointed" be
tangibiles, and ' may be ;' nay, in some case, be *tangendi*,
and ' ought to be touched.'

Num. 16.   God Himself in Korah's case and Dathan's (who went
21, 24.   about to touch Moses and Aaron, not in their persons, but
estates only) sheweth us the best way.   He gave order, that
a general *Nolite tangere* went out against him and theirs,
that no man should come near them, but all shun them and
their company, as having them in a general detestation.
God's course would be followed ; that seeing their consciences are seared, and they fear not God's voice here from
Heaven, they might feel the full discovery of His vengeance
upon earth, and might assure themselves, upon the least
measure of but a will to touch, but a will to do that execrable act, to incur an universal detestation, to have all rise
against them, to have all the hatred of earth poured upon
them and theirs, to be the outcasts of the commonwealth,
and the *maranathas* of the Church ; yea, they and their
names for ever to be an abhorring to all flesh.   Nothing
in this kind is too much : this way, if no way else, to keep
them from it : which is less than they should suffer, but all
that we can do.

3.
God Him-   The best is, if we fail not in our duty.   Though neither
self will
join with   we, nor the " Anointed," can take perfect order against them,
them.

the Anointer can ; can, and will, as this day He did. And
the rather He will do it, in the time to come, if we turn to
Him, to thank Him for that is past. To Him then let us
turn, that He may take the matter into His own hand. If
His *Nolite tangere* will not prevail, His *Nolo tangi* will: and
if He say, *Nolo tangi*, have they never so bent a will, do
what they can, they shall not (for their lives) be able to do
them hurt.

Two points there be in this charge, both expressed in the
verse next before, *Non permisit*, " He suffered none to attempt it ;" *sed corripuit*, " but them that did, He put them
to rebuke." " Put to rebuke," we turn *corripuit* : it is
properly to take up short, and that is, by a touch, or rather
by a twitch. And so He hath ever done, and so He will
ever do. *Tangentes tangentur*, or rather *tangentes corripi-
entur*, ' If they touch, they shall be twitched, be taken short,
and cut short for it,' all the sort of them. Have been,
I am sure.

I begin with *corripuit ;* for that never faileth : for sure, God By *cor-*
will not suffer His " Anointed ;" nor Christ, His synonyms, *ripuit.*
those of His name, to be touched for nought: if not His Name
itself to be taken, neither those that bare it to be touched
in vain. And there is nothing more kindly, than for them
that will be touching, to be touched themselves, and to be
touched home, in the same kind, themselves thought to have
touched others. You may see it in the first, in Pharaoh,
the very first, that touched the Patriarch Abraham. It is
said, God touched him for it (and it is the very same word
which God useth here in willing not to " touch"): God
touched him, and touched him *tactibus maximis*, with many
a grievous touch: we read, " plagued him with many plagues." Gen.12.17.
And indeed He touched them so, that He plagueth them
that have been busy in this kind. Grievous are the touches
they are touched with here on earth ; of pincers red-hot [1], [[1] Ravail-
and boiling lead : but who knoweth the touches of the place, lac, the
whither (being unrepentant) they must needs go ? which, of Henry
besides that they are *maximi*, (in another manner of degree IV. was
than these here,) are *æterni* withal, and not ended in an tured.]
hour or two, as these are. *Tactibus maximis tangentur*, they
shall be touched indeed thoroughly, as the first was.

SERM.   And look, as He began in the Patriarchs, so hath He ever
III.   held on in His "Anointed," the Kings that ensued.   The
2Sam.4.12. first that ever touched His Kings, Baanah and Rechab, were
touched for it; and cut shorter, both by the hands, wherewith they touched, and the feet, wherewith they went about
1 Kings   it.   Ask the rest, if it were good touching.   Shimei touched
2. 46.
Est. 2. 23. but with the tongue; his neck was touched with the sword.
Bigthan and Teresh said nothing, did nothing, but only with
their will; their necks were touched with the halter, *tactibus
maximis*, the greatest touch or twitch that is here.   And so,
(to make short,) were all the rest, even to those two, that
were this day put to a foul rebuke, and cut short in their
going about it.   Besides the Cherubim's wings then, to protect Kings; here you have, in *corripuit*, the blade of a sword
shaken, to keep the way to them.

By Non   But what comfort is it, if *corripuit* come to the malefactor,
permisit. if he be cut short, and if the King miscarry withal?   Baanah
and Rechab, they that killed Ishbosheth, were cut short,
shorter by the heads; but Ishbosheth, he died for it.   I confess, there is small comfort in *corripuit*, unless *non permisit
nocere*, go withal; in shortening them, without saving His
Anointed.   And that is our comfort, the comfort of this day,
which we meet to give thanks for, that both these went
together, *Non permisit nocere*, and *corripuit* both.

The   You know, at the beginning I told you, besides that it is
thanks-
giving.   a commandment, it is also a thanksgiving.   It is so, in that
it is a verse of a Psalm of Hallelujah, the first Psalm of
Hallelujah of all the twenty.

1.   Now in that He hath placed this duty, and set it in a
Ps.119.54.
Psalm, His will is, men should come to it with pleasure,
cheerfully, and as it were singing.   When we speak of it,
we do it speculatively; when we sing it, that would be with
affection.

2.   In that it is in the first Hallelujah of all, it sheweth, as I
think, that God's "Anointed" are the persons, which, saith
1 Tim.2.1. the Apostle, *ante omnia*, "before all," we are to pray for:
which, saith the Prophet here, before all, we are to praise
God for: for them, and their keeping out of evil hands.
Their safety we are to put in our first Hallelujah.

3.   This Hallelujah is a Psalm purposely for the bringing home

of the ark. And that sheweth His ark and His "Anointed" [1 Chron. 16. 1.]
are allied; and that no sooner is the ark well come home,
but this commandment goeth forth straight from it, first of
all, before all other: that all may know, what account they
were to make of this duty, how high regard to have His
"Anointed" in, in that the ark's welfare and theirs are so
inseparably knit together. And indeed, experience hath
taught it: the well setting of the ark dependeth much upon
the safety of the prince.

Now this Psalm, as it was sung with all the music could 4. [1 Chron. 16. 5, 42.]
be invented, of wind, of hand, and of voice, to shew, the preservation of kings is a benefit extraordinary, that requireth
so solemn a thanksgiving:

So besides, it is ordered every day after, to be sung *jugiter* 5. [1 Chron. 16. 37.]
coram arcâ, that is, to be the ordinary anthem of their daily
service, to shew it is a duty perpetual, that needs so daily
a remembrance, to wit, the care of their preservation.

For last of all, that all the praise and thanks here in the 6.
Psalm are for this *Nolite*, that all the Psalm was set to come
to this verse, it is plain. There be thirty verses more in the
Psalm itself (it is the hundred and fifth Psalm). But as
soon as ever they once come to this verse, all the rest, all
the verses following, are cut off; they go no further in the
Psalm, than till they come to it; and then break off all
those behind, and straight go to another Psalm (for this is [1 Chron. 16. 23.]
all of the hundred and fifth, and the next verse is the first
of the ninety-sixth Psalm). So that, this verse, plainly,
was the end and upshot of all the Psalm besides.

Of this verse then, of His *Nolite tangere*, and of His *Nolo
tangi*, besides of a famous *Non permisit nocere* in this kind,
this day is a memorial to us, and to all our posterity, even
to the children yet unborn. In God's "Anointed," not
touched I cannot say, for touched he was, and more than
touched; but in the touch there is no great matter, we said,
but for the hurt; so that, in the end, not hurt is as good as
not touched. As good, nay better, for a Hallelujah. For to
be touched, as he was, and to take no hurt, is a greater delivery far, than at all not to be touched. To go through the
Red sea, and not wet a thread; to have been in the furnace,
and no scent of the fire: that is the miracle. So, to have

S E R M. been touched, and taken by the throat (that the mark was
III. to be seen many days after); to be thrust at, and thrown
down, as he was, and yet no harm : *hic est potentia,* 'here
was the power' and here was the mercy of God ; here it was
certainly, and that so sensibly, ye might even touch it.

1.   And here, Hallelujah first : and we to praise Him, That
when *Nolite tangere* would not serve in word, made *Non
permisit nocere* to serve in deed : came forth, first, with *Non
permisit nocere,* as with His shield, and so shielded him, that
He suffered him not to take any hurt at all : anointed the
shield, made it slippery, their hands slid off, their touch did
him no harm. *Non permisit* was as His shield, that He
brought forth to save him. But besides it, He brought

2. forth His sword too, and cut them short : *corripuit eos,* was
His sword, touched them with it, and twitched them for
touching His " Anointed :" touched them with Pharaoh's
tactus maximi, that the marks of it will be seen upon them
and theirs, for ever.

3.   For either of these severally, a several Hallelujah : but
especially for not severing them, but letting them meet and
go together; *eripuit,* and *corripuit,* both jointly arm in arm.
Not either alone, this or that. Not *permisit nocere, sed corripuit,* 'suffered them to do hurt, but rebuked them :' no,
but *Non permisit, et corripuit* both, ' suffered them not to
do any hurt ; and rebuked them, and cut them short too
besides.'

And this happy conjunction of these both is it, which
maketh the special increase of our thanks this year, more
than the last, or any before. For that, since, and very
lately, God, That suffered not him, hath suffered some other
King to be touched, as far as his life. True ; he that did
that execrable act, *corripuit eum,* God touched him, touched

Ps. 144. 5. him as he did the mountains, *Tange montes, et fumigabunt,*
touched him, till he smoked again. What of that ? In the
mean time a great prince is fallen. But *permisit nocere,* He
suffered the King to take hurt : and as for *Non permisit
nocere,* God did not him that favour.

1.   Not him, but ours He did : and did it, for the manner,
not without miracle, if we compare the cases. For, he was
then sitting in the midst of divers his nobles. No likeli-

hood, that any would come near him, to offer but to touch him: if he did, there was odds, there would have been many a *Non permisit*, he should never. have been suffered to do it. One man, for all that, one, and no more, did it; divers were near him: none of them, all of them kept him not from his harm. But ours was all alone, shut up, and so left as one forsaken; not many, nay not any, no help at all near him. And not one alone, and no more, but three there were to touch him: yet even then, even in that case, God *Non permisit nocere*, suffered not, not any of them, nor all of them, to touch him, so as they did him any hurt.

And even in the manner of the *Non permisit*, God shewed Himself more than marvellous: for, it was not, God only suffered him not to be hurt; but miraculously He made, that of them that came to break His *Nolite*, even of them, one, that was set, that was ready armed to have touched, and to have hurt him, he, even that party, *non permisit*, 'would not,' did not 'suffer' the other to do him any hurt; *sed corripuit*, 'but rebuked him,' gave the *Noli tangere* to the other, spake this very text, and stayed his hand, that would have done it. This was a *Non permisit* indeed, worth a Hallelujah; and after it, came there at the least three other *Non permisit*s more. But I have presumed too much already: I will not enter into them, but end.

The more they were, the more are we bound to magnify God, and to bless His Holy Name; yearly, yea weekly, yea daily to sing our Hallelujah of praise, and thanks to Him for this day's *Non permisit*, and for this day's *Corripuit*, for them both. That, what He speaks in this text, He made good upon this day: shewed He would not have His "Anointed" touched: shewed He was displeased with them, that did touch him: kept him without hurt, and cut them short: shortened their arms, they could do him no harm, shortened their lives for attempting to do it: "scattered" them, first, in "the imaginations of their hearts;" and then, [Luke I. after, made them perish in that their wicked enterprise: 51.] and hath made this *Nolite*, this precept, to us, *præceptum cantabile*, "a precept Psalm-wise," that we may sing it to Ps. 119. Him. There is another, in another place, of another ditty 54. and tune, wherein he takes up a doleful complaint, thus:

S E R M.
III.
Ps. 89. 38,
44, 45.
" But Thou hast cast off Thine Anointed, and art displeased with him." "The days of his life hast Thou shortened, and cast his crown down to the ground." With them indeed it is *præceptum flebile,* but with us *cantabile.* Praise we Him for it.

And withal, pray we also, that as this day he did not, nor 1 John 5. 18. hitherto he hath not; so henceforth *malignus ne tangat eum,* "the malignant wicked one may never touch him :" never may any have the will ; or if have the will, never have the power to do him hurt. Suffer him not to be touched, or, if suffer him to be touched, suffer not their touch to do him any harm, no more than this day it did ; make all *nolentes,* with His *Nolite ;* if not, come with his *Non permisit,* that he may ever be safe ; and straight after, with His *corripuit,* that they may ever be taken short, that offer it. This day He suffered them not : nor let Him ever suffer any. This day He cut those short ; so may He ever do them all : and ever make this statute our song, all the days of our pilgrimage. This is now the tenth year, and so these the *Decennalia* of it ; that as this day it is, so it may still be celebrated, from ten years to ten years, many ten years more. Which God grant, &c.

A SERMON

PREACHED BEFORE

THE KING'S MAJESTY AT BURLEIGH, NEAR OAKHAM,

ON THE FIFTH OF AUGUST, A.D. MDCXIV.

PSALM lxxxix. 20—23.

I have found David My servant; with My holy oil have I anointed him.

My hand shall hold him fast (or stablish him;) *and Mine arm shall strengthen him.*

The enemy shall not be able to do him violence; the son of wickedness shall not hurt him.

But I will smite down his foes before his face, and plague them that hate him.

[*Inveni David servum meum; oleo sancto Meo unxi eum.*
Manus enim Mea auxiliabitur ei, et brachium Meum confortabit eum.
Nihil proficiet inimicus in eo, et filius iniquitatis non apponet nocere ei.
Et concidam a facie ipsius inimicos ejus, et odientes eum in fugam convertam. Latin Vulg.]

[*I have found David My servant; with My holy oil have I anointed him:*
With whom My hand shall be established: Mine arm also shall strengthen him.
The enemy shall not exact upon him; nor the son of wickedness afflict him.
And I will beat down his foes before his face, and plague them that hate him. Engl. Trans.]

WE have found here a text, wherein (we see) God "found David:" and wherein David found God. God "found David His servant:" and David found God, his good and gracious

SERM.
IV.

Lord: first, to anoint him, then to deliver him. So to deliver him, as his enemies did him no hurt: nay so, that the hurt came to themselves; and they (as we read) were smitten down before him.

And do not this text and this day somewhat resemble one another? To my thinking, they do. For, who is there that hearing in the Psalm this, that violence was offered to David by a "son of wickedness;" but withal, he shall think of the wicked attempt of this day? Who, that (for all that) they did David no harm; but your Majesty's like delivery will come into his mind? Who, that David's enemies were smitten down; but it will lead him straight to the very same end of yours. And who can doubt, that it was the same "hand" and "arm," and of the same God in both? And that He, That did the one, did the other?

King David, he is in Scriptures, not *persona Regis* only, 'the person of a King;' but *persona Regum,* 'a person representing all Kings' to come after him; such specially, as, with David, serve and worship God in truth. We do safely therefore, what is said to him, apply to them all, since he is the type of them all.

But most safely, to such a King (if any such be) where there is a correspondence of like events between David and him: that, what was covenanted to the one, is performed to the other. For there God Himself is our warrant, and even points us so to apply it.

As here now; I find a prophecy, or a promise. A prophecy of Ethan, (his is the Psalm,) or a promise of God. And I find this prophecy fulfilled, and this promise made good to your Majesty. What promised to David, made good to you; and made good this day: what is said in the text, done on the day. What doubt we then to apply it to the present? And since it fell on this day, what better day than this, for me to treat, or you to hear, or for us all to thank God for it.

The sum.

The text hath the name from the first word of it, "I have found." A finding it is.

Two ways, may a thing be "found:" one, when a thing is "found" at first, and never was before: another, when it is afterwards lost, and "found" again. Both here: David is twice "found."

"Found" first, and "anointed," at the first verse. "Found," again, and delivered, at the third. God "found" Ps. 78. 71. him first among his ewes, took him thence, "anointed him," and of a shepherd made him a King. And being a King, "found" him after among his enemies, in danger to lose both crown and life : and so, being as good as lost, "found" him again. It is hard to say, whether of these is the greater : we will not strive; both are in the text. And either hath his day ; I sought but for one day, but I found two ; and both for our turn.

According to which (somewhat strangely, but for our purpose, fitly) I may divide it into the twenty-ninth [1] or twenty-fifth of July, the day of your first finding, for your anointing or coronation ; and the fifth of August, the day of your later finding, for your deliverance or preservation.

[1] The King was crowned in Scotland, July 29th, 1567; and in England, July 25th, 1603.]

The verses are four : the points in them eight (two in each) : of which eight, some be past, some to come in the text : all past with you. Past two, 1. *Inveni*, 2. *Unxi*, the finding, the anointing. To come, all the other six : all in the future, shall or will. Two shalls, 1. "My hand shall," 2. "My arm shall." Two shall nots, 1. "The enemy shall not," 2. " The son of wickedness shall not." Two wills, 1. "I will smite," 2. "I will plague." And all six comprised in a league or covenant, which God is pleased to make with David, upon his anointing : and are so many clauses or articles of it.

Which league is made, *pro et contra*. *Pro*, ' with and for' David, in the second : and *contra*, 'against' his enemies, in the two last. And that, both defensive, in the third ; and offensive, in the fourth. So, a perfect league.

We shall pursue it thus. I. Of his finding, first. II. Then, of his anointing. III. Thirdly, of God's covenant-making with him. IV. And to this of the covenant-making, we will add a fourth of the covenant-keeping. Which is indeed out of the text, but not out of the day though. And, we preach on the day, as well as on the text. Which keeping of the covenant I hold to be a part full as necessary, though it be without, as the making of it, though it be within the text. That then be our fourth, and this our order.

The division.

The first word is " I," that is, God. He is the speaker and bespeaker : the finder and the anointer : the fast-holder and

I.
" I," that is, God.

the strengthener. the rescuer and the revenger of David, and in him (as the type), of all Kings. Not one of these, but is within the very letter of the text. For this first person " I," goeth clean through to the end, and (as it were) engrosseth them all to Himself. Of the finding first.

The points in it are four: 1. The person first, God it is That "found." 2. Then the manner, *Inveni*, "found" by seeking. 3. Thirdly, the cause why he "found David;" for He "found" him *servum Meum*. All these three are *inventio*. 4. And, having "found" him, lastly, He proclaims it here, cries *Εὕρηκα*, " I have found," that is, *inventi prædicatio*.

God
" found
David." All Kings are "found" by God; but in David, there is somewhat singular. He was not a King only, but a King (as we may say) of the first head. For, before He was " found," he was a private man. God "found" him, and " anointed" him: that is, of a private person made him a King. His seed also were to succeed him, by virtue of the entail, verse the fourth. But, he was the first King of his race: as in every race of Kings, there was such a one, that at first was "found" out. In him, in such a one, finding is most needful. In them that succeed, there shall need no such seeking; they are "found" to his hand: only anoint them, and no more ado.

1. This then we find first: that Kings were of God's finding at the first. God, we see, takes it to Himself: " I have found." They are then no human invention, devised or taken up by man; but "found" by God. They came not out of man's brain; but *ex cerebro Jovis, inventum Dei*, of, God's finding forth.

As of His finding, in this verse; so of His exalting, in the very next before: " I have exalted one, one chosen out of the people." Look you, there comes two at once; "exalted" and "chosen." Neither "chosen," nor " exalted" by the people; but by God, out of the people. Not they, out of themselves; but God, out of them. Mark that point well.

As for His finding in this, and exalting in that; so (within a verse or two following), of His adopting too. There God saith, "He," that is, the King, " shall call Me, Thou art my Father." Where we see, whereto he was chosen, whither exalted; even to be the son of God. And not every son neither; but His heir, His eldest. For, so it followeth, " I will make him My first-born." So *filius Dei* he is, *primogenitus Dei :* and what would we more? Then is not David *filius populi :* God forbid. Never father him upon them. No adoptive, no foundling of theirs. His finding, choosing, exalting, adopting, God takes them all to Himself.

Shall I let you see it *ad oculum,* this; that it was none but God? Not the people (no colour for them). Full little knew they, or any of them; nor the elders of Bethlehem: nor did ever imagine any such thing in hand, when Samuel went about it, when David was first " found." 1 Sam. 16. 4.

Nay, nor "the Saints" found him not neither, till God (as it is in the verse next before) " spake to them in a vision," and told them of it. Ps. 89. 19.

Nay, not he, of whom there is most likelihood, the Prophet himself, Samuel: he found him not, he could not find him, till God did it for him, and said to him, " This is he." All this is in the first of Samuel, the sixteenth chapter. Thus, God, in David, would let us see at first, that it was He That " found" Kings, and none but He. If Samuel the Prophet had been let alone, it had not been King David, but King Eliab: he would have found him. If Abiathar the High Priest had had his will, it had not been King Solomon, but King Adonijah, it is well known. So then, neither people, nor Saints; nor Prophet, nor Priest; but God it was, of Himself, and by Himself. He to have the honour of this invention. 1 Sam. 16. 6, 12.

1 Kings 1. 7.

And if Kings be the invention of God, then are not their inventions of God (these I mean that have been broached of late), that find Kings, or found Kings upon any but God: that make Prophet, Priest, or people, King-finders, or King-founders, or ascribe this invention to any, but to Him in the text. This for the Person, " I have found."

How found (The second) : by hap? No, it is *Inveni :* in that word is the manner of it. Every tongue hath a proper word to sever things sought and so found, from things found without seeking: you know—*Tu non inventa reperta es.* David then was not, Kings are not *reperti,* ' hit upon at adventure,' or stumbled on by chance: they are not τῶν τυχόντων. No, they are *inventi :* first sought, and so found upon search.

2. " Found him," *Inveni.*

[Ovid. Met. I. 654.]

SERM.
IV.
1 Sam. 13.
14.

Will ye hear it *totidem verbis?* *Quæsivi Mihi hominem*, saith God of David, " I have sought Me out a man."

Not that any is hid from Him, that He need seek him; it is but in our own phrase, to express to our capacities, how God stood affected to the having of Kings. So set to have them, that rather than not have them, He would do as we do, even take the pains to seek them out. Now, the endeavour to seek is from no velleity, no faint will : no, it is from a desire that fain would find. And that desire is from no mean conceit (if it come, so it is; if not, no great matter); but from some special good conceit we have of that we seek for; that we hold it worth the time we spend, worth the labour we bestow about it. All is but to shew us the worth of this invention. For it is no mean thing, we may be sure, that God will seek. Seeking them, He shews He holds them for such, as He would not be without them Himself : He would not have His people in any wise be without them. And that He would not have them thought as good lost as " found," but esteemed for such by us, as if we had them not, we would, by His example, set ourselves to seek them seriously, and never leave, till we have found them. This for the manner.

3.
" Found"
him His
" servant."

But then, thirdly ; seeking, why " found" He David, rather than any other ? We find the reason of that in *servum Meum*, because He " found" him His " servant." For a servant He sought, to whom He might commit the highest point of His service, the care of His people. And He " found" him so zealous for His flock, to keep them from being a prey to strange beasts, as He thought him meet to be made of *pastor ovium, pastor hominum.* He " found" him so devout at His service, that He set him in such a place, as if he were the servant of God, he might make ten thousand more beside himself.

These two words then, we may not slip over; the claim of the Covenant (after) lieth by them. And if the Covenant hath not been kept with any, it hath been for default of this, that He hath " found" him ; *him*, but not him, His " servant."

Yea, if any King be " found" by God before he do, or by course of nature can do Him any service (suppose in his cradle); yet even to such a one is not this word without fruit. It hath his use, this, not only in making them to be "found," but in keeping them from being lost. For the same, that was the way to be "found" at first; the very same is the way, not to be lost ever after. And it concerns David, or any, as nearly, not to be lost again, as it doth at first to be "found."

Now if David look well to these two words, and lose them not, God will not lose him (he may be sure), but be at hand still ready to defend him. Unless David lose them, he cannot lose God: and unless he lose God, he cannot be lost. David ever lost them, before his enemies could do him any harm. All Balaam's cursing will do him no hurt; nothing Nu. 31. 16. but his wicked counsel, to unmake him His servant, and so to lose God, and so to be lost of God, and so to be lost, utterly lost. Lay up this then : the way to *servari a Deo*, is to *servire Deo*. And lay it up well: it is the only article of covenant on David's part. Upon these two words depends all that follows (upon *servum Meum*). If they be sure, all is sure. And this for *inventio.*

But I find here *inventi prædicatio* besides. To find is one God tells thing, to cry *Εὕρηκα, Inveni,* " I have found," another. One it, "I have found." may find, and keep his own counsel (so men do for the most part). But God here proclaims His finding; tells all, He hath "found." And none do so, but such as are surprised with joy : as the party in the Canticles, *Inveni quem quæsivit* [Cant. 3. *anima mea,* "I have found whom my soul sought," and I 1—4.] would the world knew it, I am not a little glad of it. Commonly, where there is care in seeking, as before, there is joy in finding. Joy then : and it is not joy alone (for one may *gaudere in sinu,* ' keep his joy to himself) ;' but *gaudium cum gloriâ,* this. For, he not only joys in his invention, but glories in it, and even boasts of it, that doth *inventum prædicare.* The word which he useth, *Εὕρηκα,* is made famous by Archimedes ; who, in a great passion between glorying and rejoicing, first cried it, when he had found the secret of King Hiero's crown. But no less famous, by St. Andrew ; who, Joh. 1. 41. upon the finding of Christ, came running to his brother St. Peter, with Archimedes' cry, " We have found" Him " (the Messias)," we have found Him. Messias in Hebrew, is nothing else but anointed : and we shall see David " anointed"

SERM.
IV.

straight. And sure, next to the joy of Christ, *Christus Do-minus,* we may place the joy of *Christus Domini,* and take up our next Εὕρηκα for him. God's word will well become us, to use.

Joy to His
"saints"
by it.

And to whom is this? To "His Saints:" to them He tells it (look the last verse before). As if they had their part in this finding, so invites He them to the fellowship of the same joy. Tells them, that such a one He had "found;" and for them, and for their good He had "found" him. They, to reap special benefit by it, by this finding; therefore, they to take special notice of it, they specially to rejoice with Him for it.

1.
Joy of the
finding.
Ps. 89. 15.

And what should I say, but as this Psalm saith a little before, *Beatus populus qui scit jubilationem,* "Blessed are the people that can skill of this joy," that can skill of their own good : what it is to have a King, a King found to their hand; but specially, a King that is God's servant. Verily, if God's joy be our joy ; it is to be with us, as with God it was; this Εὕρηκα, the Εὕρηκα of joy. And truly, all this text, both that which is past, His care in seeking, and His joy in find-ing ; and that which followeth, His honour in anointing, His mercy in making this covenant, His truth in keeping it, His rescuing them from, His revenging them upon their enemies : all is but to shew us how much He doth ; and, if we will do as He doth, how much we are to do, even to set by, even to joy and glory with Him, in *Inveni Davidem servum Meum.* And this for His finding. Now no more ado, but proceed to His anointing.

[II.]
Found to
anoint.

To what end then, "found?" To anoint. Very many are "found," very few so "found," scarce one of many millions. But they, that are so "found," are *eo ipso* the greatest per-sons, and of the highest calling upon earth. So much is

God the
Anointer.

there, in this word anointing. And this also God takes to Himself : *Unxi,* no less, than the former, *Inveni.* Finds, and anoints both.

The "oil"
is God's.

And both the act His, and the oil His. *Unxi,* I did it; and *oleo Meo,* "My oil" it was I did it with. So finds Kings, and finds oil, and finds fingers, and all. Nothing goeth to them, but it is God's.

It seemeth otherwise. Samuel could not find him indeed;

but we find, he did anoint him though. He did so, but not
as of himself: what he did, in the Person of God he did it. 1 Sam. 16.
And the law is, what one doth by another, not that other, 13.
but himself is said to do it, to be the author of the deed.
For this must stand true, that God here saith Himself,
that whose fingers soever were used, God it was That
"anointed" him. And "anointed" him with "oil," "holy
oil," His holy oil.

"Oil." We can never find Kings in Scripture but still we   1.
find this word with them. We find them in "oil," and "oil" "With oil."
is for continuance. The colours of the crown are not water-
colours, to fade by and by; they be laid in oil, to last and to
hold out all weathers. So, in "oil," not in water.

And in "oil," not in wine. For though the Samaritan Lu. 10. 34.
have both, and there is use of both, in time and place; yet
here, only with "oil." There is no acrimony, nothing corro-
sive in it: it is gentle, smooth, and suppling. All to teach
them, a prime quality of their calling, to put in "oil" enough;
to cherish that virtue, that the streams of it may be seen,
and the scent of it may be felt of all. For that will make
David to be David: that is (as his name is) truly beloved.

"Oil," and "holy oil." "Holy," not only to make their   2.
persons sacred, and so free from touch or violating (all agree With "holy oil."
of that); but even their calling so also. For holy unction,
holy function.

Now this "holy oil" troubles the Jesuit shrewdly, and all
those that seek to unhallow the calling of Kings. For if the
"holy oil" be upon them, why should they be sequestered
quite from holy things, more than the other two, that have
but the same oil? Indeed, (as they say,) if they were but to
deal with common matters, common oil would have served
well enough (and so they would fain have it); but this place
chokes them: this holy oil here. And their calling, by virtue of this, being holy, what should let them, in their kind
to deal with those, either persons or matters, that are but as
the oil is, wherewith they are anointed? How fond is it
to imagine them to be "anointed with holy oil," to deal
only in unholy matters, and not to meddle with any thing
that holy is!

"Holy oil," and "His holy oil." For "His holy" is

SERM.
IV.

3.
With "His
holy oil."

[Mat. 3.
11.]

Ps. 45. 7.
Joh. 3. 34.

more than "holy." "His" is another manner "oil" than the material in the Prophet's horn, or in the Priest's vial. "His" drops immediately from the true Olive, the Holy Ghost (He the true Olive, as Christ the true Vine). Samuel's is but a ceremony; this, the substance of the anointing. It is, in this, as in Baptism; there, John "with water;" Christ "with the Holy Ghost:" and that is the soul of Baptism. So here, Samuel sheds on the oil of the Tabernacle; God He adds His from Heaven: the same and no other than Christ was anointed with. That oil is it: that, the anointing indeed. He indeed, "above His fellows," for He had "the Spirit above measure:" but He so above them, as He with them, and they with Him; with His, with the same anointing, both.

2.
Joy of the
anointing.
Ps. 45. 7.

And it is not from the purpose, that His oil is by the Psalm called "the oil of gladness:" that, as we are glad even now, for his finding; so may we also now, for his anointing. And by and by, glad again, for his delivering. And so, glad in him God makes us, for them all. It is a day of joy: I would not omit any thing, that might tend to it. And this for the first verse, finding and anointing, and (if ye will) for the twenty-ninth of July. Now to the second verse.

[III.]
Ps. 89. 21.
The
league.

Having "anointed him," the first thing he doth, is to enter a league with him. And we are glad of that. For, having "found" him now, we would be glad to keep him. And there is no surer way for that, than to join him in a league with the mightiest King (by far) of the whole world, the King of Kings, God Himself.

And God Himself is willing with it, offers it. And sure He hath reason so to do. Seeing He hath "found" him, He will not see him lost. David serves Him, He will *servare servum*. He "anointed" him, and made him holy; He will not see him used profanely. But the Eye that found him, shall watch over him: the Hand that "anointed him," shall be at hand to defend him.

It is a
league or
covenant.

So hitherto, God "found" David. Now, David finds God willing to undertake his quarrel; and even to covenant with him, so to do. For it is not a bare promise this: it is a "covenant," and so termed expressly at the third and twenty-eighth verses. And that, a covenant solemnly sworn, bound with an oath, at the third and thirty-fifth. And here now *manus Mea cum eo,* He giveth him His hand upon it. His covenant, His oath, and His hand, what can there be more? This covenant is made as sure as can be; and as surely kept, we shall see anon.

The first article of this covenant, the article of *imprimis,* is that His " hand shall hold him fast," or establish; the second, that His " arm shall strengthen him :" that is, covenants for the continual presence, and assistance of His power, ever to join with him, and still to be aiding to him.

The first and second articles of the covenant, pro, 'for' David.

This power of itself is but one, as God is one; but is set down thus, here and elsewhere, in two words : the " hand" and the " arm," the " mighty hand" and the " outstretched arm," to set forth two degrees of it. Both great, but one greater. That of the " hand" is great; as we read, the thirteenth verse before, yet but ordinary. That of the " arm" is greater, and cometh forth, but upon extraordinary occasion : every thing we put not to the arm's end.

God's " hand." God's " arm." [Deut. 26. 8.]

Not that these degrees of difference are in the power itself, which is entire, *quoad se;* but only, to proportion it, and make it answerable to our perils : which are not always alike, but less or more, at one time than another : and so seem to us to require a degree of power according. For the less, the " hand" seems enough; but for the more, the " arm :" a greater degree of power, as our peril is greater.

No day goeth over our head, but the horse we ride on, the stairs we go up and down by, the very meat we eat, we are in danger, lest it go the wrong way. For these, for every day's dangers, we cannot miss the " hand ;" and the " hand" is enough, if it do but " hold" us " fast."

But this day, the fifth of August, and such another, the fifth of November, the case is altered. Then, " Rise up, rise up, thou arm of the Lord ;" rise up, and stretch out thyself : another manner of jeopardy, then. So, in a word, the " hand" for all the year; the " arm" for the fifth of August. Now there is no jeopardy so great, but the " arm," if it stretch itself out, will serve to preserve us. And this " arm" is ever stretched out, when God vouchsafeth some strange miraculous deliverance, as this day He did. For this was *dies brachii,* on it " the arm of the Lord was revealed."

Isa. 51. 9.

Isa. 53. 1

" Hand,"
to " sta-
blish"
him.

" Arm" to
" strength-
en."

The third
and fourth
articles
contra,
' against'
David's
foes.
Defensive.

The
devil's
finding or
invention.

Both these: and either hath His proper attribute: the " hand," to " establish;" and the " arm," to " strengthen."

To " establish:" that is, to make steady, that he stand fast, and be not moved. It is ἰσχὺς, ' the passive power' to resist; such, as of the anvil, or the rock.

To " strengthen:" that is, when we are further to en-counter our peril actively, and are too weak for it; for that giveth δύναμις, ' the active power,' that strikes them down: as the sword, or halberd, in the hand of the mighty.

Both these: and both necessary, for the performance of this league: which is, both defensive, in the next verse, to keep them, that they take no hurt: and offensive, in the last verse, to pay their enemies their due, and to strike them down.

This then is the sum of the two first articles. The " hand" shall never be off him, but on him all the year long, for every day's danger. But, if further need be, if some very great hazard, if the fifth of August, then out comes the " arm." But so, as both: both " hand" and " arm," and every sinew in them, are ready still, and at hand, as occasion shall be, to " stablish" or " strengthen" him. This, for the second verse, the league: and all this is for him, *pro.*

Why, what needs all this? this holding, this fortifying? Is there any harm toward? I cannot tell: it was somewhat a suspicious word, (in the verse past,) of holding him, and hold-ing him fast; as if there were some shoving at him. The Greek is more full, συναντιλήψεται. For, in that word, there is λῆψις, God holds him: and then ἀντίληψις, as it were, another plucks at him: and then, συναντίληψις, God holds him harder or faster than before. This was but suspicious. But here now, it is past all suspicion; for here are a couple making toward him; 1. " the enemy," and 2. " the son of wickedness:" it is to be doubted, for no good. Here is now the fifth of August: here comes God's second finding him. For in his enemy's hand now he is, get out how he can.

I told you before, that Kings were God's invention: here now comes the devil's invention. For, as God finds Kings, so the devil finds traitors. God finds David; the devil finds Absalom. God, your Majesty; the devil, those of this day.

And, (as evil ever is more fertile,) for one King there are

two, in the text: and there were two on the day: and I would to God, two were all. But this is to be counted of: Satan the arch-enemy (so signifies his name) will be sure to find Kings enemies. The father of wickedness will find his whelps ready ever for so wicked an enterprise.

And now, these are they, *contra quos,* ' whom against' this league is made: for by virtue of the league, God and David, they have friends and enemies in common. Enemy to one, the King; and enemy to both, God and the King. 1. Of the parties first; 2. then of their attempt; 3. and last of their success.

The parties. Two titles they have in the text, 1. "the enemy," 2. "the son of wickedness." *Exegetice* some take them, both for one: and then, the latter glosseth the former: and then the meaning is, that David's enemies are, all of them, the sons of wickedness. And indeed such they were, and none but such. For God forbid any good man should be David's enemy. In this sense it is true. For all of them *qui vias dant ad perdendos Reges,* but much more, *qui vias docent;* that would have them lost, whom God even now with such joy found; that seek to deface God's invention: you may boldly pronounce of them, they be the sons of wickedness all: as flat against God, as *perdere* is against *invenire,* perdition against invention; and their will, against His will. For His will is, *Quos Deus invenit, homo ne perdat;* and, *Quos Deus invenit, homo perdat,* say they. And this, if both be for one.

1.
The parties.
" The enemy."
" The son of wickedness."
" Son,"
exegetice.
Prov. 31.3.

But if (as the words give, and the best writers take them) they stand for a pair, for two distinct; then, by "the enemy," is meant he that is so professed. Plain by the fifty-fifth Psalm, "It was not an open enemy:" where the word is the same that here, that is, such a one as Goliath was. But by "the son of wickedness," is meant the close hollow traitor, such as was his wicked son.

" The ene-
my," " the son of wicked-
ness," two distinct.
Ps. 55. 12.

And it is good, they know their pedigree, these fellows, of what lineage they are. That is, wickedness' own sons: as if the other, "the enemy," were but allied to it, in some degree; but these, the true offspring, the lively image of the devil. For if they be the sons, and he the father, they be as near of blood as may be. So, they see their true descent, sons of wickedness.

They be the sons of wickedness.

SERM.
IV.

What
wicked-
ness it is.

Joh. 15. 25.
Ps. 109. 5.
And it is worth the while to know, of what wickedness. Evil it is to be wicked, upon what pretence soever. But, *oderunt Me gratis* is worse; for that is of mere malignity. But *mala pro bonis* is worst of all. And such are these, such their wickedness. Sons of עולה : which עולה, the Hebrews tell us, is properly the naughtiness of some evil-natured children, that bite the nipple which giveth them milk. That is עולה right (the worst and most wicked wickedness of all others). To bite and suck, both at once. But such there are, the better they be dealt with, the worse still ye shall find them.

" The son
of wicked-
ness" the
more dan-
gerous.
Now, of the twain, these are far the more dangerous; as you may see, by the very course or standing of them in the text. For, *referendo singula singulis*, as we use to do; the "hand" before, as the former there, properly refers to " the enemy," as the former here; but the " arm," the latter there, that refers to the sons of wickedness, even by the course of the two verses. As if, for " the enemy," " the hand" were sufficient; but for these, " arm" and all were little enough.

And, sure, ye shall observe, that David, that the son of David, Christ; that *Christus Dominus*, and *Christus Domini* both, hath ever been most in danger of this kind of cattle. David, he was once in danger, and never but once, by 2 Sam. 21.
16. Ishbi-benob, an open enemy. But his great dangers were by these here, the sons of wickedness, his wicked son Absalom, his wicked counsellor Ahithophel. And indeed all his great were by this second sort.

And our Saviour Christ's furious enemies, they that would Lu. 4. 29. have thrown Him " headlong down the hill," they that would Joh. 8. 59. have " stoned" Him, they did Him no hurt; but that false Joh. 10.
31. harlot Judas, that " son of wickedness," he did. And I pray to God, He may; and I beseech David heartily, he would take this to heart, and take heed of these. The danger of these, the sons of wickedness, it was the danger of this day.

2.
Their
attempt.
" Vio-
lence,"
" wicked-
ness,"
" hurt."
2 Sam. 15.
8.
Will ye now see their proceedings and practices? They be in these three words; 1. " violence," 2. " wickedness," 3. " hurt." " Violence" they mean, that is their end; and with " wickedness" they cover it, that is, with one wicked pretence or other, the better to make the way, to do the hurt they intend. Alas, nothing but " a vow" at Hebron, said

wicked Absalom, when he vowed indeed to deprive King David both of his kingdom and life. Not lose the sermon for any good, said he of this day ; when he had in his heart " violence" and " hurt ;" no less " hurt," than the loss of your Majesty's life. This is the way of them all : " violence" wrapped about with a vow or a sermon, or I wot not what ; that before it be seen, it may do the mischief that is meant. This holy " wickedness" is simply the worst of all. O Lord, what dangers are they in, that are in this case ! How near being lost ! Now, the success.

For at the name of " violence," at but the mention of " hurt," every good heart is moved, and come running in about David, to see if any " hurt." But there is no " hurt" done, God be blessed, none done : whatsoever meant, none is done. And he falls (if you mark) : no " violence ;" nay, not so much as the least " hurt." For they be two, these, " violence" and " hurt :" and " hurt" is the more larger. Any " violence" done ? Nay, none. Any hurt at all ? Nor that neither. Neither ? all is safe then. _{3. Their success. No " violence," no " hurt." [*i. e.* no violence befalls him.]}

Where, ye see, the first use of this " hand," and " arm ;" to repel and keep back " violence," to bear off the blow, that should do them " hurt." This is the defensive part. And it is much to their comfort, that this " hand" so holds them, and this " arm" is so over them, as it is still between them and their harms : as it lights on God's " arm" and " hand" and must " hurt" them, before it come at David. But them it cannot " hurt," neither violent wickedness, nor wicked violence prevail against them : and so be they safe, from both. And no way to prevail against Kings, but to bind this " hand" first, and pinion this " arm." Otherwise, evil men there may be, and evil meaning ; but no evil success, for all that.

But, I would pray you, to take good heed to the tenor of this covenant. No promise is here made, but that such he shall have : and shall have of both sorts, open and secret ; open, to offer " violence ;" secret, privily to seek his " hurt." No, though he be David, that is, " lovely," or as lovely as ever was he, yet he shall have those that hate him ; hate him gratis, hate him though favours done them : though they lie in his lap, and are fed with his milk, yet bite him _{1. Not, there shall be no enemies, no sons of wickedness.}

SERM.   for all that. No part of the covenant this, but such he
IV.   shall have, but such there shall be.

2.   Nor, no promise neither, but as they shall be, so they shall
Not, they   be doing, as we say : not sit idle, but be plotting and prac-
shall not
be doing.   tising, ever and anon.   It is but, *Non proficient,* so read the
Fathers this verse, the covenant in the text : it is not, *Non*
[S. Aug.   *facient.*   No : *Facient, facient quod suum est iniquitatis filii,*
in loc.]
(saith St. Augustine well :) 'The sons of wickedness shall be
doing, and do their kind, that is wickedly :' intend violence,
pretend some wicked wile or other.   No part of the covenant,
but such there shall be : nor no part of the covenant, but
thus they shall do.   Let it not seem strange : look for it.

3.   But, this the covenant, and this is all.   The former part,
But they
shall not   be they shall, and be doing they shall, *sed non proficient in*
do it.   *eo,* 'they shall do no good on him' (in their sense), that is,
no evil (in ours).

Non pro-   And very fit is the word, *Non proficient;* that is, though
ficient in
eo.   they go to school all their days about it, yet shall they prove
but non-proficients, and never proceed so far, as to do it.   So
Non appo-   in the latter part, *Non apponent nocere ;* not, *Non proponent.*
nent no-
cere.   Not, shall not have the purpose ; but, shall not have their
purpose.   Not, shall not have the will ; but, shall not have
the power to do hurt.   Proffer they shall, but not profit.
Ps. 21. 11.   Devise, but what they devise, not be able to perform :
Lu. 1. 51.   imagine, but be "scattered in the imaginations of their
hearts."   So that, come when they will now, they come a
verse too late : David is provided of a "hand" and "arm"
(in the verse before) that will see him take no hurt : that
will be "hurt" themselves, rather than he take any : that
will so fence him, as neither fury shall be able to do him
any "violence," by force ; nor "wickedness" to do him any
"hurt," by fraud.   Near lost, as good as lost, as may be ;
but quite lost, he shall not be ; God shall find him again.
And so to the last verse.

Ps. 89. 23.   Very well then, David is escaped from their "violence"
The fifth
and sixth   and "hurt;" but shall they escape so? No: there is a further
Articles   matter in it.   All this is but the defensive part ; but the
contra.
'Against'   league (we find) was not only so, but offensive too ; as well to
his ene-   offend and annoy them, as to defend and rescue him.   And
mies, of-
fensive.   here now is the active power, we spake of before, of the

strengthening of the " arm." That there is not only work for the " hand" to stay him, or hold out a shield, to bear off, that so no " hurt" to him; but for the " arm" also, to draw out a sword and lay on, that so all the " hurt" shall come to themselves. And so their imaginations not only scattered, but returned upon their own heads. For " violence" they intended, and were brought themselves to a violent end. " Hurt" they meant, and they are hurt themselves, and that incurably, smitten down and perish.

margin: " I will smite down."

margin: Ps. 7. 16.

Three points I touch only. What? smite them down, and no harm done? Yea, no matter for that; down with them though. To lift up a hand or a heel here, is enough. To offer " violence," but to intend " hurt," here enough. That there was none done, thanks be to God and the good " hand" that held them : Bigthan and his fellow, hang them up though. Not, *quia nocuerunt :* no : upon no other indictment, but *quia voluerunt,* " they would have done" the King hurt, though they did him none. That is enough, " smite them down."

margin: 1. Yea, though no harm done, yet " smite down." 2 Sam. 20. 21. Ps. 41. 9. Esther 2. 21, 22, 23.

Again. What? at the very first, " smite them down?" Yea, these, at the very first. With others, He proceeds not so roundly: smites them first, before He " smite them down;" smites them a blow with the " hand," in mercy; before He " smite them down" with the deadly blow of His " arm," in rigour. But these, down with them, at the very first. Wot you why? Abishai, he desired he might have but one blow at the King, he would never desire a second. Pay him with his own money : let him have but one blow; but the first, and no more.

margin: 2. Yea, at the first " smite down."

margin: 1 Sam. 26. 8.

And what blow is it? to astonish him, or to fell him, for the time? No: it is ἐκκόψω, say the Seventy. The nature of which word is, not to fell the stem or the trunk of the tree, but to hew in sunder the very roots, that it never grow again : so to " smite them down" as they never rise more. " I will smite down."

margin: 3. How " smite down."

And as if this were not enough, he follows them yet further. Before, he fell : no " violence:" nay, not any the least " hurt." Here, he rises, " smite" them, nay " plague" them, that is, smite them down with the plague, which is yet more fearful. And it is truly turned, for מגפה is properly the stroke of the plague.

margin: " And plague them."

SERM.   The plague is a death that we would not die of, to choose;
IV.
———   if smitten down, not smitten down with that axe. Not, because it is deadly for the most part, and past recovery ; that
is not it: but because they that be so smitten, there goeth
from them a pestilent noisome vapour, that makes all shun
them, or, as the Seventy's word is, τροπώσομαι, " run away,"
"Plague   yea and fly away from them. And even so, from these there
them" in   goeth a scent, as from a plague-sore, (you will bear with it,
this life.
          it is the Holy Ghost's own term :) that taints their blood,
          corrupts their name, makes them and their memory odious,
Isa. 66. 24. yea, even " an abhorring to all flesh." Say what they will,
The   this is the plague of plagues, when all is done. And it is
plague
in God's   God's own will, God Himself would have us so reckon of
account.
Num. 16.   them. Of Korah, (the first we read of in this kind,) God
24, 26.   calls to Moses, " Charge the people all, that they get them
from about them." And Moses he cries, " Away, away from
their tents, touch not any thing that is theirs :" as if he
should say, They have the plague, it is infectious. So God
would have us think of them : and so, I pray God, all may
take warning from Him, and so think of them, and shun
them as persons contagious, that have sores running on
them.

Plague   Now this is but their plague on earth (to be plagued in
them in   their end, their blood, their name) ; but all this is nothing
the other
life.   to their plagues in hell : whither certainly they go, so many
as in *flagranti crimine,* 'in the very act of treachery,' are
Ps. 73. 18. taken away. No man shall need to wish them more hurt :
[P. B.   " they perish, and come to a fearful end." It is truly said
vers.]
by them, " I will plague them."

1. That   Yet one more, that makes up all. For, if ye mark, the
is, God   person is changed. The last verse, it was, They shall do no
Himself
"will   " violence," they shall do no " hurt :" consequently, he should
smite."
He "will   have gone on, They shall be smitten, they shall be plagued :
plague."   that had been enough. It is not so, but, in the first person,
" I will smite," " I will plague :" as if God Himself would be
the doer of it, and do it even αὐτόχειρ, *propriis manibus,* 'with
His own hands.' And surely, so sensible hath been the de-
monstration of the " hand" of His power, in the fall of these,
that, (to hold us to the term of plague,) God's tokens have
Ps. 144. 7. been seen upon them : as if He had sent His " hand from on
high," to plague them indeed. Upon these, this day ; upon

others since these, God hath from Heaven shewed, how much
these attempts displease Him, by making even the prints of
His hands to be seen upon the attempters ; that men have
been even forced to acknowledge, it was no human or earthly,
but some supernatural divine power, that brought it to pass ;
and that though other hands were in it, yet God it was,
That struck the stroke. This is the end, that, in the end, shall
come to all these from the Lord, so many as have any hand
in the " hurt" of " the Lord's Anointed." He That is the
founder of Kings will be the confounder of all conspirators.
Carry it as closely as they can, His " hand" shall find them
out, find them out and " smite" them, " smite" them and
" plague" them, plague them here and for ever. This is the
covenant here made with David, in the name of Kings.

And, I promise you, this is a fair covenant and a full : but
might we see some proof of it, how it was kept? For that
is *sal fœderis*, the proof, the keeping of it. For many fair
covenants here in the world take wind, for want of this 'salt
of the covenant,' the true keeping. [IV.] Applica-tion to His Majesty.

Of David, there is no doubt, it was kept with him ; but
the time will not serve. And this time requireth rather, to
shew the proof of the presents in your Majesty. That this
whole text, *mutato nomine*, hath been kept with you, from
point to point : " and the faithful mercies of David," as
Esay calls them, as faithful to you, as ever they were to him.
Of that, then. Isa. 55. 3.

I find then, both these days, and on them, both these
ways, you were " found" by God ; " found," the twenty-
ninth of July, and " anointed ;" " found," the fifth of August,
and delivered.

" Found" first : and that, sooner a great deal than David ;
for in your cradle. There He " found" you, and " anointed"
you. David was come to years of discretion first, to do Him
service : but you, by His preventing grace " found," before
you were, or could be in case, to do Him any. An antece-
dence even in this. 1. The twenty-ninth of July, " found" in the cradle and " anoint-ed."

Nay He " found" you twice, to anoint you. Once, before
you did, or could serve Him ; and after you could, and did,
once more. " Found" you, the twenty-ninth of July, and
the twenty-fifth both. David was twice " anointed" too ; but 2. The twenty-ninth of July, and the twenty-fifth both :

SERM.
IV.
twice
"anoint-
ed."
2 Sam. 2.
4; 5. 3.

3.
" Found"
in the
womb,
and de-
livered,
before
ever " an-
ointed."

4.
Delivered
before
"anoint-
ed :"
delivered
again the
fifth of
August.

5.
" Anoint-
ed" the
second
time the
twenty-
fifth of
July, and
deliver-
ed after
the fifth
of Novem-
ber.

Applica-
tion to the
fifth of
August,
the day
itself.
Ps. 19. 2.
Then
" found,"
and
" found"
by God.

he, but of two pieces of one kingdom; but you, of two entire kingdoms, or (indeed) of three, the least of them greater than that of his, when both pieces were together. So an anointing also, more than he.

Some difference I find, but with vantage still, on your side. For, in the text, David is first "anointed," and after delivered. But you were delivered, before ever "anointed." For, before He "found" you in your cradle, there to anoint you, He "found" you in the womb, (before ever you came into the world,) there to deliver you. Even there, His hand was over you, that, even there, "a son of wickedness" did you no hurt. This is more than is in the text; more than ever David could sing of.

But He not only thus delivered you before your birth, and so before your anointing; but after it also, no less: witness this fifth day of this month. So were you delivered first, and then "anointed:" and then, delivered again from this day, and from being lost on it. And thus far the text.

But then, were you "anointed" again after that, and delivered again after that, from a fifth day too, though of another month. For, either of your anointings have had a famous delivery, to second it. So we double the point here. A deliverance in the womb, an anointing after that deliverance; a deliverance after that anointing; and then, an anointing again; and then a deliverance again, upon that. So upon the matter, four findings with you; twice to anoint, and twice to deliver; beyond David, beyond the text here. So the text kept with you, over and over again.

But to let the rest go, and to hold us to this day. This day, if days could speak, (and days can speak, saith the nineteenth Psalm,) would certify, that this covenant was kept with you, in every clause of the six, on this your finding-day.

For, your finding-day well may it be called; well may it be said, you were "found" on it, and "found" by God on it. "Found;" for sure you were lost. And "found" by God; for men had lost you. They that gladly would, knew not how to find you, or get to you. Great odds then, but you had been quite lost. It was God That "found" you then, and made you to be "found" of them, not by any skill of their own, or by any direction but His. By hap, it might

seem: but yourself do, and we all acknowledge the hand
of God in it. His providence, that so guided them; His
doing it was, that they did it. So that God it was, That
"found" you then, or we had not now found you here. It
may then truly be called your finding-day; and God truly
say, the second time, *Εὕρηκα,* "I have found." Of it then,
of this day.

We shall fail a little, in the first point. Here is an
"enemy" professed: and you had not then, you never had
any, professed. To make amends for that, there is but one
"son of wickedness" in the text: you found not one, but
two; and they found you.

Sons of wickedness well might they be called. For if
no religion, taking religion upon it, be wickedness, (as it
is double wickedness,) a "son of wickedness" he was. If
witchcraft be wickedness, (as it is wickedness in the highest
degree,) he was a "son" of it, it was found about him. If
to do evil gratis; to do evil for good, be wickedness, (and it
is the wretchedest wickedness that can be,) you had done
them many favours: and tó bite the breast then, that had
given them milk, these are they in the text right, בני עולה,
if ever there were any.

These then, "violence" they intended, and with "wickedness" they covered it. Wickedly they enticed you, and drew
you along, till they had you fast shut up: and then violent
hands they laid on you (the marks were to be seen many a
day after). And were you not then, within the compass of
the text, of "violence" and "hurt," that is, of "hurt" by
"violence?" Yes, so near you was the "hurt," that the
hurtful point touched your naked breast. Was David ever
so near? Never: he was indeed hard bested and forced to
fly, but he never came in their hands: you did. He never
was under lock: you were. He never had the dagger's point
at his heart: you had. And when you had, all the world
then certainly would have given you lost.

Did they you any "harm" for all this? Not any, to speak
of. We may take up that before, *Fuerunt et fecerunt, sed
non perfecerunt;* so far from that, as *non profecerunt.* Such
here were, and doing they were, but it would not do; for it
was not done, the violence they intended. *Proposuerunt*

Marginal notes:
1. No "enemy" professed, but two sons of wickedness for it.
2. "A son of wickedness" he was.
3. Meant "violence," wickedly covered it. How near the doing it.
4. Yet did it not. Non proficient. Non apponent.

SERM.
IV.

nocere, sed non apposuerunt; a purpose they had, an offer they made; that was all: further they went not. You were not lost, we find you here now, and we find you serving God, safe and well (thanks be to the great Finder of Kings) as ever you were.

5.
The cause they did it not.
The "hand" and "arm" of God to "stablish" you.
The defensive part of the covenant.

5. What was it then, that it came so near you, and yet did you no "hurt?" It was the good "hand" of God, His holy "arm" that was upon you, held you, held you fast; you fast, from taking "hurt;" and them fast, from doing any.

Can any doubt that it was the "hand" of God? He that stood there armed for that end, when he was so stricken suddenly, as he had neither heart nor hand, to do that he came for; was it not the "hand" of God, that so struck him?

2. When his hand held the other's hand, that was ready to give the deadly blow, *ut non apponeret nocere* (they be the very words of the text): and was it not the "hand" in the text then?

3. That you were so stablished as to resist, that you were so strengthened as to prevail (the two effects, set down in the verse both): and yet was it not the "hand" there specified?

4. The popular tumult that rose after this, enraged by odious
Ps. 65. 7. surmises, was it not God's "hand" that laid the raging of the waves then, that stayed "the madness of the people?"

5. When the "violence" was over, "the hurt" was not. The lewd tongue of Shimei doth hurt, no less than the sword of Abishai. It would not be believed, that all this was true,
Ps. 89. 51. there were that "slandered the footsteps of His Anointed" (David's case, in the end of this Psalm). Was it not God then, That so touched the heart of him that was escaped unknown, that he had not the power, to be true to himself, to keep it in, but was even driven by remorse to betray himself, though with evident hazard of his own life: was not this *digitus Dei?*

And since that, by a further strange discovery, hath He
Ps. 63. 11. not set your innocency in the sight of the sun? that now "the mouth" of all wickedness is "stopped," so that neither Abishai's sword, nor Shimei's tongue now, can do you any "hurt?" And was not the "hand" and "arm" of God in this? Yes, the whole "arm," and every joint; the whole

"hand," and all the fingers of it. Yet lack we the last verse.

Here was the "hand" with the shield; but where was the "arm" with the sword? Here too; and it smote them, smote them down, down it smote them both, both in the very place where they designed your "hurt," and in the very wickedness of the act: both were smitten down stark dead, and there stark dead you saw them both lie before you (as the verse is), "before your face." *Non profecerunt;* nay, *defecerunt, et in ipso scelere perierunt,* "their sword" went through "their own heart," and their blood was upon their own heads. God "found" you then, and you found Him, certainly. O, let Him ever find you His servant, Whom you then found your so gracious good Lord.

But they must be plagued too (to make the text up full). So were they: for, as if they had been smitten with some pestilent foul disease; so, from them, from their mention, there goeth an odious scent, odious, and abhorred of all: yea, the very house, as if the plague of leprosy had been in it, razed down: and, that there might no infection come from this plague of theirs, their very name put out from under Heaven. And, all this, so done, and with such circumstances, as all that hear it must acknowledge it was "God's doing," and that from Heaven came the "hand" that did it: *Factum est, et a Domino factum est,* both.

And so, you are found; and they (as the children of perdition should be) are lost. Here are you; and where are they? Gone to their own "place," to Judas their brother. And (as is most kindly) the sons, to the father of wickedness: there to be plagued with him for ever. The same way, may they all go; and to the same place, may they all come: all, that shall ever once offer to do the like. Thus, to the very last syllable of the last verse, is this text found true in you; and this covenant made good to you. All the six points of it, all of them *in futuro*, in the text, "shall" and "shall be," comes me the day, and puts them all *in præterito* to you, changeth "shall" and "shall be," into was and did. That, thus we read it now: His hand did hold you fast, His arm did strengthen you: "the enemy" was not able to do you any "violence," no more was "the son of wickedness" to

6.
The "hand" and "arm" to "smite them:" the offensive part of the covenant.
To "smite them down" "before your face." Ps. 37. 15. 1 Kings 2. 32.

7.
To "plague them."

This done by God Himself. Ps. 64. 9. Ps. 118. 23.

Acts 1. 25.

SERM.
IV.

"hurt" you. But He did "smite down" your "foes," and did "plague them that hated" you. So, the covenant was fully kept with you, and sealed, even with the blood of them that brake it.

3.
Joy for
your de-
livering.
Lu. 15. 6,
9, 32.

And now, let all them, that took any joy in the first finding and anointing, here renew their joy afresh for this second, when you were thus in a manner "lost and found" again. When it was, just as in the Gospel, *Periit et inventus est*. And if he in the Gospel for his "sheep," and she for her "groat," called all their friends together, and cried, *Congratulamini mihi :* how much greater a *Congratulamini* be-

Mat.22. 20.

longs to this? where not a groat, but he that is "the image and superscription" of all our groats, yea, all our coin, silver and gold, is found again.

To find
some
praises of
God for
this find-
ing.
[Isa. 55.3.]

And what? shall this be all? No, I trust. Having thus, at the hands of God, found "the faithful mercies of David," we will stay a little, and look out some of the faithful prayers of David, to render Him for this, for such a finding. Let us do so, I pray you. And we shall not need to go far, nor any farther than our own Psalm, and but even to the very first

[Ps. 89. 1.]
The first
verse of
the Psalm
Cantabo.
Ps. 145. 9.

words of it, *Misericordias Domini in æternum cantabo.* Upon another, no less worthy deliverance, I well remember, you then took up the like, *Misericordiæ Domini super omnia opera Ejus.* Very fitly that; but this agrees rather with us now : for it is the beginning of the Psalm, whereof the text is a part : made, as it were, the anthem for this sermon.

"Mercy"
in making
this cove-
nant.
"Truth" in
keeping it.

Will ye see how it agrees? There was "mercy," in making this covenant, there was "truth," in keeping it. See then, how aptly he hath set it : "My song shall be always of the mercies of the Lord" (That made it) ; "with my mouth will I be shewing His truth" (That kept it) "from one generation to another." And shall not we sing of His "mercy?" And shall we not set forth His "truth?" Sing of His "mercy," That made this covenant; shew forth His "truth," That made it good, every article, and suffered not one word of it to fall to the ground?

The second
verse of
the Psalm,
Ego dixi.

But, if we cannot well sing it, for lack of a quire; he hath taken order for that too. For, the very next, the second verse of the Psalm, that he begins with, *Ego dixi,* "I have said :" that if we cannot sing it, we may yet say it. And it is but

the same over again : " I have said, Mercy shall be set up for
ever, Thy truth shalt Thou stablish in the heavens." What
" truth ? " It followeth in the third verse, this " truth " of
His covenant to David. To sing that, and to say this : to
make our songs, on this ground ; and our sermons, on this
theme. He hath said it, to " set up " His " mercy ; " He
hath done it, to exalt His " truth."

Ever to do this, *in æternum : in æternum* is the word of the To do it *in*
verse, (if our dulness could endure it,) all the days of the æternum :
specially
year. But, of all the days in the year, this day not to fail this day.
Lu. 19. 9.
of it. *Hodie salus facta est domui huic,* nay, *Regno huic,*
nay *Regnis his :* this day then, not to fail of it. For, having
" found" this " mercy," and felt this " truth," this day ;
shall we not, at the least, this day, thank Him for this day?
Shall the sun of this day arise, and go down upon us, and
not see us together, to render Him praise for this so loving
a " mercy," for this so faithful a " truth ? " Shall He find
" hand" and " arm," to succour and to save us ; and shall
not we find mouth and lips, to bless and magnify Him
for it ? God forbid.

Let us then sing that : " My song shall be always of the Applica-
mercies of the Lord :" record it, at least. Or, for default of tion to us.
it, say this : " I have said, Mercy shall be set up for ever,
Thy truth shalt Thou establish in the heavens." Be they
never so false upon earth, Thou in heaven shalt stablish it.
Say it, *per modum concionis :* so we have. Say it then, *per* By way of
modum orationis : so let us do, and so an end. preaching.
By way of
Even so Lord, so let it be. Set up this Thy mercy for prayer.
ever, for ever stablish the truth of this Thy covenant, with
Thy servant our Sovereign, that it never fail him, as not
this day, so not at any other time. Let Thine " hand" be
still upon him, and Thine " arm" about him for ever, between him and his harms. " Violence" and " hurt" never
come near him, the sons of wickedness be ever far from him.
Let them be non-proficients, all the sort of them, that study
or practise this wicked lesson. Never lose Thou him, or
suffer him to be lost ; ever find him, good Lord, to succour and save him ; and let Thy " right hand " find out [Ps. 89. 23.]
his enemies, to " smite" and " plague them," with the same
blows Thou didst smite, and with the same plagues Thou

didst pour on these of this day.   The destiny of this day
come on them all!

And for him, let his anointing still be fresh on him, and
his crown still flourish on his head.   Let him all the day
[Ps.89.15.] "walk in the light of Thy countenance," and at night rest
under the covering of Thy wings.   This day, as once it did,
and as ever since it hath, so let it, long and many years, rise
prosperous and happy to him.   This day, and all days.   That
he, that we all may sing Thy "mercy," and set forth Thy
"truth," all the days of our life.   Hear us, O Lord, and
grant it for Thy Son's sake, our Saviour, &c.

A SERMON

THE KING'S MAJESTY, IN THE CATHEDRAL CHURCH AT SALISBURY,

ON THE FIFTH OF AUGUST, A.D. MDCXV.

PSALM xxi. 1—4.

The King shall rejoice in Thy strength, O Lord; exceeding glad shall he be of Thy salvation.

Thou hast granted him his heart's desire, and hast not denied him the request of his lips. Selah.

Thou hast prevented him with the blessings of goodness; and hast set a crown of pure gold upon his head.

He asked life of Thee, and Thou gavest him a long life, even for ever and ever.

[*Domine in virtute Tuâ lætabitur Rex; et super salutare Tuum exultabit vehementer.*

Desiderium cordis ejus tribuisti ei; et voluntate labiorum ejus non fraudasti eum,

Quoniam prævenisti eum in benedictionibus dulcedinis; posuisti in capite ejus coronam de lapide pretioso.

Vitam petiit a Te, et tribuisti ei longitudinem dierum in sæculum, et in sæculum sæculi. Lat. Vulg.]

[*The King shall joy in Thy strength, O Lord; and in Thy salvation how greatly shall he rejoice!*

Thou hast given him his heart's desire, and hast not withholden the request of his lips. Selah.

For Thou preventest him with the blessings of goodness; Thou settest a crown of pure gold on his head.

He asked life of Thee, and Thou gavest it him, even length of days for ever and ever. Eng. Trans.]

UPON a day of joy, here is a text of joy. Upon a day of joy for the King, a text of a "King" in joy. For so, we see, there is in the text a "King;" and he joyful and "glad."

SERM.
V.

Ecclus.
47. 6, 7.

2 Cor. 11.
10.

2 Cor. 6. 2.
Isa. 49. 8.

"Glad" first, for "strength" shewed by God, in saving him; "glad" again; for "goodness" shewed by God, in satisfying, yea, (more than satisfying,) preventing his desires; and that, in the matter of his "crown," and of his "life," both.

This "King" was King David no doubt: the very title of the Psalm sheweth as much. And the son of Sirach, (of whom I reckon as well or better, than of any Commentary,) these very words here he applies to King David.

Originally then, he; but neither solely, nor wholly he. His meaning was, not to make this saving his own case, alone; nor to engross this joy, all, to himself: ye may see it, by the very setting it down. It is not, as of himself ('I will rejoice);' but, (as of a third person,) "The King shall:" "The King," indefinitely. So, entailing it rather to his office, than to his person; and leaving it at large, appliable to any other, a King, as well as himself.

To any other King, I say. Specially any other such King, that should be as strangely saved by God's "strength," as fairly blessed by His "goodness," as ever was he. That should find the like favour that he did; and be vouchsafed the like gracious deliverance that he was. Any such King, in such wise saved, to be equally interested in this joy with him; and to have this Psalm serve for a sermon, or for an anthem, no less than he.

And, by this, we hope in God, this rejoicing here shall not be shut up against us. For that which is here left indefinite, we suppose, we can definitely apply to a King, (in whose presence we stand,) to whom the same "strength," and the same "goodness," of the same Lord, have shewed forth themselves, in saving him, saving both his crown and life, no less than David's.

This comes well to the text. But what, doth this concern us now, more than any other time? Yes; for here comes the day, and claims a property in it. How that? Remember ye, how the Apostle, when he had cited the place out of Esay, "I have heard thee in an accepted time, in the day of salvation have I helped thee;" "Behold," saith he, "now is the accepted time; behold, this is the day of salvation." The same, (for all the world,) saith this day. "The King shall be glad of thy salvation:" *Ecce hodie dies salutis hujus,* 'Behold, this is the day of that salvation." For, so it is, indeed. The very salvation-day itself, this.

For, this day, was his life sought, and he set on, to have been shamefully made away : and this very day, saved he was; and *in virtute,* "mightily" saved; and *in virtute Dei,* by the mighty hand and help even of God Himself.

Since then, this blessing fell upon this day, if we will take a time, (and a time we will take to rejoice and to give God thanks for it,) that which the day pleads for is most reasonable; that you will take this day, rather than another: for if *hodie dies salutis,* if 'to-day, the day of salvation ;' no reason in the world, but to-day the day of rejoicing for it.

But I will forbear to take any notice, or to mention any but David, at the first going over; the text, that requireth a survey of course, first, and shall have it. But then, if the day shall pray a review after, I see not how, in right, we can deny it.

Be these then the two parts : [I.] the survey, and [II.] The division. the review. And in either of these, two principal points I. present themselves. II.

1. The joy, 2. and the ground or causes of it. The joy, in the front of the text; and the causes, in the sequel of it.

The causes are, as the number of the verses, four : 1. The saving of the King, by the "strength" of God. 2. The satisfying, yea, the preventing his "desire," by the "goodness" of God. 3. The setting on his "crown," by the hand of God, *Tu posuisti.* 4. The prolonging his "life," by the gift of God. These four.

Now every of these (the joy and the causes, and indeed the whole text) seems to stand upon triplicities. In the last verse of the Psalm, God is said to "exalt" His "strength." His "strength," in exaltation, makes the joy, in triplicity.

The triplicity of joy, first. "The King 1. shall rejoice," 2. "shall be glad," 3. "exceeding glad shall he be." 1. *Lœtabitur,* 2. *exultabit,* 3. *vehementer.*

The like, in all the causes. Why "glad?" First, for "the King" 1. was saved, 2. saved by God, 3. by "Thy strength, O Lord." 1. *Salute,* 2. *virtute,* and 3. *Tuâ, Domine.*

Upon this, of "strength," followeth a new triplicity of "goodness." Therein, 1. "the desire of his heart," 2. "the

request of his lips;" and besides them, 3. "the blessings of
goodness." Of these three, the first "granted;" the second
"not denied;" and "prevented" with the third.

Of 1. which "blessings," there are two set down in particular: 1. his "crown," and 2. his "life."

His "crown," and the triplicity of it. 1. *Corona*, 2. *coro-
natio*, and 3. *coronans*: the 1. "crown," 2. 'the coronation,'
or setting it on by another; 3. and that other, God: none
but He, *Tu posuisti*.

His "life:" and there another (the last) triplicity. 1. "Life,"
2. "long life," and 3. "life" *in sæculum, et in sæculum sæculi*. "Long life" in this world, "life for ever" in the world
to come.

And for this "strength" in thus saving; and this "goodness" in thus satisfying his desire, in the safety both of his
"crown" and his "life;" is all this *lætabitur* and *exultabit*,
all this joy and jubilee of the text.

This survey done, the day will further pray a review:
trusting it will fall out (all this) to prove the case of the day,
just. That all these causes will *coincidere* into it: 1. *salutem
misit*, 2. *desiderium concessit*, 3. *coronam posuit*, and 4. *vitam
dedit*: and if these, then the joy too (without fail).

And that, two ways: upon two powers, that be in the
word, "shall." 1. "Shall," the bond *de præsenti;* binding us
to accommodate ourselves to the present occasion, to this joyful season of God's sending. 2. And then, "shall," the tense,
which is not the present, but the future: and so "shall," not
only for this present day, but "shall" still; still "shall," for
many days of many Augusts, in many years more; the
same *lætabitur*, the same *exultabit*, still. So we all wish
it may.

I.
The sur-
vey.
1.
The joy.

Domine lætabitur. We begin with joy. *Auspicatum principium*, a fair front onward, a lucky beginning.

In joy: and that not single, but three in one, a triplicity
of it. We will but touch at it, now: we shall come to it
again: ere we end. Begin and end with to-day: so may
we begin, and so end, ever.

In this triplicity, two words there be, to express this joy:
1. *lætabitur*, and 2. *exultabit*: and one to give it the size or
measure, 3. *vehementer*.

The two former (1. *lætabitur* and 2. *exultabit*) are as it were the body and soul of joy. The first, *lætabitur*, the soul. For the nature of that word, and the use, noteth joy within: joy of the bosom, say the heathen: joy of the spirit, the Scripture: "And my spirit hath rejoiced." There, in the spirit, is the fountain of true joy. If there it be not, how well soever the countenance counterfeit it, it is but counterfeit, for all that. And no joy right, if we cannot say the two first words, *Domine lætabitur*, to God: and we cannot say them to Him, if there it be not, within.

There then, to begin; but not there to end. *Lætabitur* is not all, *exultabit* is called for too: which is nothing but an outlet or overflowing of the inward joy into the outward man; of the heart into the flesh: "My heart and my flesh shall rejoice." Not one, without the other. Joy, to be seen and read in the forehead ("the joy of the countenance)." To sound forth, and be heard, from the lips ("the voice of joy and gladness)." This doth *exultabit* add. There is the body and soul of joy, now.

But it is not every mean degree will content in these. Not any "glad," but "exceeding glad." The Hebrew is, *O quam!* "O Lord, how wonderful is Thy Name!" saith the eighth Psalm, the first verse. So here: "O Lord, how joyful and glad shall he be!" The meaning is; so very glad, as he cannot well tell how to express it. Else, asking the question, why doth he not answer it? but that he cannot: but that he hath never a *tam* for this *quam;* but is even fain to leave it, to be conceived by us. So do we; but σφόδρα, *vehementer*, "exceeding" it must be. So say the translations, all.

Thus have you a brief of the triplicity of joy: 1. joy within, 2. jubilee without; 3. both, *mensurâ supereffluente.*

And (which is somewhat strange) these not only permitted, but even enjoined, given in charge: "shall rejoice, shall be glad:" a necessity laid on him; but a blessed necessity, to be bound to that, our nature and we, in all our liberty, so well love and like of.

And now, to the causes. For "exceeding" joy, without a cause somewhat suitable, is but exceeding folly; but as "the crackling of thorns under a pot;" great noise, but no great cause, for all is but a whin-bush. If there be an "exceeding"

1. *Læta-bitur.*
שׂמחה

Lu. 1. 47.

2. *Exul-tabit.*

Ps. 84. 2.
Ps. 21. 6.

Ps. 118. 15.

3. *Vehe-menter.*
מה מאד

Lu. 6. 38.

2. The causes of it.
Eccles. 7. 6.

SERM. in the joy, there would be an exalting in the strength: if
V.
_____ excess in that, no defect in the ground. We take measure
still, of one of these, by the other.

Have we then a good ground? that have we: four (for
failing): every of them suitable, in each respect. For a triplicity in either of them.

The cause. The ground of all (the first) is, "salvation" or being saved:
1. "Salva- and that is ground sufficient. For who doth not rejoice, is
tion," or
being   not glad, "exceeding glad," that is so saved? But specially,
saved.
Salus.   (which was David's case here,) saved from a sudden and a
secret mischief, imagined against him. There is no joy, when
all is done, to the joy of one so saved. Be it who it will;

[Mat. 25. even *unus de minimis his:* any, "any one of the meanest."
40.]
Salus   But the person adds a great weight to the joy; that it is
Regia.   *Rex in salute, salus regia,* 'a salvation royal,' for the saving of
a King. For he (by the Scriptures' own valuation) is set at

2 Sam. 18. "ten thousand." There be ten thousand salvations in one,
3.
when a King is saved. That as *Rex* is the person, above all;
so *salus Regis* is the sovereign salvation of all.

2.   Saved then. And secondly, how? *In virtute,* saved by
Saving by "strength." For though it be good being saved by what
"strength."
means we can; yet if we might be at our choice, we had
rather have it by means of strength; rather so than by craft,
or by running away. For that is not *in virtute. Salus in
virtute,* is ever the best saving. And a King, if he have his
right, would be saved no other way: not by sleight, or by
flight, but *in virtute, Rex.*

So have you two, *virtus* and *salus,* "strength" and "salvation." Note them well: for not *virtus* without *salus,* nor
salus without *virtus;* neither without other is full; nor both,
without *Tuâ Domine.*

Virtus in   *In virtute* is well, so it have *in salute* after it. For, no, not
salute.   in "strength" is there matter of joy, every way considered.
No, not in God's "strength:" no joy *in virtute Dei,* if it have

Ps. 21.   not an *in salute* behind it. They, in the latter part of the
Psalm, found God's "strength," but smally to their joy.
This makes it up; that it is not only *virtus,* "strength;"
but *virtus ad salutem,* 'strength to save.' "Strength," not

Ps. 89.23. as to the King's enemies, to "smite them down," and
"plague them;" but "strength," as to David himself, to

save and deliver him. "Strength" is indifferent, to both; but *in salute* following, it determines it to the joyful side.

Now then, turn it the other way. For, as *in virtute*, if it end with *in salute*, is just cause of joy; so, *vice versâ*, in *salute*, if it go with an *in virtute*, makes the joy yet more joyful. I mean, that as it is *virtus in salute*, 'strength to save,' might to deliver; so it is *salus in virtute*, 'a strong salvation,' a mighty deliverance. No petty common one; but a strong and mighty one. This reciprocation sets it higher yet: that not only "strength," set forth; but "strength" to save, protect, and preserve; nor that neither, *quovis modo;* but mightily to save, strongly to protect, and strangely to preserve: so as the "salvation" may justly be said, *Tuâ Domine,* God's own saving. *{Salus in virtute.}*

For, yet we are not, where we would be. It is much to the matter of joy, whose the "strength" is, from whom the salvation, who the party. For, not *undecunque*, or *abs quovis*, yields full joy: not by every one, hand over head. The better the party *per quem*, the more the joy still. The "salvation" is made the more precious, by the Author of it. That as it is *salus Regia*, on his part that receives it; so it is *salus divina*, on His That gives it, that is, *Tuâ Domine*. *{3. By God's "strength," Tuâ Domine.}*

But to this, *Domine*, there belongs two *Tuâs*. To *virtute* and *salute*, either of them, a *Tuâ : virtute Tuâ* and *salute Tuâ :* and this doubling of the point, we shall find, concerns the joy much.

For, that it may not be, as Jonas' joy in his "gourd," up in one night, and down in another: that is, vanishing and unsure; but sound and permanent; it is best our Hosannah be in the highest: best, that the hypostasis or substance of this our rejoicing be in the "strength" of the Lord. Not "in chariots and horses:" we see what became of them, the Psalm before. *Hi ceciderunt,* "down they went," and down went their joy with them. That was *in virtute alienâ*. *{1. Virtute tuâ, not alienâ. Jonah 4. 10. Ps. 20. 7, 8.}*

Nor in his own "bow" or "sword," or number of his people: that proved not well neither: that was *in virtute suâ : in virtute Tuâ*, we shall find, is the safer. *{Nor suâ. Ps. 44. 6. 2 Sam. 24. 10.}*

Not but that in these human strengths we may rejoice in some sort, with some caution; but that they be all subject to the "worm" (Jonas' gourd was), mortal and mutable all: *{Jonah 4. 7.}*

SERM. not so soon had, but as soon lost, and sooner a great deal.
V. There is no hold of them; *quotidie diffluunt:* we find it, we
feel it, daily.

Therefore well fare *in virtute Domini,* "the might of the
Almighty." In it, there is the sound joy. O, it is a good
rejoicing in the strength of the arm that shall never wither
Ps. 36. 7. or wax weak; and in " the shadow" of those " wings" that
shall never cast their feathers : in Him, That is not there
Heb. 13. 8. yesterday, and here to-day: but "the same yesterday, and
to-day, and for ever." For as He is, so shall the joy be.
In virtute Tuâ, then, and *salute Tuâ* too.

2. *Salute*   Nay, *virtus Tua,* but *salus sua.* The power, that may be
tuâ.   God's; but the "salvation," that is the King's (one would
think). And so it is; but he rejoices not in it, as it is *salus
sua,* (at least not so much), as that it is *salus Tua,* God's : of
and from God, Who wrought it, and brought it to pass.
Nay, even *in salute Tuâ* itself: not so much *in salute,* as in
Tuâ : in the gift, as in the party That gave it. So doth no
worldly man : he goes no further than *in salute* (that he hath
it, that safe he is), cares for no more, for no *Tuâ* he. But
David's joy, and the joy of the godly, is not so much that
Ps. 68. 28. he is saved, or had strength so to be; as that it was God
sent forth His "strength," so to save him. Nay, nothing so
Lu. 1. 47. much *in salute,* as *in Tuâ;* in the "salvation," as " in God
his Saviour."

And why so joyful for this *Tuâ Domine,* more than the
rest? I shall tell you why : for this is the very exaltation,
the highest point, of the whole triplicity.

There was none of the Emperors, upon such an escape as
this, but he took to himself presently, as a high honour, the
title of Θεοφύλακτος, 'Preserved by God;' and used it ever
after, as an addition to his style, as glorious as Alamannicus
or Parthicus, or any title of them all.

A King thus saved by God is more than a King: I mean,
more than another King, not so respected by God. More, I
say, than another. 1. More to be set by, in the sight of his
own people : *tanquam speculum propitii Numinis,* 'as a mirror
of God's favour;' when they see him, thus taken into God's
special protection. The very next words are, " His honour
Ps. 21. 5. is great, in this salvation."

2. As, of his own people; so more esteemed of his neighbours, when they see their own thrust in with knives, and so
cast down and fall; but him, after he was cast down, to rise,
and stand upright: *Hi ceciderunt* helps it much. Ps. 20. 8.

3. And lastly, more feared of his enemies; when they see
the eye of God's providence, the shadow of His wings, the
strength of His arm, still over him: still set to save him,
and do him good; they will be afraid to plot aught against
him, when they see, it is in vain, God still defeats them, and
upholds him still: when they see *Tuâ Domine* in great letters upon him.

And, now are we come to the spring-head, to *caput lætitiæ:*
Tuâ, Tuâ, Domine. And when we have brought our joy up
thither, up to Him, we turn it loose, let it exceed then.
Nowhere else; but, in Him, let it. If it be *gaudete in
Domino,* nay then, *Iterum dico gaudete,* saith the Apostle. Phil. 4. 4.
Then, to it, again and again: double it, and treble it, and
spare not. Good leave have you.

Now then, for this *salus Regia* and *salus Divina,* both,
join the triplicities; see if they suit not, this and the first
(of joy). *In virtute,* God's "strength," the very promise and
hope of it, yields joy within; there is *lætabitur.* But, made
apparent *in salute,* is further matter of *exultabit,* without.
But *Tuâ, Tuâ, Domine,* to that belongs *ó quam!* there is his
place. O, how greatly shall David rejoice within, triumph
without, in the Lord; being saved by Him, so mightily, and
so marvellously saved by Him! These two triplicities are in
the first verse, both.

There is new joy, in the second verse, upon a new ground, The second cause.
the "goodness" of God. And "strength" and "goodness"
do well together; neither without other saveth. "Strength" In satisfy-ing "the desire."
alone, it could well; but will not, till "goodness" come to it.
Both did it here; for, in this verse, saved by "strength;" 1. Of his "heart,"
and in the seventh verse, "In the mercy of the Most High 2. Of his "lips."
he did not miscarry." By "strength;" that, by no arm of
flesh: by "mercy;" that, by no merit of his own.

But, His "goodness is over all His works," over "strength" Ps. 145. 9.
and all. For it sheweth itself, not in saving only (which is
a matter of necessity); but over and besides that, in satisfying his desires (and that is matter of mere bounty).

SERM. And indeed, no way doth His goodness so shew itself, as
V.   in sending us our desires. Nor nothing is so properly the
name of joy, as the " desire" sent. The denying of our
" desire;" nay, the but delaying it, is an abatement to our
Prov. 13. 12. joy; but the " desire" accomplished, that is the " tree of
Gen. 2. 9. life," saith Solomon. And " the tree of life" was " in the
midst of the garden;" the very centre of Paradise, and all
the joys there. The satisfying his " desire."

To satisfy is one thing; and to satisfy by prevention another. Between them two, they make up a new triplicity.
For the former, of satisfying the " desire," is set down,
either as conceived in the " heart," *desiderium cordis ;* or as
expressed with the " lips," *prolatio labiorum.* It is much, to
satisfy these two. His " goodness" gives satisfaction both to
the one and to the other : satisfaction, to the " heart," by
granting the " desire;" satisfaction, to the " lips," by not
denying " the request." And upon these two, in the verse,
there is a Selah. For these two, one would think, were able
to content any.

But this Selah is no Selah to God. He hath a Selah, or
an Elah, above this Selah. He hath not only a satisfying,
but a satisfying by prevention : not expecting either, but
preventing both : granting that, which neither the " lips"
ever mentioned, nor the " heart" once imagined : never
came out of the mouth, nay, never came into the mind.
And this is the *prævenisti* of His " goodness."

As for the " heart" and the " lips," we will not be curious,
nor stand scanning their order, which should stand first, the
Ps. 45. 1. " heart" or the " lips." I know, though the " tongue" be
" the pen" of never so " ready a writer," the heart can indite
faster, by much. But what skills it which is first? Both
together, I am sure, can desire more than either alone; and
He will satisfy them both.

Mat. 7. 7. Satisfy the " lips." *Petite et dabitur*, " speak and speed."
Ps. 81. 10. Satisfy the " heart." *Ave et habe*, ' wish and have.' Not only,
" open thy mouth;" but enlarge thy heart, never so wide, and
He " will fill it." This is able to satisfy David, I think, and
to make him sing Selah, which is their διαπασῶν.

3. In pre- This may satisfy David. But this satisfies not God, in
venting His " goodness" to David. No *satis* with him, but *satis*
both, with
His "good-
ness."

superque. And indeed, both these (make the best of them you can) are still but a *post-venisti,* the "heart" and the "lips" go before, and God's " goodness" comes after. Nay, till Isa. 30. 18. His " goodness" get before, till it be a *prævenisti,* it satisfies Him not. And that is ; not when He stays for us till we come to Him with our petitions ; nor till He meet us, He with His mercy, us with our prayers ; but, when He prevents us, before we stir a foot ; and hears us, not when, but *antequam,* "before" we request ; and answers us, not Isa. 65. 24. while, but ere even we desire : opening, sending, and giving, Mat. 7. 7. before we seek, knock, or ask : that, lo, is the *prævenisti ;* that " the blessing of goodness" indeed.

" The blessing of goodness." And as to satisfy is one "The thing, *quovis modo ;* to do it by prevention, another ; so, to blessing of goodness." prevent with goodness is one, and " with the blessing of goodness," another. For that is (as the fat of the sacrifice) the best, the most chief, the most choice, the most blessed part of it : blessed itself, and making David blessed, to whom He vouchsafes it.

Not but that the other, the granting, the not denying, are good blessings, and very good ; but in them, though there be the goodness of God, yet not it alone ; there is somewhat of David too, his devotion (at least) in making his request. But in this, God's goodness is all alone : David doth nothing, neither speak nor think. That he never asked, never thought to ask, before any, without any asking, he is prevented with, by this blessed goodness : and without any cause else. The Fathers read it, *benedictio dulcedinis,* and well : for while we stand waiting for the *post venisti,* our eyes fail many times, our heart pants, we float between hope and fear : and this relishes not well with us, it is a little bitter. In *prævenisti* there is none of these. And the cutting off of these makes it *benedictio dulcedinis* indeed, as having none of that unpleasant mixture with it. This is *benedicta bonitas.*

But (all this while) we see not, what need of this preventing. It is more than needs, sure. The other two, the not denying but granting, might serve our turns well enough. Yes, there is more than need of it, in the matter of saving, many times. The danger comes upon us, and surprises us so, of a sudden, as we have no time to gather ourselves together: the "heart" no space to think, nor the "lips" leisure to frame a "request." Both fail us.

And this holds chiefly in secret plots and practices. No man suspects, or misdoubts them : no man prepares for them. Unawares, on a sudden, they break out, and even oppress us, so as they prevent "lips" and " heart," and all. Such was the danger, in the Psalm : such, the danger of the day. In these, if it should be put to a *postvenisti*, we were gone. A prevention must be. In these preventing dangers, then, is the time ; there, is the place of this preventing goodness of God. Who seeing, what David would do, if he were not taken short, supplieth, of His blessed goodness, that defect, and before either of both, relieves and saves him. This is the blessed goodness, and blessed be God for this goodness, above all : we all, at some times or other, fare the better for it.

Will ye see now, how these three come again exactly to that of the joy ? The inward " desire of the heart," for that " granted," *lætabitur*, the inward joy of the heart : the outward " request of the lips," for that " not denied," *exultabit*, the outward voice of gladness. But " Thou hast prevented" them both, (both mental and vocal petitions,) without suit at all. O how glad shall David be for the other twain, but for this third especially ! For this is the goodness, O *quam !* This exceeds all.

The specialities of that goodness.
1. In his " crown."
2. In his " life."

Well; but all this while we walk but in generalities : might we see some speciality of this " blessing of goodness" thus preventing him ? Yes, we may. There follow more ; but here, in the text, are two particulars, both matter of God's prevention, both matter of His " desire." For, what would a King desire to have saved, or wherein to be blessed, but in 1. his " crown," and 2. his " life ?" And here, they be both. And in either of both, a several sort of preventing : " granted," and not asked at all, as in his " crown :" more " granted" than asked, as in his " life."

2. His " crown" first.

But first ; will ye mark that here, *Corona prævenit vitam*, ' the crown takes the place of his life,' hath the precedence of it : that his desire is carried straight to his " crown" first, before to his " life," as to the blessing, of the twain, more to be desired. Thus we find them : and we may not stir them,

they are of the Holy Ghost's own marshalling. Thus sets
He them down, as if His will were, they should so be
apprized: the "crown" before "life."

Mark well: *Posuit coronam,* and then *vitam petiit:* with
his crown on, so he desires life. But *coronam deposuit,* take
away his crown, and then *vitam non petiit,* he will not ask
"life;" he will not think it worth the asking. If he would
ask it, it would not be given him: he that takes away his
"crown," will have his "life" not long after. Fond to
imagine otherwise: and it is the poorest comfort and conceit
that ever was, to tell them, their "crown" they must part
with, but be of good cheer, their "lives" shall be saved,
that they shall. No: *vivis et regnas,* take *regnas* and take
vivis too: both, or neither here.

This is the "crown." And this "crown" in David was
a *prævenisti,* clear: a *posuit* without any *petiit.* For when
"he followed his ewes great with young," little dreamt he
of any "crown." It never came into his "lips," it never
entered into his "heart:" his "soul," as himself saith, was
"weaned" from any such matters, from so much as once
fancying them; the "crown" was in him a mere prevention.
2. That "crown," a *prævenisti* in David. Ps. 78. 71.
Ps. 131. 2.

Nay, two crowns, we read, he came to. First, Saul's
"crown:" the Amalekite brought him that, and his brace-
lets. To shew, it was a *prævenisti* merely; not so much as
an Israelite brought in. That was "set on," first. Some
thirty years after, we find he came to another "crown," the
King of Ammon's "crown," at the winning of Rabbah: a
more massy "crown," finer gold, richer stones in it, than
his first. That was "set on" too. This here in the verse was
the second, say all the interpreters: and this a *prævenisti*
likewise. If you will but remember what case he stood
in to Godward, at the coming of this second "crown" (it
was presently upon the matter of Uriah and Bathsheba), you
will say, he was rather in case of *Miserere mei Deus,* than of
aught else: that crowned him then, in "mercy and loving-
kindness." At this second "crown," it was *veniam petiit,*
and nothing else.
And his second "crown." 2 Sam. 1. 10.
2 Sam. 12. 30.
Ps. 51. 1.
Ps. 103. 4.

And at his first "crown," it was *vitam petiit,* and nothing
else. All he asked then, was his "life;" it follows straight,
next verse. And sure, time was, in the days of his prede-

SERM. cessor, when partly by Saul's own jealousy; but much more,
V. by the wicked suggestion of Doeg, and such like, he needed
to ask it. There was often, to use his own words, "but a
1 Sam. 20. step between him and death." He asked "life," then; and
3. so that might have been assured him, would have strained
his prayer no further.

We must think, when he was cooped up, one while in such
a cave, another in such a wood; put to fly for his life to
Moab, to Gath, I wot not whither: in danger still to be made
away, by one treachery or another; when he received every
2 Cor. 1. 9. hour "the sentence of death" in himself; all his mind ran
upon *vitam petiit* then. Then, this "crown," or "the gold"
of it, or the fineness of the allay, never troubled his head, ye
may be sure: "life he asked" then, and more he asked not,
and well had been him, if he might have had but security of
that; I say, security of his "life," and let the "crown" go.

3. The Behold, then, the blessed goodness of God, That gave him
"crown set both. Both, that he asked, "life" (we come to it by-and-by);
on" by and the "crown," and another "crown" too besides, that he
God. asked not. Satisfied him, in that; "prevented" him, in this;
nay, "prevented" him, in both; as ye shall see straight.

But ere I pass to that, here is a point or two about crowns,
I think good not to pass. 1. The first is, against usurpers of
the crown, *nemine ponente, nisi se ipso,* God not setting it on,
none setting it on, but themselves: that not *ipse sibi, sed
Deus ipsi;* not, *ipse posuit super caput suum,* but *Deus super
caput ipsius.* 2. The second is against usurpers of a power,
to take off that, they never set on (*deponendi quod non
posuit*), and thereby intruding upon, *Tu posuisti.*

1 [*i.e.* 1. First, the "crown," he raught[1] not at it, caught it not,
reached.] and clapt it on himself: it was brought him, he came orderly
The im- to it; it was set on, not by himself, but by another. And that
posing other was the right setter, *Tu posuisti,* God. Who will never
God's set it on a wrong, never but on the right head, if it be of His
only. setting; and if it be not of His setting, it will never prosper,
Isa. 62. 3. never flourish, be sure. *Tuâ Domine,* here too: the "crown"
is in God's "hand," saith Esay, and His hand sets it on
David's, sets it on all their heads, that lawfully wear it. It
made the Emperors to stamp their coin with a hand coming
out of the clouds, holding a crown, and putting it on their

᾿leads: and accordingly, to style themselves Θεοστεφεῖs, *a Deo coronatos,* 'crowned by God:' as well they might (this *Tu posuisti* here is their warrant).

2. Secondly, against usurping of a power to depose. God alone is in the *posuisti,* at the setting it on. None but He, there: God hath set it on. Now what God hath set on, let not any presume to take off. Not any, but He that set it on. What, by Him alone done, by Him alone, to be undone. The law is, *Ad quem institutio, &c.* 'To whom the institution belongs,' to him, and none other, the destitution. To whom the imposing, to him, and none other, the deposing: none to interpose himself in that business, but he.

And the deposing.

And now there comes a *Tu interposuisti;* and he will have to do with that, this *Tu posuisti* put on. Hath not *potestatem ponendi* (he confesses, and all the world knows); and yet would have *potestatem tollendi,* to take up that he laid not down. But if no *ponent,* no *deponent.* If none but God, at the *posuisti,* at the setting it on; none, but He then, at the *deposuisti,* at the taking it off. The "crown," the coronation, the coronant, all three, "blessings of His goodness:" but the last, the chiefest, the *Tuâ Domine* and *a Te,* the tenure of it of Him, and Him only.

Now then, to join these three to the first three. Allow the crown a *lætabitur,* and to the coronation, or setting it on, an *exultabit:* but *O quam!* is for *Tu posuisti,* the coronant, to Whom they owe it; of Whom they hold it, without any *Tu interposuisti* at all: and now, to his "life."

For what is *coronam posuit,* without *vitam dedit;* a "crown," without "life" to wear it? Here is that then: and that, in a new triplicity, 1. "life" itself, 2. "a long life," and 3. "a life for ever."

God's "goodness," in granting him 1. "Life."

Vitam petiit. Is not his first *vitam petiit,* this (we spake of even now, in Saul's time): it was after his second "crown" was set on; as is evident by thus standing after it. And this *vitam petiit* bodes no good matter. For by *petiit* it should seem, by all likelihoods, he was in case to ask it, and so in hazard to lose it; it, and crown, and all: a worse matter than any yet. It was not for nothing, the last verse before this text, they cry, "O Lord, save the King:" belike, the King was in some danger of perishing. And so he was, as ap-

Vitam dedit, but *vitam petiit* first.

[Ps. 20. 9. Vulg.]

SERM. peareth by the sequel of the Psalm, and that by a mezimma,
V. "a secret mischief" imagined against him: were it that of
Ps. 21. 11. Absalom, or some other like exigent. But "hard bested" he
מזמה
[Isa. 8. 21.] was, when it touched his life.
Ps. 119.   In that strait, here was the sum of the "desire of his
175.
1 Sam. 26. heart," of "the request of his lips:" "O let my soul live,"
21. O let the soul of Thy servant be precious in Thy sight.

And now, upon this *petiit*, as upon a ground, follows
straight *vitam dedit.* And herein first appeared the "goodness" of God, in granting his "desire," in not denying his
"request." *Vitam petiit*, and *vitam dedit; "*life he asked,"
and "life" he had: no sooner asked, but obtained. This
was satisfying.

2. "Long   But then, He stayed not there, but "prevented" him fur-
life." ther: gave it him, with advantage, with that he asked not.
"Life" He gave him, so far his petition, so far no prevention:
but He gave him "long" too: long was not in the petition,
and so a mere prevention, the second kind of prevention, that
before we spake of. "Life" was in the request, "long" was
Ps. 61. 6. not; He gave it him, with "long" too, *dies super dies Regis
adjiciendo*, "adding days to the King's days," till it was
length of days, that is, "a long life," and a long reign both.
Which very point of "long" makes that this text will not
fall in fit with every King, unless he have lived and reigned
as long (David's time, that is, forty years): for so he must,
ere *dedisti longam* can be said or sung of him.

3. "A life   But yet, here He stays not neither; but heaps upon him
for ever." more still, and goes on to *vitam in sæculum sæculi.* For, to
say truth, what is "long life," yea, never so "long," if it be
not St. Hierom's long, *Nihil longum quod finem habet?* If ye
speak of "long," that is truly "long," that shall last for ever,
that never shall have an end. Our "long" is but a short
"long;" which goes but by comparison of a shorter. Else,
what is it to live out the full compass of man's uttermost age,
if he live not so, in this life, as after this, he may live for
ever? The meaning is, What is "long life," without it be
a religious life; without it be with the true fear and worship
of God? which only hath the promise of *in sæculum sæculi:*
without which a short life is better than a long life; and no
life at all, but an untimely death, better than both. Other-

wise, the heathen have hit upon *coronam posuit*, and *vitam dedit*, yea, and *longam* too : they be but *lætitiæ gentium* these. But the "life for ever," that is a *non omnibus datum ;* Matt. 19. they among the heathen never had it : that is *lætificans* 11. *Davidis*, that, the blessing of blessings, the transcendent blessing of all, to have the end of this life the beginning of another life, that never shall have end : and that by the true service of God, in His sanctuary.

Reckon this then, *instar omnium*, even worth all, and the 1 Chron. very *consummatum est*, the highest perfection God can bestow c. 13. on David, that God gave him, to bring back the ark, to pitch c. 28. a tabernacle for it, to lay up and leave a great mass of treasure c. 25. for the building it a temple, himself devoutly to worship, and c. 26. to make laws and set orders for a more solemn and seemly worship of God, than he found : he said himself, this was the joyfullest day he saw in all his life; that "one day worth a Ps. 84. 10. thousand." And for this his care of the sanctuary, came this "help" to him "out of the sanctuary" (see the second verse [Ps. 20. 2.] of the Psalm before) that saved him, saved him both his "crown" and "life;" and that after received him to "ever- Lu. 16. 9. lasting tabernacles," to a crown and life, that shall endure for ever. And further than this, we cannot go.

So have we the particular of that was sued for and granted : and of that was granted, and not sued for, by the special privilege of God's preventing goodness. Himself saved, his "desire" satisfied, his "crown" fast, his "life" assured, here and for ever.

And judge now, whether David had good cause to rejoice or not. And whether we may not here again (for a farewell) once more, over with our first triplicity of joy again. *Lætabitur* to go to *vitam*, if you will; and, if need be, *exultabit* to *longam :* but *O quam*, to be reserved for *in sæculum sæculi.* There it is in kind : so it was never before. There it is *O quam !* indeed. For there, is a crown, life and joy that exceed all that we can desire : and there he shall receive them, and say *O quam !* indeed.

And what shall we say now of all this? truly no more than II. must needs be said : no more than the text itself draws from The review us. Here is a fair major, laid forth to our hands. A King, tion to His that hath in this manner found the "strength" of God shew Majesty.

SERM. forth itself in his saving; and felt the "goodness" of God in
V.   thus preventing his desires, touching both his "crown" and
his "life." Any such King may (for he hath good cause);
nay shall and ought (for he is bound) to be "exceeding,"
both joyful and "glad." The Holy Ghost gives His word;
says, he shall so be.

If this be King David, he; if any other, he too. King
David's we have surveyed, as the time would give us leave.
Shall we now pray a review, to see if any other may be found
besides, as deep in the causes as he? For, if as deep in the
causes, as deep in the effect; if the same *in virtute*, and the
same *in salute*, the same *lætabitur* (all will grant).

Ps.40.9,10. And here now, choose, whether we will refrain our lips,
and keep back God's "mercy and truth from the great congregation." If we would so, and hold our peace, the day,
Ps. 19. 2. even this fifth of August would not; but would, as the Psalm
saith, *eructare verbum*, break forth and tell us, that such a
King there is, and who it is. That if there be, or ever there
were a prince upon earth, that found and felt this *virtutem*
and *salutem Dei*, the mighty hand and help of God in saving
him, saving him miraculously: verily this day saith, (not as
2 Sam.12.7. Nathan, *Tu es homo;* but) *Tu es Rex,* 'you are that King'
certainly; even in all these four, in the text, from point to
point.

1.   For your saving, first. This day, you were like to miscarry,
In his
saving. in danger to perish, to lose your "life," and (that which to
Ps. 21. 7, you is dearer than your "life,") your "crown," by some that
8, 11.
מזמה   hated you, and had contrived a mezimma, "a dangerous
practice" and plot against them both. You being then and
there overset with strength, came this *virtus Dei:* you then
being upon the point to perish, came this *salus Dei*, and saved
you strangely. There is the first verse.

2.   For your desire satisfying. In that distress, I doubt not,
In the
satisfying but you might and did lift up your soul to God, in some short
his desires. Hosanna; that of Hezekiah, *Domine vim patior,* "Lord I am
Isa. 38. 14.
Mat.14.30. oppressed," succour Thou me; or, that of the Apostle sinking,
"Help Lord, I perish." If you did so, He "granted" your
"desire," He "denied not" your "request:" set a "Selah"
then. But if being surprised with the extreme suddenness of
the assault, you did not, you could not do it; then did He

more, even prevent you with His "goodness," His sweetest,
His blessedest "goodness" of all.

And besides your saving (which you had reason to desire)
that which you never would have desired, I dare say; that
gave He you too. Exalted His strength, that you might
your triplicity. And those same Zamzummims, the con- זמזמים
trivers of the mischief, His hand found them, and they found Ps. 21. 8,
12, 9, 10.
it; He set His "strings full against the face of them;" destroyed them in His wrath, even in the very place; hath
cast them into the fiery furnace, where even now they fry;
rooted out their "fruit" from the earth, and their name
"from among the children of men." All these are, word
for word, every of them in the sequel of this very Psalm.
All this He did: you desired not all this, not their eternal
destruction, I know; yet even with this also He "prevented" you.

For your "crown:" this is sure, if ever any were "pre- 3.
vented" with a "crown," he was, that was so in his cradle; In the setting on his
had it set on his head there: when he was not as a weaned "crown."
child, morally; no nor a weaned child, literally; but indeed
a child, not yet weaned, not so much; had neither lips to
speak, nor heart then to desire any such thing: he was
"prevented" sure.

Further yet: if any found favour in setting on his "crown," 4.
yea "crown" upon "crown," and saving upon saving: after In giving
and pro-
his first "crown," in danger to miscarry, and even thrown longing his
"life."
down (as upon this day): and after his second, in danger
again to miscarry, and to be blown up, (upon another day,)
and saved in both: he was fairly blessed by His "goodness," say I. Which very saving (upon the matter) was a
second crowning: even a new setting on that, that was
sliding off. So that, *Tu posuisti,* the second time, may truly
be affirmed of this day.

And what should I say? If any, that his "crown" saved,
and his "life" saved (under one); saved and prolonged both;
so that now these fifteen years together, you have held this
day with joy; and, which is worth all the rest, besides length
of this life, blessed with God's holy truth, the pledge of everlasting life, the best of His blessings: such an one, this text
doth warrant us to say, hath cause, great cause, exceeding

SERM.
V.

Lu. 1. 46,
47.

great cause his soul to " magnify the Lord," and his " spirit" to " rejoice in God" his " Saviour." Such an one, to perform all the three here specified : so many triplicities of favour would have more than a single rejoicing.

And shall not I add this? As to rejoice in God, so to seek and set himself, to devise and do somewhat for which God may rejoice in him : somewhat for the sanctuary ; from thence came his help, and from no other place : somewhat I say, that this joy may be mutual, as of you in God, so of God in you again.

Sure, there is a bond, an obligation to it, in *Lætabitur*. " The King shall rejoice," " shall be glad," shall do it, shall not be dispensed with, not to do it : shall not please God, if he do it not.

Our duty.

But, where are we all this while ? excluded from this rejoicing? " The King shall," it is said : what, and none but he ? None is mentioned, but he : we would not let him, I dare say, do it alone ; there be many thousands of us, that would not stand by looking on, if we had any warrant to rejoice too. Give me leave then to look out a warrant for us : we would be loth to sit out, and to lose our part in this joy.

[See the
Vulgate.]

This Psalm, and the Psalm next before it, are two sister-Psalms. That, a prayer for the King's safety: the last words of it are, " Lord, save the King." Why, the King is saved, they have that they prayed for; and shall not then their Hosanna resolve into a Hallelujah ? Their careful Hosanna, into a joyful Hallelujah ? Yes, and so it doth, in this. For, as the last words of that Psalm are, " Lord, save the King ;" so the last of this, " So shall we sing :" sing for very joy of it.

[Ps. 20.5.]

They promised as much, there (in that Psalm) to "rejoice," at the fifth verse. " We will rejoice in Thy salvation." *Lætabitur Rex*, here it is ; *Lætabimur nos*, there. They promise it there ; and they will be as good as their word : and so they are : for even in this Psalm, *Lætabitur Rex* is the first verse ; *Cantabimus nos* is the last : that if he " rejoice," at the first ; we come in, at the last. If his at the beginning, ours at the end.

2Sam.20.1.
1 Kings
12. 16.

" We have no part in David," is the voice of a rebel. All good subjects have a part, have an inheritance in him, or as the new taken-up term is, a birthright in him; and in him, before his law.

In the second of Samuel, chapter the nineteenth and forty-third verse, they fall there to share the King among them, (the tribes,) and to reckon up, what part and portion each hath in him. Have they a part and portion in him? Why then, in his grief, and in his joy. And if they in theirs; we, in ours. So that, to use the Apostle's phrase, if he be 2 Cor. 2. 2. "sorry," who can make us "glad?" and if he be glad, to use the Apostle's phrase again, he may truly say, (and so may every good King, of his people,) "This trust have I in 2 Cor. 2. 3. you all, that my joy is the joy of you all." Thus come we to have our part in his joy. And if (as it is well noted) Judah is in David : the very name of the one (with a very small transposing) in the other's name : if Judah, in David; then Ps. 53. 6. Judah's joy, in David's : that if it be true, *lætabitur David*, it will also be, *lætabitur Juda, et exultabit Israel*, "Judah will rejoice, and Israel be right glad." Look ye, there is now a warrant, there is Scripture for it.

Now then, if we have Scripture for our rejoicing, let us 1. do it; and do it thoroughly : even by and through all this tripartite joy.

Begin with *lætabitur :* "rejoice" in the spirit within. A good sign we do so, if we can but say the two first words here, *Domine lætabitur*, unto God. The whole text is a speech directed to God: He made witness of our joy. Therefore see it be hearty and true : there is no halting with Him: see it be so, or tell not Him it is so: He will find you straight, and give you your "portion with hypocrites," if Matt. 24. you say to Him, Lord, Thou knowest thus I am, and yet 51. thus you are not.

In very truth, the Psalm seems to be penned for the nonce, that no dissembler might say it. He, to whom it is to be said, is not man, but God : and He can tell, whether we speak as we think or not.

But all true hearts will say it, and say it with confidence, and that even to God Himself, That knows the ground of the heart : Lord, Thou knowest what is within me, Thou knowest that I am truly joyful, even there within.

There within, we must have it first; but there within we 2.

SERM. must not keep it : nay, there within, it will not be kept, if
V. there be this spirit and life of inward joy in it. Out it will,
with an *exultemus :* and even so God would have it. No
Rev. 5. 5. concealed joy, no Apocrypha to-day. All "the seven seals"
of it opened. Shine out, as a beam ; flow forth, as a stream,
into a visible and audible exultation : shew itself as God's
joy doth, in the sixth verse, in " the joy of the countenance."
That if any tell you he is glad within, (that he is,) and hath
the clouds in his forehead : if it will not serve ; you may ask
him, But where is your *exultabit ?* we must see you are so.
1 Cor. 5. 8. There is some "leaven" of malignity within, if there be not
Ps. 118. 15. " the voice of joy and gladness," that it may be heard to the
ear ; if there be not the habit, gesture, and other signs of it,
to be seen to the eye ; that it may give evidence, to both
senses.

Both these ; and both in no scant measure ; no pinching
3. to-day ; but " good measure," "running over:" " exceeding"
Lu. 6. 38. is the word of the verse. Exceed first, in this least and
lowest of all ; in the low voice of joy and gladness, in these
panegyrics of praise, and joyful acclamations. But, exceed
we them. How ? by *cantabimus,* the hymns and music of
the Church (that is louder); and to help them to exceed, all
the organs and other instruments of the quire below. But
exceed we them, too. How ? with the bells, the instruments
of the steeple above ; and with the sound of the trumpets,
that will be heard further off. And yet exceed them too.
How ? With a peal of ordnance, (if it be to be had,) that
will be heard farthest of all.

" Exceeding" is the word in the text. " Exceeding" to be,
in and through all ; that our Hosanna may be in the highest
to-day. And so for the other senses ; in shows and triumphs,
feasts and fires, and other signs of jubilee ; whatsoever we
use, when we use to exceed in gladness ; when we would
shew we exceed in it : that so, *O quam !* may be said of it,
it doth so exceed. All are but due to this deliverance, to
thus many triplicities in it.

We to exceed : for God Himself, we see, exceeds here.
His ordinary is, but to give leave, or, at most, to call us to
rejoice. But here, He doth not give leave, or call us to it,
with a *jubilate :* nay, " shall" here is more than a *jubilate.*

That but exhorts; this binds us : "shall be glad," that is, neither will nor choose, but be so. Yea, He makes us speak to Him, *Domine ;* and makes us promise Him, we will so : and having promised, looks we should make it good. God enjoins it : and if God enjoin it, the day doth most justly *intercedere,* even 'plead' for it, that if ever we will do it, we would now do it, on the salvation-day itself. And never may he see day of joy, that joyeth not in this day ; nor have cause of gladness, that for this cause is not glad. And this for " shall be glad ;" and for the bond, *de præsenti,* that is in " shall."

But besides it, there is a tense, *de futuro,* in " shall" too. We may not lose it, for fear of *tolletur a vobis ;* but, ad- Joh. 16.22. monished by that tense, bethink ourselves how to draw it further than the present tense, even into the future (still " shall ").

Lætetur or *lætabitur Rex :* the Hebrew will bear both. But ours, and so all translations choose *lætabitur* rather. Not *lætetur :* that is not so well ; for, that is true, if it be done now, and but now, for the present, for this once ; *lætabitur* is better ; for there, the doing it is in the future still, still to come : still more joy behind.

For, "The King shall rejoice" of this day, will be over soon at night. What, shall we end our rejoicing then, with this day ? No, I trust. But by virtue of this " shall," shall rejoice next year again ; and when that is come, shall the year following ; and so then again, the year after that : and so from year to year, *donec cognominetur* " shall," so long as it Heb. 3. 13. is called " shall ;" so long as we look into our books, and find " shall rejoice" there. So long, and no longer.

Now, that the joy may so continue, the causes must continue too : there is no remedy. It is they must keep our *lætabitur* still alive. The causes were, *salutem misit, desiderium prævenit, coronam posuit, vitam dedit.* To perform our vows then, (*vota publica,* I trust,) to desire that this chain of causes may keep whole still, and not a link of it be broken, or lost ; that they may pass into the future, all : still *salutem mittet, desiderium præveniet, coronam ponet,* and *vitam dabit.*

I will not go through them all ; only touch the Alpha and

S E R M. Omega, the first and the last: and so I have done. *Læta-*
V. *bitur*, and *vitam dabit*, still.

Prov. 14. *Lætabitur*, joy first; if it be but for *vitam dedit*. For, joy
30.
Prov. 16. is a prolonger of life, *Dulcedo carnis et sanitas ossium*, as
24. Solomon calleth it : and even for that cause, we begin with it.
But (to say truth) leave out *lætabitur*, and what is there wish-
worthy ? Truly, without it, neither saving, nor " crown," nor
" life," worth the wishing. For who would be saved, to live
still in sorrow ? And the " crown" itself, it is not *corona
desiderii*, if it be not *corona gaudii*. Yea, and who would
wish "life," but to take some joy and comfort in it ? I will
Gen. 3. 8, say more. Let one be in Paradise, as Adam was : even there,
10. when Adam had lost his joy, Paradise itself was no Paradise :
as good in a dry desert, as in it : without joy, Paradise itself
is not worth wishing. Joy is all in all. Let that then be
Ps. 45. 7. *caput voti ;* that "the oil of gladness" may run down through
them all, and over them all : make his saving precious to
Ps.132.18. him ; " his crown flourish ;" his life, *vitam vitalem*, and worth
the desiring. That joy may be the unity of this trinity,
1. *salutis*, 2. *coronæ*, 3. *vitæ*.

But then, last, because all four of them hold upon life ; to
the end, they may hold, that that may hold ; hold, and hold
long. Some think it is long enough already : and so, long
may they think. I know not what to think : for (I cannot tell
how) long and short are said but *comparative :* that so a life
may be long, and not long, diversely compared. To stand
rating it, as the law doth, seven years to a life ; so, seven
lives already : so compared, it is (in a sense) long. But we
will none of that. Nor, as compared with the Princes round
about him : for he hath stood them all, and longer than any
Ps. 89. 27. of them all : and hath had the honour long to be *primogenitus
inter Reges terræ*, God's " first-born now of all the Kings of
the earth :" and long may he have it. Long, if thus. But
then again ; not long, if compared with the desires of our
hearts, with the requests of our lips : not long, if compared
with that that may be : and whatsoever may be in this kind,
we wish, it might be, even as long as nature can possibly
draw it out. Let this then be our Omega, our *summa voti ;*
and that, in no other words than the usual words of the old
councils to the Emperors or Kings then present among them.

Jacobo Regi, a Deo coronato, a Deo custodito, vitam longam, annos multos.

'To King James, crowned by God, preserved by God, many years, long life.' So long, till he change it for a longer; till there come eternal salvation, an immortal crown, life *in sæculum sæculi,* nay in *sæcula sæculorum,* and make all consummate. And so I end.

But before I end, in any wise let us not be so ravished with our *lætabitur,* but that we remember *Tuâ Domine* withal. He, That sent this salvation, fulfilled this desire, the setter on of these crowns, the giver of this life. So rejoice, as, in every of them, our joy come up to Him. So take *calicem salutis,* Ps.116.13. as we term it (I pray God we so term it, and so take it aright) : but aright we shall do both, if we forget not to call upon His Name, even "the Name of the Lord." That He, Which saved to-day, may so save ever : That fulfilled his "desire," may keep it still full : that He That "set on" his crowns, may hold them on, hold them on fast : and last of all, add to the "crown," "life;" and to "life," "long :" and to "long," "for ever and ever."

And even so, conclude we, as the Psalm doth : addressing our speech to Heaven.

"Be Thou exalted, O Lord, in Thine own strength." Thou wert so this day : be so still, again and again. "So shall we sing and praise Thee" for it. We now do so, for this day's salvation, and all the joyful triplicities of it. So may we still : so may we long : so may we ever.

And, good Lord, exalt Thou this Thy "strength," and treble these Thy triplicities to us; that we may, for these Thy exultations and triplicities, double and treble our thanks and praise to Thee : as this day, so all the days of our life. And this, with one heart and voice, beseech we Thee to grant, &c.

A SERMON

THE KING'S MAJESTY, AT BURLEIGH, NEAR OAKHAM,

ON THE FIFTH OF AUGUST, A.D. MDCXVI.

ESTHER ii. 21—23.

In those days, when Mordecai sat in the King's gate, two of the King's eunuchs, Bigthan and Teresh, were wroth, and sought to lay hands on the King Ahasuerus.

And the thing was known to Mordecai, and he told it unto Queen Esther, and Esther certified the King thereof, in Mordecai's name.

And when inquisition was made, it was found so : therefore they were both hanged on a tree : and it was written in the book of the chronicles before the King.

[*Eo igitur tempore, quo Mardochæus ad Regis januam morabatur, irati sunt Bagathan et Thares, duo eunuchi Regis, qui janitores erant, et in primo palatii limine præsidebant, volueruntque insurgere in Regem, et occidere eum.*

Quod Mardochæum non latuit, statimque nuntiavit Reginæ Esther, et illa Regi ex nomine Mardochæi, qui ad se rem detulerat.

Quæsitum est, et inventum ; et appensus est uterque eorum in patibulo. Mandatumque est historiis, et annalibus traditum coram Rege. Latin Vulg.]

[*In those days, while Mordecai sat in the King's gate, two of the King's chamberlains, Bigthan and Teresh, of those which kept the door, were wroth, and sought to lay hand on the King Ahasuerus.*

And the thing was known to Mordecai, who told it unto Esther the Queen ; and Esther certified the King thereof in Mordecai's name.

And when inquisition was made of the matter, it was found out ; therefore they were both hanged on a tree : and it was written in the book of the chronicles before the King. Engl. Trans.]

SERM.
VI.

"IN those days ;" so begins the text. In these days ; so may we begin. Nay, come yet nearer, on this very day. For, on this very day, there fell out that hath made, either beginning may well serve: "In those days," or, In these days. *In diebus illis,* we read there was a King, and he in danger: in danger to have hands laid on him, and that by two, two of his own people: for no cause, but that they were angry; and it appears not why. And the issue was, the King delivered; and they that sought his, brought to a wretched end.

As we have read, so have we seen *in diebus his.* One of the same condition, a King too; and in the very same danger of hands laid on him, and by the same number, two: and of his own subjects and servants; and for no cause, but they were angry; and for no cause, that neither. And the issue here again, the King preserved, and they also came both (as these here did), though not to the same, yet to a far more fearful end.

I speak before understanding hearers; and, I know, there was not any but upon the reading of the text, his conceit did lead him presently, who was meant by King Ahasuerus, and withal did even think of the Bigthan and Teresh of this day: and so made the comparison with your own selves, before I could make it.

We shall gain, this year, by this text, somewhat onward The sum. more than the former we did. Till now, we have been all in divinity: that a heinous sin it is there, this attempting on Princes; but now shall we go to the common law, what it is there. For, here is an assize brought against two, and the matter enquired, and a verdict found, and they had sentence and were executed. For what? even for *voluerunt insurgere,* as the fathers read it; or, as we, *quæsiverunt mittere manum:* for but seeking, for but having a will, "to lay hands on" the King.

And that, not the Jews' law. There we were, in the years past; now, we are not in "Jewry," where "God" was Ps. 76. 1. "known;" we turn us to the Gentiles: we are in Persia now. And this we do, by the Prophet's warrant. "Get you," Jer. 2. 10. saith he, "to the Isles of Chittim and behold, send to Kedar and enquire," if there were any such thing sought there, and were not condemned. For if there, *ad erubescentiam vestram* 1 Cor. 6. 5. *dico,* "I speak it to your shame," that would be held the people of God, if any such thing should be found with you.

They are worse than pagans, that so seek : we will empannel
no Christian; a quest of heathen men shall serve to attaint
them.

This is no law of the brain; it is written : twice written :
1. written down, first in " the chronicles" of Persia, by direction from the King. 2. After, written out of them, and
enrolled here in this place, by direction from God. Enrolled
I say, and properly : for, this of Esther is not called a book,
as others are: not the book, but the roll of Esther. Originally it was but Persian law, this : and it had not been
much, if that had been all; but by virtue of this enrolment,
it is made the law of God also. That, from henceforth, it is
clear at both laws, the law of the Jews, and the law of the
Gentiles : the law of man, and the law of God : that all
seekings of like nature are made criminal and capital, and
the sentence of *suspensi sunt* upon them, holy, and just,
and good.

Lastly : written law, and old law. For of this, (whether
divinity or law,) this we may safely say : it is no new Por-
tugal divinity, this, almost three years old, taken up *in
diebus his.* Nor no new law of *heri* and *nudiustertius :* nay,
Mat. 19. 8. not of Edward the Third then, *et a principio non fuit sic.*
No : it is old this, *in diebus illis,* " in those days." And
" those days" are as old as the second monarchy, the famous
monarchy of Persia : the reports of which nation are more
ancient than any, save those of the Jews : no book, but the
Bible, so ancient as they.

And this methinks is not amiss, when we can bring this
book to justify the justice, or any way to give strength to
the law of the land : it is pity, but it should be so : either
support other mutually, *facultas juris,* and *facultas theologiæ.*
As here now, we have the roll of Esther, and in it a report
of Bigthan's case, long before there were any year-books or
reports at the law. We are willing to bring forth this roll
of ours, (which till an ancienter can be shewed, must be the
leading case, to make *voluerunt* treason,) to shew the country
law, in this, to be no other than God's is : that it is no otherwise at the one, than at the other; treason by law, treason
by divinity, by both.

Well may we talk of law, the law of the land ; but when

all is done, never do men rest with that quiet and full contentment, as when they see it is warrantable by the word of God : hath the ground there, as this hath the ground there. Every word here hath in it his warrant : *quæsitum est,* for the trial; *inventum,* for the verdict; *suspensi sunt,* for the execution.

The main points are, as the verses are, two : 1. the King's The division. danger, in the former, the verse of danger; 2. the King's delivery, in the latter, the verse of delivery.

In either, the means of either. His danger : 1. of what, I. 2. by whom, 3. what moving them.

1. Of what? of having hands laid. 2. By whom? by Bigthan and Teresh. 3. What moving? nothing, but angry they were.

His delivery : 1. by what means, 2. of whom, 3. and how. II. 1. By what means? by notice taken and given of it. 2. By whom? by Mordecai. 3. How? even casually, as he was sitting in the gate.

But the King's delivery, it is not meet it should go alone : it is therefore attended with their ruin, that sought his.

That is, as it were, the train borne up after it.

His danger by Bigthan and Teresh. In them two things : 1. what they " sought," and 2. what they found.

1. What " sought" they? " To lay hands on the King." What found they? One laid hands on them for it; *appensus est uterque eorum in patibulo.*

2. His delivery by Mordecai. In him, two more : 1. his notice taken, by casual overhearing them, sitting as he sat. 2. His notice given, by his faithful discovery of the whole to the Queen ; and to the King, by her means.

Then should follow the legal proceeding; but I will spend no time in it. It is all out of our case this day. Our Bigthan and Teresh had no enquiry : no jury went on them, they were not executed in form of law. No further goeth our case, than the King's danger, his delivery, and the cutting off those that sought his life : and no further we will follow it : not that.

But this we will, the solemn setting down and recording III. all this, 1. in the King's chronicle, as a memorable accident : 2. in God's roll, as a famous case : 1. of the treason of the

SERM.
VI.

two, to their eternal infamy: 2. of Mordecai's good service, to his everlasting praise: 3. of the King's happy delivery, to the universal joy of all his subjects.

And there, come we in. For, we may not, nor we will not forget *in diebus his.* And I shall make it appear, I trust, that, whether we take the Kings, or the parties; the danger sought, or the delivery found; *diebus his* will match and overmatch *diebus illis,* in all points. And so the joy of this day, our joy, to do the joy of them accordingly.

I.
The King's danger.
Esther 3. 6.

It is a delivery, they and we celebrate: no delivery, but from a danger precedent; so was there here. The King in danger evidently. And he no sooner out of danger of these two, in this chapter; but the Queen in danger of Haman, in the next. So, the estate of Princes is not exempt from danger.

1. Of hands laying on him.

And of no small danger neither: no less matter, than having hands laid on them, that is, even of being made away. This King here, saith the Apocryphal book of Esther, saith Josephus, say the best writers, was Artaxerxes, surnamed Long-hand. If he; his father was slain by Artabanus. The father was: and the son, we see, was sought to be: near it, escaped it narrowly.

2. By his own.

And by whom this? neither by enemy, nor by stranger, but by his own. Of his own subjects, of his own household, of his own chamber, and the chief of his chamber then, too.

3. Because they were angry.

And why? for no evil of his. He was, for his moral parts, (as all write of him,) a good Prince. That would not serve: his life was sought though. And no cause, but they "were wroth;" and no cause appeareth. All which sheweth princes; that for all their might and greatness, for all their innocency and goodness, for all the favours they vouchsafe others, it is not in them, their safety consists. It is in the "mercy of the

Ps. 21. 7.
Ps. 89. 21-23.

Most High they do not miscarry." "His hand, that holds them fast; His arm, that strengthens them, that the enemy is not able to do them violence, nor the son of wickedness to hurt them." To look up to Him, to hold good terms with Him, Who in all their danger, either by Mordecai, as in the text; or without Mordecai, as in the day, can work their deliverance.

The danger.

Deliverance from danger. Danger, whereof? delivery,

wherefrom? executed, wherefore? All leads us to the fact 1. The lay-ing hands on any, a sin. next; which indeed seems no fact, for nothing was done; sought only to have been.

"To lay hands" is one thing; to but "seek to lay" is another. "To lay hands" is, of itself, I know, a thing indifferent, thereafter as the hand is. It may be a helping hand, as God's is; and then *Mitte manum*, saith the Psalm, lay it Ps. 144. 7. and spare not. But if it be Satan's *Mitte manum* upon Job, Job 1. 11. to do mischief; then stay it, lay it not. And such were these hands here: for it is said, they "were angry and sought to lay hands." Angry hands, it is well known, are hurting hands. Either Jeroboam's, "Lay hands on him," to sur- 1 Kings 13. 4. prise his person; or Herod's, Lay hands on Peter, to do by Acts 12. 3. him as he did by James, to murder and to make him away.

So to "lay," is a sin certainly, be it on never so mean a Specially on the King. person. But *in Regem*, is a sin of sins. For, the sin (we know) is still by so much the more grievous, by how much the party is the more eminent, against whom it is. Now there is not on earth a person more eminent; nay, so eminent, as the King. *A Deo primus*, saith Tertullian, *post Deum secundus:* 'Count not God, he is the very first: count [Tertull. Apolog. c. 30.] God, and he is second.' None so high as he; and so, no sin so high as it. To "lay hands" on him? it is too rank that: away with it.

But that is not the case. It is not *miserunt* here: none The seek-ing "to lay hands," is a sin. were laid. No matter for that; it is *mittere quæsiverunt*, and that is enough. To "lay," and to "seek to lay;" though one be worse, both be naught, even *missio* and *quæsitio* both.

Seeking is a plowing for sin; and that is sin, saith Job. Job 4. 8. It is a hatching of a "cockatrice egg;" and that, saith Isa. 59. 5. Esay, is poison; no less than that comes of it.

Sin, to "lay;" sin, to "seek to lay." As to "lay," though you hurt not; so to "seek to lay," though you lay not. Ever, in what degree soever, Ahasuerus' danger is Bigthan's sin: the King's danger; their sin, that seek it.

But if that be all (sin); we shall do well enough. What A capital sin. care men for sin, if there be no action at the common law for it? None but Westminster-hall sins do men care for. God saw it would come to this: men learn no more duty, than penal statutes did teach them. He took order therefore, to bring it within them too.   We say further then, by virtue of this text, besides that it is a grievous sin, prejudicial to the state of the soul, it is a heinous crime, a capital crime, amounting to *suspensi sunt*, as much as their neck is worth, to seek this.   It will bear not an action only, but an indictment of life and death.

If upon
the King.
But it must be *in Regem* then, against him : against others, it is not so.   This is a prerogative royal.   And, as many other ways, so hereby appeareth, what a King is.   That whereas, in other men's cases, as touching the law of life and death, to " seek to lay," and to " lay," are much different ; in the King's case, they be all one.   *Quæsiverunt*, if it be no more but so, the law, in that case, to any other, is (I take it) favourable ; and for a bare purpose, if no hurt ensue, no man shall suffer death.   Not so, with the King : *voluerunt*, against him, is death, if it may be discovered ; and *quæsiverunt*, if he but seek, though he find it not.

Ps. 82. 6.
This helps us to understand the text, *Ego dixi, dii estis.* *Dii*, for other causes ; and this for one, that they participate this divine privilege : that, as against God, so against them, the heart is enough.   *Quæsiverunt*, the seeking, whether they find or not.   *Voluerunt*, the will, whether the deed follow or

Eccles. 10.
20.
not.   Thou shalt not speak evil of the King.   How ? not with thy lips ?   No, not in thy secret thoughts, saith the Preacher. If not speak evil in heart ; do evil in heart, much less.

Two commandments (when time was) we said there were

Ps.105. 15.
in *Nolite tangere ;* 1. " Touch not," the act ; 2. " Have not the will to touch," the intent.   Two cases there be upon

2 Sam. 4.
5—12.
these two : 1. Baanah and Rechab's that did lay hands upon King Ishbosheth.   2. And Bigthan and Teresh's case here, that did but seek it, to King Ahasuerus.   Both guilty, both suffered.   Yea, Baanah and Rechab, hang them, and well worthy ; they murdered the King.   But Bigthan and Teresh ? Nay, and them too ; hang them, though they found it not ; only for seeking.

This then I would have all bear away ; it is the substance of the text : *distillatio favi*, as I may call it, drops of itself without any straining.   We find here in the Bible a ruled case.   Bigthan's case, that held up his hand, not for laying his hand, but for seeking to lay it, *plane suspensus est uter-*

que, ' put to death they were both.' Why ? *quæsiverunt,* for nothing but that they " sought" to do it : they did it not ; they might plead *non est factum,* they did it not. It would not serve, they died for it, for all that, upon no other indictment than *quia voluerunt. Voluimus* is enough to attaint any : if that can be proved, no pleading not guilty.

And this is the law, not of the Persians alone (which yet was the law of a hundred and twenty-seven provinces) ; nor ours alone (and so may seem to be the law of nations) ; but, that which strikes it home by virtue of this enrolment here, is the Law of God : God, by thus recording it, hath made it His own; that if there were no law for it, they might be executed by this book, and this verse of it. Sit still then, and seek it not : for if you do, this is your doom, expressly set down here by the pen of the Holy Ghost. Take it as a sentence from God's own mouth : *Qui quæsiverunt, suspensi ; qui quærent, suspendendi sunt,* ' They that sought, went ; they that shall seek, to go the same way.'

Yet for all this, sought it was then, and since, even the King's life; *sed væ per quos.* And that *per quos,* ' by whom,' is the next point. The crime is bad ; *in Regem* makes it worse : but the seekers, worst of all : for they, of all other, should not have sought it.

2. The parties, by whom.

Two they were in number : for I know not how, but for the most part they go by twos : Simeon and Levi, to the murder of Shechem ; Baanah and Rechab, to that of King Ishbosheth ; Jehozabad and Jozachar, to that of King Joash ; Bigthan and Teresh to this attempt here against Ahasuerus ; and the very same number, to that of this day. Treason is in Hebrew called קֶשֶׁר, a binding together. Two there must be, to be bound, at least : two, to conspire, or put their breaths together, to make a conspiracy. Upon the point, there is, in all, never less than three : for *inter duos proditores diabolus est tertius.* All that do conjure, conjure up a third to them : the devil makes them up three; for he is one still : he the faggot-band, that binds them : he the spirit, that inspires all conspirators. For indeed, these unnatural treasons do not so much steam or vapour up out of our nature, (bad though it be,) as they be *immissiones per angelos malos,* sent into it by some messenger of Satan,

Two, in number.

Gen. 34. 25.
2 Sam. 4. 5.
2 Kings 12. 21.

or rather by Satan himself. *Postquam misit Satanas in cor Judæ,* "after Satan had put it in his heart." For, he it is that puts in their hearts, to *seek* to do it; and to *do* it, if God break not the band, choke not the breath of them; as here He did choke it in these, with *suspensi sunt.*

Two in number, what were they? Nobly born, I doubt not, to be in the place they were.

What place? There be that think, Bigthan and Teresh were not their proper names; but the names of the rooms they held. And they have reason for it: Bigthan, as the word goes in that tongue, is *Dapifer,* Teresh is *Pincerna.* Those, we know, were rooms ever counted of special faith and trust.

But plain it is, they were of his chamber. Not of his lieges alone, or of his household; but, which is more, of his chamber. It is a wonderful thing, the state that the Persian Monarchs kept. No man, upon pain of death, to come so near as into their inner base court uncalled; if he did, he
died for it, unless the King, by holding forth his sceptre, pardoned him his life. You will easily then imagine, in what place they were, that had free recourse into his innermost chamber, to go and come thither at their pleasure.

Not only to do so themselves, but to be those, by whom all others were to go or come : no man to come thither, but by them. For that is meant by lords of the threshold, or *qui in primo limine præsidebant,* as the Fathers read it, the very chief over his chamber.

The Septuagint, who should best know the nature of the word, they turn it ἀρχισωματοφύλακες. Φύλακες first, 'keepers;' σώματος, 'of the body.' And many they had (for many such Kings need have) : but these two, they were ἀρχὶ, the chief, the arch-keepers : had, if any more than
other, the chief charge, the very principal of all. "God do so and so to me," saith King Achish to David, "if I make not thee the keeper of my head :" and in so saying, thought he promised him as good a place as he had. He could make him no more. To this place had the King advanced these two : and these two were they, that sought this. That it should be sought at all, evil ; that these should seek it, too bad. They, that if others have sought it, should have

stayed their hands; these to lay on their own, to seek it themselves !

All men know, it was no mean preferment, early and late to be so near Ahasuerus' person; they had means thereby to do themselves much good. So had they, to do others much hurt, if they were not the better men. But for others' hurt it skills not, if they had not thereby had the means to do Ahasuerus himself: if the devil prevailed so far with him as he did. Of his chamber, *Dapifer,* his dish; *Pincerna,* his cup: keepers of his body, principal keepers : if they seek " to lay their hands," they will soon find what they seek : the more dangerous they, the more his danger by them, a great deal. And is not this heaviness to death, when they that were so honoured, prove so unkind ; when they that so trusted, so untrue : and may we not take up the Wise Man's O, " O wicked presumption, whence art thou sprung up to cover the face of the earth ! " Ecclus. 37. 3.

Stay a little, and look upon them, as ye would upon a couple of monsters. 1. To seek this, *in regem* alone, were too much : to break their duty to their liege lord, if there were no more but that: "to lay their hands" on him, for whom they should lay down their lives. 2. Add then: not to a King only, but to such a King; nor to their liege lord alone, but to so good and gracious a lord, that had done them so great favours, placing them so near him, trusting them so far, honouring them so greatly. (For, no honour, to trust; no trust, to the chief trust of all.) More than heathenish wickedness this, to render evil for good : and whose wealth they of all other bound to seek, to seek his ruin. 3. And they came not to that place, but they were sworn: to vilify their oath then, and to tear in pieces the strongest band of religion: the hands that had taken that oath, those hands to lay on him ! 4. To betray their trust to him, that had laid his innocent life in their hands, and to make their trust the opportunity of their treachery ! 5. In a word: of the chief keepers of his body, to become the chief seekers of his blood, the chief enemies of his body, and life, and all ! What can be said evil enough of these ? Say it were lawful in any case (it is not lawful in any ; but say it were) to lay hands on a King; yet they (in all reason) of all others should not have

S E R M.
VI.
been the doers: *Etsi ille dignus perpeti, at non tu qui faceres tamen.* Were not these monsters then? was not their condemnation just? It grieves me, I have stayed so long on them; yet if I have made them and their fact odious, it grieves me not.

3.
The cause wherefore.
They were angry.
What was the matter? what could move them, thus to play the wretches? Why they should not, many and good reasons we see. Why they did, none in the text, but that they were angry: and that is no reason, but a passion, that makes men go clean against reason many times. Bigthan was angry, and Teresh as angry as he.

Yet, if it be but a little anger, it will over. Indeed (such it may be) it will. What manner anger was it? The word Ephes. 4. 26. is a shrewd word; signifies an anger, will not go down with "the sun," will not be appeased. What speak we of the word? their deeds shew as much. We see, nothing would satisfy them, but his life: nothing serve, but "lay hands on" him. That, they sought; so angry they were.

What angered them then? No cause is set down. And none I think there was. If there had, we should have been sure to have heard of it. For men to be angry without a cause, and even with superiors, it is no new thing.

Well: if no cause, some colour yet: if not that, some shadow at least. Somewhat we are to seek, why they did seek this.

If there be in the text any thing to lead us to it, it is in the first words, or not at all: "In those days." "In those," angry they were: as much to say as, before "those days" they were not; but, "in those," then they were. Else, there is no cause to mention that, of the "days," but to make this difference: out of the text, nothing can be picked else.

Angry for Ahasue-rus' choice of Esther.
Why, what "days" were "those?" That goes immediately before: the "days" wherein Ahasuerus had made choice of Esther, to match with her, and make her his Queen; and had made a great feast upon it. At the feast, it seems, they surfeited, they could not brook that match, at any hand. Some ambitious desire of theirs disappointed by it: likely, that was the cause. This was fain to serve for the occasion, for lack of a better: a bad one, we say, is better than none.

What, the great King of Persia find no match in all his own brave nation ? Never a Persian lady serve him, but he must to this vile base people, the Jews, his captives, his slaves, to pick him a match thence? What a disparagement in this, to all the Persian blood ! It would make any true Persian heart rise against it.

Nay then, a worse matter : (now ye shall see them grow godly on a sudden, and wax very zealous, as the fashion is.) Nay then, now we shall have a Queen of a contrary religion, we shall now be all Jews. One that cares neither for Mithra nor Oromasdes : one by all likelihood brought in to be the utter ruin of the ancient religion, established in Persia, ere she came there.

This was it, (they tell us,) and like enough so to be: as (ever) ye shall observe marriage-matters are made occasions oft, to serve to many purposes. For Ahasuerus may not marry but where Bigthan and Teresh appoint. Else, they will be " wroth," and fall on seeking. If any be in the text, this was it. And was not this (trow you) a goodly occasion, and a substantial, to make them quit their allegiance, forget their oath, cast behind them all his favours, betray their trust, truth and all ; lose all these ? For all these must they lose, before they could seek that they sought.

But, why found they it not ? It was not so easy for them to find at first : by reason, that for any to come there, in the King's presence, with a weapon, nay, but having his hands out to be seen, not having them hid, held close under their garments, it was death : Cyrus put two of his kin to death for it. That so they might well seek : and so I leave them seeking that, I pray to God, they may never find. But the true cause was, God was angry with this anger of theirs, that their seeking succeeded not.

And now are we come to the catastrophe, or turning about of all. For by this time *innotuit res Mardochæo,* " Mordecai came to the knowledge of it :" forth it came. Nay, if it come forth, the King shall do well enough. To discover the treason, is to deliver the King.

This was by Mordecai : what was he? No Persian (to begin with) ; but a stranger by birth and by religion ; and a captive besides : one that had better reason to have sought

II.
His delivery.
1.
The means of it. By notice given.
2. By Mordecai,

S E R M. it, than they.   He had as great causes, as any are by them
   VI.   alleged, that favour such seekings.   For this King held him,
          and all God's people with him (to use Esther's own terms)
          in bitter captivity, as a tyrant.   And this, worse he was (at
          least as evil) as a heretic ; for he was an idolater.   One
          would think it had been a work meeter for him, this : he,
          to seek ; and they to keep him from finding that he sought ;
          they him, not he them.

3. As he   And how came he to it?   It skills not how ; but as he
"sat in   "sat in the gate," he came to it.   This is all : he stirred
the gate."
            not, but "sat" still.   And "sat" not in any lurking corner,
            but even in the broad "gate ;" and there came he to it, or
            it to him.   This was God's doing sure.   Their anger boiled,
            (so signifies קָצַף,) and boiled over it should seem, and brake
            out into some words.   Else how should Mordecai take notice
            of it? they would never trust him with it, ye may be sure,
            being a stranger.   A Jew, with their displeasure at the
            match with a Jew, never : but some big words came from
            Bigthan, that by Mordecai were overheard.

            What, in "the gate," in presence of a stranger?   The
            Targum (the most ancient exposition we have) saith, God so
            took away their wits, as they forbore not to talk of it, he
            sitting by ; but did it in a foreign strange language.   Knew
            him a Jew ; thought he could speak no language but his
            own, or a little broken Persian perhaps : not the tongue
            they had their conference in.   Which (it fell out) Mordecai
            understood as well as they.   And thus all came out : God
            would so have it, Who so assotted them, to make a way,
            as to His mercy, for the safe-guard of the King : so, to His
            justice, to bring that upon their own heads, they sought to
            have brought upon the King's.

            And Mordecai, when he had it once, he kept it not : made
            it known, not to him he next met with, but discreetly, where
            he knew he well might, to the Queen.   She was, by blood
            and bringing up, faithful to him ; and so did she shew her-
            self : for what he brake with her, she told the King, not in
            her own, but in Mordecai's name.   The fashion is otherwise
            with some : to tell it in their own names, and never speak
            a word of Mordecai, from whom in truth it came.   Well :
            the issue was, what she told the King seemed to him no idle

fancy of some vain man, but such as was meet to ground an equity [1] upon. So, they were apprehended, and committed, and so to the law we leave them. Well: by this means the danger is over, and the King safe, thanks be to God.

And many ways doth God give just cause to mankind, to admire His high providence, in bringing to light such attempts as this against His Anointed: such variety, so divers strange means He hath, to effect it by; as here, in this, I note four unto you.

1. The party first, Mordecai, that by him. That this health should come to the King of Persia neither by Mede nor Persian: not by any of his own people, but by a stranger, who was none of his lieges, born out of his allegiance, a Jew, a mere alien; that this should come forth by him, and by no other means. But so is God wonderful in His ways; and will, by an honest stranger sometimes, save that, a bad subject would destroy. That in default of his own, God would have saved him by a stranger, rather than not at all.

2. Observe again: that to this stranger it came no otherwise, but as he "sat in the gate." We may not pass that; it stands in the front of the text, as the special means of all. That it thus came, and no other way, as he "sat" still; still, and went not up and down searching: "in the gate," a public place, not any private corner or lobby; he not diving into their bosoms, but only there sitting, it should thus happen; he should overhear them talking together in a strange tongue (though to him not strange); by a mere casualty one would think, all this: indeed by a high and wonderful disposition of God's heavenly providence, this; that, even as he there "sat," it should be brought to him thus.

And very oft doth God betray bad enterprises by such (one would think them) mere casual events. But *in maxime fortuitis* there is *minimum fortuiti, et quæ fortunâ fieri videntur, fato fiunt.* It seems chance, that is (indeed) destiny. And never let them look for other (all the Bigthans of them). One shall be by a wall, or at a window under the house' eaves, near one cranny or other; God will so dispose, somebody shall be within the hearing, when they full little think. For God will have it out certainly: rather than not, by some

S E R M. mere accident, some that sits by chance in the "gate," some
VI. that goes by the "gate," shall bring it out, rather than it
shall not be brought out.

3. And may I not add this for a third, that all this came out
by occasion of that which they pretended for their occasion.
That very match, which was so great a mote in their eye, that
they so maligned, as they must needs swear the King's death
for it; that very match was the means that brought Mordecai
thither to the gate: for thither he came to hearken, not for
any such matter as this, but how the new Queen (his niece)
behaved herself, what report went of her. And as it fell
out, this, which he came not for, there he heard: his thither
coming, by this hap, was the happy means for this happy
discovery: happy for the King; happy for the whole land.
But all came by his resort thither, by means of the marriage.
So, that they made their occasion, was made the occasion of
their ruin.

4. And let this be the last, that even from their own
selves he brought it. They that go about the like, their
own hands shall make them to fall, they shall be "ensnared
in the words of their own lips:" rather than it shall not come
forth, it shall come forth *ex ore tuo serve nequam*, come out
at their own mouths, as here it did. Their own tongues
shall fall on babbling, their own pens on scribbling: God
will have it out certainly; even by themselves disclosed,
rather than not at all. And this, for God's mercy, He had
here, and still hath, to bring such plots to light, marvellous
in our eyes.

Now of Mordecai, the means of all. For though, as this
day's delivery was, we have no great use of him, there was no
Mordecai, no discovery there (this day's was another manner
of delivery, of a higher nature than so); yet is there great
good use of him for all that. Indeed, *Mardochæus exemplum
nostrum*, he is 'our pattern:' ours, that be true men. He set
before us a mirror of a faithful good subject, one according
to God's own heart. For this is a perfect Scripture, we
have in it both what to fly, and what to follow. As there
be in it, two bad; so, thanks be to God, there is one good.
To avoid them: to be like to him.

Like to him three ways: 1. like him in his *innotuit;*

Marginal notes:

Ps. 63. 9, 10.
Prov. 6. 2.

Lu. 19. 22.

Mordecai
to be our
example.

2. like him in his *nunciavit;* 3. but above all, like him in
that which was the ground of all: that he was a faithful
subject to a strange and to a heathen Prince.

Like him first, in his *innotuit.* Not to turn the deaf ear
to Bigthan and Teresh, as if we heard them not; nor to look
through our fingers at them, as if we saw them not. None
knew, he understood the language they spake in: he might
have carried it slily, made as if he had known nothing, not
known that, he knew: nothing to compel him, but his conscience, to take notice of it. But Solomon ran in his mind,
" Save him that is designed to death, Wilt thou not deliver him
that is led to be slain?" Any; but the King more than any.
"If thou sayest I know not of it, He that ponders the heart,
doth not He understand? He that keeps the soul, doth not
He know" the contrary? And shall not He pay every man,
and so thee, according to thy work? Well: for *innotuit*, since
from the "gate" it came, good therefore that Mordecai sit
there, or, which is all one, that they which sit there have
somewhat of Mordecai in them: be, if not curious and inquisitive, yet vigilant and attentive. And yet curious and
inquisitive I would allow, in the case of a Prince's safety.
And the King and the Queen to have their eyes and their
ears abroad (both of them) and all little enough. We see,
for all the King's wise men, that knew the times, never a
one of them knew this time. This good, we see, came by
Mordecai, came on the Queen's side.

Like him in his *innotuit,* to know; like him in his *nun-*
ciavit, to make it known. Careful to get notice, faithful to
give notice of it in due time. God, Whose will it was, it
should thus happily come to him; His will it was, it should
as faithfully come from him. He knew, by the law he was
bound, if he heard the voice of conspiracy, and uttered it not,
it should be sin to him. He knew, by the Psalm, what it was
to partake with other men's sin, what to have his part with a
thief or an adulterer; and if with them, with a traitor much
more. He knew by the Proverbs, he was now in as deep as
they, as good lay his hands on him, and seek it, as lay his
hand on his mouth, and not seek to prevent it, keep it in and
conceal it. He knew (for he told it Esther after) that if he
had not bewrayed it, God wanted not his means to have

1. In his
innotuit.

Prov. 24.
11.

Prov. 24.
12.

2. In his
nunciavit.

Lev. 5. 1.

Ps. 50. 18.

Prov. 24.
12.

Esther 4.
14.

brought it out some other way. And last, he knew by the
Prophet, God would have "set His face" against him for so
cloking it, and have rooted him out. All this he knew; but
the mystery of the seal of iniquity, the seal of confession, it
seems he knew not. It was not graven then, that seal; nor
many hundred years after. That shuts up treason, as a
treasure, under a sacred seal, at no hand to be broken: no,
though all the Kings' lives in Christendom lay on it. This
act of Mordecai's mars the fashion of that seal quite.

And, this may be said of him, he would never have laid
any hands on, himself; for then he would have let it proceed, and not hindered it, by his betraying, as he did. This
also: he that did thus disclose, for a need would have taken
an oath to disclose. Sure I am, would never have taken oath
or Sacrament not to disclose it: would never have stuck at
the oath of allegiance (that is once); but it may be, would have
stuck at the seal of confession, for ever coming upon his lips.

3. In his
loyalty to
Ahasuerus
a stranger.
This for *nunciavit*. And all this he did, yea though himself were no subject born to Ahasuerus, nor he his natural
Prince; but born out of his dominions, far off, in Jewry.
Did it, not for Josiah, or Jeconiah, or some King of his own:
did it for Ahasuerus King of Persia, one that held him and
his countrymen captive and thrall; yet to him he did it.

A Heathen.
Yea, more than that yet: this did he to Ahasuerus, not
only a stranger, but more than so; to Ahasuerus a heathen
man, an idolater, one that worshipped the sun, and the fire,
every day. As that did not hinder him, that of a diverse
nation; so neither did this, that of a diverse, and that of a
false religion. For though he were of a diverse religion from
the King, yet was he of God's true religion, that teacheth
men to be true to their Prince. Be he Jew, or be he Gentile,
Assyrian, Persian, or what he will; be he a right worshipper,
or be he an idolater; be his nation, or be his religion, what it
will be: though the King be (as Ahasuerus) a Pagan, though
they be (as Mordecai) the only true Church and people of
God; to be true to him though. But none of that religion,
that is fast to the Catholic, loose to the Heretic. If it be
Josiah, O then stay your hand; but if Ahasuerus, if *ethnicus*
or *quasi*, if excommunicate, then set Bigthan and his hands
freer to seek and to find, and to lay them on and spare not.

This religion was none of Mordecai's; nor let it not be any of yours : witness this act of his, a holy and good act. For which, though not presently, yet not long after, he was highly rewarded by the King, and for which he is set here (his name and his act both) among the righteous, to be had in everlasting remembrance.

Of the train now a word. I said I would tell you what they "sought," and what they found. That they "sought," they found not. Not that : but pity it is, but they should find somewhat, seeking as they did : and so they did. They found somewhat instead of it, which had been better lost than found ; they found a halter, scarce worth the finding : they found their own perdition, and the worst kind of it, *perditio tua ex te*, themselves the authors of it. *Ex ore tuo,* by that which came from themselves, out of their own mouths : the devil's *quærite et invenietis*, right.

The train.

What Big-than and Teresh sought and found.

Hos. 13. 9.

Lu. 19. 22.

And will you see how fitly every thing fell out ? They "sought," and they were sought into ; *quæsitum est.* They "sought," and found not ; they were sought into, and found. They were "wroth" with the King, and God with them : the heavy wrath of God was upon them. They would have "laid hands on the King," hands were laid on them for it : up the gibbet they went, and off they went, and the world was well rid of a couple of traitors. Before they could find, they were found themselves, and their fact found : the law was not to seek ; that was found, and founded long before. A law, that now hath received the approbation from God : and so now a right Persian law, never to be altered.

Dan. 6. 15.

Have we done ? not yet, this must be entered first, "written." Nay, "written" over twice, a duplicate of it. 1. "Written" first in "the Chronicles." And that "before the King :" of such importance the King thought it. 2. And then this writing here of the King is here "written" over again, a new order from God. So two *constat*s ; one in the King's "chronicles," the other in God's canonical Scripture, of this act. Two copies extant, one *in rotulis registri*, the other *in archivis Ecclesiæ ;* one among the King's records, the other in the Church's monuments. What should this mean ? Something there is sure, in the adding of this clause, about the writing it up. I know no meaning, but that God

III.

The solemn recording of this.

S E R M.
VI.

liked well of the writing of it in the King's, that He would have as much done in His own records.

Why the King would have it chronicled, is easily seen. It was a very memorable event, worthy to be set down there. But why God? Sure He saw, these "chronicles" would not last so long, as His will was, this example here should. And indeed, they being now lost, we had been little the better, if it had been there only: He made it therefore to be entered into His own *chronica chronicorum*, that never should be lost. Well it was, it should stand in the Persian story while it did last; but God, for failing, provided further, to have a memorandum of it in His own sacred story, that last, as long as the world should last. That, that is there, is *ad perpetuam rei memoriam* indeed.

Another reason. Being in these "chronicles," it would have spread no further than Persia, or the hundred and twenty-seven provinces at the farthest. God's eye looked farther: that not Persians only, but Jews; nor both those, but Christians too: not the hundred and twenty-seven provinces alone, but all the provinces in the earth should take notice of it. 1 Cor. 9. 9. I speak with the Apostle, Hath God a care of Persia? either writ He not this for our sakes? Yes, for our sakes no doubt He wrote it, that we also might be the better for it.

The better, two ways: 1. First, to know God's censure of both these, *in diebus illis*, for the present: the due praise of Him, by Whom the delivery, the just condemning of them, by whom the danger; that none that so seek shall be saved by His book: for that, we see here, brings them to the gallows, and there leaves them. 2. Or rather, there leaves them not, but by this *scriptum est* sets up their quarters, there to stand and be seen by all that look in it, to the world's end. And this is worse than hanging, yea, in chains; for the carcasses of those in time will consume and drop away and come to nothing; so shall these never, but remain as fresh still, as the first day they were set up, to all generations to come. It is that, that grieveth the noble generous nature, I dare say, more than the execution itself, there to hang upon the file in Bigthan and Teresh's infamous black roll: their names to be read there for ever.

But this was written also for them that come after, and a double use there is of it that way: as the parties and their facts be good or bad, that there are registered. If bad, then, as in the seventy-eighth Psalm, *ne sint sicut,* "not to be like" Ps. 78. 8. this Bigthan and Teresh. *Ne sint sicut,* "not to be like" them, in their wicked attempt; *ne sint sicut,* "that they be not like" them, in their wretched end.

"Not like them;" but like Mordecai (a *sint sicut* there): that coming to the notice of so wicked a design took himself bound in conscience to detect it; yea, though it were against a stranger to him in nation, a more stranger in religion to him, yet to do it. Here, *Inspice et fac,* saith God in His Exod. 25. Law: *Vade tu et fac simile,* saith Christ in His Gospel. In Lu. 10. 37 a word: this was written, to the end, to tie up all hands from seeking as they did; and to open all mouths to disclose as he did: to make men loyal to their Princes, though heathen idolaters, such as Ahasuerus.

And if this were the end; if any shall go quite cross, in a manner, in their *scriptum est*s, to this *scriptum est,* in all these three: 1. Let loose the hands to that these here sought, and are condemned for it: 2. Stop up the mouths from disclosing of that Mordecai here did, and is commended for it: 3. And both these, not in the case of Ahasuerus, but even of a Christian Prince; what think you by them? What do they say in effect, but *sint sicut Bigthan et Thares, ne sint sicut Mardochæus?*

I report me to your consciences. God thus scoring up these, that but "sought to lay their hands" on a heathen King, would He ever approve of such, as underhand set on subjects, to go past seeking, even "to lay their hand" on Christian Princes, Most Christian Princes, their own Princes, own by nature and nation, own by mass and religion too, as *in diebus his* we have seen two in France, (a Bigthan and a Teresh both,) one after another?

And what for Mordecai? They swear men, they give them their Maker upon it, never to disclose that, which Mordecai is here honoured for disclosing. Yea, and approve, nay more than approve of some, for doing clean contrary to that Mordecai did here; even for concealing, nay for sealing up, (and that under a holy signature,) as foul and wicked a treason as ever was.

This hath been done. But, we are in writing, what say ye to that? Will ye compare but the writing of *diebus illis*, with ours *in diebus his?* Let there be a book written, saith God, (this of Esther,) that no man ever do the like to these two; that no man ever seek to conceal those that shall so seek. Let there be a book written, saith somebody else, as it were an anti-Esther to this Book of Esther, to set men on to seek that, these here sought, and to teach them the way how to find it: to point out, who shall be Bigthan, when and how they shall "seek to lay," and "lay" both: as it might be a book written by Suarez in defence of Teresh, (his name of [¹ In Latin the two names nearest ¹,) in some case to license the seeking, *Thares.*] and to command the close keeping of such gear as this.

But yet, we have not all. Writing a record, making up a roll, is more than writing a book. Every authentic record (as is this) is of the nature of a precedent, to do the like; of a copy set for us to write by. So, here we have further, a warrant, to make up our records by this record; to record all that "lay their hands," for such as Bigthan and Teresh; and all that disclose them, for such as Mordecai. Ever, upon like occasions, to make like entries. Shall we do it? Write them down, saith the King, in "the Chronicle." Write them down, saith God, in the Bible, for traitors, these two. Write me down some such as did the like or worse, for other manner persons in another manner register, even for no less than martyrs: you know, who it is.

[Pope Six-
tus V., in
a speech
to his Car-
dinals,
justified
and com-
mended
the mur-
der of
Henry III.
of France.] Register me Mordecai, saith the Holy Ghost, for a party well deserving, for uttering his knowledge of so wicked a treason. Paint me up such an one, saith another ghost, straw and all, and in the border print me him Holy Martyr, for not disclosing as foul a treason, nay fouler a great deal.

But trow you this to be God's Vicar, that thus makes act against act; checks God's records with counter-records of his own; affronts God's chronicle with his new calendar on this
Mat. 26.51. fashion? Or St. Peter's successor? Nay not his: of all others, his least. He laid his hand on his weapon, for his master: so would he teach, and not otherwise. Judas, he

indeed laid none himself, but he it was gave the watch-word, "This is He, lay hands upon Him." So that Judas' crew, it Mat. 26.48. seems, they be, that so do; and no better than Judas himself, that so teach. No Apostle bid ever lay hands, but Judas: he did: his disciples they be; his successors, not St. Peter's, that bid it.

We may and will then, by this warrant, be so bold as to enter them traitors in "the chronicle before the King:" by what warrant they may register them for martyrs, in the calendar before the Pope, let them look. Ours we shew; let them shew but the like, and carry it. Else, if he see, allow, and print books with privilege, that tend to the manumising of Teresh's hand, and to the sealing up of Mordecai's mouth; if under confession he animate Teresh, and with his seal of confession muzzle up Mordecai; if God write one way, and he another, in effect; write King, write God, what they will, write me him "martyr;" we will be so bold as to write him up with St. Paul for ἀντικείμενος, "one that opposes himself" 2 Thes.2.4. flat against this book, and the writer of it: which book stays all hands from laying, and opens all mouths to the betraying such as these.

I will pray you, I may rather forget myself a little, than The comforget *in diebus his* after all this: we promised to shew that paring of diebus his they match and overmatch *in diebus illis*. That they match with *diebus illis.* in many points. 1. That Kings both, both in danger, in the same danger both; by the same number, and by those of the same rank; and upon the same motive, great anger for little cause. Again, that both were preserved, and both strangely; that the seekers in both, instead of finding that they sought, found their own confusion.

But, as in many, they match; so, in many more, doth this day overmatch those days. More degrees in our dial than in theirs; the day goes beyond the text: and not this text here alone, but any other, that ever yet I could find. The more, say I still, are we all bound to God for His goodness, That hath so magnified His mercies toward His Anointed, and in him to us all, as He hath vouchsafed him such deliveries *in diebus his*, as He never vouchsafed *in diebus illis* to any King of His own peculiar chosen people, or of any other under the sun. Such to be found in our "chronicles" as not the like in the "chronicles" of Persia: nay, not of the Kings of Judah or Israel: but are *sine exemplo,* ours; none coming home, all falling short of them.

Which, methinks, I can let you see sensibly; and so, that we have greater cause to rejoice in this of ours. In the Kings first. The King *in diebus illis,* make the best of him, was but a Pagan, a worshipper of idols: these be bars in his arms. The King *in die hoc,* neither heathen (I am sure), nor that can have the least touch of idolatry fastened on him: he that shamed not to say, No Christian, and hath been fain since to eat his word, he durst not say, An Idolater; that would soon have rebounded back upon himself. And no Idolater is a Christian; nor Christian, an Idolater, I am sure.

This first vantage then we have here yet. Always the very state of Kings, in itself, without any other addition, is dear unto God, we see. Ahasuerus here doth assure us of that, who was thus preserved, only because he was a King, and for no cause else. But I hold clearly, a Christian King to be more than a King; more than a Pagan King: and so *major Ahasuero hîc,* and *de majore majus gaudium;* and so we, of the twain, more cause to rejoice.

Next, as both Kings, yet not both like; so both in danger, and that not like, neither. The danger of *in diebus illis* was but of hands laying; the danger of this, of hands laid. On Ahasuerus, no hands were laid: it came not to that. It came to that, here. On they were; come off how they can. Those in the text but "sought;" they on the day found what they sought. It was past *quæsiverunt;* it was plain *miserunt.* That was the case, this day. No such things in "those days." Ahasuerus was not offered the point of a naked dagger; not taken by the throat; not grasped and tugged with, till both lay on the floor. All his danger was but *de futuro;* "sought" to have been, and might have been; but was not. This was *de præsenti,* present danger, of being presently made away, in a corner, by the hands of bloody wretches; that not only "sought to lay," but found that they sought, and did lay. Now, the greater the danger, the greater the joy for the delivery, ever; and so our joy the greater. For, no comparison between the dangers: that is clear.

No more was there between the actors by whom the danger grew. Bigthan, bad enough, I grant; but behold a worse, a bigger than Bigthan here. Bigthan and his fellow might have gone to school to them. They were angry, and so shewed themselves to be, and the less dangerous for that. These were as angry as they, but shewed it not. They brake forth in terms, that it came to Mordecai's ear. These had learnt their lesson better; not an evil term came from them, no show of anger appeared, but fair and false semblant all. So much the more likely to do mischief, say I: so much the more like Judas' treason, the worst that ever was. For, no betraying, to betraying with a kiss. Give me angry Bigthan, rather than fawning Judas; to welcome one kindly, and set Mat.26.48. one privily, with Judas' watchword, "This is he, lay hands on him:" from such, God deliver us. The more the parties such, the more our joy, you escaped out of their hand.

Both Kings were delivered: so far, equal. But then again, great inequality in the manner; very great. That, "in those days," by a Mordecai: all was regular, went the common ordinary way, upon a discovery. *Quotidiana sunt hæc*, to be seen, to be read in every chronicle. But on this day, there was never a Mordecai to discover aught: Mordecai failed here. A conceit there was, somewhat should have been discovered in another kind; but the plot itself, no discovery of it, till the very instant, till one appeared in arms, till out went the dagger, till the dagger discovered itself. God was fain to be Mordecai, to supply his part: though he were wanting, God was not. By Whom, it is true, Ahasuerus was delivered; but you delivered after a more strange manner. (I report me to all.) Now the more strange the manner, the more the joy ever. Then, Mordecai did somewhat toward it. This came merely from God; neither Mordecai, nor any else; sitting in the gate, or out of it; there or any where else.

Yet let me add this: that you might be beholden to God even that way too, He hath fitted you that way also. This fifth of August, without a discovery: the fifth of November, with a discovery. So, with Mordecai, and without Mordecai, hath God wrought for you, *in diebus his:* that we might every way be bound to Him, and that, every way, our joy might be full.

Now, in both, as the hand of God was stretched over both

Kings to save them; so was the same hand stretched out against those that sought their lives, to bring them to evil ends: both which may ever be the ends of such beginnings. There was no wonder in theirs; there, all was done by a legal course, a fair judicial proceeding, they indicted, convicted and executed by course of justice. Good Lord, with what ease was Ahasuerus delivered, even sitting still! There was no wonder, in this, at all. So was it not here. Here was old[1] pulling, and wrestling, and weapons out, and drawing of blood; and a kind of battle fought *dubio Marte* a good while, but at last the victory fell on your side. And this winning of it, as it were, and seeing your enemies lie dead at your feet, made the delivery the more wonderful; and so the more welcome; and so your joy the greater. And if one might take joy in the fall of his enemies, the fall of yours was worse for the manner. For, they died not like subjects, but as open enemies or rebels; not as penitent sinners, but as damned reprobates, lost not only their lives, but their souls too.

[1 *i.e.* great, or, more than enough.]

Thus, every way, doth this day go beyond those: the King beyond, as a Prince Christian; the danger beyond, for the extremity nearer. The parties that sought, beyond; for the less they appeared, the more perilous they were. The delivery beyond, for without any Mordecai at all. And their fall beyond, for stricken down in the place like rank rebels, and tumbled into hell like reprobates, without space or grace, without fruit or sign of repentance. And if thus many ways beyond, allow for every of these a degree of joy, and I have that I would.

Of this writing, one special end was for joy. A double joy; for either verse, one. 1. In the former, *Rege incolumi gaudendum,* 'joy for the King's safety.' 2. And in the latter, *stratis hostibus gaudendum,* 'joy that his enemies lay where they lay,' on the floor.

For the King's safety, we to rejoice; but without a Mordecai. He parts not with God, in ours; it is entire without him. So it is not in the text. God and Mordecai, there; here, God alone, and joy in God alone.

Then for *stratis hostibus,* in regard of them. First, that they sped not; then, that they were sped themselves: that their anger was *vana* and *sine viribus,* did no hurt: that God's

anger to them for it, was both sure; paid them home: and
swift; did it out of hand. That they fell, and fell before
him: he saw them lie slain at his feet. That his eye saw his
"desire upon his enemies;" nay more than his "desire," Ps. 92. 11.
that he was fain to pray for them, that had not the grace to
do it for themselves.

A little after in this book, for the saving of the Queen from
the laying on of Haman's hands, we find there was great joy
and a double feast, the fourteenth and fifteenth of Adar. And Esther 9.
can we imagine, but there must needs be as great, nay, *fes-* 17—22.
tum magis duplex, for the King here? If for her, a stranger;
for their own natural liege, much more. Was so with them
in diebus illis, and with us to be *in diebus his*.

Or rather *in die hoc*; for, there, it was plural, more days
went to it than one; many days in doing: here, it was dispatched sooner. No *diebus* here; begun, acted, ended, all
in a day; nay, half a day, between noon and night. And
this shall be the first, that it was not long in doing. Short
as it was, yet may I take upon me, there is as great odds
between this day and them, as is between the fifth of August,
ours, and the fifteenth of Adar, that is, December, theirs:
that is, between a long and a short, a summer's and a winter's day.

There is not, in all the Scriptures, a book that expresseth
so plentiful joy, for the saving of a Prince, as doth this of
Esther: the whole ninth chapter, in a manner, is spent in it.
There is *gaudium*, and *lætitia*, and *hilaritas*, and *convivium*, Esther 9.
and *tripudium*, I cannot tell how many times over; and the 22.
day christened by the name of *dies festus*, 'a festival day.'
There is joy in Shushan, the city; there is joy in the vil-
lages; there is joy in the hundred and twenty-seven, every
province of them; joy all over: and all this allowed, nay, a
statute made, to keep it. So, a day of joy to all posterity,
and all this chronicled so. A joy in "the chronicles:" what
would you more?

Hence have we warrant for this day of ours; and for all
and every of them, on this day of ours; the same joy full out,
the same that was for that in every degree, let be for this;
and more for this, as this is more, as hath been shewed; as
by the season of the year, the day is longer, the sun brighter,

the sky clearer, the weather fairer, in August than December. As this case more famous, God's might and mercy more marvellous; more fit for a chronicle, more worthy to be engrossed in the great roll, ours than theirs.

And in one we shall be above them, that we begin our joy in the house of God; whereas they in Persia had none to begin it in : here do we begin it, as God would have us begin it, in the house of prayers, with prayers.

A prayer for Bigthan and Teresh we cannot (either these of the text, or those of the day) : but a prayer, that by their examples both *ruina præcedentium* may be *admonitio sequentium,* 'the destruction of those that are gone before, may be the instruction of all those that shall come after.' This the first part; and if this will not be, the second. So may they ever find, that so seek ; if seek as they "sought," find as they found.

A prayer for Mordecai, that for his so sitting in the gate, he may sit in a better place : that so, many may follow him in his good example.

A prayer for the King. But first a praise (the principal cause we come hither for). Praised be God ever, That saved, in Persia, Ahasuerus from his two ; That saved, in Scotland, your Majesty from your two : the Saviour of Kings, *maxime fidelium.* Then, the prayer : that "those days" and these days may never fail him, nor he ever see other.

No more Bigthans, good Lord, but Mordecais for them. That Mordecai may never fail him ; but, if he do, that Thou wouldst not, no more than this day Thou didst, but ever save, ever deliver, ever preserve him, and make them that seek his ruin find their own. Either hang aloft, as these in the text ; or lie on the floor, as those of the day.

And even so, let the end of this be the beginning of the other, even of the joy of the whole day. For the day, for it, for this happy event on it ; for the King, the subject of it ; to the cause of it and of all our joy, God the Father, by Which, and through Christ in the unity of the Holy Spirit, be all blessing, honour, praise, glory and thanksgiving, this day and all days, for ever and ever.

A SERMON

PREACHED BEFORE

THE KING'S MAJESTY AT WINDSOR,

ON THE FIFTH OF AUGUST, A.D. MDCXXII.

----

1 SAMUEL xxiv. 5—8.

*And the men of David said unto him, See the day is come
whereof the Lord said unto thee, Behold, I will deliver thine
enemy into thine hand, and thou shalt do to him as it shall
seem good to thee. Then David arose, and cut off the lap of
Saul's garment privily.*

*And afterward, David was touched in his heart, because he had
cut off the lap which was on Saul's garment.*

*And he said unto his men, The Lord keep me from doing that
thing unto my master the Lord's anointed, to lay my hand
upon him, for he is the anointed of the Lord.*

*So David overcame his servants with these words, and suffered
them not to rise against Saul. So Saul rose up out of the
cave, and went away.*

[*Et dixerunt servi David ad eum, Ecce dies de qua locutus est Dominus
ad te, Ego tradam tibi inimicum tuum, ut facias ei sicut placuerit
in oculis tuis. Surrexit ergo David, et præcidit oram chlamydis
Saul silenter.*

*Post hæc percussit cor suum David, eo quod abscidisset oram chlamy-
dis Saul.*

*Dixitque ad viros suos, Propitius sit mihi Dominus, ne faciam hanc
rem domino meo, christo Domini, ut mittam manum meam in eum,
quia christus Domini est.*

*Et confregit David viros suos sermonibus, et non permisit eos ut con-
surgerent in Saul. Porro Saul exurgens de speluncâ, pergebat cœpto
itinere.* Latin Vulg.]

[*And the men of David said unto him, Behold the day of which the Lord said unto thee, Behold, I will deliver thine enemy into thine hand, that thou mayest do to him as it shall seem good unto thee. Then David arose, and cut off the skirt of Saul's robe privily.*

And it came to pass afterward, that David's heart smote him, because he had cut off Saul's skirt.

And he said unto his men, The Lord forbid that I should do this thing unto my master, the Lord's anointed, to stretch forth mine hand against him, seeing he is the anointed of the Lord.

So David stayed his servants with these words, and suffered them not to rise against Saul. But Saul rose up out of the cave, and went on his way. Eng. Trans.]

SERM. VII.

Ecce dies venit, "Behold the day is come:" so begins the text, so say David's men. And, "Behold the day is come:" so may we begin, and as truly so say of this day, as ever did they of that. The first words agree well: so do the last. *Abiit Rex viam suam,* "the King rose up and went his way:" so ends the text, and so ended this day too. And not only the first and last words, but the midst and all fall out as fitly. For, indeed, what is the whole text, but a report of a King, in danger to have been made away, and that closely in a cave, and a motion made to that end, and a knife drawn, and David's men up against him and all? Yet, see the goodness of God! the King did well enough for all that; and "went his way," without any hurt done him.

And comes not this home to the day? Saul at Engedi, in the cave there, may he not seem, as I may say, a type of His Majesty at St. Johnston, shut up (to use Saul's words) in the close corner there? Instead of a knife, was there not a dagger drawn there, and somewhat else; and more sought, than a corner of his cloak? And, as David's men rose here; so, rose there not a popular tumult there?

And yet, being in that extremity, was he not delivered out of their bloody hands? and did not all end, as the text ends, "The King rose up and went his way?" And this our meeting now, in this public solemn manner, is to no other end, but to rejoice together in the presence of God, and to render unto Him our anniversary sacrifice of praise and thanks, that *Ecce dies venit,* "Behold the day is come," wherein he escaped so fair, and went his way so happily.

And shall we not withal put our incense to our sacrifice, that is, add our prayers to our praises; that, as this day, there was, so still and ever, a way may be made him, to escape all his dangers?

King Saul, here, in the text, was the first King that ever the people of God had. In him, the first, would God have all succeeding Kings to read their destiny : that as they are placed high, so their high place is no exemption from danger : a provoking it, rather. Here now, Saul is in danger in the vale Engedi. Once before had we him in as great a plunge ; and that was in the hill Hachilah. Abishai would fain have had a blow at him ; and but one blow. But David came then between, with his *Ne perdas.* ^{1 Sam. 26. 8.}

That did not so well fit our turn. It was night then : Saul was in his bed asleep. That was not our case : this here comes nearer. This fell on the day. Saul was awake : so was His Majesty. We may say, *Ecce dies,* Behold it was day, and that day is now come. Between them both, they make up thus much : that sleeping or waking; by night or by day; in Hachilah the high lands, in Engedi the low valleys, out of danger they go not, if the hand of God be not over them, as here over Saul it was.

First and last, we may recapitulate the whole text into one word. It is all but a delivery. *Ecce tradam in manus,* a delivery into their hands ; *Ecce abiit,* a delivery out of them. Which two make the two main parts of the text. The former, the delivery into, lasts to the last verse : and, in the end of the last, comes the latter, the delivery out of : "The King rose up out of the cave, and went his way." ^{The division.}

Ecce tradam in manus is of two sorts ; 1. into David's hands, and 2. into his men's hands. Or thus : Saul's danger here is double : 1. one the danger of David's men's motion ; 2. the other of their commotion (for rising they were, and David suffered them not to rise). ^{I.}

1. In their motion. 1. What was moved to David by his men : and 2. what David did upon it. That which was moved was, *mittere manum,* "to lay hands" on the King. That he did upon it, was, he went and laid his hand on Saul's mantle, and cut off an end of it, and that was all. This, the fact : then, the censure of this fact.

SERM.
VII.

When David had done this, what he thought of it: 1. what he, and 2. what his men.   He thought not well of it, he did penance for it, his heart smote him for doing but so much. His men thought not well of it neither; but *ex alio capite* they, for not doing more than so.

2. What followed of this?   The neglect of their motion turned his men to a commotion: they were rising against Saul, if they had not been stayed.   The second danger, this: far the worse of the twain; the rising of David's men, than the drawing of David's knife.   Thus far the *epitasis*.

II.   Then follows the catastrophe.   For the issue was, David's men were stayed by him, and kept from rising: David's victory.   And how? by certain words speaking.   Those words are in the third verse: David's spell I may call them.

And upon all this followed, the King was saved, twice saved, from both dangers, (thanks be to God!) and away he went, safe without any harm.   Only, lost a piece of his mantle: and I would never greater loss might come to him.

III.   Thus lie the parts in this order; which, when all is done, we must crave leave to reflect upon, and review again: to shew, that the *Ecce* of this our day is far above the *Ecce* of that of theirs.

Now, by the special providence of God, it so fell out, that all this was not passed and done in silence.   There was arguing the point, reasoning on both sides.   The whole text is but a kind of dialogue between David's men and him, what was to be done with Saul their enemy, now they had him in the cave; kill him, or let him go?   And it fell out well, that this point was thus argued.   For, out of this their debate, might those two wretched men this day have learned, if they had had grace, and may all true men and good subjects learn, what to do or not to do, in like case.   For a clear resolution here is, to be held for ever, taken out of David's *absit* here: God forbid that ever any should lay his hands on "the Lord's Anointed."   Yea, though he should catch him in a cave (or as good as a cave, as this day he was).

Nay further, God so providing, here falls a matter in upon the by, (of Saul's mantle,) that removes it from the main (Saul's person) quite.   Saul's person, David touched not; went but to his mantle.   And even for going but to that,

" did his heart smite him." Which (by *a minore ad majus*) puts this question past all question, as being a protection for the King's robe : and, if for it, for his person much more.

And let me say two things of this text to you : one, that as Saul was the first King, so, this the first case that ever was, wherein the making away of a king was put to the question. So, the leading case (as they call it) to all the rest. Resolved here by David (and we cannot resolve ourselves by a better) ; and resolved once, resolved for ever. No more queries of it now.

The other, that it is the only case, this, that ever I read 2. of in Scripture, of *dixit Dominus* alleged for killing a King : of killing Kings, by divinity. The more worthy it is your attention, the nearer it comes to the late phrensy of this age of ours.

And two uses there be of it, as the chief persons in it are two. 1. In Saul, to let Kings see their danger ; 2. in David, to let subjects see their duty. To let Kings see their danger, that they may look up continually to their Deliverer out of evil hands. In David, to let subjects see their duty, and the extent of their duty, as to themselves, so to others.

Two dangers were like to befall Saul here. From David first. His men persuaded him to dispatch Saul : persuaded him but prevailed not ; he did it not : so Saul escaped once. Second : when that would not do, they were upon rising (themselves) to have done it. David dissuaded them : dissuaded them, and prevailed ; they did it not neither : there scaped twice.

In which two, David is two ways our example, to learn us the two duties I spoke of. 1. Would not do it himself : 2. would not suffer others to do it : would not be persuaded by others to it : did dissuade others from it. I will say with our Saviour, *Vade tu et fac similiter*, let every good subject Lu. 10. 37. " go and do likewise." Neither do it, nor suffer it to be done : and he shall be according to David's, who was a man according to God's own heart.

Saul was now in the cave. What David's men would have I. had him do to Saul. Even what was good in his eyes (a good The first delivery : mannerly term) ; but even what pleased him. What is that ? *Ecce tra-* What meant they by it ? The meaning is, they would have *dam in manus.*

SERM.
VII.

had him lay hands upon Saul.   Plain by David's answer.
What? lay hands on him?   God forbid.   More plain yet, by
David's report of it to Saul, (the tenth verse,) "And some
bade me kill thee."   Lo, there ye have it in plain English.

To make this motion seem good in his eyes, they use here
a perilous motive; or rather three in one : 1. *inimicum tuum,*
the motive of enmity or deadly feud ; 2. *Ecce dies venit,*
" now is the time come," the motive of opportunity ; 3. and
de quo dixit Dominus, the motive of God's word, of doing it
by divinity.

1.
Inimicum
tuum.

Inimicum tuum.   That is the ground of all (a motive well
beseeming them that make it, even fit for a soldier's mouth) ;
he is " your enemy," he would kill you ; what should you do
but kill him ?   should not we kill them that would kill us ?
This goes current in the camp, this is *bonum in oculis,* ' a
good motion in their eyes.'

Now if this hold for good, if an enemy be to be slain ; it is
sure Saul was David's " enemy :"   God Himself calls him so,
inimicum tuum :   they be God's own words ; one that (even as

1 Sam. 24.
11.

David saith himself) " hunted for his soul."   And, even at this
very instant had him in chase, and was so eager on it, as up

1 Sam. 24.
2.

the " rocks" he went after him, among " the wild goats," and
followed him so hard, he was fain to take a cave (here).   In
which cave, what taking he was in, ye may read in the fifty-
seventh Psalm, (made when he fled into this cave,) even at

Ps. 57. 1.

Miserere mei Deus, miserere mei :   one *miserere* would not
serve him ; in a greater agony of fear.   For, if Saul had but
known it, David had never gone his way thence, as Saul
did his.   It is well known, Saul sought his life.   That was
not all : there was a further matter than so.   Will you hear
it from Saul himself?   Look to the twentieth verse : " I
know," saith Saul, " thou shalt be King after me."   Yea,
" shall !" then was it *inimicum tuum* (indeed) in another
sense ; then was Saul's life an enemy to David's rising.
David stands in his own light, if he do it not.   Do it then ;
and besides the assurance of your life, the crown is yours.
These two laid together, any would wonder what eyes David
had, that this seemed not good in his eyes.   And this for
inimicum tuum.

2.

But, many an enemy escapes with his life, because we

meet not with an *Ecce dies,* a fit time and place to do it in. *Ecce dies venit.*
Verily, opportunity itself is a shrewd motive. The common
saying is, *Occasio facit furem :* that which one was far from,
would never have imagined, there will come so fair an offer,
such a fair shoot, (as they say,) as will make a man do that,
which, but for such an occasion, he would never once have
thought on. We are all to pray to God to take from us the
opportunity of sinning: so frail we are, it is no sooner offered,
but we are ready to embrace it (God help us). What say
they then? Why, *Ecce,* here is a time, and here is a cave, as
fit a place as can be for such a motion. Such an opportunity
as, if you take it not, you shall not meet with again, all your
life long. To have your enemy light into your hands, in a
dark cave, where you may dispatch him, and nobody the
wiser, who did it, or how it was done. Well then, wisdom
is seen in no one thing more, than in taking opportunity.
Go to, shew yourself a wise man: you know what you
have to do.

Nay, it is not only *Ecce dies,* but *Ecce tradam ;* and there, *Ecce tradam.*
is an *Ecce.* For there is much in *tradam :* he is even delivered, even taken, and put into your hands: I weigh the
word *tradam.* It is one thing to say, your enemy is fallen ;
another, to say, he is delivered. Falling is casual; delivery
imports a deliberate act of an agent to do it, to deliver him.
So this is more than chance, more than hap-hazard: it is not
cecidit, it is *tradam.*

Again, one thing to say delivered ; another, delivered by *Ego tradam.*
God : now I weigh the person. *Ego tradam,* it is God That
speaks it. One may be delivered, and by man, by some false
traitor (it was not Saul's case this, it was the King's). But
here, God is the deliverer, נְתָן, the giver. Take him then as
donum Dei. God hath even given you him, and having given
him, would have you take him, and I hope it will seem good
in your eyes so to do, and not let God give you him for
nothing.

Nay, yet there is more. Now I come to weigh *dixit* 3. *De quo dixit Dominus.*
Dominus. For one may be delivered by God, seeing it, and
saying nothing to it, but suffering it: by God's permission.
So are all things. Of many of which though, God saith
nothing, speaks never a word: but of this, God spake to you

S E R M. before, spake to you with His own mouth, and spake it with
VII. an *Ecce, Ecce tradam :* gave you warning of it, gave you His
word for it, "I will deliver him:" and is now as good as His
word, hath delivered him. See if He have not.

Will ye collect these three? 1. Not casually fallen into
your hands, but purposely delivered; 2. and delivered not
by man, but by God Himself; 3. and by God, not *quovis
modo*, 'at adventure,' but plainly prophesying and promis-
ing He would so do. Of this (sure) God must needs be the
author, that He foretells thus, and promises beforehand. So
have you here God made accessory, nay principal, to the
murder of a King.

And now are we come indeed to the perilous point of all.
This, lo, is it. They would have Saul made away ; and for
this, they allege *de quo dixit Dominus,* as if God had bespoken
a set day for the doing of it. This goes to the quick. *Inimicum tuum* is but a revelation of flesh and blood, that; but
dixit Dominus, that is the will of our heavenly Father. So,
not only lawful now, but a matter of conscience, to kill Saul:
אמר, God hath said it.

Where, first, you see, it is no new thing this, to kill Kings
by divinity. This gear is but newly raked up from hell again.
It is but the old devil new come abroad, that had been in the
world before. For, ever since there have been Kings over
God's people, this, hath been abroach; broached first in the
cave here at Engedi, and *dixit Dominus* pretended for it, you
see, in the first King's days of all.

The grief is, they were not Saul's, they were David's men,
the better side, that allege this. But David's men all, are not
Mat. 9. 14. of David's mind : John's disciples sometimes are found with
Acts 20.30. the Pharisees ; and the Apostle saith, " Of ourselves there
shall arise men speaking perverse things." Therefore never
marvel at it. Go not after the men; go after the master,
David himself.

Well yet, I must needs say for these good fellows here, they
go roundlier to the point, than doth Suarez, or any of them
that have been blundering about this gear of late. They be
all triflers to David's men here. For upon the matter, all they
Jud. 3. 21. have been able to say, is, It hath been done. King Eglon
2 Kings was killed ; so was Athaliah. Neither of them a true lawful
11. 16.

Prince (as God would have it); usurpers both. So, nothing to the matter. But, say they had been lawful; yet all this is but *homo fecit;* it is not *Deus dixit.* Never a *dixit Deus* comes from them. Nothing but poor *Pasce oves ;* which sure is a Joh. 21. 16. full unlikely text to persuade a man to become a butcher, and cut his sheeps' throats. One *Absit* of David's here, one *Ne perdas,* one *Quis erit innocens ?* able to dash twenty such, and all they can say, to pieces. Not one of them comes off to the point, as do these in the text, with *dixit Dominus,* God's express word for it.

There is no remedy, we must stay a little at this, at *dixit Dominus.* What He saith, we may : nay, we must do. To His *dixit,* there is no *contradixit.* If God speak once, " let Zech. 2. 13. all flesh keep silence."

I will not trouble you with, when God spake this, or where. Extant it is not. Yet seeing David traverses it not, denies not but that God spake it, we will take it for good, that they truly alleged God. For, it is not unlikely, that at some time when David was in some great distress, God might send to him by the hands of Nathan or Gad, his seers, he should take a good heart to him, he should be so far from being delivered into Saul's hands, as the day hould come, Saul should be delivered into his, to do with him what seemed good in his eyes.

Well then, take it, God said all this; and all this might God say, and yet Saul not touched. Ye shall see as little force in this *Dominus dixit,* as in their *Homo fecit.* Neither of them, to the purpose they are brought. You shall see withal, what it is when swordmen will be meddling with *Dominus dixit,* with our profession ; what trim consequences we shall have, to make, what seems good in David's eyes, and to murder Saul, to be all one. And withal, that it is good for Kings to be learned, and to be learned in God's law. For, had not David been the better diyine, he might well have been overtaken, and made believe, there is a way to destroy Kings, even by the word of God.

To scan them a little. *Dixit Dominus,* "God said." What said He? ' The day should come :' well, it is come. 'That God would deliver Saul into his hands :' well, that is done too. ' And David should do to him,' What? ' What seemed

S E R M. good in his eyes.' What is that? To destroy Saul? No
VII. indeed : *bonum in oculis* will bear no such matter. We
might dispatch all in a word, all is put upon David's eyes,
and in his eyes it seemed not good. But to touch them
shortly.

Facies ei   First, *Facies ei* here enjoins nothing, leaves him but to
quod bo-
num est in himself : that is all can be made of it. Nay, they desire no
oculis tuis. more, but so to be left. And when one is so left, what
then, may he do what he list? Suppose, he list to do that
which is evil or forbidden? Adam will tell you, No : that
consequence we all pay full dear for. It undid him and us
all. God's so leaving us gives not any leave to do any thing
that evil is; puts but power in our hands, to try how we
will use it. For, when power is so put, *ipsa ratio dictat*,
even by the rule of reason, we are so to use it, as we take
the better, and leave the worse ever, and reach not our hand
to the forbidden tree.

Not bonum   When God leaves a man to do that which is good in his
in oculis :
but in ocu- eyes, he had best wipe his eyes, see they dazzle not. If
lis tuis. they do, that may be *bonum in oculis* which is not *bonum*
indeed. They be not all one, these two, 1. *bonum in oculis*,
and 2. *bonum :* take heed of that. That which is evil may
seem good to an evil eye. And no man is so fond, to think
God would have any evil done.

Therefore He saith not, *bonum in oculis,* and stays there ;
but He adds *tuis, in oculis tuis.* For, much is, as the party
whose the eyes are. For, as the party is, so is his eye. And
the party here is David. God would not have said this to
every one. To David He did, and He knew what He did,
and that Saul was safe enough for all that. He knew his
eye was single and good, that nothing that was evil in God's
eyes would seem good in his. He would never have said
so much to Saul, of David; nor to David's men, of Saul.

In oculis   Never have said to David, *quod bonum est in oculis tuorum.*
tuis not
tuorum. If it had been what seemed good in their eyes, Saul had
been gone. No, He had not so good a conceit of their
eyes; of David's He had. To him therefore He said it :
and he deceived not God's expectation. *Pepercit tibi oculus
meus,* saith he at the tenth verse. All then resolving into
David's eyes; it seemed good in his eyes to spare Saul.

.

And, this is sure, they have not David's eyes in their heads, to whom it seems otherwise. For, to do what seemed good in his eyes, was to do Saul no harm. Look to *tuis* then, that the eyes be David's, and all is well.

Then, seeing David's eyes are so clear and so good, how were it to be wished, David would see with no other eyes but his own: would still do what is good in his own, not in his men's eyes.

So this was their elench. It seemed good in their blood-shotten eyes to lay hands on Saul; and they strongly imagined, what seemed good in their blood-shotten eyes, would have seemed so in his too. The sequel shews, it did not. Why stand we any longer then upon it? but leaving the motion, let us now see how it moved him, what he did upon it.

Some think it moved him, till he came to the very push; and then God struck his heart, and his " heart struck him," and so his mind changed. Others think, that it stirred him not a whit (for the blow came after all was done). Yet, as if it had moved him, he moved upon it. Somewhat to satisfy them, he would seem to do somewhat. So, up he rose, and toward Saul he made, בלט, as softly and as secretly as he could. And when he came at him, close behind him, out went his knife, as if he meant to use it. (His men, I dare say, hoped to some other end.) Stay here. And he that had seen David thus, in this wise, coming close behind the King's back with his knife drawn in his hand, would he not have taken him for Ravaillac? What difference? I promise you, this was not *bonum in oculis*, no very good sight. And then knowing Saul was his mortal enemy, and even now, at this very instant time, come forth to seek his life, and seeing them thus in a blind cave, and David hard at his back with a naked knife, would he not have given Saul for dead, past (for ever) *Abiit viam suam?*

1. Well: when all came to all; first, it seemed not good in David's eyes, to use spear or sword, but his knife. Why, a knife will do mischief enough. 2. Then, to go to work with it, not *punctim*, but *cæsim*, not ' with the point,' but ' with the edge' only; thrust not, cut only. Yet that will hurt too. 3. But cut, what? Neither flesh nor skin; not

[marginal note: What David did upon this motion.]

them.   Nay, not his shirt or doublet; his mantle only, and
but a piece of it.   4. And, it was no great piece neither, he
cut no skirt: it was so small, it was not missed.   Saul's
fellows spied it not, till David came after them, called to
them, held it up and shewed it them : and then they looked
well, and saw a piece was gone, but not before.   The word
כנף, πτερύγιον, *ala*, signifieth "a wing :" and those, we know,
are but additionals, no part of the entire garment; the
garment is whole without them.   So, it was not in the
whole cloth neither, he cut.   His knife he drew, but drew
no blood with it; went not to Saul himself, his person, but
to his mantle; took but an edge of that, and away he goes :
and so may Saul go his way, for any hurt David hath done
him.   And this, lo, is all came of the motion; and more
than this seemed not good in David's eyes.

His cen-
sure of it.
What, and is it but this ?   This, and no more ?   No more
but a shred of his mantle: and is that all ?   All, yea: and
too much of that too.   For, now it follows, in the second
verse, when David reflected upon what he had done, how
this he had done seemed in his eyes.   It seemed good to
them to do but thus much, or rather thus little, and after it
was done, it seemed not good to him, not this little he had
done neither; but it even seemed good to him, to repent
when he had done it, as little as it was, or as it seemeth to
us to be.   Repent?   Yea, that he hath done no more.   Nay,
that he had done thus much; had cut his mantle, had cut
at all.   That which any would think was highly to be commended in him, he went no further, you shall see him do
penance for it, as if he had gone too far, as if he should not
have gone so far as that.

Will ye see David do penance indeed for it ?   Penance, I
say, in all the parts the schoolmen make of it: 1. *contritio
cordis*, in this verse, his heart smote him for it: 2. *confessio
oris*, in the next, "The Lord keep me" from doing more :
this was too much ; 3. *satisfactio operis*, in the last verse, in
making amends, by not suffering his men to rise, but con-
verting them from so sinful a purpose.   And besides, in
leaving behind him *ad perpetuam rei memoriam*, a monu-
ment of all this, a Psalm, מכתם, that is, " a golden Psalm,"
(so he calls it), the fifty-seventh Psalm, made, as the inscrip-

tion shews, at this his being in the cave. Of it, and there, both in word and deed: of saying "Destroy him not," which is the title of the Psalm. Though ye get Saul in a cave, yet "Destroy him not." Other Psalms there be of the same title; but the fifty-seventh, that is the first of them all, purposely set upon this occasion, and at this time and place.

For his contrition. It is said, after he had done it his heart smote him, and told him why. Even but for making a hole in Saul's mantle. It is strange, that his heart, that (one would think) should have sprung for joy, that he did no more but that, falls to strike and to beat him for doing but that: instead of exultation, that he had done well, done the King no harm, a palpitation, a pang or passion of fear takes him, lest he had done more than he could well answer. And, it is the more strange, the great valiant David, one of the nine worthies, whom neither the bear daunted nor the lion; who without all fear encountered the giant, great Goliath, and smote him down; whose heart served him, fainted not then; here, for doing I wot not what, a shred of Saul's mantle, it serves him not; but beats and throbs, as, in fear, it is usual for the heart to do. *His contrition, Percussit cor suum.*

Bonarum mentium est, saith Gregory, 'Good minds will sometimes fear and acknowledge a fault, where none is.' Peradventure, David doth so; is more scrupulous than needs. Nay indeed. For to do but this to the garment of any private man, such as ourselves, to cut or to mar it, is a trespass (I take it), and will bear an action. And if so; then must it needs be a higher, a more heinous offence, to offer it to any of the King's robes; to mangle or deface them in any sort. The material part of it cannot (sure) be justified. Only the formal part, (as in schools we speak,) *non tam quid quam quo animo,* that may in some sort seem to qualify his act, and help to excuse him; that he did it, with no other mind, nor to no other end, but by the little shred taken off, to make it appear he did not so much as he could have done, if his mind had been so bad to Saul, as Doeg and such as he would fain make him believe: *teste vel segmento hoc,* which he gave in by way of evidence, "When I cut off this lap, I killed thee not;" as, going a little farther, I might have done: might have done, but did not. Might have gone otherwise to work: *1 Sam. 24. 11.*

S E R M. with a sword, and not a knife; with the point, and not the
VII. edge; thrust, and not cut: or, if cut, taken away a collop of
his flesh, as well as a corner of his cloak. Yet, for all this,
though his heart were privy to no evil intent, it smote him
though. For, in cases touching the King so near, it is not
enough to say, I meant not that, but this. So, a fault it was;
and, as for a fault, his heart smote him.

There is no smiting, but for a fault. Specially, not of the
heart. For the heart strikes not us, but it is itself stricken
first. And if you ask, who strikes it? that doth God; for,
this (of the heart) is nothing else but the reverberation of
God's stroke, His knock at our hearts, to forethink us of what
we have done amiss, when we have cut where we should not.

And it is no light fault, the heart suffers for. The heart is
the chief part, and the blow of it is the greatest blow. Give me,
Eccles. 25. saith the Wise Man, πᾶσαν πληγὴν, " any stripe," any grief
13. rather than "the grief of the heart." *Cardiaca passio* is the
worst passion of all. Therefore, as a fault; so, no light fault
it was.

We may pattern it with the numbering of the people, after.
2 Sam. 24. Then, it " smote him" too; and then he cried, *Peccavi valde :*
10. and the same reason is of both, as misgiving him in both, he
had in both done far otherwise than he should. But this
(here) was the first blow, the first discipline given him, as if
Ps. 105. 15. he had gone too near Saul; as if *Nolite tangere* did reach
further than the person, even to the robes royal.

Lu. 18. 13. And herein is his contrition. For, we use to strike our
breasts, with the Publican, because we cannot come at our
heart, to strike it, for not striking us, when we made a fault.
But, when the heart needs not be stricken for it, when it
1 Kings 8. strikes us first, when we feel *plagam cordis*, (as Solomon calls
38. it in express words,) upon making a fault; that our heart
corrects us, gives us discipline for it; then is our penance
begun, then is our contrition in a good way.

Now good Lord, if but for a slit in Saul's cloak his heart
went and came thus; how would it have taken on, how con-
trite would it have been, if his hand had happened to swerve
a little, and done him any hurt! How many blows then,
what sharp penance for that!

Will ye now lay these together. How scrupulous, how

full of fear David was, good men were, in that world : not his mantle or cloak ; not an edge of it. And how desperately audacious, how past all fear some are grown in this : not cut now, but thrust ; or if cut, cut through cloak, coat, skin and all. And their heart never smites them for it. Nay, there be, whose hearts would have stricken them, they had stricken no deeper, as did his, that he had hit the tooth [a], and missed the throat : and that, if the knife had been in their hands, would have cut his skirts so close, the blood should have run down the reins of his back.

To such, David (in effect) saith thus. It was a less matter far that I did, than laying hands on Saul : if you will be ruled by me, meddle not so much as with laying hands on his mantle : if you had felt such a blow at your heart, as I did at mine, you would never offer. What ? not *mittere manum in illum ?* nay, not in *pallium illius.* Never talk of his person : so far from that, as not to the very corner but of his cloak.

And this is the remove I told you of at first. Thus did God suffer this *a minore ad majus* to fall out in this first attempt upon a King, that we might infer thereof a further matter, and yet no other than our Saviour Christ's own inference. May not a man put a knife in Saul's raiment ? by this blow of the heart (here) it seems he may not. May he not ? and " is not the body more worth than the raiment, Mat. 6. 25. O ye of little faith ? "

Alway, this we may count of, and so conclude this point : that he whose heart did thus smite him for doing this, he would not do that, his heart smote him for, if it were to do again. Not go thus far, since he felt it at his heart, his going but thus far ; though nothing so far, as his men would have had him. And so much for *percussio cordis,* David's contrition.

All this while we go but upon collection ; feel but by his 2. pulse, how his heart beateth. Will ye have an *ore tenus,* a David's confession. full and a flat confession from him ; hear him distinctly speak 1 Sam. 24. his mind to this very point, of laying hands on Saul ; and 6. give you the true reason, why he did it not ; why, neither

[a The life of Henry IV. of France was attempted by John Chastel, Dec. 26, 1593, when the King was stabbed with such violence in the mouth, that one of his teeth was forced out. Mod. Univ. Hist. vol. 9. 308. Folio.]

SERM. **they,** nor any should ever do it? That follows now in the
VII. third verse.

What
David's
men
thought
of it.

But first, let me tell you, this cut of David's was not well
taken, of either side. David (we see) thought not well of it :
no more did his men. He, that he had done so much ; they,
that he had done no more. Evidently to be gathered, that
his men, when they saw he made no more of their motion
than so, that he came back with his knife in one hand, and
a snip of Saul's mantle in the other, and his knife had no
blood on it ; and that he had done as much as he would do,
and no more was to be looked for at his hands (for he looked
like one heart-stricken, that if it had been now to do, would
not have done that, neither) : they fell into a rage, a mutiny,
a plain rising ; as resolved, if he would not, they•would : if
it were not good, in his eyes, in theirs it was. It was not
an end of a mantle should serve their turn ; they would
make him sure for ever going his way : as knowing, if he
went away, he would prove worse than ever, as, indeed, so
he did. So, when David was down, his men were up.

2.
Saul's
second
danger:
David's
men's
commo-
tion.

Here now, is there a second danger toward Saul from
David's men, a multitude ready to rise and run upon him.
Plain : for it is said in the next verse expressly, David
"suffered them not to rise." Which could not be said
properly, unless they were on rising. But, an insurrection
there was toward, and at Saul they would have been, had
not David interposed, and opposed himself, with these words
which now follow, and with those words "overcome them,"
and stayed them, that they did not rise.

David's
dissuasive
to them.

So that the words we now come to, serve for two purposes :
not so much for an apology for himself, that he did it not,
(though that they do too): as for a dissuasive or retentive
to them ; and in them, to us, and to all, that none should
ever attempt it. You saw even now, how evil his heart
brooked it : you shall hear now his mouth utterly renounce it,
ever to hold that for good, that seemed good in their eyes.

First, a flat denial it is. But, that is not so much ; the
manner of it is all. It is not soberly and coldly, No, I will
not do this thing. No : but it is with very much vehemency,
as the manner of men is, when they speak in great passion.
If ye mark it, it is with short turns. "God forbid." What,

do this? "To my liege lord?" To God's "Anointed?"
"Lay my hands on him," and he God's "Anointed?" A
pause, at every word; as if he were half out of breath, as if
his heart did beat still. Weigh them a little, חלילה לי מיהוה.
There is not, in the Hebrew; there is not, in any tongue, so
earnest, so passionate an abnegation, abjuration, abrenun-
ciation, as it: it was the word they used when they rent
their clothes at blasphemy. We turn it, as our tongue will
bear, as the poverty of it will suffer us. To turn it to the
quick, there is more in it, than can in any one phrase be
expressed. So, not being able to do it in one, the interpreters have essayed to do it in more than one. Every one,
as their own idiom will best bear. "The Lord keep me from
doing this thing," saith ours. So, it is of the nature of a
prayer against it. *Μηδαμῶς*, "Out upon it," "Away with
it," "By no means:" or, *Μὴ γένοιτο*, saith the Greek:
"Never let me, let any, never let it be done." So, it is
an utter detestation. *Absit mihi a Domino*, saith the Latin,
"Never let me come where God hath to do, accursed be I
of God, all evil come to me," if ever I do as you would
have me. So, it is a bitter execration. It bears all. Under
one, it is both a hearty deprecation or prayer against it,
a deep detestation, and a fearful execration, if ever he be
brought to do it, to lay hands on Saul. These three will
amount to an oath of allegiance at least.

You will say, here is passion indeed; but it is reason, and
not passion, must carry things, when all is done. Nay, here is
reason too, and reason upon reason, couched in these words,
why not to do it. *Domino meo*, first; to his "liege lord" or
sovereign: not to him. Then if that will not hold, *Christo
Domini*, "to the Lord's anointed," not to him: that will.
For, two he alleges, *Domino*, and *Christo Domini*: the first is
from the earth, earthly: *Domino meo*, his earthly "lord." The
second, *Christo Domini*: *Domini* is "the Lord from Heaven."
The first He stands not on; this second, that he stands on,
that he iterates once and again, sets up his rest upon that;
as indeed, when we have studied all that ever we can, we
shall never be able to find a more forcible. It can never be
answered, if we care either for heaven or earth, *Christus* or
Dominus, 'Christ or God;' any thing at all. It cannot be,

*The rea-
sons of it.*

*1. Domino
meo.*

*2. Christo
Domini.*

[1 Cor. 15.
47.]

the Lord of heaven should ever endure, where His hand
hath been to anoint, any hand should be, to violate, to do
any violence to that party. Do but see how he utters it.
" Lay hands" on him? and he God's " Anointed?" and so
breaks off; as if he held it for a foul indignity, for a gross
absurdity in reason, once to question it. So, for laying
hands but on his mantle, David's heart checked him; but
for laying hands on his person, that is past *cor pœnitentis*,
it is *vox clamantis* that, *Μὴ γένοιτο, Absit*; " Far be it from
me;" Never that, never.

Will ye now observe, how, in this speech, he returns upon
them and their three motives? " God forbid," saith he, to
that, for which they alleged *dixit Dominus*. To their " God
said," he says, " God forbid;" answers *Dominus dixit* with
Dominus interdixit. Of which " God said," No, no, " God
forbid," and that חלילה לי, " forbid with a curse." And what
God did then forbid, He doth forbid still; what to him He
did forbid, He doth to us, to every good body, that cares
either for His bidding or forbidding it. They that " lay
their hands" care for neither. Do that, which (as we use
to say) is against all God's forbode.

Then, for *inimicum tuum*, he replies to that with *Christum
Domini* : opposing, as his " God forbid" to *Dominus dixit;*
so, " the Lord's Anointed" to his " enemy," to weigh down
that. And so it doth : there is, there will ever be, more
virtue in *Christum Domini* to keep him alive, than in any
inimicum tuum, any enmity in the world, to destroy him.

Last, where they say, *Ecce tradam in manus*, he is now
even " put into your hands," but not *mittere manum*, (saith
he,) not to " lay hands on him." So that, for all *Dominus
dixit*, or *inimicum tuum*, or *Ecce tradam in manus*, David is
still where he was, answers with reason every part of their
reason : " God forbid," for any of them, or for all them,
Saul should have any harm, but go his way quietly for him.
And this for his confession.

3. David's
satisfac-
tion.
But, you will remember I told you, all this was spoken,
not so much for David's defence, why he did it not, as to let
them see a good ground, why they should not do it; to keep
them from rising. For rising they were, " rising," say the
Seventy, *θανατῶσαι αὐτὸν*, " to have slain Saul." They

starting up, as it were, in a kind of indignity that David had thus served them, to do that themselves, which they hoped he would have done, but did not : for done it should be, if not by him, by them : that was resolved.

Sure, had David had any edge to Saul's making away, here now was another, a second, a fair opportunity offered itself: as plausible a pretence as he could have wished, to have let Saul been taken away in a military tumult, a mutiny of soldiers. As for David, he had refused it, he had good witness of it : if they rose rudely and ran upon him, what could he do withal? it was their fault, not his; he had no hand in it. But, in all this, he shewed himself a most loyal subject, in thus putting himself between Saul and them ; in taking pains, and even striving, till he had appeased them. Which sheweth plainly, his heart was up-right in all this business, in saving the King's life now *secundo.* Else, what he listed not to do himself, he might have let them do.

So then : do it he will not; nor suffer it to be done, neither : neither *per se* nor *per alium,* ' by himself or any other :' thought it not enough to say, I will have no hand in it; but neither his own, nor any man's hand else, if he can stay it. Not only *Absit a me,* but *Absit a meis;* first and last, *Absit,* saith David to both. Not, *Non faciam* only, Let not me do it; but Μὴ γένοιτο, *Ne fiat,* Let not any, Let it not be done. And what? not only not *mittere manum,* but *mittere de manu* or *de manibus,* rather, ' send him out of their hands,' send him away safe. To this second end, were these words spoken by him, and (as the text is directed to his men) to quiet them, and not only to clear himself. Now to David's victory.

Et vicit verbo hoc, and he even " overcame them with these words," saith the text. Here is David's victory. But, if he " overcame" them, then was there a strife. So he even strove to save Saul. And if he suffered them not to rise, then were they bustling up at least, and ready to have risen.

II.
The second delivery.
Ecce abiit.

The text-word in the Hebrew is full of force : שִׁסַּע, it is to " cleave" properly, or to " rive in sunder." So, either they were clustering, (as the manner is in mutinies, to run to-

gether on a heap,) and he made them shed and sever themselves, and return to their places again; or ye may refer it
to their hearts, that with these words were even smitten or
cleft quite, and broken of their purpose, for proceeding any
further in so bloody an enterprise. Their motion did not
so much as enter into him; his did into them : entered
into them, and as his heart smote him, so, he smote theirs :
smote them, and even cleft them; made them leave, and let
go their resolution quite, and let Saul go.

The Seventy say, ἔπεισε, that is, he " persuaded them"
with these words (the best overcoming ever by words, by
persuasion). " Overcame them," our text turns it; and so
David had here a victory : nay, a double victory. 1. Over
himself, one ; and that is a great one : great victors have
failed of it. 2. Over his men, another ; he kept them too.
And so, by these two, saved the King twice. And many
victories he had; but of them all, none like this : this the
greatest. For in those other, he but slew his enemies; but
in this here, without a drop of blood shed, he saved his
Prince's life. And now, this victory obtained, David and
his men are agreed ; and they are satisfied, not to rise, but
sit still, and let Saul rise quietly, and go his way. By
which, some amends was made for the piece of his mantle.
This, for David's satisfaction, and for his victory, both in
one. For this victory was, in a sort, his satisfaction, and
served for it.

And now we have set the King safe, that he may go when
pleases him, would I beg a little leave to return to David's
words ; to his spell, if I may so call it, to this cleaving word,
שמע : that David did not only " smite," but even " cleave"
his men's hearts. With what axe did he this? (for it is
the act of an axe properly.) Even with these words, (they
were David's axe :) Shall we do this? shall we so ? "lay
hands" on him ? and he God's " Anointed?" And the edge
of his axe were these two, *Christus Domini:* they did the feat;
all the force was in them. And (indeed) of great force they
seemed to David, and were of great use with him, came
from him oft. To his companies, here. To Abishai (a chapter after). To the Amalekite (the next book after, the
first chapter). Twice, here: thrice, to Abishai: twice, to

the Amalekite. Seven times in all. And still, nothing
but *christus Domini;* as if they had been a kind of spell,
to charm any from rising, to any such end.

[1 Sam. 24.
6, *twice;*
26. 9, 11;
to *Abner.*
1 Sam. 26.
16; 2 Sam.
1. 14, 16.]

And, sure, a marvellous energy there seems to have been
in these words. David's men (here) were rising: these words
kept them down, they rose not. Abishai after, he was even
striking: they stayed his hands, he struck not. David himself, he was but thinking a thought that way: they smote
his heart, made it to ache, made him give over.

Now, when I fall to consider what virtue these words had
in those times, to hold men's feet from rising; their hands
from striking; yea, their very heart from thinking any such
thought; O, I am forced to wonder, they should not have in
our times the force they then had. David could not overcome some men now: his men would rise, do what he could:
feet, hands, and heart, fly loose now, these words notwithstanding. They have not the power to break men; men
have rather the power to break them.

David's men were brave soldiers; Abishai one of his three
worthies; himself more worthy than they all. Power they
had, to stay these so many men of arms; and have not now
the power to make a silly Friar hold his hands. What is
become of their virtue now? Of the cleaving force they then
had? It should seem, David's men were othergates men
than many (I will not say of our soldiers, but) of our Jesuits
and Friars are of late; had *magis subacta pectora,* ' breasts
of a better mould;' had at times been brought by David to
know what God was, what it was to be God's " anointed,"
how " precious" their blood was in His sight, how no man
could lift up his hand against them, and be innocent. So,
they soon took an impression of this his *Absit,* so passion-
ately, so pithily (withal) delivered by him.

2 Sam. 23.
18.

Ps.116.15.
1 Sam. 26.
9.

Men's breasts are now made of a tougher metal, the words
meet with harder hearts in the cloister now, than here they
did in the camp. Some men's hearts now leave not striking
them, till they have stricken Saul to the heart. Turn
David's *Absit mihi a Domino,* into *Adsit mihi a Domino
facere rem hanc:* turn his execration into a prayer, nay,
into many prayers, rosaries, and masses, for God's assistance, to an act, which His very soul abhorreth. And this

is the reason.   The words are not rebated ; they have not
lost their edge ; but men have instead of hearts now, flint
stones.   Else, the words being the same, the same effect
would still follow, if the hearts also were the same.

For the same effect doth still follow, in all whose hearts
God hath touched, on whom the Spirit of God is come.   For,
where the Spirit of God is, there the word of God will work:
and where it works not, we may safely say, there is no Spirit
to work on.

1 Chron.
12. 18.
To try then, on whom the Spirit of God is come, there
comes to my mind a pregnant place, (it is the twelfth chapter
of the first book of Chronicles,) full to this point, and it will
even bring us home to our own text again.   Amasa there,
when the question was asked, whom they would take part
with, he and his ; cried, " Thine are we, O David, and on
thy side, thou son of Jesse."   And it is there in express
terms affirmed, that the Spirit of God came upon him, That
made him thus to cry.   If then the same Spirit of God be
upon us, That was upon him, it will make us take up the
same words, " Thine are we, and on thy side, O David."

1 Sam. 13.
14.
Thou hast a testimony in holy writ, to have been " a man
according to God's own heart ;" what was in God's heart,
was in thine : then are we to think, say, and do, as thou
didst, and so the Spirit of God is upon us, indeed.

Will we then be as David, with him, on his side ? If God's
Spirit be upon us, we will.   Now come we to our text.   For
here is in this our text, a vive anatomy of David, in each
part : his eye, his hand, his heart, his mouth and all.

1. His " eye," full of compassion to Saul his sovereign.
It was not good in his eyes, to do him any hurt ; good to
spare him.   *Pepercit tibi oculus meus,* the tenth verse.   There
is David's " eye."

2. His " hand," not able to stir, not *mittere manum in
Christum Domini,* to lay any " hands" on him.   *O ne sit
manus mea super te,* he twice cries, verses twelfth and thirteenth, " Let not my hand be upon thee."   There is David's
" hand."

3. His " heart smote him," we see, for putting but his
knife into the edge of Saul's mantle.   There is David's
" heart."

4. His mouth: from that we hear *vox clamantis, Absit mihi a Domino,* with great vehemency of passion. There is David's mouth.

5. So says David: and will ye hear how he sings? hear it upon his harp? how his heart and harp agree? hear him say it and sing it both? Ye may: for to keep for ever this day in memory, he made a Psalm of Saul's being in the cave here, and of his escaping out of it: and gives it this title, " Destroy not;" no not in the cave: " Destroy not." By this means to sing into the men's minds, their duty in this point. And not into theirs alone, but into the hearts and minds of all posterity, not to give their ways to destroy Kings: no, though they have them in a cave, as these had Saul. Even there, to sing, " Destroy him not." *Ne perdas,* in the cave, is worth all.

So have you David at full: if any be of his side, thus to see, and say, and sing, and think, and do. . . . *Sic ille oculos, sic ora ferebat.* If you would know, what his heart believeth touching this point, *percussit eum cor;* that gave him a shrewd check, for but a shred taken off Saul's cloak: he believes, he did not well in it. If, what his mouth confesseth, *Absit mihi facere rem hanc. Absit,* saith his mouth; *Ne sit,* saith his hand; *Ne fiat,* saith his heart; *Ne perdas,* saith his harp. All keep time, all sound one way; this way, all.

[Virg. Æn. 3. 490.]

It seemed not good in his eyes to do it: that is the text. Nor to his " hand;" let not that be " upon him." Nor to his mouth; he spit it out with an *Absit.* Nor to his " heart;" least of all to that, that for a less matter, for but drawing his knife, though without mind of drawing a drop of blood, fell on beating, and cast him into a cardiac passion. And any, who thinking but a thought that way, if his heart smite not him, let him smite it hardly. Else is he not according to David's; and so, not to God's heart.

Thus have our ears heard of a King delivered in the text. And the like, may our eyes see, of a King delivered on this day. *Sicut audivimus, sic et vidimus,* is the Psalm; but *plus vidimus quam audivimus,* may it truly be said of this day of ours. I report me to you, if it may not: if there be not a greater *ecce;* nay, many greater *ecce*s on this day, than on that.

III. The *Ecce* of this our day. Ps. 48. 8.

S E R M. Many ways, I know, the balance is even. Kings, both: in
VII.   danger, and danger of *ecce tradam*, both. Both in a cave
(for all caves are not under ground, some above stairs).
And of a knife, or worser than a knife, both. And of a
tumultuous rising, both : and yet both preserved from both.
Thus far, even. But then, in other points, they are not: no,
nor even in these. For, weigh them well, and Saul will be
Dan. 5. 27. found (as Balshazzar was) Tekel, *minus habens:* "too light
in the balance." And this of ours, to overweigh, to weigh
him and all his down, many ways.

To reflect a little on this. I have said a great deal: I
have said nothing, if nothing be said of this. It is the life
of all. If, of the twain the *Ecce dies* of this day be the
greater, if more *Ecce*s upon it; the more of them, the more
Behold*s*, the more beholden are we to God : the more marvellous His mercies have been to us, the more plenteous our
thanks be to Him for them.

The *Ecce dies* is as the *ecce diei*. Ever, the more remark-
able the day, the more the things are so, that happen upon
it. The *ecce diei* is of two sorts: 1. *Ecce tradam*, 2. *Ecce
abiit Rex*. *Tradam*, the delivery into the danger; *Abiit*, the
delivery from it.

And ever this we hold, the worse the *Tradam*, (that is,
the danger,) the better the *Abiit*, the escaping from it; and
the better it, the more is our joy; and the more our joy is,
the more our thanks should ever be *Jehovæ Liberatori*. And
O that such an *Ecce* might be on our thanks, as there is on the
day, as it and the *Ecce*s of it do well deserve at our hands.

1. To shew them, the *Tradam* is worse; I begin with the
Tradent, or *Traditor*. *Ecce tradam*, "Behold, I will deliver
him;" it is God that saith this : this was God's doing,
Saul's delivery into. Here is no treachery in the text. Into
the cave he came of his own accord; was casually found
there, not guilefully drawn thither. So, was it not to-day;
but the King trained thither most treacherously. *Ecce;*
"Behold," then, it is far worse, when wretched men by
[¹ *i.e.* wicked alluring means shall tole¹ one, meaning no harm at
decoy.]] all, into a secret corner, as evil as Saul's cave every whit,
and there set on him. Worse, I say; for here the devil
betrays; God delivers not. Suffers, I grant; but is not

agent in it. God never co-operates with treason. So then, no day this, *de quo dixit Dominus :* rather *de quo dixit diabolus,* a day (in respect of them and their treachery) of the devil's own bespeaking. This then the first odds, that *a Domino factum est illud, a diabolo factum est hoc :* that of God's ; this of the devil's own *Tradam :* and so the *traditor* worse, I am sure, with an *Ecce.*

And, who was delivered? *Inimicum tuum,* an "enemy" in the text. Some reason in that. Saul was so indeed, David's "enemy." You were not theirs; they were yours, without a cause. Nay, cause to the contrary : nay, causes more than one. And, in that regard, worse. Worse, to deliver an innocent, than a deadly enemy.

And delivered, whither? The text is, into a cave. Where Saul indeed saith, he was shut up; but to say truth, simply he was not so; the cave's mouth was open, he might have come forth, his men might have come to him at his call. But, with us, in our cave, the King was *secundum literam,* 'in the literal sense,' shut up indeed. Many locks and doors fast upon him, no going out for him, no coming in for others. The worse his case. Nay, a worse could not be. So doth the Holy Ghost describe the hardest case of all, by these 2 Kings three : 1. *Conclusus,* 2. *derelictus,* 3. *et non erit auxiliator.* 14. 26. All three, here : "shut up," "quite left," "none to help." In far worse taking, than ever was Saul in the cave.

There is no hurt in a cave, if there be no hurtful thing in it. But David saith in the Psalm, his was : and sure it is, Ps. 57. 4. your soul was there "among lions." The text is, *Tradam in manus tuas. Tradam in manus;* I ask, into whose "hands?" for in danger, it is ever good lighting into good hands. Into what "hands" light you? No comparison, there. Saul light into David's hands : his *in manus tuas* were David's, and David's were gentle hands. His heart smote him, for doing but so much as you have heard. If their heart smote them this day; it was not for doing so much, but for doing no more. David was touched with his duty to his Sovereign, stricken with the majesty of *Christus Domini :* these, they trod under foot, duty, and majesty, and *Christus* and *Dominus,* and all. Nothing like David ; quite contrary, worse with an *Ecce.*

Nay, not like David's men. For first, in the text, here is a dispute between them and David, and the parties divided. Saul the more likely to escape : as he did. Where the enemy is divided, the danger the less. But to-day, in the Kings, no debate at all. It was *conclusum in causâ,* resolved on both sides, long before, what to do with him if ever they got him. No way but one then.

Again, David's men (however evil-minded at first, yet) after relented, were overcome. These of the day, of far another spirit; their malice invincible. David's men's overcoming was with words; here, it came to blows and to gripes, and all would not serve. David's men, they were overcome willingly, and did yield; these were overcome too (thanks be to God); but it was maugre their wills, they never yielded, till they both lay dead on the floor. The more the parties, the more their hands such, the more your peril; the more it, the more the fair grace of God, you escaped such parties' hands.

Now to *et facies illi;* what was done. At Saul there was a knife drawn; or rather, not at Saul, but at his mantle. A dagger, not at your mantle, but at you. Between these two, a dagger and a knife, there is some odds; but certainly, between a dagger's point, and a knife's edge, there is. And, this was your case.

And what to do with it? (that sets it further yet.) To do nothing to Saul, and no great thing to his mantle : left a piece of that behind. His dagger, with far another mind, and at far another mark, than David's knife. More was sought here. You to lose more than so. What talk we of a piece? I would, a cloak; I would, a whole wardrobe would have served the turn, would have satisfied them, or excused you. No cloak-matter, here. Your best blood was sought; your breast aimed at; and not the edge, but the point bent, and too near you.

And, to be short, for the last point, *bonum in oculis.* No more than a shred seemed good in his eyes; no less than your life seemed good in theirs.

Thus every way, from point to point, the *Ecce* still greater, in *Tradam* the delivery to: in *Ecce abiit,* in the delivery from, how holds it there?

In his extremity, Saul found one yet to cry, *Absit,* to deliver him. Never an *Absit* here. Never a one? Yes: one

there was, and that a strong one. When that wretched creature, that was set to do the fact, in a sort hindered it for once.
But so faint a one it was, as that would not serve, as David's
did Saul. God was fain to step into David's room: and,
when there was never a tongue on earth to say it, to say it
from heaven; thence to give the true $M\grave{\eta}$ $\gamma\acute{\epsilon}\nu o\iota\tau o$, *Ne fiat,* ' I
would not have it done.' From heaven He sent you help;
not by the cave's mouth, but miraculously another way, by
them that knew not whither they went, but unwittingly were
led by God, to the place of your danger.

Let me see: at the most, there were but two attempts
against Saul. So, he scaped but twice. Two and two against
you. Twice and twice escaped your Majesty, four times in
all: four distinct dangers, and as many preservations. 1. That
of him that stood ready armed; 2. that of the dagger of the
first; 3. that of the sword: nay, more than one, *Ecce duo
gladii,* of the second brother. 4. And that of the popular
tumult, worst of all. These were but upon rising, in the
text; they rose not: they were not upon rising, but were
risen up indeed. So, two *Ecce*s more in yours.

And, of all this peril, Saul had no sense at all. Awake he
was, but he might even as well have been asleep. Of all that
was said, he heard not a word; of all that was done, he
perceived nothing: had an easy escape, he. So was it not
with your Majesty. You heard, and saw all, and felt somewhat of that was said and done; escaped the peril, but not
the fright and fear, oftentimes worse than the peril itself.

Upon the matter, in Saul's, somewhat was offered to be
done, but nothing acted: no doing. Here, there was doing
and suffering both.

In Saul, it never came to *manum mittere,* not on his person :
hands were laid on his cloak; his person, that not touched.
Yours was: hands were laid, blood was drawn, the marks on
your jaw, the hurt on your hand remained, to be seen a good
time after. So, Saul's comes not home; falls short in every
point. More *Ecce*s in yours; your day, your danger, your
delivery: the more of them, the more is God still to be
magnified by you, and by us all.

All fell out well in the end though, with both. It was
meant, you should neither have risen; Saul, nor you. You

both rose.   And either of you went *viam suam ; viam,* not
eorum, but *suam ;* went not the way, they would have sent
you, the wrong way ; but *viam suam,* your own, the right way,
the way of safety and peace.   And thus ended Saul's danger,
and thus yours : thus the text, and thus the day.

Nay, yours ended not so.   The goodness of God stayed
not there.   Yours had a *plus ultra,* another, a further, a
greater *Ecce* yet, beyond that of Saul.   There, as Saul went
his way, so did his enemies their way too : he scaped them,
Ps. 1. 4. and they him.   *Non sic impii, non sic :* it was not so with
Ps. 92. 9. yours.   You scaped them ; they scaped not you.   *Quia ecce
inimici tui, Domine, Ecce inimici tui,* for " Lo Thine enemies
O Lord, lo Thine enemies shall perish" (and so they did) ; and
" all the workers of wickedness shall be destroyed" (and so
they were) : *Misit manum in manum mittentes,* ' He stretched
His hands against them, that stretched theirs against you.'
And because their hearts smote not them in this so foul an
attempt, they were smitten to the hearts, the sword went
through both their hearts.   The very place they had designed for yours, became to them the place of their perishing :
perishing here, and perishing eternally.   The day, of which
they said, " Now is the day come," it came indeed ; but came,
and proved a dismal day to them : the rubric of it written
in their own blood, with an *Ecce ;* the last *Ecce* of all, Behold
our fearful end, and let every one fear to do the like.

They said not, *Absit nobis a Domino :* God therefore said,
Absit Dominus a vobis.   And so He is : He from them, and
they from Him, as far as the bottom of the nethermost hell
is from the top of the highest heaven.

And ever the same hand of God be so laid on them, that
shall offer to lay hands on God's Anointed.   So may they all
shut their eyes, as many as it shall seem good in their eyes,
to do the like.   So, may their hearts be smitten, that ever
hatch in their hearts any thought that way tending.   And
Isa. 55. 3. " the faithful mercies of David" be upon them, whose eye and
hand, heart and tongue, shall see, and say, and think, and do,
as he did.   And let the King live, live yet many years, to
see the renewing of this blessed day, and to refresh the
memory of God's mercies, upon it, shewed him ; and in him,
shewed us all.

And now to return to the beginning. We may, I trust, now say, *Ecce dies venit,* " Behold the day is come," with a higher accent. A day, in regard of the delivery into their hands, *de quo dixit diabolus;* but in regard of the delivery from them, *de quo dixit Dominus,* which God did bespeak. Bespeak, but in a better sense. Not thus; *in quo tradam in manus :* but rather *in quo eripiam de manibus :* not, ' deliver you into,' but ' deliver you out of their hands.' And yet, it is *dies in quo tradam* too : but the edge turned toward them. Not, *in quo tradam te illis;* but *in quo tradam illos tibi :* not, ' deliver you into your enemies';' but, ' deliver your enemies into your hands.' The beginning was, they made full account, you had been given over into theirs; and that the good should have been in their eyes. The end, as is happily proved, they were given into your hands, and the good was in yours; removed thither : and you have done, and they suffered, what was good, not in their, but your own eyes: heaven and earth approving it, and rejoicing at it.

Now then, as, if they had done to you that was good in their eyes, it had made many weeping eyes, it had been *Ecce dies funestus :* so, seeing they have suffered what was good in yours, and even in God's eyes; and thereby made many a glad heart, shall it not be *Ecce dies festus,* a day " of joy and health Ps. 118. in the dwelling of the righteous;" wherein "the right hand 15, 16. of the Lord" had " the pre-eminence, the right hand of the Lord" brought this "mighty" alteration to "pass?" As they meant it, it had been a day, the devil had marred : as it fell out, this was " a day that the Lord hath made," and " let us Ps.118.24. rejoice and be glad in it," " with the voice of joy and thanks- [Ps. 42.4.] giving, among such as keep holy-day."

" Holy," I say : for let God have the honour of the day, for setting so many *Ecce*s upon it. For which, all days, but specially as the day itself returns, we to make return of our thanks upon it. Even upon it, upon this day, for this day, for the many *Ecce*s of this day; to God the author of them, for the King and his safety, the *subjecta materia* of them ; for the *Ecce surrexit e speluncâ,* his rising out of the cave, in effect as good as his rising out of the grave, or (as David in this Psalm calls it,) his delivery from the lions' den : thence Ps. 57. 4. he rose. And for *Ecce abiit viam,* that a way was made him,

SERM. that he was not made away, but that his way he went. Then
VII. went, and many a way since hath gone, and many more may
Ps. 91. 11. still go, and the Angel of the Lord take charge of him, to
"keep" him in all his "ways," and the Lord Himself preserve his going out and coming in, from this time forth for
evermore.

There is a Psalm, (as I said,) the fifty-seventh, purposely
set (of his being there in the cave, and escaping thence) : the
Psalm is like the day, represents it fitly. The fore-part of it,
Ps. 57. 1,4. full of danger and fear : *Miserere mei Domine, miserere mei,*
and "My soul is among lions :" well befitting you, when you
were under their hands. But the latter part, the catastrophe,
full of joy and triumph. When you were got out of the cave,
and were now upon your way, then it was, I trust, and ever
Ps. 57. 8-
11. will be, as there it followeth : "My heart is ready, O God,
my heart is ready, I will sing and give praise. Awake up my
glory, awake lute and harp, I myself will awake up early.
I will praise Thee among the people, I will sing unto Thee
among the nations : for Thy mercy is great toward me, it
reacheth even up to the heavens, and Thy truth above the
clouds. Set up Thyself, O Lord, above the heavens, and
Thy glory over all the earth :" as this day Thou didst indeed.
So ends the Psalm, and a better end there cannot be. So,
will we end, with glory and praise, blessing and thanks, to
all the three Persons of the glorious Trinity : to Whom, for
this day, and the *Ecce* of this day, be ascribed this day all
these, even this day, and for ever.

A SERMON

PREPARED TO BE PREACHED

ON THE FIFTH OF AUGUST, A.D. MDCXXIII.

Genesis xlix. 5—7.

Simeon and Levi, brethren in evil; the instruments of cruelty are in their habitations.

Into their secret let not my soul come; my glory, be not thou joined with their assembly: for in their wrath they slew a man, and in their self-will (or fury) they digged down a wall.

Cursed be their wrath, for it was fierce; and their rage, for it was cruel: I will divide them in Jacob, and scatter them in Israel.

[*Simeon et Levi fratres; vasa iniquitatis bellantia.*

In consilium eorum non veniat anima mea, et in cœtu illorum non sit gloria mea; quia in furore suo occiderunt virum, et in voluntate suâ suffoderunt murum.

Maledictus furor eorum, quia pertinax; et indignatio eorum, quia dura: dividam eos in Jacob, et dispergam eos in Israel. Latin Vulg.]

[*Simeon and Levi are brethren; instruments of cruelty are in their habitations.*

O my soul, come not thou into their secret; unto their assembly, mine honour, be not thou united: for in their anger they slew a man, and in their self-will they digged down a wall.

Cursed be their anger, for it was fierce; and their wrath, for it was cruel: I will divide them in Jacob, and scatter them in Israel. Eng. Trans.]

I HAVE read you a text out of a piece of Genesis: a part of Jacob's last words, before he went out of the world; or (as they call it) a clause of his last will and testament. There is in it a censure upon a couple of his sons. In which censure, I take it, I have read the destiny of another couple : in attempting, both, of a like foul design, they as these, and these as they : as Simeon and Levi, the brethren of the text; so these two, the brethren of the day.

To open the case here in the text : the day will open itself sufficiently. You are to imagine, you see Jacob, being now about to go out of the world, lying at the very point of death ; lifted up in his bed, (for so he was,) his sons standing before him, all twelve in order, according to their several ages, as they came into the world. He had somewhat to say to them (it should seem) ; and coming to these two, (his second and third sons,) he called to mind a foul outrage by them committed, upon Hamor and Shechem, and the whole city. Of which you may read before, at the thirty-fourth chapter.

This, though it were done and past many years before, that it might seem to have been forgotten, yet it comes fresh to his mind, and troubles him now at the hour of his death. The nature is such, ever, of the sin of blood.

This fact of theirs, he did not think good to slip over in silence ; but, even then, to tell them of it, and to tell them his mind about it. No time, to keep it from them now. He was going to God ; and so, stirred in spirit, not to leave the world, till he had left a good testimony of his deep dislike of attempts in that kind. It was the will of God ; so, as he spared not his eldest son Reuben, for a foul act of another nature, for incest ; so neither did he these two, for another, of blood-guiltiness. Blood and incest, take heed of them.

Besides, it might prove dangerous (he knew) if he did not declare his mind, and set a censure upon that, and the like attempts ; and that he could not discharge his conscience, if he had said nothing to it. That others therefore, hearing of it, might fear to do the like ; 1. first, he condemns their counsel with a *Ne veniat*, "Let never my soul come" into any such counsel or company ; 2. then lays his heavy curse on the fact itself, and on their thirst of revenge, the cause of it ; 3. and lastly, censures them doubly for it : 1. by disherison, depriving them, and not them only, but all their posterity, for ever having lot of inheritance of their own, as all the other tribes had : 2. and then scattering them abroad up and down all

Israel. For, these are two distinct : 1. to disinherit is one thing ; and 2. to scatter abroad is another.

The sum is, Jacob their father's curse, and the disherison The sum. of these two brethren, Simeon and Levi ; for consulting first, and after pursuing so wicked a counsel, as the murder of Shechem.

Culpa and *pœna* will divide the text; 'the fault' and 'the The di- punishment.' In it do but add the persons, to make the vision. parts three ; Simeon and Levi, the parties that made the fault, and upon whom the punishment came.

The fault was either the fact itself, or two weighty circum- I. stances of it. 1. The fact was, " they slew a man, they brake down the wall." This for this fact, and for the two things in it : 1. first, that there was a meeting and consulting before, about the doing of it : 2. then, that there was cruelty after, shewed in the doing of it. Consulting, and plotting, before ; rage and fury, after.

The punishment or censure is of two sorts : you may thus II. reduce them. 1. The one is a Church censure ; 2. the other, a civil penalty : and so the sentence of both courts. 1. *Male- dictus*, of one court, that is spiritual ; and 2. *Dispergam*, of the other, that is temporal.

You shall observe, all here stands upon twos. 1. " Simeon, III. and 2. Levi :" 1. they, and 2. their bloody weapons. 1. In the plot, two : 1. counsel, and 2. company ; whence Jacob removeth two, 1. his " soul," and 2. his " glory." 2. In the fact, two : 1. murder, and 2. burglary ; done upon two ; 1. upon the men, 2. and upon the very walls. 3. In the manner, two : 1. anger, and 2. fury. And they two, two epithets ; the anger 1. strong, in the beginning ; and the rage 2. indurate, in pursuing : killed the men, in their anger ; brake down walls, in their fury. 4. In the censure, two : 1. the curse, 2. and the penalty. One looks back ; the other looks forward ; one, to the fact, the curse ; the other, to the persons, the penal part. In the penalty, two : 1. the dividing, and 2. the scattering ; dividing their persons in the family of Jacob, scattering their posterity in the commonwealth of Israel.

What is now the use we have of it ? First, the not coming to any such counsels ; the condemning of all such attempts, the holding for accursed all such outrages as this was. Which,

SERM.
VIII.

I trust, we will now do at the last. We have seen it condemned in Persia, in Jewry, and now in Egypt. In Persia, by the heathen; in Jewry, by Kings and Prophets; and now in Egypt, by the patriarchs. By the heathen, in the case of Bigthan and Teresh; by the Kings and Prophets, in the case of Absalom and Abishai; and now by the Patriarchs, in the case of Simeon and Levi. And all this even up as high as Genesis, up before the Prophets, before the Law, long ere Moses was born, in the Patriarchs' days: and now, higher than Genesis, further than the Patriarchs, we cannot go.

Kings and Prophets you have heard: to-day, you shall hear a Patriarch lay his curse upon it; and not, in his lifetime only, but at the very point of death. All, to shew, how hateful a sin this is; and how God will be sure to require it at their hands, " whose feet are swift to shed blood." And, this was a good doctrine then, and hath been ever since, till our unhappy days; wherein, some that have attempted it have escaped the Patriarch's *maledictus,* and have much ado to escape the Pope's *benedictus,* and being made Saints for it.

Isa. 59. 7.
[Rom. 3.
15.]

" Simeon and Levi" are the parties. He joins them together in the process, for so they were in the fact: either as deep as other, and so their causes proceeded in jointly.

The parties: two.

Two they are: and two are more than one. It is " hand in hand" this; a double-twisted cord. " Hand in hand" is the stronger: double, than single iniquity.

Prov. 11.
21.

And this is true of any two; but more yet of these two; for these two are " brethren." And that very bond of nature and natural affection works yet more strength. For, strong as the bars of a palace, so is *frater qui a frater adjuvatur* (saith Solomon).

Two " bre-
thren."

Prov. 18.
19.
[See Vulg.]

The first thing, that makes us muse, is, that Jacob calls these two " brethren," as if the rest were not so: were nothing of kin to them. They were " twelve brethren;" themselves say so to Joseph. But, not of whole blood, you will say. True: but six of them (these two named, and four besides), they had all the same father, Jacob, and the same mother, Leah. And why then these two, two " brethren," and not they? We must seek out somewhat, wherein these two were, and the rest were not. And we will not stir a whit from the text. They two were " brethren," first, 1. in wear-

Gen. 42.
32.

ing of "weapons of violence" (in this verse); 2. and (in the next) "brethren" in wicked counsel; 3. and third, in the rage of revenge; 4. and last, in a bloody murder. And, as in these, that make up the fault; so, in the punishment. In all these, were these two, "brethren," and these two only: the other, nothing of kin to them, no fraternity in these.

If Rabbi Solomon be right, that μάχαιρα in Greek be all one with *mechera* in Hebrew; then it is, the swords they were girt with were "weapons of violence." But if (as others take it) *mechera* be a 'tent;' then it must be, the "weapons of violence" were to be found in their tents: that in their tents they had them, though not at their sides. The other were of a more quiet disposition: so were not these; but their swords "Brethren," out, ready to offer violence upon every occasion. The other in wearing had weapons too, but not "weapons of violence:" and tents weapons. they had, but cruelty dwelt not in them. "Weapons of מכרה cruelty" then, is their first difference.

Why, may not one, for a need, have by his side, or in his house, weapons? Yes: but these were *chele chamas*, that is, כלי חמס "weapons of violence:" and violence implies wrong, ever. Weapons, he may; of wrong, he may not. All, even our very hands and "members" themselves, are to be "weapons Rom. 6. 13. of righteousness." God never intended to arm injustice. 2 Cor. 13. 10. There is no power given to destroy, or do violence withal. The law allows no *chele chamas:* no man to have them in his house, no man to wear them by his side. No sword is allowed to private fury or revenge: *Mihi vindictam,* "re- Deut. 32. venge" is God's, for He will do justice. The "sword" of it 5. [Rom. 13. is His; and no man's, but whom God girdeth with it, by 4.] virtue of the words in Genesis, "By man shall his blood be Gen. 9. 6. shed." But, that man is not every man: that sword hangs not at every man's girdle; nor is by every hand to be drawn forth.

There is one case only, where the party would, and cannot stay for the magistrate's succour: the assailant comes on him so fierce and furiously, that either he must use it, or lose his life, and yield it to the rage of his enemy, being a private man as himself. In that case, if he cannot otherwise keep off violence from himself, it is lent him *pro hâc vice tantum;* and the use of it made lawful by the unwritten law, the law

SERM.
VIII.

of nature, *vim vi*: yet, as we speak, *cum moderamine incul-patæ tutelæ*, or, as our law, *se defendendo*. And never, but upon that occasion: and, in that case, the sword is but a weapon of defence, to keep off violence. And out of that case, this one except, not to be allowed. Even they that carry the sword in their name, (*Gladiatores*,) we call them Fencers: and so do they themselves their science, the Science of defence, that is, skill to use their weapons only to that end. For (ever) a Cherethite is *eo ipso* to be a Pelethite. These two are but one: their weapons, to defend and save: to deliver from wrong, to do none. To make the sword the weapon of cruelty is to abuse the sword. Every abuse is naught: and so, these two, "brethren," *non tam naturâ quam nequitiâ*, 'not so much in nature, as in naughtiness.' As, we know a place, where many such there be: no kin at all by nature, yet sworn brethren they call themselves: making *sacramentum pietatis, vinculum iniquitatis*: binding themselves by the oath of God to serve the devil: as they

Is. 59. 7.

all are, "whose feet are swift to shed blood." So, the Patriarch implies thus much: that of all his sons, these two were of a revengeful nature, of a bloody disposition. And as they were, so were their weapons. For, who will blame the sword, or lay anything to the weapon's charge? The weapon is, as the man is; as he will use or abuse it. Of itself not violent, if he be not so, that wears it. But these were so: and so, the fault in the men, and not in the weapons. Brethren of blood they were; and not so, but "brethren" in blood. And so pass we from this blood.

2. In counsel.

You may guess at their dispositions, not so much by their weapons, as by their counsel; *in consilium eorum*. He tells of a council taken about it, where they met, and said one to another, their swords should do violence: their sister was wronged, they would be revenged: and no revenge serve them, but death and destruction; death of the men, destruction of the town, yea, of the very walls of it. It was a plot or conspiracy then: a very match made between them.

And what was their counsel? *In dolo*, 'deceitfully' contrived. Marry they would their sister to Shechem; and all should be well, if they would be circumcised. Whereas, their purpose was, when they were sorest of their circumcising, when the wound was at worst, and they could not stir; then, to set upon them, and to make a massacre of them all.

Here, Jacob cannot contain himself, but burst out : From such matches God keep me. At the very first, at the doing, Jacob misliked it : misliked it then, and ever after ; and even now, at his death, he cries, *Ne veniat*, "Never let my soul come" among them, or have to do with them.

It troubled him much, at the time it was done. He saw, he lost his reputation by it. Lo, here is the holy patriarch! Here be imps of his breeding and bringing up! That they made him even "stink" (you will bear with it, it is the Holy Gen.34.30. Ghost's word :) before the nations round about.

Beside, they put him in fear and hazard of his own, and all their lives. Very like it was, they would all have been over-run by the bordering people, but that God, seeing Jacob's innocency, even for his sake sent His fear into the heart of the nations adjoining, that they pursued them not to death with the like cruelty. These were motives for the present : but here now, so many years after, he takes it on his death, he was never party nor privy to it. Never was he, to that; nor ever would be to any such, as we see by his so deeply detesting it, and protesting against it. For, it is, as if he should say : I here declare openly before God and the world, it went against my very soul, this counsel of theirs : I had no hand in it, neither art nor part, as they say : neither had, nor ever meant to have; but was, and ever will be, innocent from all that belong to it, violence, counsel, and all. Never let my soul come among such.

And why not come in any such counsel? For where two or three are at counsel about any such matter, *inter duos pro-ditores diabolus est tertius*, 'where two are consulting of any treachery, the devil is the third.' *Misit Satanas in cor*, was Lu. 22. 3. in Judas, is the rule of all traitors. The first mission, the first motion, is ever from him : he the prime counsellor of the three. And blame not Jacob, if he would not be one of, or one at, any counsel of his, or have his soul at the end of any such treaty.

This, on their parts, makes it the more heinous, that they did it not of any sudden passion, but *consulto*, in cold blood : slept upon it, rose upon it, were in it three days : did all advisedly, of malice pretensed : met about it, took counsel how to effect it, the "counsel of the ungodly;" put off the execution, till after three days.

Jacob's
twofold
abhorring
of it.
1. *Non
veniat
anima in
consilium.*
2. *Non
sit gloria
in cœtu
eorum.*

On Jacob's part; two things he speaks of : 1. that neither "his soul should ever come in such counsel" (so, it is a soul-matter; a counsel, and an act, which brings with it the hazard of the soul): 2. nor his "glory" or reputation (so that it is a thing which toucheth one's honour and reputation near: a blemish to the glory of a man). As pollutes his soul, so taints his blood; is the loss of both. To save both these, he doth, we see, and we must disavow all such counsel and counsellors. All are bound under the same pain, to make the same protestation : to say the same *Ne veniat anima mea,* all that are of the Israel of God; Let never my soul come into any such counsel, let never any such counsel come into my soul. Mark those two words : 1. his "soul," 2. his "glory :" the two things of highest regard with all; 1. what shall become of our souls, 2. what name we shall leave behind us. All, to think, that in such company, they do but cast away their souls, they do but lose the honour of their name for ever.

סוד קהל

And yet, a farther matter there is. For mark these two words, council and assembly, *sod* and *kahal :* for by them two several partakings he seems to set out. 1. One, of their secret privy meetings, that is *sod.* 2. The other is *kahal,* which is any public meeting or assembly of theirs : and namely, their Church and congregation. He speaks to his "glory," never to make one in any such assembly, never to be joined to any such congregation : so, makes a matter of religion of it. Never, of that Church, which shall give countenance, that there may be any meetings, to any such end. It is no *kahal,* no Church, no religion for Jacob, that favours any man that is so minded.

חלילה לי

If then we will like or dislike with the King and Prophet David, we must say *Chalila li,* God forbid, I should once lift up my hand to any such act. If we will like or dislike with the Patriarch Jacob, we must say, *Ne veniat in consilium anima mea.* You observe, the Patriarchs and the Prophets agree well; Jacob's *Ne veniat,* with David's *Absit mihi a Domino.* Not only to have clean hands from it, not to lift them up, or stretch them out to the act; but a clear soul; never once to consult, but to detest, not only their consultations, but even the congregations of such consulters, that be that way given. Neither civilly nor ecclesiastically; neither in church nor market (as they say) to have to do with them.

And for a farewell to this point, let me tell you; there be, that interpret Jacob's speech, in this sense. Not, Let not me, nor my soul be present, or partaker of any such; but, Let not my soul or life be the matter or subject of any such consultation; *Ne tractent de animâ meâ in consilio tali, ut sicut Sichemitis fecerunt, sic facerent et mihi,* God keep my soul, save my life from any such consultors, for ever coming to be treated or debated of by any such. Let never any such meet in council about my soul or me. Both will stand well : 1. neither I, about any man's; 2. nor any, about mine : either 1. to consult about the life of any other; or, 2. my life to be consulted of by any other like them.

From the counsel we come to the fact, to the hatching of it. There is too much in the counsel; that was fault enough, if no fact followed : but here followed a fact too, and that a foul fact. Which is of two sorts : expressed first in two words, 1. *interfecerunt,* and 2. *suffoderunt,* that is, murder and burglary : and two more; "killed," whom? it is said "a man," *virum,* in the singular, but one; the number doth but aggravate, the fact is all one, one or more, both to be condemned. *(marginal: II. The fact, 1. Murder. Interfecerunt.)*

But sure, Jacob in saying *virum,* "a man," meant but and aimed but at one, principally. *Virum : at quem virum?* 'what man was it?' Hamor the chief "man," the ruler, the lord of the city, and the territory about. Of no great circuit, perhaps : that comes all to one; but, being the sovereign ruler and lord, such a "man" is worth many men; that, in killing him, they may be said in one to have killed many. And, as if Jacob thought, they might be quit of the rest, so they had let that man (the chief magistrate) alone. *(marginal: Virum.)*

But they killed more than one, even every mother's son, "all the males" in the city. This is an outrage : not to leave a man to kill; to kill them all, as if they were but one man; to leave no one alive ! *(marginal: Gen. 34. 25.)*

SERM.
VIII.
Gen. 34. 2.

And why? what was the offence? Shechem had deflowered their sister. Say, there was a fault in Shechem: what, no remedy, but kill and slay him? But, if his were the fault, let him alone be slain. But, what was his father's fault? He sought to make amends, by marriage, for the wrong done, and gave them a blank for her jointure, to put in what they would: agreed to be "circumcised," he and all his people: all that ever in reason could be required. Why was he, then, slain? For being his father. Nothing else can be alleged. But all the men in the city, the poor people, what had they done? They went about their business, meddled nothing in the matter: yet, they went to the pot too. So, it is murder of many, and those many, innocents all. Innocent and nocent together, to be swept away? "Shall the Judge of the world do" it? shall any judge in the world do that, which the Judge of the world would not do? They said, should he "abuse" our sister? No: but, should he do it, and all they suffer for it? But, what had their wives and children deserved, that they should be led captive, and all they had, either in house or field, taken for a prey, made spoil of, and carried clean away? But, what had the walls and houses hurt them, that not only the house-walls, but even the town-walls must be laid flat for it? was there ever heard of a greater havoc?

Gen. 34.

11, 12.
Gen.34.24.

Gen.18.25.

Gen.24.31.

And, so eager upon it they were, that, to commit the murder, they commit burglary first: first, down with the house-walls, that after, down with the men. So greedy to kill, as break down walls, break up houses, to make their slaughter. For, either it must be, they broke through the houses to come at the men and kill them: or, when they had killed the men, they pulled down the houses and all. Both, it may well be, they did: but, one it must needs. And, that one is too foul and barbarous.

2. Bur-
glary.
Suffode-
runt
murum.

Now, put to the circumstances, which are ever of importance, (specially in a story,) and well worthy to be weighed, in a matter of fact. Here was no war, wherein such things are done: for the name of war covers many a foul fault. But war it was not; but a treaty of peace. So, they "shed the blood of war," that is, that blood, which but in war should not be shed: made spoils as in war, razed down towns as in war; and all this "in peace."

1. Kings 2.
5.

Nay, not only a treaty of peace, but of a match and marriage, contracting affinity, of a firm league, of amity perpetual. Nay, of unity in religion, taking upon them the same seal of the covenant. That they violated all three, 1. *jura fœderis*, 2. *connubii*, 3. *religionis.* And, that in all these, their counsel was fraudulent, *bemerma*, without any good במרמה meaning, coloured only with these three pretences. Which they did not only violate; but, above all, abused the holy 1. ordinance of matrimony, 2. abused the Sacrament, 3. and made the sacred "seal of righteousness" a cloak for their [Rom. 4. bad and barbarous intent. 11.]

They would seem to pretend justice: but, even in justice, the rule is, *pro mensurâ peccati* there should be *plagarum modus.* Here was no measure kept. A whole city sacked, a whole country spoiled, all the men slain, all the rest led away as prisoners: and all for a fault, to which they were no ways accessory.

And that, all this they did, with a kind of contempt of Jacob their father, and his authority: never acquainted him with it, never consulted him about it. He was bound not to come in their counsel: they were bound to come to him for his; who, if they had come, would have counselled better.

The conclusion is: reason they had none, nor colour of reason. Only, it is said, *birtsonam*, for their will and pleasure, ברצנם did they all this. A wretched pleasure, to take delight in so wicked a design.

To this, add the root of all, set out in two words, 1. rage, The root and 2. outrage, or anger and fury. That their anger shewed of these: itself cruel; that their fury shewed itself indurate. It was 2. Fury. not *aph* only, that is, anger; but *gebrath*, which is past אף anger, gone beyond it; indeed, very fury. They did it עברה furiously. And, that fury was hard, hard as stone; cast off all compassion, without pity or mercy, spared none: not the poor people, that made no fault: not the women and children, but made booty of them: no, not the walls, but down with them too. And, which is the worst of all the rest, spared not God neither: did all these in the very act of religion. If they had done it, when they were yet heathen men, it had been the less: but now, in their being circumcised, to do it,

SERM.
VIII.
as they were coming on to be the people of God, and were within the covenant, by receiving it, already: now to do it, inferreth well, "Cursed be the wrath," yea, thrice accursed that outrage; for the like was never heard.   Anger, we know,

[Hor. Ep. 1. 2. 62.]

is *furor brevis;* and, *si gravis, brevis,* being so vehement, it should not be long by course of nature: but this was long too, continued: not to be satisfied, but implacable; nothing could appease them, or turn them from their outrage, till they saw walls and all lie flat upon the ground.   Here, we look

בלי

back.   Their weapons, above, were *chele,* which is, properly, *vasa,* "vessels."   So as, their passion was not poured out, like water, and so let run away; but it was kept or reserved, as liquor in a vessel: barrelled up, to be broached, when they saw cause.   Without reason, in the beginning; without appeasing, in the end.   Such was the malice of these men: such, theirs of this day.

III.
The censure.
1. A *maledictus* to the fact.
Deu. 27. 24, 25.

Now, such "rage," so outrageous, justly deserves a *maledictus:* such "wrath," so qualified beyond all account, so exorbitant, so insatiable.   On such "wrath," Jacob lays his curse, curseth them here.   Which curse was, after, by God renewed in Mount Ebal: "Cursed be he that smiteth his neighbour secretly."   Again, "Cursed be he that lieth in wait to shed innocent blood."   The two last and heaviest curses there, to which all Israel was to say "Amen."

From Jacob.

While it was but in consultation, Jacob cries, *Ne veniat,* Away with the counsel, come not at it.   But, when it comes into act, then he cries, *Maledictus,* "Cursed" be the execution; at no hand, be an actor in that.   Nay, not only have no part in it yourselves, but condemn them that have so, and hold them as people accursed, even by Jacob's own mouth.

Weigh a little this *Maledictus* of Jacob.   *Maledictus* is a word, we would not hear from the poorest and meanest body, that is.   But, there is much in the party, who is here a Patriarch; and they virtuous, holy, and grave persons.   To be cursed of one of them is much; for, whom they curse,

Nu. 24. 9.

God curseth also.   And not only a Patriarch, but a father, to whom God hath given power to bless and to curse; and Whose curse ever accompanieth a father's; especially such a father, as is like Jacob.   So that, this puts them under God's curse certainly.

Weigh also the circumstance, the time. For, this time was the time of blessing: lying on their death-beds, men commonly give their last blessings to their children. So did Jacob to Judah here, and so to the rest. At this time, then, to do it, is somewhat yet more strange, than at another; nay, than at any other time. Blessing-time with others is cursingtime with them. When he blest others, to curse them, and that there, on his death-bed! For, the curse of the death-bed is of all other the worst: such as are so cursed, some evil will come to them.

On his death-bed.

Yet somewhat to ease it. This curse, if you mark it, is not on their persons: their nature, as men, is not touched; but only by reflection upon their affection of anger. And yet, not on that neither (for there is good use of them also; for one may be " angry and sin not") : but as it was transcendent, too much and too long; passed the bounds of all reason and moderation. And this was their punishment spiritual.

Eph. 4. 26.

Maledictus, that goes to the fact, *Dispergam* to their persons; which he denounceth, shall fall upon them. And he doth not this by way of prophecy, They shall be divided and scattered; but pronounced it by way of sentence. Not, It shall be done; but he will do it himself. It should be his own act, and he would never leave it, till he see it put in execution. And, though it were not done in his time, yet it was as good as done; as certain and sure, as if, at that time, it had had the performance.

2. A dispergam to the persons.

You may refer *Dividam* to Simeon, and *Dispergam* to Levi. Simeon was divided into pieces: a piece, in Judah; a piece, in Dan; a piece, in mount Seir of the Amalekites. Levi was scattered here and there, up and down in every corner of the land. Or, (if you will refer it to both,) they were divided, while Jacob continued a family : they were dispersed, when they after came to be a state.

And, if you mark, the punishment is very proper, and well proportioned to the fault. The fault was a bad union; their punishment is a just division. Their fault was " hand in hand," they were too near; their punishment is, they shall be set far enough asunder, for taking any such counsel more. So, whom the devil hath joined, God puts in sunder. And a righteous thing it is, it should so be. For, punishments

[Prov. 11. 21.]

SERM.
VIII.

should have in them the nature of a medicine : they cure ever, by contraries : heat, by cold : drought, by moisture. Even as this doth ; an evil joining, by a just dispersion.

There was great wisdom in this punishment. For, them that be evil, if we destroy them not, we must take order to weaken them : and to separate them, is to weaken them. United force is the stronger ; disunited, the weaker still. Undo the faggot-band, and when the sticks be severed, you shall, stick by stick, deal with them, and keep them under. A stick will easily be broken ; a faggot will not. So as, to scatter them, is to weaken them.

And so to be, is good for " Simeon and Levi" themselves. It takes from them ability to do hurt: pares their nails, breaks off their horns, doth them good against their wills. For, if the worst come to the worst, they can hurt but singly, or by one. And therefore we say, *Consultum est malis, ut a sociis dividantur :* 'They that are ill affected, it is good for them and their fellows to be put asunder.'

And, if it be good for them ; certainly, for the other tribes, much more ; they shall all live the more quietly. For, if these two should still continue together, they might the sooner, the more easily, again in like sort combine, and confederate themselves together against the other tribes, if they gave them but the least occasion. Now, they shall be so scattered, and set, where they shall do no great harm any more : as no more they did. And so, as it was good for them, so we say, *Consultum est reipublicæ ut dividantur socii ad malum :* 'Good for the commonwealth, if any be that way given, to remove them either from other at least.' So, they the weaker, and the rest the safer. But scattering will not always serve : for, even scattered, some do mischief enough. And therefore, it is as good policy to coop them up, if scattering they do harm ; as it is, to scatter them, if they prove the worse for being together.

The grievousness of the punishment. 1. Disinheriting.

To speak a little of the grievousness of the punishment : these degrees are in it. 1. First, it concludes the disherison of them, the loss of having any lot at all of inheritance of their own, as the rest of the tribes had. It kills not the men, but it pulls down their wall, and lays them to the common, wherein every man had as much right as they. And sure,

God, of His goodness, not intending to proceed the way Him-self had set, that, having "shed man's blood, by man should [Gen. 9. their blood be shed" (for so they should have been rooted 6.] out clean, and two tribes had been lost in Israel): the next was, to let them have no inheritance, entirely by themselves, as had all the rest. As the Psalmist saith : " Slay them Ps. 59. 11. not, lest my people forget" any such thing was done; but " scatter them abroad," and so put them down that way, as chaff is either to be burnt, or the wind to scatter it, no man can tell whither.

A second degree is, not only to be disinherited, but to be 2. Scatter-scattered : for, that was Cain's punishment, divided and cast ing. Gen. 4. 12. out from God's presence : all his life long, to wander up and down he knew not whither. That was for blood too, the blood of Abel. It is the Jews' punishment (and that was for blood too, the blood of Christ), that they are scattered all over the earth (as to this very day they be); and never could get together, to make an entire state, no more than these did.

The third degree is, that all this did light upon their whole 3. Even of posterity, rather than upon their own persons. For, to have their pos-terity. all that came of them so dispersed abroad, was a more heavy hearing to them, than if it had lighted on themselves : of that I make no question. It is the course God holdeth in His Law, " to visit the sins of the fathers upon the children." But, this Exod. 20. is yet heavier : for, there, it is but to " the third and fourth;" 5. but this to endure throughout all generations. The father, which is little moved with his own loss; if it shall turn to the damage of his children, it will move him the rather : as this ever hath done, and ever shall.

And let this be the last, that Jacob's *Maledictus* and his 4. And *Dispergam* do remain and stand thus of record, and so shall that upon record. stand to the world's end. The curse on their heads, a blot on their names, a scattering upon their seed and posterity for ever.

But, let me add this : that, though it appears, their nature was none of the best; they were no good-natured men, as given to blood, and so to be disliked : yet was not their nature exempted from grace though, but place left for grace, and so, they to be relieved that way. For, it may well be thought, this so severe a censure, especially at this time now inflicted, and by their own father, being to go out of the world; that it wrought upon these two brethren, and wrought in them deep contrition of that their outrage. Wherewith God being appeased, turned their curse into a blessing: *pœnam dispersionis in præmium sacerdotii,* say the Fathers. For the curse which Jacob inflicted, Moses reserved (not for their dispersing, which came through their father's fault): scattered they were, but scattered with honour: one having the office of Priesthood, and teaching men; the other, of scribes and schoolmasters, training up their children all the tribes over.

The application of the text.
Let us see now, if you can find in these men, the men of this day; and in this fact, theirs; and so, for the punishment likewise. 1. Two they were, this day: so the number agrees. 2. And "brethren" they were, as nearly allied. 3. And "weapons" they had both. 4. And made of the same metal ("of violence") that theirs here. 5. Counsel they took, into which Jacob's "soul" would never have come. 6. And coloured it with false semblance, *bemerma,* no less than these (one, of discovering of I wot not what secret; the other, of not being from the sermon in any wise; his sermon, like their circumcision). 7. Did as much as in them lay, to execute their counsel: offered to strike, offered to bind, lay hands, grasped, fell to the ground. 8. And from the same root they came both, from desire of revenge. Their fury no whit less, no less cruel, no less implacable. Thus far, their likeness holds.

But now, in two things, dislike: 1. one, these in the text had some cause: their sister was deflowered. Not the least colour, here. Their sister was honoured; themselves dealt with but too well. No cause in the world, they. Dislike, in this first.

2. And then, if you come to the issue; in that, dislike too. It was not *interfecerunt* indeed (we thank God for that it was not): yet they did their good will, *birtsonam.* And it was a judged case in Persia, *voluerunt* was enough.

דרצנם
[Esther
2. 21.
See the
Vulgate.]
But, when we come to the *virum,* there, I am sure, is great odds. Ours, another manner of *virum* than theirs, and put Hamor and Shechem both together. Many a year after this, there were in that land thirty-one Kings, whereof Hamor (at

the most) had but one part : the least of your three kingdoms is greater than all the thirty-one put together. So, there holds no proportion in *virum*.

Will ye see now the punishment? that though "hand were in hand," they were not "unpunished." Jacob's legacy came [Prov. on ours too. Under Jacob's curse they died, his curse upon 11. 21.] their souls, under which their souls lie, and so shall for evermore. And upon their glory and honour; for that is gone and lost for ever; and, as their souls, so their memory accursed. And upon their tribe or house; for, that is scattered as dust before the wind, and come to nought.

And one degree further, wherein ours were dislike. "Simeon and Levi," for all this, lived out their time : slew, but were not slain. But, here this day with these, instead of *interfecerunt*, it was *interfecti sunt*. This Simeon and Levi, they lay both dead on the floor, with their weapons of cruelty in their hands, with their wicked counsel and purpose in their hearts. Which hearts of theirs, the weapons of just defence went through; and their counsel turned to their confusion.

And now our *Benedictus Deus*, to God. Blessed be He for this *Maledictus* of Jacob, for the Patriarch's curse, that light upon them and theirs. And yet our *Maledictus* too, to them, their weapons, their counsel, their fury, their souls, and their memories. And from such blood-thirsty cursed men, God ever bless you !

Let me tell you this, for a farewell. Jacob doth here two things : 1. delivers us a document; 2. and denounceth a dreadful punishment. His document is, *Ne veniat anima mea;* his punishment is, *Maledictus* and *Dissipabo*. And choose, they that will not say *Ne veniat* with him, he will say *Maledictus*, his curse be upon them. But, as Jacob said, so we to say all, all to say after him, *Ne veniat*, both passive and active. Passive: Never be their counsel taken about Jacob's soul; or his soul that is to us Jacob, even the Feeder, the Pastor, and Stone of Israel, never come his soul to be the subject or matter treated of in any such counsel. Active: And never let any true subject's soul come in any such counsel; nor ever any good Christian come in that Church, wherein such counsel or counsellors are harboured and

S E R M.
VIII. maintained; or that hold any doctrine that favours any such consultations.

But if any will not thus say Jacob's *Ne veniat;* we to be so bold as to say Jacob's *Maledictus,* to him, his soul, his seed, his memory and all.   Let all such inherit the curse, let it be Ps. 68. 1, 2. their legacy. *Exurgat Deus et dissipentur inimici,* " Let God arise, and these His enemies be scattered."   As the stubble before the wind, and as the "smoke," let them vanish and come to nothing.   Let their lives be for the sword, their names be put out; their souls for the curse, their houses Judges 5. 31. pulled down and desolate.   " So perish all Thine enemies O Lord," &c.

SERMONS

OF THE GUNPOWDER TREASON,

PREACHED UPON THE FIFTH OF NOVEMBER.

A SERMON

PREACHED BEFORE

THE KING'S MAJESTY AT WHITEHALL,

ON THE FIFTH OF NOVEMBER, A.D. MDCVI.

PSALM cxviii. 23, 24.

This is the Lord's doing, and it is marvellous in our eyes.
This is the day which the Lord hath made; let us rejoice and
be glad in it.

A Domino factum est istud, et est mirabile in oculis nostris.
Hæc est dies quam fecit Dominus; exultemus et lætemur in eâ.

[*This is the Lord's doing; it is marvellous in our eyes.*
This is the day which the Lord hath made; we will rejoice and be
glad in it. Engl. Trans.]

To entitle this time to this text, or to shew it pertinent to
the present occasion, will ask no long process. This day of
ours, this fifth of November, a day of God's making; that
which was done upon it was "the Lord's doing." Christ's
own application (which is the best) may well be applied
here: "This day, is this Scripture fulfilled in our ears." Lu. 4. 21.
For, if ever there were a deed done, or a day made, by God
in our days; this day, and the deed of this day, was it. If
ever He gave cause of marvelling, as in the first; of rejoicing,
as in the second verse, to any land; to us this day, He gave
both. If ever saved, prospered, blessed any; this day, He
saved, prospered and (as we say) fairly blessed us.

The day, we all know, was meant to be the day of all our
deaths; and we, and many were appointed, as sheep to the
slaughter; nay, worse than so. There was a thing doing
on it, if it had been done, we all had been undone. And the

SERM.
I.

Ps. 118. 7.

Ps. 111. 4.
[P. B. V.]

Exod. 12.
3, &c.

Esther 9.
26.

[Exod.
12. 23.]

The di-
vision.

very same day, (we all know,) the day wherein that appointment was disappointed by God, and we all saved, that we
might "not die but live, and declare the praise of the Lord:"
the Lord, of Whose doing that marvellous deed was; of
Whose making, this joyful day is, that we celebrate.

This "merciful and gracious Lord" (saith David, Psalm
the one hundred and eleventh, verse the fourth,) "hath so
done His marvellous works, that they ought to be had,"
and kept "in remembrance." Of keeping in remembrance,
many ways there be: among the rest, this is one, of making
days, set solemn days, to preserve memorable acts, that they
be not eaten out by them, but ever revived, with the return
of the year, and kept still fresh in continual memory. God
Himself taught us this way. In remembrance of the great
delivery from the destroying Angel, He Himself ordained
the day of the Passover yearly to be kept. The Church,
by Him taught, took the same way. In remembrance of
the disappointing of Haman's bloody lots, they likewise
appointed the days of "Purim," yearly to be kept. The
like memorable mercy did He vouchsafe us: "the Destroyer" passed over our dwellings, this day: it is our
passover. Haman and his fellows had set the dice on
us, and we, by this time, had been all in pieces: it is
our "Purim" day.

We have therefore well done, and upon good warrant, to
tread in the same steps, and by law to provide, that this day
should not die, nor the memorial thereof perish, from ourselves or from our seed; but be consecrated to a perpetual
memory, by a yearly acknowledgment to be made of it
throughout all generations. In accomplishment of which
order, we are all now here in the presence of God, on this
day, that He first, by His act of doing, hath made; and we
secondly, by our act of decreeing, have made before Him,
His holy Angels, and men, to confess this His goodness, and
ourselves eternally bound to Him for it. And, being to confess it, with what words of Scripture can we better or fitter
do it, than those we have read out of this Psalm? Sure, I
could think of none fitter, but even thus to say, *A Domino
factum, &c.*

The treaty whereof may well be comprised in three points:

I. The deed or " doing;" II. " The day;" and III. The I.
duty. The deed, in these : " This is the Lord's," &c. " The II.
III.
day," in these: " This is the day," &c. The duty in the
rest : " Let us," &c. The other two reduced to " the day,"
which is the centre of both. The " doing" is the cause ; the
duty is the consequent: from " the day" groweth the duty.

To proceed orderly, we are to begin with " the day." For
though (in place) it stand after the deed ; yet, to us, it is
first : our knowledge is *a posteriori*. The effect ever first,
where it is the ground of the rest. Of " the day" then first.

1. That such days there be, and how they come to be
such. 2. Then of the " doing," that maketh them : wherein
1. that this of David's was ; and 2. that ours is no less, rather
more. 3. Then of the duty, how to do it : by rejoicing and
being glad ; for so, *gaudium erit plenum*, these two make it
full. How to take order, that we may long and often do it,
by saying our Hosanna, and *Benedictus ; for gaudium nos-* Joh. 16.22.
trum nemo tollet a nobis, those will make, that " our joy no
man shall take from us."

" This is the day :" " This?" Why, are not all days made   I.
by Him? Are there any days not made by Him? Why Of " the
day."
then say we, " This is the day the Lord hath made?" Such days
there be.
Divide the days into natural and civil: the natural, some
are clear and some are cloudy ; the civil, some are lucky
days, and some dismal. Be they fair or foul, glad or sad
(as the poet calleth Him) the great *Diespiter*, ' the Father [Hor. Od.
of days' hath made them both. How say we then of some I. 34. 5.]
one day, above his fellow, " This is the day," &c. ?

No difference at all, in the days, or in the months themselves ; by nature, they are all one. No more in November,
than another month ; nor in the fifth, than in the fifteenth.
All is in God's making. For, as in the creation, we see, all
are the works, and yet a plain difference between them for
all that, in the manner of making : some made with יְהִי, *Sit*,
" Let there be light," a " firmament," " dry land ;" some, Gen. 1. 3,
with *Faciamus*, with more ado, greater forecast and framing, 6, 7, 9, 26.
as man, that masterpiece of His works, of whom therefore, in
a different sense, it may be said, This is the creature which
God hath made (suppose, after a more excellent manner). In
the very same manner, it is with days: all are His making,

SERM.
I.

all equal in that; but, that letteth not, but He may bestow a special *Faciamus* upon some one day more than other; and so that day, by special prerogative, said to be indeed a "day that God hath made."

Now, for God's making, it fareth with days as it doth with years. Some year, saith the Psalm, "God crowneth with His goodness," maketh it more seasonable, healthful, fruitful, than other. And so for days: God leaveth a more sensible impression of His favour upon some one, more than many besides, by doing upon it some marvellous work. And such a day, on which God vouchsafeth some special *factum est,* some great and public benefit; notable for the time present, memorable for the time to come, in that case, of that day (as if God had said *Faciamus diem hunc,* shewed some workmanship, done some special cost on it) it may with an accent, with an emphasis be said, This verily is a day which God hath made, in comparison of which, the rest are as if they were not; or at least were not of His making.

Ps. 65. 11.

As for black and dismal days, days of sorrow and sad accidents; they are and may be counted, saith Job, for no days: nights rather, as having "the shadow of death" upon them; or, if days, such as his were, which Satan had marred, than "which God had made." And for common and ordinary days, wherein as there is no harm, so not any notable good, we rather say, they are gone forth from God, in the course of nature, as it were, with a *fiat,* than "made" by Him; specially, with a *faciamus.* So, evil days no days, or days marred: and common days, days; but no "made" days: only those "made," that crowned with some extraordinary great favour, and thereby get a dignity and exaltation above the rest: exempted out of the ordinary course of the calendar with a *Hic est.* Such, in the Law, was the day in the Passover, made by God the head of the year. Such, in the Gospel, of Christ's resurrection, "made" by God, *Dies Dominicus;* and to it, do all the Fathers apply this verse. And we had this day, our Passover, and we had a resurrection or παραβολή, as Isaac had. But I forbear to go further in the general. By this that hath been said, we may see, there be days of which it may be safely said, "This is the day," &c. and in what sense it may be said. Such there be then; that

Job 3. 3, 5, 6.

Exod. 12. 2.

Heb. 11. 19.

this of ours, one of them : that if it be, we may so hold it, and do the duties that pertain to it.

David's " day" here, was one certainly, *dictante Spiritu;* and they, that are like it, to be holden for such; so that, if ours be as it was, it is certainly *dies a Deo factus.* Now then, (to take our rule from the former verse,) *Factum Domini facit diem Domini,* 'It is God's deed that maketh it God's day:' and the greater the deed, the more God's day. There must be first, *factum est,* some " doing:" and secondly, it must be *a Domino,* He the doer; and thirdly, that somewhat must be somewhat " marvellous ;" and fourthly, not in itself so; but, " in our eyes." These four go to it; these four make any day a day of God's making. Let us see then these four: first, in David's here, and then in our own ; and if we find them all, boldly pronounce, " This is the day," &c.

First, the *factum est,* in David's : what " was done," set down at large in the fore-part of the Psalm. It was a deliverance : all the Psalm runneth on nothing else. Every deliverance is from a danger ; and, by the danger, we take measure of the deliverance. The greater that, the greater the delivery from it ; and the greater the delivery, the greater the day, and the more likely to be of God's own manufacture. His danger first : what should have been done. He was in a great distress. Three several times, with great passion he repeats it, that his enemies 1. "came about" him ; 2. "compassed" him round ; 3. "compassed" and "kept" him "in on every side ;" were, no swarm of "bees" so thick : that they gave a terrible lift or thrust at him, to overthrow him; and very near it they were. And at last, as if he were newly crept out of his grave, out of the very jaws of death and despair, he breaks forth and saith, I was very near my death : near it I was, but *non moriar,* "die I will not" now, for this time, but live a little longer, to "declare the works of the Lord." This was his danger : and a shrewd one (it seemeth) it was. From this danger he was delivered. This, the *factum est.*

But man might do all this ; and so it be man's day, for any thing is said yet. Though it were great, it maketh it not God's, unless God (God, I say, and not man, but God Himself) were the doer of it : and if He the doer, He denominates the day. This then was not any man's, not any Prince's

Marginal notes:

II. David's "day" was such.

In it there was 1. a *factum est,* a deliverance.

From danger.

Ps. 118. 10, 11, 12.

Ps. 118. 13.

Ps. 118. 17.

2. *A Domino.* By God, not by man.

Ps. 118. 8, 9.

S E R M. doing, but God's alone; His might, His mercy, that brought
I.
it to pass: not any arm of flesh, but God's might; not of
any merit of his, but of His own mere mercy. This was done
Ps. 118.15, by His might: thrice he tells of it; it was "the right hand
16.
of the Lord," that brought "this mighty thing to pass."
Ps. 118. This was done by His mercy, His ever-enduring "mercy:"
1-4.
four times he tells us, it was that, did it. With that he begins,
and makes it the key of the song. Then, as we have *factum
est*, so we have a *Domino :* the deed, and the doer both.

3. God's doings are many, and not all of one size. The Pro-
Et mirabile,
"and mar- phet Zachary speaketh of "a day of small things;" and, even
vellous" it in those "small," must we learn to see God, or we shall never
was.
Zech. 4. 10. see Him in greater. Yet, so dim is our sight, that unless they
be great, commonly we see Him not: nay, unless it be great
usque ad miraculum, so great, that "marvellous" withal, we
count it not worth a day, nor worthy God, unless it be such.
Ps. 72. 18. But, if it be such, then it is God's, *Qui facit mirabilia solus*,
"Who only works great marvels;" then, man is shut out;
and God's must the day be. *A Domino factum, et mirabile.*

4. And yet this is not enough. The truth is, all that God
*In oculis
nostris*, doth, all His works are wonderful; *magna, sed ideo parva
even "in quia usitata*, 'great wonders, all; but, not wonderful: seem
our eyes."
small to us, because they be usual.' His miracles are no
more "marvellous" than His ordinary works, but that we see
the one daily, and the other not. Therefore he addeth, "in
our eyes," for a full period. His doings, all "marvellous"
in themselves; but, not "marvellous in our eyes," unless
they be rare, and the like not seen before: but then, they
Exod. 8. be; and then we say, *Digitus Dei est*, "It is the finger of
19.
God;" nay, "the right hand of God," that brought this
"mighty thing to pass." Then we give the day for God's,
without more ado. Now then, we have all that goeth to it:
1. a deliverance wrought; 2. wrought by God; 3. a wonderful deliverance; 4. and that, even "in our eyes." These
make David's "day," a "day" of God's making.
Our day Will these be found in ours, and then ours shall be so too?
was such.
These four They will, all of them certainly; and that, in a higher degree,
in ours.
Factum est. in a greater measure; match David's day, and overmatch it
1. A de- in all. 1. We were delivered, and from a danger: that is
liverance
from a clear. How great? (for that makes the odds). Boldly I

dare say, from a greater than David's. Thus I shew it, and danger,
a greater
danger.
go no further than the Psalm itself.

1. David called upon God in his danger; he knew of it
therefore. We did not: we imagined no such thing; but
that all had been safe, and we might have gone to the Parliament, as secure as ever. The danger never dreamt of, that
is the danger.

2. His was, by compassing and hemming in; that is,
above ground, and may be descried from a watch-tower.
Ours was by undermining, digging deep under ground; that
none could discern.

3. One cannot be beset, but he may have hope to break
through, at some part. But here, from this, no way, no
means, no possibility of escaping. The danger not to be
descried, not to be escaped, that is the danger.

4. His were a swarm of "bees" (he calleth them so): they Ps.118.12.
buzz and make a noise, when they come. Ours, a brood of
vipers, *mordentes in silentio ;* still, not so much as a hiss, till
the deadly blow had been given.

5. His was but of himself alone; so he saith, I was in
trouble, "They came about me," "kept me in," "thrust Ps.118.11,
13.
sore at me :" but one person, David's alone. Ours, of a far
greater extent: David, and his three estates with him. Now
though David himself were valued by them at "ten thou- 2 Sam. 18.
3.
sand" of themselves (and not overvalued neither; for he is
worth more; and all Kings like him no less worth); yet he
and they too must needs be more than he alone. Not only
King David had gone, but Queen Esther too; and not only
they, but Solomon the young Prince, and Nathan his bro-
ther. Nor these were not all. The Scriptures recount, 2 Sam. 20.
24.
[2 Sam. 8.
17.]
David had Jehoshaphat for his Chancellor, Adoram his
Treasurer, Seraiah his Secretary, Zadok and Abiathar, and
twenty-two more, the chief of the Priests, Admo his Judge,
Joab his General, all had gone: his forty-eight worthies or 2 Sam. 23.
8.
[1 Chron.
11. 20-47.]
nobles, all they too. The principal of all the tribes in the
kingdom : all they too; and many more than these; no
man knoweth how many. It is out of question, it had
exceeded this of David's here.

6. One more. His danger, he confesseth, was from man:
he goes no further, "I will not fear what man doeth unto Ps. 118. 6.

SERM.
I.
Rev. 9. 3.
me." This of ours was not merely man's : I deny it; it was the devil himself. The instruments (not as his, a swarm of "bees," but) a swarm of "locusts" out of the infernal pit. Not men, no not heathen men : their stories, nay their tragedies, can shew none near it. Their poets could never feign any so prodigiously impious. Not men : no not savage wild men : the Huns, the Heruli, the Turcilingi, noted for inhumanity, never so inhuman: even among those barbarous
1 Cor. 15.
32.
[Vid. Aris-
tot. Ethic.
vii. 1.]
people, this fact would be accounted barbarous. How then? "Beasts :" there were, at Ephesus, "beasts" in shape of men; and θηριότης, 'brutishness' is the worst, philosophy could imagine of our nature. This is more than brutish; what tiger, though never so enraged, would have made the like havoc? Then, if the like, neither in the nature of men nor beasts to be found (it is so unnatural), we must not look to pattern it upon earth ; we must to hell : thence it was
Joh. 8. 44.
certainly, even from the devil. "He was a murderer from the beginning," and will be so to the ending. In every sin of blood, he hath a claw ; but all his claws, in such an one as this : wherein so much blood, as would have made it rain blood ; so many baskets of heads, so many pieces of rent bodies cast up and down, and scattered all over the face of
Joel 2. 30.
the earth. Never such a day : all Joel's signs of a fearful day, "blood, and fire, and the vapour of smoke." As he is
Mark 9. 26.
a murderer, so we see (in Mark), by his renting and tearing the poor possessed child, he is cruel; and in this, all his
Exod. 1.
16.
Mat. 2. 16.
[Gen. 32.
11.]
[2 Kings
25. 8, &c.]
[Esth. 3.
5, &c.]
Ps. 137. 7.
Job 1. 18,
19.
Lam. 2. 9,
10; 5. 12.
Jer. 31. 15.
cruelties should have met together. Pharaoh's and Herod's, killing innocent and harmless children; yet they spared the mother: Esau's cruelty, smiting mother, children, and all : Nebuzaradan's, not sparing the King, nor his lords : Haman's, not sparing Esther nor her ladies: Edom's cruelty, not sparing the sanctuary nor the walls—"Down" with them "to the ground:" his own smiting "the four corners," and bringing down the house upon the heads of Job's children. Put to all the cruelties, in Jeremiah's Lamentations, the not honouring the faces of nobles, priests, judges; the making so many widows and orphans ; the "voice in Ramah," of Rachel comfortless : cruelty, more cruel to them it spared and left behind, than to those it took away. It irketh me to stand repeating these: that ever age, or

land; but that our age, and this land should foster or breed such monsters!

That you may know it for that perfectly, consider but the wickedness of it, as it were in full opposition to God, and you must needs say, it could not be His doing. God forbid, saith Abraham, "Thou shouldest destroy the righteous with the wicked." Kill not dam and young ones both, saith Moses in the Law. You shall "not touch Mine Anointed," saith God in the Psalms. You shall not pull up the good corn; rather let the tares stand, saith Christ in the Gospel. You shall not do evil that good may come of it, saith Paul in his Epistles. But, here is Satan flat contrary, in despite of Law, Prophets, Psalm, Epistle and Gospel: *Hoc est Christum cum Paulo conculcare,* to throw down Abraham, and Moses, and David, and Paul, and Christ, and God and all, and trample upon them all.

One more yet: that this "abomination of desolation" (so calleth Daniel, so calleth our Saviour, the uttermost extremity of all that bad is: so may we this truly): that this "abomination of desolation" took up his standing "in the holy place."

I. An "abomination:" so it is; abhorred of all flesh, hated and detested of all that but hear it named: yea, they themselves say, they should have abhorred it, if it had taken effect. It is an "abomination."

2. Every "abomination" doth not forthwith make desolate. This had. If ever a desolate kingdom upon earth, such had this been, after that terrible blow. Neither root nor branch left, all swept away: strangers called in; murderers exalted; the very dissolution and desolation of all ensued.

3. But this, that this so abominable and desolatory a plot stood "in the holy place," this is the pitch of all. For, there it stood, and thence it came abroad. Undertaken with a holy oath; bound with the holy Sacrament (that must needs be in "a holy place"); warranted for a holy act, tending to the advancement of a holy religion, and by holy persons called by a most holy name, the name of Jesus. That these holy religious persons, even the chief of all religious persons (the Jesuits) gave not only absolution, but

[Margin notes:]
Gen.18.23, 25.
Deut. 22.
6.
[Lev. 22. 28.]
Ps. 105. 15.
Matt. 13. 29.
Rom. 3. 8.

Dan. 9. 27.
Mat. 24.15.

SERM.
I.

resolution, that all this was well done; that it was by them justified as lawful, sanctified as meritorious, and should have been glorified (but it wants glorifying, because the event failed: that is the grief; if it had not, glorified) long ere this, and canonized, as a very good and holy act, and we had had orations out of the conclave in commendation of it. (Now, I think, we shall hear no more of it.) These good fathers, they were David's "bees" here, came hither only to bring us honey, right honey they; not to sting any body;

Ps.118.22.

or, as in the twenty-second verse, they, as "builders," came into the land, only for edification; not to pull down or to destroy any thing. We see their practice, they begun with rejecting this stone, as one that favoured heretics at least, and therefore excommunicate, and therefore deposed, and therefore exposed to any that could handle a spade well, to make a mine to blow him up: him, and all his estates with him to attend him (the corner stone being gone, the walls must needs follow). But then, this shrining it, such an abomination, setting it "in the holy place," so ugly and odious; making such a treason as this, a religious, missal, sacramental treason; hallowing it with orison, oath, and eucharist; this passeth all the rest. I say no more, but as

Mat.24.15.

our Saviour concludeth, when you see such an "abomination" so standing, *qui legit intelligat;* nay, *qui videt.* God send them, that (not read of it, but) see it, and had like to have smelt of it, to learn that they should, by it: and so I leave it.

Tell me now, if this were not his doing; and if it should not have been a day of his making, the devil's own making.

This should have been done; this, the danger: what was done? This the *factum fuisset;* what the *factum est?* All these were undone, and blown over; all the undermining disappointed; all this murder and cruelty and desolation defeated. The mine is discovered, the snare is broken, and we are delivered. All these, the King, Queen, Prince, Nobles, Bishops, Judges, both houses; alive all; not a hair

Dan. 3. 27.
Ps. 68. 26,
27, 28, &c.

of any of their heads perished; not so much as "the smell of fire" on any their garments. "Give thanks, O Israel, unto the Lord thy God in the congregation, from the bottom of the heart. Here is little Benjamin thy Ruler, the Princes of Judah" &c., that they are here, and we see them here, and that the stone these builders refused is still the head-stone of the corner. That should have been done; this was done: and we all, that are here this day, are witnesses of it, witnesses above all exception of this *factum est.*

But by whom, whose "doing?" Truly, not man's "doing" *A Domino.* this; it was "the Lord's." *A dæmone factum est illud,* or *fictum est illud.* It was the devil's doing or devising—the plot: *A Domino factum est hoc,* this was "God's doing"—the deliverance. The blow was the devil's; the ward was God's. Not man, but the devil, devised it; not man, but God, defeated it. He, That sat in Heaven all this while, and from thence looked down, and saw all this doing of the devil and his limbs; in that mercy of His, which is over all His works, to save the effusion of so much blood, to preserve the souls of so many innocents, to keep this land from so foul a confusion, to shew still some token, some sensible "token Ps. 86. 17. upon us for good, that they which hate us may see it, and be ashamed;" but especially, that that was so lately united, might not so soon be dissolved; He took the matter into His own hand. And if ever God shewed, that He had a hook in the Leviathan's nose; that the devil can go no farther than his chain; if ever, that there is in Him more power to help, than in Satan to hurt; in this, He did it. And, as the devil's claws to be seen in the former; so God's right hand, in this mighty thing He brought to pass, and all the fingers of it.

1. To shew it was He. He held His peace and kept silence, sat still, and let it go on, till it came near, even to the very period, to the day of the lot: so near, that we may truly say with King David, "As the Lord liveth," *uno tan-* 1 Sam. 20. *tum gradu, nos morsque dividimur,* "there was but a step be- 3. tween death and us." We were upon the point of going to the hill, all was prepared, the train, the match, "the fire," Gen. 22. 7. "wood" and all, and we ready to be the sacrifice, and even then and there, *in monte providebat Dominus,* God provided Gen. 22. 8. for our safety, even in that very place, where we should have [14.] been the "burnt offering:" from Heaven, stayed the blow. It was "the Lord's doing."

2. When treachery hath his course like water, and creeps

SERM.
I.
———

Ps. 58. 8.
[Ps. 118.
12.]

Ps. 58. 9.

Ps. 58. 11.

Eccles. 10.
20.
Ps. 64. 8.

Prov. 16.
10.

[Gen. 41.
45.]

Gen. 41. 38.

along like a "snail," (it is the fifty-eighth Psalm,) then to make it "like the untimely birth of a woman," never to "see the sun:" not, as in this, *arserunt sicut ignis in spinis,* was but a blaze, as in a bush of thorns; (nay if it come so far, it had gone wrong with us:) but, as in that, *priusquam intelligerent spinæ,* or ever the thorns gat heat, or the powder, fire; then, saith he there, *dicet homo, Utique est Deus,* men shall say, "Verily there is a God," and this was His "doing."

3. And not only, that it was bewrayed, but that He made them the bewrayers of it themselves; and even according to the place, Ecclesiastes, chapter the tenth, made things with feathers to disclose it: when, as in Psalm sixty-four, "their own tongues," or, which is all one, their own pens, "make them to fall;" all that consider it shall be amazed; and then "all men shall say, This hath God done; for they shall perceive" it plain, "it is His work." They shall be charged in confession, they shall swear, they shall take the Sacrament not to do it; and yet, contrary to all this, it shall come out by themselves. Was not this "God's doing?"

4. Yet further, to shew it was so: this which was written was so written, as divers, of profound wisdom, knew not what to make of it. But then cometh God again, (God most certainly,) and as in the Proverbs, the sixteenth chapter, and tenth verse, puts קֶסֶם, a very "divination," a very oracle in "the King's lips," and his mouth missed not the matter; made him, as Joseph, "the revealer of secrets," to read the riddle: giving him wisdom to make both explication, what they would do; and application, where it was they would do it. This was God certainly. This, Pharaoh would say, none could, unless he were filled with "the Spirit of" the holy "God." It was *a Domino factum.*

5. Lastly, as that when it was come forth they were not reclaimed; not then, when they saw the hand of God was gone out against them, and that it was even God they strave withal: no, but even then, from hidden treachery fell to open rebellion, and even perished in it, (if God shewed not a miracle of His mercy on them,) perished there, and perished eternally: as this I say did: (that it was *factum a dæmone,* who never left them till he had brought them thither); so

that (before they came thither) God cast their own powder
in their faces, powdered them and disfigured them with it;
and that their quarters stand now in pieces, as they meant
ours should: it is the case of the hundred and ninth Psalm, Ps. 109. 27,
"And hereby shall they know, that it is Thy hand, and that ²⁹·
Thou Lord hast done it." How? in that they are thus
"clothed with their own shame," and even "covered with
their own confusion;" that they fall as fast as they rise; are
still confounded, and still Thy servants rejoice. These five
(as prints) shew it was God's hand: it was "the Lord," That
"made" the "day;" it was "the day, that the Lord made." Ps. 21. 13.
"Be thou exalted Lord in Thine own strength:" it was Thy
right hand, that brought this mighty thing to pass.

This will not serve the turn. His "doing" makes it not 3. *Et est*
"the day:" His doing a miracle; that makes it: and that *mirabile.*
it is too. I take no thought, to prove this point; by the
Law, the Prophets, the Gospel. To put them to it. Moses:
"Enquire now of the days that are past, that were before us, Deu. 4. 32.
since the day that God created man upon earth, and ask
from one end of Heaven to the other, if there came to pass
such a thing as this, whether any such like thing hath been
heard;" and, if we cannot suit it, or set such another by it,
we must needs yield it for one. By the Prophets: "Go to Jer. 2. 10.
the Isles and behold, send to Kedar and take diligent heed,
and see, if you can possibly find the like:" if not, confess it
for "marvellous." "Come hither," saith David, and "be- [Ps. 66. 4.
hold, how marvellous God is!" and what is that? that such P. B. V.]
as are rebellious are not able to exalt themselves. We need
not go so far; we have it here to see: we may say to him,
"Come hither." By the Gospel: for so do they there acknowledge our Saviour's for miracles: "Sure, we have seen
strange things to-day;" "We never saw it on this fashion;" Lu. 5. 26.
"The like was never seen in Israel:" therefore "marvellous" Mark 2. 12.
certainly. It is now no miracle, no strange thing, to have a Mat. 9. 33.
King delivered: every other year, we see it, and therefore
wonder not at it. But, to see King, Queen, their seed, all
their estates delivered, that is *mirabile*, that is "a new thing Jer. 31. 22.
created on the earth." I conclude: as that was the devil's
doing, and was monstrous in our eyes; so, "this is God's
doing," and it is "marvellous in our eyes." And again,

SERM. upon all these marks, that as this was a day, the devil would
I.   have marred; so, "this is a day, that the Lord made."

4. *In oculis*   "Marvellous" then it is: yet hath it not," as we say, his
nostris,
"in our   full Christendom, unless it be so "in our eyes." For the
eyes."
Ps. 126. 1.   time, it was; and that (of the Psalm) fits us well: "When
God," saith he, "turned away the captivity (say we, the
destruction) of His people, then were we like to them that
dream." No man, but stood in a maze, as if he knew not
well, whether he saw it waking, or dreamt of it, it was so
strange.

In the   And let me go further. Not in ours only; for, sure I am,
eyes of   that which followeth there is true ("Then said they," *inter
others.
Ps. 126. 2. *gentes*) "of other nations, The Lord hath done great things
for them:" and we are to blame, if we answer them not with
Ps. 126. 3. the echo there following, "Yea, indeed, the Lord hath done
great things for us, for which we have cause to rejoice." If
strangers think it strange, and say and write, *A sæculo inau-
ditum,* 'The like was never heard before;' if it were "marvellous" in their eyes, it were very "marvellous," it should
not be so "in our eyes" too.

Of the   I add, they that were the actors of it, in their eyes, it is
very actors. so; and that of the Apostle may fitly be applied to them:
Acts 13.
41.   "Behold, ye despisers, and wonder and vanish, for God hath
wrought a work in your days, a work which you yourselves,
that were the doers, shall scarce believe, when it shall be
told:" that even astonished themselves, to see it go forward
so long, and so suddenly cast down. Nay, I go further, to
make it a miracle consummate. I doubt not, but it was
strange news, even in hell itself, insomuch as even that place
had never hatched the like monster before. You see the
welcome they in hell gave him of Asshur: What, art thou
Isa. 14. 16. come, "that makest the earth to tremble, and dost shake
whole kingdoms?" And yet it is well known, all his shaking
was but a metaphor: he never made it shake actually, as
these would have done: and therefore, this of greater admiration, and (I doubt not, but) more wonderful in their eyes:
and ours are very dim, if in all other it be, and be not so
in ours.

III.   Then if such days there be, if this of ours be one of them,
The duty. if the fore-part of the verse do, then must the latter also

belong to us : if " this, the day the Lord hath made;" then, this, the day, wherein we to "rejoice." When He makes, we to make; and our rejoicing in it, is our making of it.

To "rejoice," no hard request, nor heavy yoke, let it not be grievous to us. We love to do it, we seek all means to do it in all cases else; then to assay to do it here. This, sure, the Prophet would not require, nor make it the office of the day, but that upon such days, God Himself calls us to joy.

And even as, when God calleth us to mourning by black days of famine or war, or the like ; then to fall to feasting or revelling, is that that highly displeaseth God : so, when God by good days calleth us to joy ; then to droop and not to accommodate ourselves to seasons of His sending, is that which pleases Him never a whit.

What (saith Nehemiah), upon such a blessed day as this ? "Droop you to-day ?" *Nolite*, at no hand to do it, *dies enim* Neh. 8. 9, *festus est*, "it is a festival day." What then? why it is essen- 10. tial, it is of the very nature of every feast, (saith God in His law,) *omnino gaudere*, by any means, in any wise, therein to Nu. 10. 10. "rejoice." And Nehemiah's promise is to encourage us, that Deut. 16. if the strength of the Lord be our joy, the very "joy of the 11. Lord" shall be our "strength."

To conclude. Sure I am, that if the plot had prevailed, it would have been a high feast in Gath, and a day of jubilee in Askelon ; "The daughters of the uncircumcised" would 2 Sam. 1. have made it a day in triumph. Let us not be behind them 20. then, but shew as much joy, for our saving, as they would certainly have done for our perishing.

Exultemus et lætemur. God loveth our joy should be full : *Exultemus* it is not full, except we have both these, the body, as it *and læte-* *mur* both. were, and the soul of joy : the joy outward of the body, and gladness inward of the soul. (So much do the two words signify, in all the three tongues.) Both He will have : for if one be wanting, it is but *semiplenum*, ' half full.'

And he beginneth with *exultemus*, the outward : not to *Exulte-* ourselves within, which we call *gaudere in sinu*, 'joy of the *mus :* *the out-* bosom ;' but such, so exuberant, as the streams of it may *ward joy.* overflow, and the beams of it shine and shew forth, in an outward sensible exultation. It is a "day :" so would he

SERM. have us rejoice, that, as by day-light, it might be seen in
1. our face, habit, and gesture : seen, and heard both. There-
Ps. 118. fore he saith, at the fifteenth verse, "The voice of joy is in
15. the dwellings of the righteous." And "in the dwelling" it
doeth well : but yet, that would not serve his turn ; but,
Ps. 118. "Open me" (saith he at the nineteenth verse) "the gates of
19. righteousness," that is, the church door (his house would not
hold him) : thither will "I go in," and there, in the congregation, in the great congregation, "give thanks to the Lord."
And that so great a congregation, that it may *constituere*
[Ps. 118. *diem solennem in condensis usque ad cornua altaris,* 'that
27.] they may stand so thick in the church, as fill it from the
entry of the door, to the very edge of the altar.' This same
joy, that is neither seen nor heard, there is some leaven of
malignity in it; He cannot skill of it. He will have it seen
in the countenance, heard in the voice ; not only preaching,
but singing forth His praise. And that, not with voices
alone, but with instruments ; and not instruments of the
quire alone, but instruments of the steeple too, bells and
[Mat. 21. all, that so it may be *Hosanna in altissimis* in the very
9.] "highest" key we have. This for *exultemus.*

Lætemur, But, many a close hypocrite may do all this, and many
the inward a counterfeit Shimei and Sheba did all this to David ; got
joy. them a fleering forced countenance, taken-on joy: and therefore the other ; that God will have His joy not be the joy
of the countenance alone, a clear face, and a cloudy overcast
heart : He will have the gladness of the heart too, of the
Ps. 16. 9. inner man ; *cor meum et caro mea,* "the heart" as well as
the "flesh," to be joyful. The joy of the soul is the soul of
joy; not a body without a soul, which is but a carcass.
Ps. 18. 44. "Strange children" may, and "will, dissemble with me,"
saith the Psalm : "dissemble" a gladness, for fear of being
noted ; and yet within, in heart, you wot what. But God
Ps. 68. 26. calleth for His *de fontibus Israel,* which we read, "from the
ground of the heart." That is, indeed, the true fountain of
Ps. 71. 23. joy, that "our lips may be fain, when we sing unto Him,
[*See here* and so may our soul, which He hath delivered." Nay, He
and else-
where the delivered both : and therefore, both the body to rejoice, and
P. B. ver-
sion.] the soul to be glad. This doth *lætemur* add to *exultemus.*
How to If then we be agreed, that we will do both, I come to the
order our
joy.

last, how to order our joy, that it may please Him, for Whom
it is undertaken. It is not every joy, that He liketh. Merry
they were, and joyful (they thought), that kept their "King's Hos. 7. 5.
day," by taking in bowl after bowl, till they were " sick"
again. So they that Malachi speaks of: there came nothing Mal. 2. 3.
of their feasts but " dung" (bear with it, it is the Holy
Ghost's own term), that is, all in the belly, and belly-cheer.
So they, that " sat down to eat and drink, and rose up to Exod. 32.
play," and there was all ; that is the calf's feast : a calf can ^{6.}
do as much. "But with none of these was God pleased ;" 1 Cor. 10.
and as good no joy, as not to the purpose ; as not to please ^{5.}
Him.

That it may be to the purpose, that God may take plea-
sure in it, it must begin at Hosanna, at *Aperite mihi portas* Ps. 118. 19.
justitiæ, at the temple-door ; there must it go in, it must
bless, and be blessed, in the house of the Lord. I will first
" make joyful in my house of prayer" (it is God by Esay) : Isa. 56. 7.
the stream of our joy must come from the spring-head of
religion.

Well then, to the Church we are come : so far onward.
When we are there, what is to be done ? Somewhat we must
say, we must not stand mute. There to stand still, that
the Prophet cannot skill of. That then we may there say
something, he here frames, he here indites us a versicle, Ps. 118. 25.
which after grew into such request, as no feast ever without
it, without an Hosanna : it grew so familiar, as the very
children were perfect in it. The sum and substance where- Mat. 21. 9,
of, briefly, is no more, but (which we all desire) that God ^{16.}
would still " save," still prosper, still bless him, that in His
name is come unto us, that is King David himself, whom all
in the house, and all of the house of the Lord, bless in His
name.

And to very good purpose doth he this : for joy hath no
fault, but that it is too short, it will not last, it will be taken
from us too soon. It is ever a bar, in all joy, *tolletur a vobis :*
subject to the worm that Jonah's gourd was. It standeth
us therefore in hand, to begin with Hosanna ; so to joy, as
that we may long joy to pray for the continuance, that it be
not taken from us : ever remembering, the true temper of
joy is (*exultate in tremore*) not without the mixture of some Ps. 2. 11.

SERM.
I.

Prov. 27. 1.

fear. For this day, we see what it is, a joyful day; "we know not," saith Solomon, "what the next day will be;" and if not what the next day, what the next year much less. What will come, we know not; what our sins call for to come, that we know: even that God should call to judgment, if not by fire, by somewhat else. If it be but for this, it concerns us nearly, to say our Hosanna, that the next year be as this. It is our wisdom therefore, to make the means for the continuance of it, that God would still establish the good work, He this day wrought in us: still bless us with the continuance of the same blessings.

And this that we may do, not faintly but cheerfully with the lifting up of our souls therefore, as far as art or spirit can do it, he hath quickened his Hosanna, that he may put spirit and life in us, to follow him in it, with all fervour of

Ps.118.25.

affection: four times, twice with *Anna*, and twice with *Na*; either of them before, and after; but eight words, and four of them interjections: all to make it passionate; and that so, as in the original, nothing can be devised more forcible; and so, as it is hard in any other tongue to express it: which made the Evangelists let it alone, and retain the Hebrew word still. But this, as near as I can, it soundeth: "Now, good Lord, save us yet still; now, good Lord, prosper us yet still." Be to us, as last year, so this, and all the years to

[Heb. 13. 8.]

come, "Jesus" a Saviour, "yesterday and to-day and the same for ever."

And three things doth he thus earnestly pray for, and teacheth us to do the like. 1. To save, 2. prosper, 3. and bless.

To save: that should be first with us; it is commonly last: we have least sense of our souls. To save us, with the true saving health (it is a word whereof our Saviour Jesus hath His name), it importeth the salvation of the soul; properly to that it belongeth, and hath joined to it

Mat. 21. 9.

Hosanna in the Gospel, *Hosanna in excelsis,* to shew it is a high and heavenly salvation.

2. Then, to prosper. If He but grant us the former alone, to have our souls saved, though without prosperity, though with the days of adversity, it is *sors sanctorum,* 'the lot of many a saint of His,' of far more worth than we: even

so, we are bound to thank Him, if, even so, we may be but saved. But, if He add also prosperity of the outward, to the saving of the inward man, that not so much as a "leaf" of Ps. 1. 3. us shall "wither," but look what we do shall "prosper;" and that, whatsoever men of evil counsels do, shall not prosper against us; if He not only vouchsafe us *Hosanna in excelsis,* but *Hosanna de profundis* too, from deep cellars, deep vaults, those that dig deep to undermine our prosperity; if He add the shadow of His wings, to shelter us from perils, to the light of His countenance, to save us from our sins, then have we great cause to rejoice yet more : and, both with *exultemus* from without, and *lætemur* from within, to magnify His mercy, and to say with the Prophet, "Praised [Ps.35.27.] be the Lord, That" (not only taketh care for the safety, but) "taketh pleasure in the prosperity of His servants."

3. Lastly, because both these, the one and the other; our future salvation, by the continuance of His religion and truth among us, and our present prosperity (like two walls) meet upon "the Head-stone of the corner;" depend both, [Ps. 118. first, upon "the Name of the Lord," and next upon him, 22.] that in His Name, and with His Name, is come unto us, that is, "the King :" (so do both the Evangelists, St. Luke and St. John supply ; and where we read, "Blessed be He," Lu. 19. 38. there they read "Blessed be the King that cometh :") so Joh. 12. 15. that neither of them sure, unless he be safe ; that He would bless him, and make him blest, that, in His blessed name, is come amongst us. The building will be "as mount Sion," Ps. 125. 1. so the corner-stone be fast ; so the two walls, that meet, never fall asunder. If otherwise : but I will not so much as put the case ; but as we pray, so trust, it "shall never be removed, but stand fast for ever."

This then we all wish, that are now in the "House of the [Ps. 134. Lord," and we that are of "the House of the Lord," do now 1.] and ever, in the temple and out of it, morning and evening, night and day, wish and pray both, that He would continue forth His goodness, and bless with length of days, with strength of health, with increase of all honour and happiness, with terror in the eyes of his enemies, with grace in the eyes of his subjects, with whatsoever David or Solomon, or any King that ever was happy, was blessed with ; him

SERM.
I.

that in the Name of the Lord is come to us, and hath now these four years stayed with us, that he may be blessed, in that Name, wherein he is come, and by the Lord, in Whose Name he is come, many and many years yet to come.

And, when we have put this incense in our phials, and bound this " sacrifice with cords, to the altar" fast, we bless you and dismiss you, to eat your bread with joy, and to drink your wine with a cheerful heart: for God accepteth your work; your joy shall please Him: this Hosanna shall sanctify all the joy, shall follow it.

[Ps. 118.
27.]

To end then. "This day, which the Lord hath" thus "made" so marvellously; so marvellously and mercifully; let us rejoice in the Maker, for the making of it, by His doing on it that deed that is so " marvellous in our eyes," in all eyes; returning to the beginning of the Psalm, and saying with the Prophet, " O give thanks to the Lord, for He is gracious," &c. "Let Israel, let the house of Aaron, yea, let all that fear the Lord, confess that His mercy endureth for ever."

Ps. 118.
1-4.

"Who only doeth great wonders." " Who remembered us when we were in danger." " And hath delivered us from our enemies," " with a mighty hand and stretched-out arm." And, as for them, hath turned their device upon their own head. And hath made this day, to us, a day of joy and gladness. To this God of gods, the Lord of Heaven, "glorious in holiness, fearful in power, doing wonders," be &c.

Ps. 136. 4,
12, 23, 24.

[Exod. 15.
11.]

A SERMON

PREACHED BEFORE

THE KING'S MAJESTY AT WHITEHALL,

ON THE FIFTH OF NOVEMBER, A.D. MDCVII.

PSALM cxxvi. 1—4.

When the Lord brought again the captivity of Sion, we were like them that dream.

Then was our mouth filled with laughter, and our tongue with joy; then said they among the heathen, The Lord hath done great things for them.

The Lord hath done great things for us, whereof we rejoice.

O Lord, bring again our captivity, as the rivers in the South.

[In convertendo, Dominus, captivitatem Sion, facti sumus sicut consolati :

Tunc repletum est gaudio os nostrum, et lingua nostra exultatione.

Tunc dicent inter gentes, Magnificavit Dominus facere cum eis.

Magnificavit Dominus facere nobiscum ; facti sumus lætantes.

Converte Domine captivitatem nostram, sicut torrens in Austro. Latin Vulg.]

[When the Lord turned again the captivity of Sion, we were like them that dream.

Then was our mouth filled with laughter, and our tongue with singing ; then said they among the heathen, The Lord hath done great things for them.

The Lord hath done great things for us, whereof we are glad.

Turn again our captivity, O Lord, as the streams in the South. Engl. Trans.]

THE word "captivity" is enough to give us light, when and why this Psalm was first indited; namely, upon their return from the captivity. Of which return of theirs, it may truly be said, it was one of the greatest; nay, it was the very greatest delivery that ever God vouchsafed His people. Their estate nowhere so miserable as there; witness the book of Lamentations. Their case never so joyful, as returning thence; witness this book of Psalms. No benefit so much celebrated; none, so many Psalms as it. Divide the whole book into four parts, one fourth part is for this return: either directly of set purpose (as here are fifteen together); or recorded in Psalms, though made upon other purpose. Still, as the greatest delivery that ever they had.

Yet, this I confess unto you, that this delivery of theirs (such as it was) falls short of that of ours as on this day, wherewith yet I shall be fain to match it. But, this I must tell you beforehand: to have this of ours fully patterned in all points, we must not look for it; the Scripture hath it not. They had no powder then, it was not found. If they had had, they would have used it, but for the murder of *persons*; they knew no other murder. But, to murder all three estates of a realm at a clap! *Facti sunt sicut somniantes;* or rather, *Facti non sunt sicut somniantes,* they never dreamt of any such. And what then is our case, think we, that have received from God such a deliverance, as we can find no match for it?

But well, though these Psalms of the "captivity" come not fully home, be not altogether like ours; yet, because there be none liker, none that come nearer, we must content ourselves with these, and either take our texts hence, or take none at all.

In taking this then, and applying it to the present, there shall need but one word to be altered, that is, the word "captivity." But for it, all else would run very clear and current: if we might but change that one word, and instead of reading, "When the Lord turned away the captivity of Sion," we might thus read, 'When the Lord turned away the blowing up of Sion;' all besides, every word else, would suit well, and keep perfect correspondency.

It is true, it was not a "captivity," that was "turned away" from us. And yet it is hard to say, whether it might not have proved to that too; and whether God, in turning it away, did not happily turn away a "captivity." But if not a "captivity," that, He "turned away" from us, was worse than any "captivity." This Psalm sheweth it: they that are captives, how miserable soever their case be, yet have hope of returning, as these had, and did. But, if this of ours had taken place, we had been sure enough for ever returning: we had been all past singing, *In convertendo.*

This one word being changed, (and that without wrong to the text, for it is for a greater,) all else will fall in and follow of itself. 1. As that of theirs, so this of ours, for all the world like a dream. 2. As they, "among the heathen," then said of them ; so, they of other nations now said of us, that God had been our good Lord, for bringing us again, if not from the captivity of Babylon, from Babylon, I am sure, that is, from a horrible and fearful confusion, which He turned away from this land, and from us all.

To set then this Psalm, first for them, and then for our- The sum selves. It is a "Psalm of degrees" (the title is so) : and two and di-vision. degrees there be in it. No new ones, but the usual; which we must still fall upon, if we deal with the Psalms. All the Psalms are reduced to them, even to those two words, Hallelujah and Hosanna, praises and prayers: Hallelujah, praises for deliverance obtained ; Hosanna, prayers for obtaining the like, upon the like need. I. The Hallelujah in the four first verses; II. the Hosanna in the last. I durst not sever them : they prosper not, where they go not together.

The Hallelujah or praise hath two degrees, which, as in all other things, so in this, make it praiseworthy ; 1. the stuff, and 2. the workmanship.

The stuff, or matter, I call the turning back the "captivity of Sion ;" and two degrees in it : 1. that Sion is suffered to go into "captivity ;" 2. That God turneth away the "cap-tivity of Sion." This is Hallelujah for the stuff.

And again, Hallelujah for the workmanship. That God did not deliver Sion *utcunque ;* but, so deliver her, as the manner was memorable. The manner is set down in two degrees : which two are as it were the embroidery of the other. 1. "Turned" it so strangely, as, when it was done, it seemed rather a dream, than a thing done waking, *Facti sumus, &c.* 2. Again, "turned" it so memorably, as the hea-then talked of it, *Tum dicebant, &c.*

SERM.
II.
Which *Dicebant* divides itself, 1. into the sound " among the heathen," in the second verse; and the 2. echo of it in Israel, in the fourth.

Then cometh the conclusion, the best conclusion of all, *Facti sumus, &c.* This their Hallelujah.

II.
Their Hallelujah is no sooner done, but close upon it cometh their Hosanna. To their knees they get them, and pray, *Converte Domine.* And in this also two degrees: 1. first, they pray to "turn" it; 2. and then, so to "turn" it, "as the streams in the South." " In the South," that is, the wilderness; likening their captivity to a desert, and their returning to streams of water. And what more needful, or what more welcome, than water in the wilderness? These are the degrees and steps, in theirs. The same steps will we tread in our own; to shew, that we may with good right convert to our own use this Psalm, *In convertendo.*

Ps. 126. 1.
I.
Halle-
lujah.
Hallelujah first for the work, then for the workmanship. The work is, "The Lord turned away the captivity of Sion." 1. First, of " the captivity of Sion;" 2. then, of the Lord's turning it.

1.
For the
work.
1. "The
captivity
of Sion."
"The captivity of Sion:" I ask first, why "of Sion?" why not "the captivity" of Jerusalem, Judah, Israel? Jerusalem, Judah, Israel, were led away captives, no less than Sion. They, the greater, and more general; why not "the captivity" of them, but " of Sion?" It should seem, there is more in Sion's, than in the rest, that choice is made of it before the rest. Why? what was Sion? We know, it was but a hill in Jerusalem, "on the north side." Why is that hill so honoured? No reason in the world, but this; that upon it the Temple was built: and so, that Sion is much spoken of, and much made of, it is only for the Temple's sake. For whose sake it is, (even for His Church,) that " the Lord loveth the gates of Sion, more than all the dwellings of Jacob." " Loveth" her more, and so her " captivity" goeth nearer Him, and her delivery better pleaseth Him, than all Jacob besides. This maketh " Sion's captivity" to be mentioned chiefly, as chiefly regarded by God, and to be regarded by His. As, we see, it was. When they "sat by the waters of Babylon," that which made them weep was, " When we remembered thee, O Sion:" that their greatest

Ps. 48. 2.

Ps. 87. 2.

Ps. 137. 1.

grief. That their greatest grief, and this their greatest joy :
lætati sumus, when news came (not saith the Psalm, *in domos
nostras,* 'We shall go now every one to his own house,' but),
in domum Domini ibimus, "We shall go to the house of the Ps. 122. 1.
Lord," we shall appear before the God of gods in Sion.

Sion, God loved and favoured high ; yet, how dear soever
Sion is in His sight, for Sion's sins, *propter peccata populi
Mei,* she sometimes is forsaken and afflicted by Him. Though
He take "not His mercy utterly from her, nor suffer His Ps. 89. 32,
truth quite to fail ;" yet " He visiteth her offences with the 33.
rod," and her deeper transgressions " with scourges :" and
among the rest, with this scourge of " captivity."

To be plagued at home, in their own land, is but "a rod"
in comparison ; " captivity" is a scourge, in respect of it, and
a sharp one. To be bereft of all we have, and of that, which
they have, that have nothing else, liberty ; to be carried into
a " strange land ;" to be made bond and thrall to the proud [Ps. 137.
commands of an enemy ; " Woe is me for Sion," saith Jeremy. 4.]
And no man shall need but to read his Lamentations only.
There is, in particular, to be seen the evil of " captivity," how
sharp a scourge it is. The book was made for that end.

But, of all captivities, none so evil as that of Babel : if any
other be a scourge, that is a scorpion. In Egypt, their case
was more tolerable : their souls were free there, howsoever
their bodies in servitude ; they might serve God yet, they
were not compelled to fall down before Isis or Osiris. Only,
" the captivity" of Babel is " the captivity" of souls, no less
than bodies. There, they must fall down before the great Dan. 3. 1,
idol in the field Dura, or be thrown into the furnace. Babel 6.
is the worst place that is, for Sion to be carried captive to.
And this is the first degree : Sion is afflicted, and that with
" captivity," with " the captivity" of Babel. Now to *In convertendo Dominus.*

" They that fell by the sword," saith Jeremy, were in 2. The
better case than they that went into " captivity," save only Lord's
that this poor hope they had left. They might return again. of it.
They might return, and so they did. Sion went into " cap- Lam. 4. 9.
tivity ;" but her " captivity" went not so far, but it turns
again. It is one of the songs of Sion : " Many a time have Ps. 129.
they afflicted me from my youth up," &c. And again, 1, 2.

SERM.
II.
"Many a time have they afflicted me," &c. that is, many and many times more; but yet "they have not prevailed against me" finally. Here is a proof of it. Though brought to Babel, yet not left there; though led into "captivity," yet restored to liberty. There may be snares for her, but the end is,

Ps. 124. 7. *Laqueus contritus est;* there may be bonds, but the end,

Ps. 116. 16. *Dirupisti vincula,* "Thou hast broken my bonds in sunder." Sion's "captivity" is still "turned" back.

But who shall turn it? *In convertendo Dominus.* Cyrus may seem to have done it; but alas, Cyrus is a great monarch, and they a sort of poor captives. Besides, he is a heathen man, an idolater, a stranger to them and their religion, no

Mark 16.3. ways like to turn, or to be turned. *Quis revolvet nobis hunc lapidem,* What engine shall bring this about? *Dominus,* "The Lord" shall. For, though the hearts of monarchs be as rivers

Prov. 21. 1. of many streams, yet *in manu Domini cor Regis,* (saith a great Monarch,) "in His hand their hearts be;" *et quocunque vult convertit,* and He can turn them, "as the streams in the South." (This verse referring to that of Solomon.) It is the Lord then, the great Καρδιοτρέπτης, the great Turner of the greatest Monarchs' hearts, that thus turned Cyrus's heart. Cyrus being turned, his decree came forth for their return.

Ps. 118. 23. *A Domino factum est istud,* it was His "doing:" they saw it, they noted it; and they had been to be noted of great blindness, if they had not noted it. But note it they did. So they

Ps. 124. 1, 2. begin one of their songs, *Nisi quia Deus:* and again they repeat it, *Nisi quia Deus,* "If the Lord had not done it," it had not been done. But for Him, they had been in Babel still. Thus much 1. for "Sion's captivity," and 2. the Lord's turning: "The Lord turned away the captivity of Sion." So have ye the work; Hallelujah for the work.

2.
Hallelujah.
For the workmanship, or manner.
And again, Hallelujah for the workmanship. To escape a "captivity" is enough, it skills not how; howsoever, it is well: thanks be to God. But it receiveth increase, and is made capable of a higher degree, by the manner: and that greatly. All captivities are grievous, especially that of Babel; and all returns joyful, especially from thence. Yet is even that made more joyful, two ways; set higher by these two degrees: 1. that it was like a dream. It is ever a sign of a very strange event, when men, at the seeing aught, though

they be awake, yet think they are not; though they do not dream, yet think they are in a dream. 2. That "they among the heathen" talked of it. It is ever a sign of a famous accident, when other men (especially other nations) speak, and speak *magnificè* of it.

Facti sumus sicut somniantes, "We were as it were in a dream," it came so unlooked for. For, so come dreams, we know, without looking for: men know not, when they go to bed, what they shall dream of. And it is a benefit to have a benefit come, like a dream, without waiting longer for it. So strange as like a dream.
1. Un-looked for.

Then, it came without any labour of our parts. That, that cometh in a dream, cometh to us sleeping; we doing nothing to it, or toward it, more than if we had been fast asleep. And it is a benefit to have a benefit come, like a dream, without pains-taking for it. 2. Without labour.

But neither of these is it; that it was unlaboured for, or that it was unlooked for. But, that it was so strange, as no man would ever have looked for it; so strange, as well might we dream of some such thing, but, awake, never any saw the like. The nature of dreams is such: men, in dreams, have such strange things appear to them, as would never come into the minds of any that were awake. They see ladders so long as will reach up to Heaven: they see the moon and stars worshipping them: they see men with heads of gold and breasts of silver, and I wot not what things: incredible things, of the fancy's figuring, but never of the senses' apprehending. This maketh things, by all likelihood, to seem like dreams. And such was their case, at the coming out of Cyrus's proclamation for their return. It was so little looked for, that ever it should come; it was so above all they could hope for, when it did come; that, what with the suddenness, and what with the strangeness, for the present, it seemed to them a dream of the night, rather than any vision of the day. Well might they say, *Facti sumus,* &c. 3. Beyond hope.

Gen. 28.
12; 37. 9.
Dan. 2. 31,
32.

A dream it was. To specify what kind of dream. Jacob dreamed, and was much comforted with it: Nebuchadnezzar dreamed, and was exceedingly frighted with it. This, here, was of the nature of Jacob's; a comfortable pleasant dream. You may see by the effects in the second verse; *Tum repletum est, &c.* And sure, the impression of the fancy nowhere A pleasant dream.
Gen. 28.
13, &c.
Dan. 4. 5.

SERM.
II.

sheweth itself more powerful, than in dreams. Men shall be so affected, as they shall even laugh out, as they shall even talk aloud; yea so, that they shall even wake with it many times. This here was such. Joyful, it filled their hearts full of joy; so full, as it even brake forth, and ran over, over into the countenance, *os risu;* over into the tongue, *lingua jubilo.* The face is a mirror, to shew how the mind is affected: the tongue a trumpet, to sound out the secrets of the heart. You might see their joy in their face, as in a mirror: you might hear it from their tongue, as from a trumpet. A sign it was, the fountain was full, when both the cisterns thus run over.

And true withal.

But, what is it for a dream to be pleasant, if it be not true withal? Nay; there is no more miserable case, than of him that dreameth the pleasant ivory dream, and when he awaketh finds it nothing so: dreams he is at a feast, and waketh all hungry; dreams he is rich, and waking, finds nothing in his hands. This was not such; it was *per corneam portam,* a true one; not to be let go for a dream, for it proved more than a dream, a real thing indeed. For when they came out of their dream, all the country about rang of it, *Tum dicebant, &c.*

[Isa.29.8.]

[Virg. Æn. 6. 895.]

And there can be no better way to come to a true judgment of what befalleth us, than by *Dicebant,* what other men say of it. Men are commonly over-sensible of their own joy: a truer estimate would be taken from them, that are no parties to it. Best hear what they say.

Especially, if it be not only *Dicebant inter homines,* but *inter gentes* too; if they be not single men, but whole nations. Their *Dicebant* is yet a degree further. For, many a deliverance there is, the world never talks of, and yet great for all that; but those, that fill the eyes and the mouths of whole nations, must needs be *primæ magnitudinis:* and so was this then. Notice was taken of this by those *inter gentes,* and no other talk, for the time, but of it. This sheweth, it might well be as strange as a dream, but was no dream indeed.

The heathen were either strangers, and regarded them not; or enemies, and maligned them. No fear, that such (especially, the latter sort) should dream too. No; envy

sleeps not. And waking and seeing it; no fear they will be
partial and confess more than truth. Commonly, their nature is to abate, diminish, extenuate: no fear of amplifying
at their hands. If they say, it is great, it is great indeed.
And here, both strangers and enemies confess it; therefore,
we may be sure, it was no vulgar or ordinary turning.

And truly, great reason they had so to say. It could be
no policy, they saw, for Cyrus to send them back. He had
them now safe, and well broken to service, by seventy years'
continuance. They might prove slippery, and revolt; and
so he repent his sending them home. Besides, he sent none
back, of all the rest of his captives; being yet of his own
religion, which these were not. They saw, then, no reason
for it in the world. Then, to let them go; and in such sort
to let them go; with so ample a commission; with so rich
rewards, to build again: this, when it came to their notice,
it made them muse, it found them talk; it even drew from
them this *Dicebant*.

"Then said they of the heathen." And, what is it they
said? It is to the purpose. In this, as in many other, the
heathen's saying cannot be mended. This they say: 1. that
they were no quotidian, or common things, but "great."
2. Then, these great things they ascribe not to chance; that
they happened not, but were "done." 3. Then, done by
"God" Himself: they see God in them. 4. Then, not done
by God at random, without any particular aim; but, purposely done for them. 5. And yet, there is more in *magnificavit facere* (if we look well). For, *magna fecit* would have
served all this; but in saying *magnificavit facere*, they say
magni fecit illos, ut magna faceret pro illis, 'He magnified
them, or set greatly by them, for whom He would bring
to pass so great a work.' This "said they among the
heathen."

And it is pity, the heathen said it, and that the Jews
themselves spake not these words, first. But, they were
so ravished with joy at the first, as they were to be borne
with. But now, finding the heathen so saying; and finding,
it was all but true, they said; they must needs find themselves bound to say at least so much (and more they could
not; for more cannot be said). So much then, and no less

2. So me-
morable, as
the hea-
then talked
of it.

Ps. 126. 2.
The sound
"among
the hea-
then."

SERM.
II.

than they. And this addeth a degree to the *Dicebant.*
That the sound of it was so great " among the heathen," as
it made an echo even in Jewry itself.

Ps. 126. 3.
The echo
of it in
Israel.

That echo then followeth in the third verse : the person
only changed, *nobiscum* for *cum illis :* there is all. And indeed, Sion should have been much to blame, if the heathen
should see those things for great, and God to be the doer of
them ; and Sion should not discern them for such : if the
heathen should say *Magnificavit Dominus facere,* and Sion
should not magnify Him for this so magnificent a work ; if
this confession should even be wrung from the heathen, and
should not come voluntary from the children of Sion, whom
it more nearly concerned a great deal.

But what, shall there be no difference between Sion's and
the heathen's *Dicebant,* but only *nobiscum ?* Yes : for though
the words be the same, there may be odds in the uttering.
God forbid, but Sion should say, in another manner key, at
the least.

The con-
clusion
*Facti
sumus læ-
tantes.*

And yet, there is some amends for Sion : the words are
not all out the same. Here is a *hemistichium* more in Sion's ;
in which they plainly express the odds between their affections and the heathen's. This it is. *Facti sumus lætantes :*
that is, the heathen say it ; but, rather wondering, than rejoicing at it. They say it, because they cannot choose but
say it, it is so evident ; but they bite the lip, when they
have done ; they could have been well content to have spared
the speech ; well content that God had not done it, that
they might not have said it. In a word : they say it without a *lætantes ;* but, Sion saith it joying, and joyeth in saying it : saith it, and in saying it, say at the end of it, *Facti
sumus lætantes.* And this, here, is true joy, grounded upon
the due consideration of the matter, by occasion of the
heathen's speech. The other, before, was like the laughing
in a dream. But this, true joy ; and, in sign thereof, it was
at the first but *Facti sumus sicut somniantes ;* but here it is
Facti sumus, not *sicut,* but *vere lætantes,* 'truly joyful' indeed. And this maketh up the Hallelujah.

Ps. 126. 4.
II.
Their
Hosanna.

Their Hallelujah thus performed, they come to their
Hosanna straight. And why so straight ? They were *sicut
somniantes ;* so they say : and dreams, we know, have this

quality, they are but short. And they were *facti lætantes;*
and joy commonly is of the same nature, lasteth not much
longer than a dream, but vanisheth quickly, "as a dream Ps. 73. 20.
when one awaketh." Dreams and joys, as soon had, so soon
lost. That therefore their *lætantes* prove not *sicut somniantes;*
to keep their joy waking, this they think their wisest way :
no sooner to make an end of Hallelujah, but straight to begin
their Hosanna; make the next verse to their thanks for *In
Convertendo,* a petition, *Converte.* And that to Him, That
granted that; to grant this. *In convertendo Dominus, Converte Domine :* that is, Hosanna to Him in the highest.

    Converte Domine : Why how now? But very now, they 1. They
praised Him for turning it away, and do they now pray Him pray to
"turn" it.
to "turn" it away? How hangs this together : to pray to
have that turned, that is turned already? They may seem
to be scarce yet out of their dream. Not so : these two *converte*s and these two captivities are not all one. St. Augustine saith well, (upon *solutis doloribus inferni,* Acts the se- Acts 2. 24.
cond chapter,) that two manner of ways, a thing is loosed :
1. either, after we are already snared : 2. or else beforehand, [S. Aug.
that we be not snared with it at all. Christ loosed those Epist. 164.
3.]
sorrows, this latter way, which is far the better way of the
twain. And even so, two ways is a captivity (or any mischief else) turned away : 1. by an after-delivery, when it is
come; 2. or by a fore-hand prevention, ere it do come.
The Grecians express it by *Prometheus* and *Epimetheus ;* the
Latins by *Antevorta* and *Postvorta ;* the schoolmen by *præ-
veniendo* and *subveniendo :* but prevention is ever the better.
Better a good buckler, to keep off the blow; than a good
plaster, to heal the hurt of it. Better never see Babel, than
return from it. "The captivity" of the first verse was come,
and is now come and gone : who knoweth whether there be
any other to come? If there be, *Converte Domine,* "Turn it
away" beforehand; take order there never come any more.
So, it is plain, for all the former *In convertendo,* they may
well pray this last too, notwithstanding. They may well
pray it; and good reason they have to pray it. "The Ps. 137. 7.
children of Edom," and the rest of their evil neighbours,
that shewed their good will in this "captivity" past, are the
same men still; still carry the same minds. No year, no

SERM.
II.

day goeth over their heads, but they wish and contrive, to bring another, either "captivity," or some mischief else, I know not what. Therefore *Converte Domine* is no more than needs.

2. The manner of turning it.

Now, as *Converte Domine* is what they wish done; *sicut torrentes* is the manner how they wish it done. "Turn" it, and so "turn" it, "as the streams in the South:" by "the South," understanding the south climate, on which side lay *Arabia Deserta*. All, southward from them, was nothing but a dry and waste wilderness. It is of the nature of a wilderness to be without water. And what streams are

Ps. 107.35.

there then in the wilderness? None, but such as they call land waters. And how are they turned or brought thither? No other way, than by melting the snow on the great high hills there, which being dissolved by the summer sun, come down so plentifully, that all the pools are filled with water, so strongly, that they turn the course of mighty rivers. Their meaning then is: 1. they have as great need of delivery, as the south climate hath of water. 2. Captivity is as congealed snow, and they frozen fast in it, that they cannot stir. 3. They would have it turned, but by no violent way, but even only by thawing and melting the hearts of Princes, (Cyrus and the rest,) set against them (whose hearts Solomon

Prov. 21.1.

compareth to these "streams") by that, rather than by any other way. 4. That never was water-stream more welcome to the wayfaring man in the wilderness, than this shall be to them. For we read of two manner of turnings they had.

Ps. 136.11.
Ps. 114. 3.
Ps.136.15, 19, 20.
Ezra 1. 1.
2 Chron.
36. 22.

1. One out of Egypt, in violent and tempestuous manner: "The sea fled, Jordan was driven back:" Pharaoh was drowned; Sihon and Og slain; very great ado there was. 2. And now this, out of Babylon; neither by an army, nor by main strength, but by My Spirit, saith the Lord, breathing upon Cyrus, and in mild and gentle manner melting his heart: and there was all. A conversion, not as that of Pharaoh, but as this of Cyrus: not, as the rivers of the north, but "as the streams in the south," is it they pray for. So pray they, and so will all pray that are well advised. Thus far their Hosanna.

The application
Our Hallelujah.

Now to alter the property of all this, and to convert it to our own use: and to shew first, that both this Hallelujah,

and then, that this Hosanna will no less agree to us, and
our choir, (if not more; but certainly more); a review must
needs be granted of all the former points. And, in them,
there is no remedy, but we must fall to measuring, that
it may appear there is great odds, between this of ours, and
that of theirs. Consequently, that we are bound to give
thanks with another manner of Hallelujah, than ever did
they. And that, whether we look to that which was turned
away; ours was worse: to the manner of turning itself;
ours was better: to the means of this turning; ours to be
preferred ; to the likeness of a dream, to the *Dicebant inter
gentes,* to the *Facti sumus lætantes :* in all and every point,
we are still beyond them.

That which was turned away, in them, was a " captivity"
for term of years ; in us, was an utter desolation : as much
odds between them, as lying in prison and flying in pieces.
" Captivity," as we see by this, is *vox convertibilis,* hath
hope to turn again ; utter desolation being incapable of
In convertendo, past all hope or possibility of ever returning more.

Our turn-
ing and
delivery,
greater
far.

1.
For that
which was
turned
away.

And what manner of desolation? For we may find captivities to match theirs : for a people to be carried away
captive, is no new thing upon earth. But this desolation of
ours puts down all that ever were. What should I say, but
as the Apostle of that which passeth the speech of all
speakers, *Oculus non vidit, &c.* The like never was seen,
heard, "nor entered into the heart of man."

1 Cor. 2. 9.

And our turning, therefore, the better : and not only
therefore; but in itself, simply. Two turnings we said there
were : 1. by prevention, ere it come; and 2. subvention,
after it is come ; and prevention the better : and that was
ours. Theirs was by *Postvorta ;* light upon them first.
Ours came not at us at all; and yet, very near us it came,
as near as could be, not to hurt us; and even then, away it
was turned. So much the better, should I think, we will
reckon of it. That the blow, or blowing up was turned, and
we not hurt ; rather than we hurt, and lie long on the
chirurgeon's hand, and at last be cured. That of theirs lay
heavy upon them for a long time, ere it was turned away ;
seventy years full. Ours was turned, in the turning of

2.
For the
manner of
turning.

SERM.
II.

a hand. And we know, it is a doubling of the pleasure, to do it at once.

As in the manner, so in the means of this turning, we pass them far. In that of theirs, the immediate cause of their 'turning, under God, was the turning of Cyrus the King's heart, which God hath in His hand, and "turneth as the streams of water." And was not ours so too? And yet still, after a more excellent manner. Theirs, a heathen; ours, a Christian Prince: theirs, a stranger; ours, our own. To the strange turning of whose heart, to turn the letter into a strange construction, next to God Himself, we may all truly ascribe our destruction then turned away. This for the 1. turning, the 2. manner, and 3. means of it.

Now at the time of this turning, if they were *sicut somni- antes*, we were more. 1. They were delivered by a procla- mation. Proclamations, we know, come not forth, till it be well on of the day, when the streets are well filled with people to hear them; but never early in the morning. But, the news of ours came betimes, when a great part of us were not out of our beds, and scarce well awake: so, it might be affirmed of us literally, we were then in good earnest *sicut somniantes*.

2. St. Peter was awake, broad awake, when the Angel made his chains fall off: he clothed himself, shod himself, girt himself, went through three gates one after another, and after that, through a whole street; yet that that happened was so exceeding strange to him, that all this while, he

thought he was but in a dream. Our case was St. Peter's, for all the world; we were truly delivered, and yet many of us got up, and were fully ready, ere we could get ourselves ready to believe, but that we did still *visum videre : sicut somniantes, et ecce vigilantes.*

3. They had sense of their "captivity," their mind ran on it; the more their mind ran on it, the more like to dream of it. We had not so much: it was the further end of our thought, and therefore more like a dream, more unlooked for.

4. They were not fast asleep, they did somewhat toward their delivery; with long, often, and earnest prayer, they did solicit God; they and their prophets for them. We prayed

not, we knew no cause to pray : nothing at all did we to it
or toward it ; it ran into our nets, while we were on sleep.

Shall I say any thing of the joy of the dream ? This **5.**
I may ; that we pass them in that. They were in a strange For the joy of the
country ; they must look more demurely, they must speak dream.
more sparingly. We were in our own, we might do it the
more freely, both in countenance and speech. And for the
time, so we did.

And, will ye now see, we pass them in *Dicebant.* Theirs **6.**
was *Dicebant;* but of ours, not only *Dicebant*, but *Scribebant* For *Dicebant.*
and *excudebant,* ' said it, wrote it, and printed it.' And what,
as this here, *Magna ?* Nay, *Magna, et a sæculo inaudita;* such,
so great, as the like was never heard before.

This for *Dicebant.* And for *inter gentes,* we pass them **7.**
there. For, who talked of theirs ? a handful of nations, in For *inter gentes.*
comparison ; but those that bordered about. They in effect
say as much : not *gentes,* not all ; but *inter gentes,* some
among them. A small part of the world, compared to ours :
more tongues a great deal went to our *Dicebant.* I may
safely say, *Quæ regio in terris,* ' What land is there' whither [Virg. Æn.
the fame of it is not gone, where it is not spoken of ? and 1. 464.]
we, by means of it, renowned and made famous over all the
earth, even to Turks and Infidels : for thither also it is come,
how God hath dealt with us. Yea, even our very enemies
themselves, I doubt not, when it was told in Gath, and published in the streets of Askelon ; even in Rome itself, even
they in the conclave, even the Pope himself, helped to make
up this *Dicebant ;* though not aloud, that their voice might
be heard in the streets, yet among themselves, in private,
were forced to say as much : that the greatness of ours received witness from the mouth of our enemies.

Our *Dicebant* is double to theirs then, and so is our *Facti* **8.**
sumus lætantes. There is, as a joy for our own delivery ; so For *Facti sumus læ-*
likewise another joy, for the fall of our enemies : they had *tantes.*
the former only ; we, both former and latter. For, in theirs,
they to whom they had been captives let them go, and there
was all ; and they were glad of it ; but they of Babylon
became not captives to Sion. But in ours, not only the
captivity was turned away ; but we "led captivity captive," [Ps. 68.
which is the greatest joy of all. They that meant ours, 18.]

instead of ours, found their own; were taken in their own turn, became captives themselves; and as they intended, our members should, so theirs now rent, and stretched one from the other. So, in every point, they fall short of us; and we, in all and every, are still beyond them.

And now let me a little stay, and say as much for ourselves, as for the Jews. If we shall but enter into our own hearts for a moment, we cannot but think thus: What, doth this our deliverance draw thus much, even from other nations, that are our enemies? Why then, belike, it must be some extraordinary great one. Why, methinks, it toucheth not them, this; it toucheth us: it is we that were delivered, and not they; and shall they say all this of us, and shall not we say as much of ourselves? Shall we come behind them, or rather, shall we not come behind them, since they are got before in this *Dicebant?* The words we cannot mend, they are so full. "Great" were the things, and very great: they chanced not; they were "done;" done by "God," He was the doer; He the doer of these great things, and we the people, for whom these great things were done: and so, a people highly magnified by Him in His mercy; and so, a people deeply bound to magnify Him for all His mercies; but for this, above all, that all the world speaks of.

And though we cannot, with other words than they; yet can, and will, I trust, with far other affections. God forbid, but *facere nobiscum* should be sounded in a higher key than *facere cum illis.* In dangers, I am sure, it is; never any men's dangers touch us as our own; never they from the shore cry so heartily, Lord save them, that they see in danger of drowning upon the sea, as they in the ship, themselves cry, "Lord save us." God forbid, but we that felt it should take up our Hallelujah in a higher strain than they that were but lookers-on; heard of it, and spake of it, but were not partakers as we were of it.

[Mat. 8.
25.]

Let this be the difference: that we say the same that they say; but they say, *Magnificavit Dominus facere cum illis,* and *facti sunt gementes;* and we, *Magnificavit Dominus facere nobiscum, et facti sumus lætantes.*

And since our case doth so many ways surpass this of the Jews, in all the points along, our Hallelujah must needs do so too. It is but reason I will require. Theirs, here, went no further than their "mouth" and their "tongue," *os et lingua :* more they mention not. But, in a certain place, the Psalmist, when he would express a far greater joy, thus he saith, "All my bones shall say, Lord who is like Thee?" Ps. 35. 10. This I think reason, that seeing our "bones" should have Ps. 141. 7. been "scattered" in every corner, like as chips, "when one heweth wood on the earth" (should have but were not); not only our "mouth" and "tongue," as theirs; but our very "bones should say," Hallelujah, "Lord who is like Thee," Who hast rid us from a danger, the like whereof never was? I add further: that if we and our "bones" would hold our Lu. 19. 40. peace, "the stones should cry it." For, timber-work, and stone-work, and all had flown in pieces, we know, then; even, as Habakkuk speaketh, "that the beam out of the timber- Habak. work, and the stone out of the wall, may cry one to another;" 2. 11. the beam to the stone, Hallelujah; and the stone to the beam again, Hallelujah, to Him, That hath kept them fast, and not made Jerusalem as a heap of stones. Even they, to cry : every bone to have a tongue; and every stone and beam to have a tongue, to put down theirs, and to make our *Dicebant,* our Hallelujah, our *Magnificavit* the louder.

And now, shall we stay here, and end with Hallelujah, Our and cut off Hosanna quite? I dare not: I seldom see Hal- Hosanna. lelujah hold long, if Hosanna forsake it, and second it not. For I ask, What, are they all dead, that sought our lives? Say, they are; is the devil dead too? If he be not, it skills not, if they were. His powder-mill will still be going; he will still be as busy as ever, in turning over all his devices, in turning himself into as many shapes as Proteus, and all to turn us to some mischief. The more it concerns us, not to be too long at our Hallelujah; but, when we have done it, before we stir, to take up our Hosanna; not to forget it in any wise. After we have praised Him for *In convertendo,* that so it is; to return to our *Converte Domine,* that so it may long be. The wheel will stand, it will not turn on still, without it.

Then, in the person of humble suppliants cry we all, Hosanna to the Highest, and *Converte Domine,* to Him, That Ezek.1.15, is Lord of Ezekiel's "wheels," and of all their conversions. 16.

The rather, for that there is no one design hath more laid open, and let us see the defects and weakness of all human wisdom and watchfulness than this. There wanted neither, but it went beyond both. No, nor any design hath let us see, how dangerous and undiscoverable plots the devil is able to possess his limbs withal. All to let us see, what need we have to turn to Him with our *Converte,* That can see what they do at midnight, in the vault, as well as what is done at noonday, on the house-top: can see, and discover; discover it, and turn it away. That He would, as many as are coming this way, turn them all away.

And turn them all away, by the way of prevention; not suffering them to light on us, as theirs did, and then after remove it; but averting it, before it come; lest after, it be too late.

And, (that we forget not *sicut,*) that He turn it by such, and no other means, than the "streams in the south;" that is, with no great ado: not, in boisterous or rigorous means, as that of Egypt; but in mild and calm manner, as this of Babel, and as our own. By the same means still; even by the turning of the heart, which is in His hands; which, as the "streams in the south," He now did turn; and so still and ever may. That, from that fountain, still may flow the streams that may give us refreshing in time of our need. That, if it be His blessed will, that may ever be the *sicut,* as now it was.

And now, "Turn our captivity O Lord," past and to come; turn both; that, as the "streams of the south," they may melt, fall away, and come to nothing; that our future dangers may still be *sicut somnia,* ever 'as dreams,' but never visions; that, as we have been now matter of praise to the nations, for our former delivery, so we never become a by-word to them, for any after calamity; but that our conclusion Joh. 16.22. may be ever *Facti sumus lætantes,* still in joy, and this joy may never be taken from us; that we still may laud and magnify Thy glorious Name, evermore praising Thee and saying, *Magnificetur Dominus.* The Lord hath magnified His power and goodness toward us this day, for which His holy Name be magnified this day, and for ever!

A SERMON

PREACHED BEFORE

THE KING'S MAJESTY AT WHITEHALL,

ON THE FIFTH OF NOVEMBER, A.D. MDCIX.

LUKE ix. 54—56.

And when His disciples James and John saw it, they said, Lord, wilt Thou that we command that fire come down from Heaven, and consume them, even as Elias did?

But Jesus turned about and rebuked them, and said, Ye know not of what spirit ye are.

For the Son of man is not come to destroy men's lives, but to save them.

[*Cum vidissent autem discipuli Ejus Jacobus et Joannes, dixerunt, Domine, vis, dicimus, ut ignis descendat de Cœlo, et consumat illos? Et conversus increpavit illos, dicens, Nescitis cujus spiritûs estis. Filius hominis non venit animas perdere, sed salvare. Lat. Vulg.*]

[*And when His disciples James and John saw this, they said, Lord, wilt Thou that we command fire to come down from Heaven, and consume them, even as Elias did?*

But He turned, and rebuked them, and said, Ye know not what manner of spirit ye are of.

For the Son of man is not come to destroy men's lives, but to save them. Eng. Trans.]

WE have here, in this text, a whole town of Samaria in danger of being destroyed; of being destroyed by fire: and they escaped it narrowly: so near it was, there lacked but *dicimus*, a word speaking. Of the disciples, some were very forward in the motion; but Christ "rebuked them;" and the end was, the town was saved. And was not this, under the terms of James and John, and a town of Samaria, our very case, this day four year? We were then in danger of destroying, and destroying by the same element fire; and so near it we were, it would have been done as soon as a letter burnt. There were then, that forwarded these fireworks, with their *dicimus*, all they could : and they said, they were disciples of Jesus's society. But Jesus shewed Himself to be, in Heaven, of the same mind He was on earth. And as He was then better to this town, than His disciples; so, to us He was better than the fathers of His society, and rebuked them too: and blessed be God, as the text ends, so did the matter; in *non perdere, sed salvare :* none destroyed, all saved.

Finding here these words *non perdere* in the text, which amount to as much as *Ne perdas,* it brings to my mind, that [1 Sam. 26. 9.] this text will second well David's *Ne perdas.* As, when time was, we had David's *Ne perdas,* to save a King ; so, here we have now the Son of David's (Christ's) *Ne perdas,* to save (a town in the text; but with us,) an assembly more worth than Samaria, and all the towns in it.

This *Ne perdas* of Christ, beside the Sabbath itself, is to Lu. 6. 1. us, this day, matter of a second Sabbath ; and so, this (like that in the Gospel) δευτερόπρωτον, " a second besides the [*The 5th Nov.* 1609 *O. S. was a Sunday.*] first," two Sabbaths in one ; wherein the voice of praise and thanksgiving is here, and is all over the land, for the happy *non perdere, sed salvare* of this day.

The sum. The whole text is a question upon a case : the case, this. Christ was journeying from Galilee to Jerusalem. Being in that country upon His way, He sent to this town, to take up lodging : no lodging would be had ; a general restraint ; no Lu. 9. 53. man to receive Him : the quarrel, " because His face was toward Jerusalem ;" would not worship with them, in their mount. Upon this case, this question : Whether this town, for not receiving Christ, upon pretence He was not of their religion, might not be consumed ? Or make the case, if you will, blown up with fire. Some little difference there is, and but little. *Vis, dicimus descendat,* say they ; *Vis, facimus ascendat,* say ours : *descendat* or *ascendat,* both end in *consumat eos,* destruction of them and us. In this question, we shall divide Christ and His company. For of them, two here named were ready to do it, and therefore resolve, it might be done. But Christ ruleth the case, for the town, that it ought not to be done; no, not for this quarrel, *Non receperunt Eum;* no, not upon these parties, Samaritans; no, not by that means done, by miracle.

It was an error this of the disciples; we see it plain by *Nescitis:* but of it may well be said, that Gregory saith of another of theirs, *O salutaris error, qui totius mundi sustulit errorem!* ' A blessed error it was; for by it the world was rid of the like error, ever after.' Rid of the error of this day: what Christ answered in this case, He would have answered in ours, *a fortiori;* if not a poor town, not such an assembly. If not by a supernatural and miraculous; not, by an unnatural and monstrous act. If not for Himself; not for St. Peter. So that, this day's case determined here by Christ, before ever it was propounded; and determined quite contrary by Jesus, to His disciples, then; or to His society, of late. We are all much bound to St. Luke, for recording it, or to the Holy Ghost rather, for inspiring him so to do. For so long as this verse shall stand in this Gospel, it will serve for a resolution to this question: whether, upon pretence of religion, Christ will allow the Jew should blow up the Samaritan? Upon *Non receperunt eos,* any of His disciples may do that, which they here would have done? This rebuke here of these will reach to all undertakers in the same kind. This *non perdere sed salvare* saves all our towns, cities, and states, from consuming by fire, from any of Christ's company.

To pass then to the entreaty. In the former verse, there is a motive, and a motion. I. The motive in these: "And when His disciples, James and John, saw this." II. The motion in these: "They said, Lord, wilt Thou that we" &c. Somewhat they saw, to move them: and what tley saw is in the verse before, *Non receperunt Eum:* Christ's suffering repulse; and for no other cause, but because " His face was to Jerusalemward:" that is, were not affected, as they were, in religion. II. The motion: 1. to have the town destroyed for it; 2. destroyed by fire; 3. by fire from Heaven; 4. from Heaven only by *dicimus,* speaking a word only; and 5. th upon warrant, *sicut fecit Elias,* Elias's example.

The division.
I.

Lu. 9. 53.

II.

In the latter, Christ's censure. First, He giveth no leave nor liking any way to the motion. 1. *Magister, vis, dicimus,* say they; *sed, Magister non vult dicere.* 2. So far from that, as He rebukes them that moved it. The rebuke of the movers is a dislike of the motion. 3. Rebukes them not, for some one point or circumstance in it, but even for the whole, for moving to Him any such thing. 4. Nay, He goeth further: likes not the motion; nor likes not the spring it comes from. 5. In His rebuke, tells them, *Nescitis,* they are much mistaken: mistaken themselves, and mistake Him both. Themselves, to move any such matter; Him, to move it to Him: it being neither meet for them, to move; nor Him, to grant. Them, to move: for they were "of another spirit," if they could hit on it. Him, to grant: for He came to another end, than either to hear or yield to motions of that nature: tells them they are not of Elias's spirit, but of His, if they be His disciples; and so, must come as He came, *non perdere sed salvare.*

But, because we come not now to learn only, but to give thanks, as the duty of the day requireth; after this, we will lay the two cases together, case by case; this of the day, to this in the text: by which it will easily appear, I doubt not, that we have as great cause every way, of joy, and thanksgiving; nay, of the twain, the greater, for the happy *Ne perdas,* Christ's *Ne perdas,* of this day.

Or ere we come to the motion, let us begin with that, that was the beginning of all this quarrel; that is, dissent in religion, between the Samaritan and the Jew. We see the fruit of it here, and what spirit it maketh men of. On the one side, Be they Jews, go they to Jerusalem? let them have neither meat, drink, nor lodging; that is to say, starve them. On the other, Be they Samaritans, sectaries? pity of their lives; put fire to them, burn them, blow them up. Mutual and mortal hatred breaking forth, upon every occasion. The woman of Samaria expresseth it by *Non co-utuntur,* "They use not," one side the other. She might even as well have said, *Co-abutuntur,* 'they abuse each the other:' so they do; forgetting humanity and divinity too, on either part. Here is the fruit: this, the spirit it breedeth. And these two, the Samaritan and the Jew, they made not an end of this, till it made an end of them. Look in Josephus, you shall see in [Vid. F. Joseph. Ant. Jud. 20. 5.] the days of Claudius (Cumanus then deputy) the very like quarrel to this here upon the very same occasion, taken wholly by the Zelotæ, and pursued hard, opened the way to the Jews' wars, which never ended, till the utter rooting out and desolation of them both. Thus it was; and thus it will be: and by this we see, how necessary Christ's *Pax vobis* is; and the Joh. 20. 26. Mat. 5. 9. peace-maker, that could make the peace, how blessed he should be! blessed here, and blessed everlastingly.

But, let me tell you this withal: this spirit was not then in all; neither all the disciples, nor all the Samaritans. Some there were, on both sides, more moderately affected. The disciples, I doubt not, did all of them (the other ten too) much dislike this discourse offered Christ; yet, all cried not for fire: two only, these two only of the twelve. On the other side; the Samaritans neither, all were not thus inhuman. Though this town received Him not, it is said, in the last verse, they went to "another town," and there He Lu. 9. 56. was received. So all, neither all the disciples, thus spirited: not all "the sons of thunder;" some the sons of rain, as Bar- Mark 3.17. tholomew is interpreted: nor all the country of Samaria; God provided better for both. All had gone to a general combustion, if all had been of this destructive spirit: and all did go, when those spirits gat the upper hand.

And for their comfort, that are such, this: that our Saviour Christ was none of the Zelotæ, but shewed Himself on that side, that inclined to humanity and peace. There was no fault in Him. It was still His desire *co-uti Samaritanis*, to use, and be used by them. He would have had water, and asked it of the "woman of Samaria:" sent His disciples to Joh. 4. 7,8. that town there "to buy meat;" and now, to this town here, to take up lodging: shewed Himself still willing to break down this partition-wall. In this very journey, after this repulse here, yet He healed (among others) a leper, yea though Lu. 17. 16. "a Samaritan." Yea so favourable that way He was, and so ready to be used, as He was counted and called "a Samari- Joh. 8. 48. tan" for His labour. Well then, let this town, and these two disciples please themselves in their consuming zeal: that other town, in the last verse, and the other ten were in the right. Christ was in the right, I am sure: and it is safe for

us, that "the same mind be in us, that was in Christ Jesus."
And so now to the motion; but first, to the motive, "And
when they saw," &c.

Let me say this, for St. James and St. John: they saw
enough, to move any to indignation. A great indignity it is,
that, which is done by common courtesy, to every ordinary
traveller, (harbour for a night,) to deny that to any. *Omni
animantium generi pabulum et latibulum,* 'Fodder and shelter,
they are due to all living creatures' by the law of nature.

Lu. 9. 58. Within a verse after, Christ saith, *Vulpes foveas habent, &c.*
Not to allow a man so much as every fox is allowed, a hole
for his head; a very great inhumanity to any: who could
choose but be moved?

2. And if to deny this to any were too much; it received
increase by the Person. It was Christ, That was thus re-
pelled: of whose well-using, it stood them upon, to be jea-
lous; and not to shew themselves cold, in putting up any
disgrace offered to their Master. We must needs allow their
zeal, in their Master's quarrel.

3. And when was this? For that circumstance adds much
here. It was even then, when He was newly come down
from the mount, from His transfiguration: immediately upon
that, came this. Him, Whom a little before they had seen
glorified from Heaven; to see Him now thus vilified upon
earth, would it not move any?

4. And who were they that did it? A pelting¹ country-
town; and they in it a sort of Samaritan-heretics, whom the
world were rid of; at whose hands, who could endure to see
Him thus used? Coming from hatred of heresy, how can it
choose but be a good motion?

5. And now, why was it, they did Him this disgrace? For
no other cause, but for His religion: because His back was
to their mount, and " His face to Jerusalem." And here, zeal
is in his prime: never so plausible, as when it hath gotten
religion for his pretence, and the Catholic cause for his colour
then they may set fire on the town. Put these now together:
1. A barbarous indignity, harbour for a night denied; and
2. denied Christ; 3. Christ so late in all His glory; 4. and
that, by a sort of heretics; 5. and only, for that He was well-
affected in religion. The case is home: when they saw this,

it moved them to make a motion. Never talk of it: the
motion cannot be misliked; specially coming commended by
the movers, "two of His disciples," and none of the meanest
of them; two "pillars" (as St. Paul calleth them); and he Gal. 2. 9.
whom "Jesus so loved," one of the two. Joh. 21. 7.

We see what moved them. Now let us see what they II.
move, and upon what warrant. They move to have them motion.
destroyed by " fire from Heaven." Their warrant, *sicut fecit* [1.]
Elias; whom they had seen a little before in the mount, and
who, they are sure, would never have endured it.

In their motion, methinks, two things they take for granted: 1. one, that destroyed they must be; no less punishment serve; 2. the other, that it should be by "fire." They
make no question of these two, nor so much as consult with
Christ of them: 1. whether it be meet they were destroyed;
2. then, whether fire were not a fit kind of death for such.
They run away with these two, and pass sentence upon them.
Die they must; die they must: and then limit the kind; being heretics, best even burn them and make no more ado.

They only advise with Christ about the means, whence
they will have their fire, and how. Whence, from Heaven:
how, by *dicimus*. And hitherto, the case like. Both, to be
destroyed; both, by fire; both, upon one pretence, they and
we. Now, they break company, Jesus's disciples and Jesus's
society. For when it comes to the means, Jesus's disciples
will take no indirect course: do it like disciples, or not at all.
They will go to work on God's name, call it down, not conjure it up; from Heaven, His own sphere; not from any infernal place, not rent the earth to bring it up. St. John, as
an eagle, flies up to the clouds; not, like a molewarp, creeps
into a vault to do it. *De cœlo* do it, like prophets; not, like
incendiaries, fetch fire the wrong way.

The like may be said of *dicimus:* not from Heaven, by
any optic instrument (as some had, before that time, fired
whole navies); no, but only by *dicimus,* saying the word and
no more. No powder, but from the clouds; no match, but
their tongue; no *vis fodimus,* no pickaxes to dig, nor boats
to carry, nor trains to kindle it; but, *vis dicimus,* by way
of miracle, or not at all. This, the motion. Now, to the
warrant.

A good warrant will do well. Christ, without it, they know, likes of nothing done. The *quo warranto* (to win Christ to be willing, to obtain His fiat) they allege, one would think a good one: 1. *sicut fecit;* so no novelty; a precedent for it; 2. and *sicut fecit* (no less Prophet than) Elias. They had seen him but lately; they did the more easily call him to mind. Moses they saw then too; but they could not serve themselves of him. He was taken out of the water; no good *sicut* for them, that were about fireworks. And he was the "meekest man" on earth: and it was no meek matter; and so he no meet man, for the purpose they were about. Elias is Scripture as well as he: the authority of so great a Prophet is enough, to do no more than he did, upon like occasion. Nay, not like; here, the occasion is greater; behold *plusquam Elias,* 'a greater than Elias' suffereth disgrace here; and therefore *sicut Elias* is but reasonable. And here again, our motioners will fall short too. For if the motion to Christ had been *vis fodimus?* whom would they have alleged, whose example or authority, *sicut fecit?* Who, who ever did the like? Which of the prophets or patriarchs? Their motion must have been without a *sicut fecit.*

For the matter, all is one, saith Sanders, all one. Elias, when he commanded fire from Heaven, might even as well have commanded any on earth: run upon them, run them through; had as great power over the metals on earth, as over the elements in the sky. And it is like enough, if Sanders had lived till Anno Domini MDCV., and had been consulted with, he would have said straight, All one, Elias might as well have bid put fire under the town, from beneath, as let fire fall on the town, from above. But, by his leave, there is great odds between these. For first, Elias must do, as his commission was to do it, from Heaven: he might not interline his commission, and put in, 'By metals, or gunpowder,' or what he listed. And again: who sees not, that Elias's fire and Sampson's foxes are not all one? God's "arrows," as lightning from Heaven, and these *tela ignita Satanæ,* Satan's trains and fireworks from under the ground. In one, the hand of God must needs be; in the other, the paw of the devil, the malice of man, the fury or treachery of forlorn creatures may have no place. No such authority, no such fear to touch the conscience, as the act of God hath; therefore, that is not *sicut Elias.* And lastly, if it were, yet is nothing gained by it; Christ repeals it by and by; and forbids, in this, either the act or spirit of Elias.

But now, they that say thus (not *Magister dicito tu,* but), *Magister vis dicimus nos,* feel in themselves, belike, no lack of strength. The cardinal cannot say of them, *Id non fuit, quia deerant vires,* 'That was not done, because there wanted force.' So that, if after, they lost any of their due, it was not, because they lacked power to maintain it. St. Paul denieth it flatly : "Having," saith he, "in a readiness," vengeance "against all disobedience." Had it; had it, "in a readiness;" and "against all disobedience." And sure, they that could thus do, call fire from Heaven, strike Elymas blind, strike Ananias stark dead in an instant, need not lose their interest, which they had forsooth in this same temporal dominion, for lack of strength. Now, it is well known, it was the case here in the text : *Discipulus potuit, sed Magister noluit.* It was for want of *vis,* this in the text; *vis* of *volo,* of will in Christ; not for want of *vis* or *vires,* power in them. It went not by *vires aderant vel deerant;* it went by *Magister vis;* Christ's will was wanting, and nothing else. That was their case, here: who therefore, (because two things go to the act, 1. their power, and 2. Christ's will,) howsoever they felt their own power, and themselves able to do it, yet would not do it, on their own heads, without His privity or leave : and so now they ask it, *Magister, vis dicimus.* By which very manner of propounding it in this confident style, it seemeth, little doubt they made to carry it clear; made full reckoning of Christ's *Volo,* and that He would be moved with their motion.

And with their motion He was moved; for, it is said, He "turned" with it; but, it was the wrong way. At the turning, it may be thought, they looked for some good turn; that Christ should have commended them, and said, I con [1] you thanks, I see you have care of my credit; you are even worthy, for it, to sit "one on my right hand, the other on my left," for shewing yourselves my champions: your motion is good; forward with it.

But, it falls out, His turning is the wrong way : He turned

2 Cor. 10. 6.

Acts 13. 11.
Acts 5. 5.

III.
Christ's censure and rebuke of them.
[1 To *con* *thanks* is to thank ; the same as *savoir gré* in French, and εἰδέναι χάριν in Greek.]
[Mark 10. 37, 40.]

SERM. on the left side, to rebuke them. This Christ did. Now I
III. will tell you, what He should have done. For, according to
the new taken-up resolution of the grave fathers of the
society, He should have taught them first, to take a pair of
balances, and weighed, whether the good that would ensue
would overweigh the loss of the town : if it would, up with
it, and spare not. That it would certainly. For, it would
strike such a fear (the burning of this town) into all the
towns about, that Christ should never after want receiving ;
and it would salve Christ's reputation much, Who had been
thought too great a favourer of these Samaritans : and it
would be much for His credit, that He had disciples could
do as much as ever could Elias.

But Christ never stands weighing these ; but, for all the
parties were Samaritans, parties not to be favoured ; for all
it is made His quarrel, *non Eum ;* for all their means should
be by miracle, which cannot be misliked ; for all this, turns
and rebukes them. Never thinks the motion worth the
answering, as being evil *ex totâ substantiâ ;* but rebukes
them for moving it, rebukes the spirit it came from ; and
rebukes them of ignorance of their own spirit ; " Ye know
not what spirit ye are of." As much to say as, If ye did,
ye would make no such motions : that you do make any
such, it proceeds from *Nescitis.* That would be marked.
They are in ignorance ; and the worst ignorance (of themselves), that move for fire. They knew not what spirit they
are of ; but whatsoever it is, a wrong spirit it is ; for here it
is rebuked by Christ.

1.
For *nesci-*
tis.
That which Christ rebuketh is *Nescitis ;* that is their fault ;
there is no word, on which His rebuke can fall, but that. It
can be no good motion, that comes from *Nescitis.* For from
Nescitis cometh no good : without knowledge, the soul itself
Mat. 20. 22. is not good. *Nescitis quid petatis,* no good prayer. *Adoratis*
Joh. 4. 22. *quod nescitis,* no good worship. And so ignorant devotion,
implicit faith, blind obedience, all rebuked. Zeal, if it be
Rom. 10. 2. not *secundum scientiam,* cannot be *secundum conscientiam ;*
matter of conceit, it may be ; of conscience, it cannot be.
It is but κακοζηλία : and κακοζηλία is not to be allowed (we
see), no not in Christ's own cause.

And it is not every ignorance, this ; not, of the act ; but

of the "spirit" He chargeth: which is more. For, *Spiri-* 2.
tuum ponderator Deus, "God weighs the spirit." Men look For nesci-
tis cujus
to the acts; He, to the spirit : therefore, try the act; but spiritûs.
Prov. 16. 2.
the spirit, rather. We may be deceived in any act, if we
know not the spirit it comes from. One and the same
act proceeding from diverse spirits, good for one; for
another, not so. Therefore *Probate spiritus* is ever good
counsel; and *discretio spirituum*, a principal part of know- 1 Joh. 4. 1.
1 Cor. 12.
ledge. 10.

And if this import us, to do in other men's spirits, not to 3.
be deceived in them ; much more in our own : that we de- For Nesci-
tis, cujus
ceive not ourselves, which is the third degree. *Nescitis* spiritûs
vos.
cujus spiritûs, cujus vos ; the foul elench of all, *ab ignoratione*
proprii spiritûs, to fall into this *fallax*. For indeed, many
blind actions come from men, by reason of ignorance of this
third. And this we are to look to the rather, for that we
see two so great Apostles like to precipitate themselves into
a bloody act, for mistaking this point.

1. There are (sure) many *Nescitis* they were in. Elias,
first, did not that, they would do; that is one. His fire took
hold of none but delinquents; every one as deep in the same
fault as another. Here is a great many women and children
in the town, not accessory to this. God would not suffer
the wicked and innocent to perish together, no not in Sodom ; Gen. 18.23.
would not suffer Nineveh to be destroyed, because there Jonah 4.
11.
were in it many that "knew not their right hand from their
left." This did not Elias.

2. Then, it was but *quod fecit Elias ;* not, *sicut :* there is
another. For, what Elias did, he did by special inspiration,
had a particular commission, and, as it were, a privy seal for
it. And, that we must ever distinguish, in the Prophets :
when they proceed by their general calling (therein we may
follow them) ; and when an act is executed and done by
them by immediate warrant : for such warrant passes not
the person ; no precedent to be made of it. Else, without
their revelation, we may do *quod fecit Elias*, and not *sicut*.
And, that is a great *Nescitis*, and doth much harm : for
many a lewd attempt, it is sought; and, if they get it once
over their heads, they think they are safe. For killing of
Kings, *sicut fecit Ehud ;* of Queens, *sicut fecit Jehoiada ;* for Judges 3.
21.

SERM.
III.

2 Kings
11. 20.
[2 Kings
8. 22.]

rebelling, *sicut Libna.* No, no ; *quod fecit,* not *sicut fecit :* what they did, they do ; as they did, they do not.

3. But, if it were *sicut fecit* too, it would not serve : it is a *Nescitis* still; and this is our Saviour Christ's, directed to their allegations of Elias. I observe, they ask of the act; and Christ answers of the spirit. So that, *sicut fecit Elias* is not enough ; is but a weak warrant : you must be of his spirit, as well as do his act. His *sicut* will not bear your act, unless you have his spirit too. It is not enough to say, Thus did Elias, unless you add, I am of the same spirit.

4. Then, it remains, they must say, they are of Elias's spirit ; and into some such fancy, it seems, they were fallen ; but that is another *Nescitis.* Why, what harm is that ? Elias's spirit, I hope, was no evil spirit. No ; but every good spirit, as good as Elias's, is not for every person, place, or time. Spirits are given by God, and men inspired with them, after several manners, upon several occasions, as the several times require. The times sometime require one spirit, sometime another ; Elias's time, Elias's spirit. As his act good, done by his spirit; so, his spirit good, in his own time. The time changed, the spirit, then good ; now, not good. For both are faulty : the act without the spirit ; and the spirit without the time. And so it may fall out, that at some time, one may be rebuked for being of Elias's spirit well enough, when Elias's spirit is out of time.

5. But why is it out of time? That is another *Nescitis,* which Christ sets down plainly, when He renders the reason : " For the Son of man is come " (for we may well make a pause there). As if He should say : Indeed, there is
" a time to destroy," saith Solomon, Ecclesiastes the third chapter; that was under the Law : *ignea Lex,* the "fiery Law," as Moses calls it : then, a fiery spirit would not be amiss ; then, was Elias's time. But now, the " Son of man is come :" " Ye know not, what manner of spirit ye are of." The spirit of Elias was good, till the Son of man came ; but, now He is come, the date of that spirit is expired. When the Son of man is come, the spirit of Elias must be gone. Now especially : for Moses and he resigned lately, in the mount. Now, no law-giver, no prophet, but Christ. Christ now, and His Spirit, to take place. You move out of time :

will ye be of Elias's spirit, and the Son of man is come?
A plain *Nescitis.*

6. The Fathers work out another *Nescitis,* out of the emphasis *Vos ; Cujus spiritûs vos. Vos* is no idle word ; it makes
a plain separation between them and Elias. *Vos,* "you:"
why, you are My disciples, I trow ; you must answer to *Cujus
spiritûs vos ? Cujus spiritûs Tu.* Christ's disciples and Elias's
spirit ? that cannot be. Choose ye now ; for, of whose spirit
ye are, his disciples ye must be. If you be his, what do you
here with Me? get you to his tabernacle. If ye be Mine, off
with Elias's mantle and spirit both. The disciples and the
master are of one spirit. To make a disciple is nothing, but
to do, as God did, at the door of the tabernacle, take off the [Deut. 31.
master's spirit, and put it on the disciples. But, if ye be of [14. [34. 9.]
My spirit, My spirit is *in specie columbæ,* not *aquilæ;* not of [Joh. 1. 32.]
the eagle, that carrieth Jupiter's thunderbolt ; but, of the
dove, that brings "the olive-branch" in her bill, the sign of [Gen. 8. 11.
non perdere sed salvare. If this spirit be in you, let all your [See Vulg.]
motions smell of the olive-branch, not of the thunderbolt ;
come from saving grace, and not from consuming zeal.

7. But yet, the worst *Nescitis* is behind. For worse it is,
to be mistaken in Christ, than in ourselves. And Him they
mistook, in that, they would move Him, to that, Whose coming was contrary, quite contrary to that, they would have
Him do. This is a *Nescitis* indeed. *Vere nescitis, qui peti-
tis a Magistro mansuetudinis licentiam crudelitatis ;* 'A *Nescitis,* to seek at the hands of Him, that is the master of all
meekness, a license to commit such cruelty.'

The very title of the "Son of man" is enough for this. For,
whatsoever as the Son of God, He may do ; it is kindly for
Him, as the Son of man, to save the sons of men. Specially,
being the Son of such men as He was ; the Son of Abraham,
who entreated hard, that even Sodom might not be destroyed. [Gen. 18.
The Son of Jacob, who much misliked, yea even cursed the [23, 24.
[Gen. 49. 7.]
wrath of his two sons, in destroying Shechem. The Son of
David, who complained much of the sons of Zeruiah, that
they were "too hard" for him. As Christ doth here of the [2 Sam. 3.
sons of Zebedee, who (as if indeed they had been born of a [39.]
thundercloud, and not of a man) were so ready to make
havoc of the lives of men. It cost the Son of man more to

SERM.
III.
Ps. 49. 8.

redeem men, than to have them blown up so lightly. And, if James and John were to pay for them, at His price, they would not be so evil advised, as to make so quick riddance of the lives of men.

Christ doth here warrant us, that to tell *cujus spiritûs,* the way is, by *ad quid venit?* what spirit is he of, by 'To what end comes he?' whither blows it, which way is his face, to *salvare* or to *perdere?* For, to the end of His coming, God hath framed His spirit. You may know it, by His first text.

Lu. 4. 18.

"The Spirit of the Lord is upon Me, to heal the broken, to deliver the captive;" to save that was lost, He sent Me: therefore He was sent, and therefore He came. You may know it, by His name, "Jesus," a Saviour; you may know it by His similes (no destroying creatures) : a "lamb," no wolf; a "hen," no kite; a "vine," no "bramble," out of which came fire to burn up all the trees in the forest. Of His coming, clean contrary to this, speaks the Prophet, "He shall come down like the rain;" speaks the Apostle, *Hic est ille Jesus qui venit in aquâ,* "That came in water," to quench; not in fire, to consume.

[Mat. 1. 21.]
Joh. 1. 29.
Mat.23. 37.
Joh. 15. 1.
Judges 9. 15.
Ps. 72. 6.
1 Joh. 5. 6.

Again, that He doth not this (*non perdere sed salvare*) by accident, as it hits; but, on set purpose: it was the cause, the final cause, the very end, God sent Him, and He came for.

In which point, to take away *Nescitis* clean for ever, he sets it down positively, and privatively both : wherefore He came not, and wherefore He came. Came not, "to destroy;" but, came, "to save:" this is plain dealing. But first, "not to destroy;" that they, which cannot save, may yet be sure not to destroy any; but, if they can, not only not destroy, but save too, as Christ doth. But, of these, Christ came but to one end; hath but one office; came not, to the other; and this would be marked. The Cardinal begins his book to the Pope, *Duplex Petri officium, pascere et occidere;* Christ had but one, to feed, to save: another there is, was *Homicida ab initio.* But, if St. Peter have gotten two offices, he hath one more than Christ. Christ came to save only, with a flat exclusive of the other.

Joh. 8. 44.

And, where they move Him, *in specie,* for a destruction by fire; He (not content to deny that alone) denieth it *in genere,* not to destroy at all ; neither by fire, nor any other way.

Here, we have a case of fire; will ye have another, of the sword? Shall we do it by fire? say James and John here; *Domine si percutimus gladio?* saith St. Peter after in a Lu. 22.49, greater quarrel far than this, when they laid hands on Him, 51. to carry Him to His passion. That, He denieth too, and in that quarrel; and saith, *Sinite,* Let alone your sword. Out with your fire, James and John; Up with your sword, Peter. So that, neither by fire, here; nor by sword, there: neither by miracle, as here; nor without miracle, as there, doth Christ like of these motions. What then? shall not Christ be received? Yes: He is most worthy so to be. I add, they that refuse it are worthy any punishment: but, that every man is to be dealt with as he is worthy, would prove but a hard piece of divinity: hard for all, and even for themselves too. If, so oft as Christ suffers indignity, fire should come down from Heaven, *Domine quis sustinebit?* we were all in Ps. 130. 3. hard case, Jews and Samaritans and all: yea, disciples; yea, this James and John, and all. The Samaritans, they received not Christ; they were gone; burnt all. For Jerusalem's sake, because His face was that way, here, He was not received. When He came to Jerusalem, how was He received there? Why, there He was murdered: worse used than in Samaria. Then, we must call for more fire: Jerusalem must be burnt too. Now, for the disciples, James and John, how carried they the matter? It is true, they had received Him; but when most need was, thrust Him from them, renounced Him, utterly denied that ever they knew Him. Then, we must trouble Heaven once more: call for fire, for James and John too. Nay then, "the world was made by Him, and the Joh. 1. 10, world knew Him not," nor "received Him not:" why then, 11. the world is at an end, *facti sumus sicut Sodoma;* all a heap Rom.9.29. of ashes, if this doctrine go forward. Best, take Phaeton out of the chariot, that he set not all on fire. Sure, this, I take it, is a *Nescitis;* for who receiveth Christ as he should? yea, who refuseth not, one time or other, to receive Him? Who, of the disciples? who, at Jerusalem? Then, all must be turned out and in; *Non venit salvare, sed perdere.* Then, this will follow; if no place for repentance, then no use of Christ. For, whom shall He save, when James and John have consumed all to ashes? But, it will be well to leave Christ some-

S E R M. body to save; not disappoint Christ of His coming, and send
  III.   Him back without His errand.

Our *Scitis*   Now, out of this *Nescitis* to frame our *Scitis.* 1. By this
out of this
Nescitis. time we know Christ's Spirit, (as He teacheth us,) by His
coming. His coming was not to destroy : they that came
a destroying, came not in His company. 2. Then, our own
spirits : if they do *spirare Christum*, they have the same
journey's end. 3. We know their spirits, that hatched alate
this question anew ; *Vis facimus ascendat ignis?* And theirs
too, that never turned and rebuked it, but gave allowance to
it, both before, and after it was done; yea, bound them to it
by oath, and set it forth, with both Sacraments, 1. of penance,
and of the 2. altar; and (what should I say?) resolved flat
against Christ, in the very same point; and did not, as He,
cast water, but put oil to the flame.

  Can these be the society of Jesus, and the spirits blow two
contrary ways, and their comings be to two contrary ends?
His, not to destroy; theirs, to destroy : His, to rebuke;
theirs, to allow of such motives?

  To know what spirit they be of, look what manner of
spirits they make choice of, and by their wills choose, and
cherish none other ; eager, fierce, boisterous spirits. O,
Mat. 21. 5; Elias's spirit is a goodly spirit ! but Christ's, *Ecce Rex tuus*
11. 29. *venit mansuetus ;* or *Discite a me quia mitis*, it is not worth a
mite : that spirit is too weak, and too faint, to forward their
fireworks.

  And, if yet ye doubt, no better way to be resolved, than
by *Ad quid venit ?* ask that, and it will resolve you straight.
[1569.] Wherefore came Doctor Morton, a little before the rebellion
[1579.] in the north ? Wherefore came Doctor Sanders into Ireland?
Wherefore Cardinal Allen into the Low-Countries in eighty-
eight ? To what end came he out of the Archduke's camp
hither ? Was it, to save men's lives, or to destroy them ? By
these marks we cannot but know, *cujus spiritús.*

  It sufficeth, that Christ rebuketh this spirit ; that if they
[2 Cor. 11. be the society of Jesus, it is *alius Jesus,* "another Jesus"
4.] than this in the text : Bar-jesus, for he, by interpretation, is
Elymas, that is, a destroyer. Christ likes no destroying : no,
though the town be full of Samaritans, He likes it not : no,
though the colour be *Non receperunt Eum*, yet He likes it not :
no, though we could miraculously do it, like Elias, yet likes

He it not. It is not God's will, in the Old Testament, that Sion should be built in blood; nor, in the New, that His Church on the ashes of any estate; nor that His not receiving should be pretence for the extirpation of any town; much less, kingdom or country.

This we learn. But we come not only for that, but to congratulate this poor town, that scaped the fire, and ourselves no less, that should have perished by the same element, though not from Heaven, yet another way; though not by *Dicimus*, yet by another means: and in public manner to render our yearly solemn thanksgiving, that we also, by the Son of man, were delivered from the powder laid ready to consume, and from the match-light to give it fire; that they were rebuked, yea (more than that) destroyed themselves, that sought our destruction. Every way, our case hath the advantage; and therefore bindeth us to greater duty. *Our duty.*

Will ye consider it, in the parties? This was against Samaritans; and, by the Apostles: came commended by the movers; they were Apostles: aggravated by the parties, against whom; they were the sect of the Samaritans. We are no Samaritans, I trust; but, they no Apostles, I am sure: no Apostles, nor of no Apostolic spirit, which would authorize that, which was rebuked in the Apostles themselves. And, for Samaritans (which falls to our turn) it may be, they count us and call us so; it is no matter, they call Christ Himself so, then. This, I say: Had we been such, as they would have us to be; such as these here, very Samaritans, we were to find as much favour, at the hands of the society of Jesus, as did the Samaritans, at the hand of Jesus Himself; if their spirit, their coming, their faces stood, as His, to *non perdere*.

But we are none. No, if we go by the marks, the Scripture sets down of them, the Samaritans will light on their side. For, let it be enquired, whether part, in the worship of God, useth more *ritus gentium*, they or we (the mark of the Book of the Kings); of whether of us it may more rightly be said, "You worship you know not what" (which is Christ's own mark). In a word: let this be the case, whether religion have more windows open to Jerusalem; whose face looks more fully that way. No: the looking to Jerusalem is not the quarrel; the not looking to Rome, that is the matter. *2 Kings 17. 33.* *Joh. 4. 22.*

s 2

And sure, this quarrel is much after one in both. That, in the text, was made a matter in religion, but was none; no more was this of theirs. *Non receperunt* is no act of heresy; *Non crediderunt*, that is. But it is not their misbelieving, moved them in the text; nor these neither. It was the not-harbouring makes all this ado. So they would entertain them, they might believe as they list. Upon the matter then, it falls out to prove, not zeal against their heresy, but zeal for their own entertainment; which will not, but, indirectly, be made matter of religion.

Now, if ye weigh the destruction, ye shall find, though in the main they agree (for upward and downward makes small difference) ; yet, ours was the worse.

Worse: for it should have been sudden, which is worse for the soul; therefore simply worse. Worse: for that would have wasted but to the ground, and there left; but this should have fetched up foundations and ground, and all. Worse certainly: for, that should have consumed but Samaritans only; but this, for the good of the catholic cause, Samaritans and Jews both. Yea, such as themselves were, disciples, and James and John too, if they had been there, for company. Worse : for this had the show of an example, *sicut fecit Elias ;* but ours, *sicut fecit* who? Not *sicut fecit Elias :* no; *sicut,* without example. Never the like entered into the heart of any, that carried but the shape of a man. So, still the advantage, on our side.

Now, for the delivery. When all is done, that which was saved here was but a poor town without a name. I should much wrong that famous assembly, and flower of the kingdom, if I should offer to compare it with that, either in quantity, (alas, like little Zoar to great Nineveh,) or in quality, when in ours (to say nothing of the rest) one there was, more worth than "ten thousand" such as they; we have good Scripture for it.

2 Sam. 18.
3

These here were rebuked but verbally, on earth ; ours, really rebuked from Heaven. Really rebuked, in their intention, by miraculous disappointing the execution; and themselves put to a foul rebuke besides : God first blowing their own powder in their faces, to write their sin there; and after, making their bowels, their merciless bowels, to be consumed

with fire, within the very view of that place, which they had
meant to consume with fire, and all us in it.

Christ came to save us : there be manifest steps of His
coming. Apparent first, in that He made them, they could
not contain their own spirits, but brought them out by their
own *Dicimus;* made them take pen and paper, and tell it out
themselves, and so become the instruments of their own destruction, which is the worst of all.

Again He came, when He gave His Majesty understanding
to read the riddle of, ‘ So soon as the letter is burnt[1]:’ to [[1] The let-
construe the dialect of these unknown spirits, and pick it ter to Lord Mont-
out of a period, as dark, as the cellar was dark, where the eagle.]
powder lay.

There is but one coming in the text, He “ came not to
destroy, but to save :” here, were two in ours ; both, comings
of Christ. 1. He “ came not to destroy, but to save” us,
in mercy ; 2. He “ came not” to save, but destroy them
(His second coming) in judgment. To conclude. This one
notable difference there is, on our side : they should have
been destroyed by miracle, and we were saved by miracle.
“ The right hand of the Lord brought it to pass ;” which is, Ps. 118. 16.
of all others, the most welcome deliverance.

And shall I then, upon all this, make a motion ? Master,
wilt Thou we speak to these whom Thou hast delivered, that
seeing Thou tookest order, the fire should not ascend to consume them, they would take order, their prayers may ascend
up, and, as the odours of Saints’ phials, burn before Thee
still, and never consume, but be this day ever a sweet smell
in Thy presence ? Their fire, they came to put under the
earth, Christ would not have burn ; another “ fire” He came Lu. 12. 49.
to put upon earth, and His desire is that it should burn :
even that fire, whereon the incense of our devotion and the
sacrifice of our praise burn before God, and be *in odorem* Eph. 5. 2.
suavitatis. We were appointed to be made a sacrifice : if
Isaac be saved, shall nothing be offered in his stead ? Shall
we not thank God, that He was better to them than James
and John ; and to us, better than those were, that will needs
thrust themselves to be of His society ? That, when this
Dicimus was said of us too, stayed it at *Dicimus,* and never
let it come to *Perficimus;* miraculously made known these

SERM. unknown spirits: that He turned and rebuked the motion,
 III.   and the spirits that made it: that He came, once and twice,
to save us, and destroy them.

Lu. 1. 46.   If we shall, let us then do it; Let our souls magnify the
Lord, and our spirits rejoice in God our Saviour: that the
beginning of the text and of our case was " fire" to " consume
them" (in the first verse) ; that the end was, *non perdere sed
salvare* (in the last). Such may ever be the end of all attempts to destroy us. So may He come still; and still, as
here He came; never to destroy, ever to save us. And as
oft as He, to save us ; so oft we, to praise Him.

And God grant, that this answer here of Christ may serve
for a determination of this case for ever; and every Christian
be so resolved by it, as the like never come in speech more,
by any *Dicimus*. But if—as we know not what spirits are
abroad; that every destroying spirit may be rebuked, and
every state preserved, as this town here was, and as we all
were, this day. And ever, as He doth save still, we may
Ps. 136. 1. praise still; and ever magnify His " mercy, that endureth
for ever." Amen.

A SERMON

PREACHED BEFORE

THE KING'S MAJESTY AT WHITEHALL,

ON THE FIFTH OF NOVEMBER, A.D. MDCXII.

LAMENTATIONS iii. 22.

It is the Lord's mercies that we are not consumed, because His compassions fail not.

Misericordiæ Domini quia non sumus consumpti, quia non defecerunt miserationes Ejus.

[*It is of the Lord's mercies that we are not consumed, because His compassions fail not.* Engl. Trans.]

THE verse is not amiss; the book suits not so well. For this joyful day of our great and famous deliverance, Christ's *Tibiis cecinimus* is more meet, than John Baptist's *Planxi-* Lu. 7. 32. *mus;* and David's harp, than Jeremiah's Lamentations. This, I know, cometh to your minds, at the mention of this melancholic book. But yet, if we weigh our case well; not, what it fell out to be, but what it was meant to have been; the very book will not seem so out of season. For, this very day, should it not have been a day of lamentation to the whole land? Was it not so marked in their Calendar? And they had had their will, would they not have given matter of making a book of Lamentations over this state; and that another manner book, with more, and with longer chapters, than this of Jeremy's? By the mercy of God, it proved otherwise. But what? shall we so intend the day, what it is, as we forget, what it was like to have been? No: the book and the verse *juxta se posita* will do well; one set out the other, as the black work doth the white. The book put us in mind, but for God's mercy, in what case we might have been. The verse, by God's mercy, what we are. And even to thank Him, that our lot was, to hit the verse, and miss the book; to fall within the one, and without the other.

The truth is, I had a desire that *misericordiæ Domini* might have their day; and this day I thought to dedicate chiefly to them. We have formerly moved and resolved the question, out of the Gospel; we have once or twice called to joy out of the Psalms. The barbarousness of the act, and the parties to it, hath been justly inveighed against; a time given to each of these. And shall we not allow one day to the magnifying of Him, and His mercies, That was the cause of all? It should have had the first day by right, and we were pointed to it by *Misericordiæ Domini super omnia opera Ejus.* Well, at last now in this seventh year, this *annus Sabbaticus*, let us make it our Sabbath, rest upon it, and put it off no longer. Be this day dedicated to the celebrating of them.

Ps. 145. 9.

To this end, though all the Scripture over, God's mercy be much spoken of; (for where shall ye light, but ye shall find it upon one occasion or other?) yet, to fit this day and our case, as it fell out this day, (in my poor conceit,) none in any other book falleth out so just, cometh so home, as this verse to this day. "It was the mercies," &c. as upon the opening will fall out. Which, though it be in the book, yet is nothing of the nature of the book.

The sum and division.

The verse is a recognition or acknowledgment: I may add, a just and a joyful recognition. And that double, 1. that "we were not consumed," and 2. why "we were not." So it standeth on two parts: 1. that "we were not," a happy effect; 2. why "we were not;" it was God's mercy, the cause of that and all other our happiness.

   1.   The effect is in these words, *Non sumus consumpti.* Of which, 1. *consumpti* is the danger; and 2. *non sumus* the deliverance.

   II.   The cause in these words, *Misericordiæ Domini quod non.* And there first: 1. *non,* we were "not;" 2. and then, there was a cause *quod non,* "that we were not;" 3. then, that cause was "God's mercy." 1. Which we take in sunder: it was God first That did it; 2. then, it was His mercy, that moved Him to it. In the mercy, three things we find: 1. *Misericordiæ,* more than one, many "mercies." 2. "Compassions," or (as the native signification of the word is) bowels, the bowels of mercy; that special kind. 3. And those have this property, they fail not, or (which is all one) consume not : not they : and so not we ; their not consuming is the cause, we were not consumed.

Then last our recognition. That seeing, His mercies fail not us, that we fail not them ; seeing they consume not, nor we, by their means ; that our thankfulness do not neither, that it fall not into a consumption. But that in imitation of the three, we render Him, 1. plural thanks ; 2. and these from the bowels ; and 3. that incessantly, without failing. And this, not in words only, but in some reality, some work of mercy, tending to preserve those that are near *consumpti,* pining away. III.

Plain it is, a danger there was ; else, vain were the recognition. That danger is set down in the word *consumpti ;* some consuming there should have been : some such matter was in hand. A word, even (as it were) of purpose chosen for us ; for it sorteth just with our danger as may be. I. The effect. 1. The danger.

Consuming may be more ways than one ; but no way so proper, as by the element of fire, *confector et consumptor omnium,* saith the heathen man, 'that makes away and consumes all things.' It is the proper peculiar epithet of that element, consuming fire ; and the common phrase of the Holy Ghost is, consumed by fire. This fits us right. Fire it was, "consuming fire," should have consumed us ; it was a fiery consumption. *Consumpti igne.* Heb.12.29. Lu. 9. 54.

Then *consumpti,* in propriety, is nothing but *simul sumpti ; con* is *simul* in composition. All taken, all put together, and an end made of all. And was it not so with us ? King and Prince ; Lords Spiritual and Temporal ; Judges, Knights, Citizens, Burgesses, and a great number besides of spectators and auditors, that day, out of all the flower of the kingdom : all cooped up together under one roof, and then blown up all. This is *simul sumpti,* and *consumpti,* both. 2. Con-sumpti, i.e. *simul sumpti.* 1. Personally.

Will ye any more for company ? This was but personal ; take the real too : lead, stone, timber, windows, walls, roofs, 2. Really.

SERM. foundations and all, must have up too : an universal desola-
IV. tion of all, both personal and real.   That "the stone out of
Habak. 2. the wall, and the beam out of the frame," if they could
11.
speak, might say, And we are in ; *simul sumpti* and *con-*
Mat. 24. 2. *sumpti* too : all laid waste, not "one stone standing upon
another." This was right *consumpti*, spent indeed, where
nothing left, person or things, with life or without : utter
havoc made of all.

Thus far might Jeremy go, and match us in these three.
I will touch two or three more beyond him, that we may see,
our case should have been more lamentable than the Book
of Lamentations itself.

1. There was no fire in Jeremy's time ; none but of wood
and coal, and no consuming but that way : and that fire
consumes by degrees, piece and piece, one piece fire, while
one is wood still : so that one may save a brand's end for a
need.   But this was a fire, Jeremy never knew of, nor many
Zech. 3. 2. ages after was ever heard of : takes all at once.   No brand
here, no pulling out of the fire, no saving any : here is quick
work, all done and past, as soon as the paper burnt.

2. Another.   In this of the Prophet's they had fair warning.   There was a camp pitched three several times in Je-
hoiakim's, Jechoniah's, Zedekiah's days : they had time to
Rom. 9. 29. make themselves ready.   But in ours, *facti essemus sicut*
Sodoma, "our destruction had been like that of Sodom ;"
no camp pitched there ; but suddenly, in a moment : to
the hazard of many a soul, that were (I doubt me) but evil
prepared, if they had been thus suddenly surprised.   And
that had been a lamentable *consumpti* indeed, of both body
and soul : the body here, the soul eternally.   A terrible
blow indeed, and we should not have known, who would
have hurt us.

3. Now we do, as hap is ; and therein we leave Jeremy
behind again.   It was not an open enemy offered this :
usually, destruction cometh from them.   So did this, in the
text : from the Chaldees, not only strangers, but in open
hostility with the Jews.   But, in ours, they were not so
much as strangers, but born subjects of one and the same
country, tongue, and allegiance.   The more lamentable, to
be "consumed" by ourselves ; to be shot through with an

arrow, the feathers whereof grew on our own wings. So they were, naturally; but, when they fell once to this unnatural designment, when they fell on consuming, they were no longer men, all humanity was quite consumed in them. And this was the danger.

To make a danger dangerous, two things are required : 1. The sureness, and 2. the nearness. If it be uncertain, we reckon not of it; nor, though it be certain, if it be far away. Let us see, both was it.

To make it certain, these are required : 1. it be soundly resolved; 2. surely bound; 3. and seriously put in execution. First, upon good resolution, a sentence given *quod eramus consumendi,* ' we were to be made away :' and rather than we should not, their own friends, allies, and kindred; yea their own dear Catholics, to go the same way, to have been in the *consumpti,* as well as we. This was to have it certain, to make sure work. *[marginal: 2. The certainty of the danger. 1.]*

Gravely resolved; and fast bound as *funiculus triplex,* the three immutable things of their religion could bind it. 1. Bound by oath : their *Sacramentum militare* they ever took first, never to discover, never to desist. *[marginal: 2. [Eccl. 4. 12.]]*

2. Bound again by their Sacrament of Penance. Thither they went in an error, as if it had been some fault; but they found more than they went for : went for absolution; received a flat resolution, it was not only no sin, but would serve to expiate their other sins. And, not only expiate their sins, but heap also upon them an increase of merit. In effect, that our consumption would become their consummation.

3. Bound last, with the Sacrament of the Altar, and so made as sure as their Maker could make it. These three; sure now, past starting, I trow.

But go to; oaths and sacraments consume nothing. True : it was therefore not only solemnly bound, but sadly set upon. They fell to their pickaxes, laid in their powder, by ten and by twenty barrels at once : and I know not how much iron, and how many huge stones; *fervebat opus,* in earnest they were. Of all which we may say with St. John, "That which we have seen with our eyes, which we have looked upon, and our hands have handled," that preach we, in *[marginal: 3.]* *[marginal: 1 Joh. 1. 1.]*

this point. That very sure it is, we were very far gone in our consumption.

3. The nearness of it.

And all this while, it may be, it was *in dies multos,* far enough away; to be done a good while after, we know not when. How near was it? *Nox una interposita,* but a night (nor that neither: neither a whole night, nor a whole day); but a few hours we had to spend. The train ready, and the match; three for failing. They stayed but for the *con,* for the time, till all were *con,* that is, *simul sumpti;* and then *consumpti* should have come straight upon all.

This was our case, thus dangerous, thus sure, thus near; insomuch as we were even given for dead. The letter shewed as much. Their being together, and waiting for it at their meeting-place, shewed as much. They made full reckoning, we were little better than even *consumpti* in the preterperfect tense. And nearer we cannot come. It is well known, David was never destroyed indeed finally, yet (often in the Psalms) he saith, he was brought back "from the deep of the earth again," from "the gates of death;" yea even from "the nethermost hell." His meaning was, he was exceeding near it. And so were we as near as was possible, and not be swallowed up of it. And this is the meaning of *consumpti.* And thus much for it.

Ps. 71. 20;
9. 13; 86. 13.

2.
The deliverance.
Isa. 37. 3.

Now are we to put *Non sumus* to it, and we are safe straight. Which two words contain our delivery. So as, though we were destinate as fuel, to this fire; though *venerunt filii ad partum,* though they were come to the point, to be delivered of that they had so long travailed withal; though like we were, and sure we were, and near we were, yet "consumed" we were not. We were not: for here we are, blessed be God. Here, and elsewhere (some few except, which since be gone to their graves in peace). The place standeth, the persons still alive. *Non sumus consumpti;* this is *ad oculum,* it admits no further discourse. But this it admits, that we may stay a little, and lay our *non sumus* to this of Jeremy in the text; and we shall find ours, another manner of preservation, by odds; that so we may provide ourselves of another manner of recognition.

1. The comparing of theirs and ours.

Non sumus consumpti, saith Jeremy: when for all that, in every corner of the streets they lay slain. Only he, and a handful more, in comparison, were spared. This served him 1. In the persons. Lam. 2. 21. to say, Yet we be not all gone : a cold comfort, God knoweth. This for persons.

For things. The gates of Jerusalem were burnt with fire, 2. In the things. and a great part of the city; howbeit not all. A remnant there was left, though but a poor one, God wot; yet enough, in his sense, to say *Non consumpti,* " All is not consumed." 1. Will ye see now them with us? With them, some few left alive, the most slain; with us, not one slain, but all still alive. 2. With them, a part of the buildings left, though the far greater part consumed; with us, neither stick nor stone touched nor burnt; nay, not so much as singed. All safe: all, *in toto ;* and all, *in qualibet parte.* 1. Upon the matter, thus it is. They were " not consumed," that is, not all; we were " not consumed," that is, not at all. All were not " consumed," with them; none at all, with us. 2. Some were saved there; both all and some here; neither person nor thing miscarried. 3. Jeremy could not say, It is God's mercy, we are all safe; he was fain to give it in the negative, " We are not consumed." We may say it, and put it in either : both in the affirmative, All safe; and in the negative, None consumed, no not one.

There be indeed two *non consumpti*s. 1. One cometh after, The difference of ours above theirs. after it is burnt a great while, with water to quench it. 2. The other goeth before, and keeps it from taking fire at all; and that is ours. In which case, *non consumpti* is no term diminuent. Nay, the precurrent negative is better by much. Ask the speculative divine, if it be not so: if *Ne* [Matt. 6. 13.] *nos inducas* be not better than *Libera nos,* " lead us not in," than " deliver us out :" not to sin, than to be forgiven it; not to fall, than to be lift up again : and (to insist in this present) not to kindle, than to quench. For the latter is from *Subsequetur me misericordia,* mercy subsequent, which is good; the former from *Cito nos anticipent miseri-* Ps. 23. 6. Ps. 79. 8. *cordiæ tuæ,* from the anticipation of mercy, which is far the better of the twain.

2. One great difference we see between the two *non sumuse*s. Another now, no whit less. For the greatest of all their miseries, and which touched Jeremy nearest, was the proud insolence of their enemies (the Chaldees) over

SERM.
IV.

Prov. 12. 10.

Isa. 33. 1.

Ps. 9. 15.

Acts 13. 41.

Ps. 30. 5.

Ps. 107. 6

them ; worse than the consuming, was their insulting upon them. This, worse than all the rest. Thanks be to God, so did not ours. They had no cause to triumph over us ; we, over them, rather. *Non sumus consumpti : non nos, at illi.* Will ye observe that ? " We were not ;" but our enemies were " consumed" themselves. *Et viscera impiorum crudelia,* " the cruel bowels of those wicked men" consumed ; and that with fire, and that, before, and in the sight of the very place, to which they had vowed destruction, and, in which, the destruction of us all. That the saying of the prophet might be taken up over them : *Væ qui consumis, nonne consumeris et ipse ?* " You that will needs be a consuming, shall not you yourselves be so served ?" In " the pit" you " digged," in " the net" you " spread," in the element you made choice of, your own bowels burned. " Behold, ye despisers, and tremble, and fear ;" your mischief is turned upon your own heads, and your consumption lights upon your own bowels. This then doubles the point : that not only we were not, but that they (our consumers) were.

3. Yea I add (for a full triplicity in this point), even that we were cured of our consumption sleeping (for so we were), and never dreamed of any danger, till we had scaped it. This also is a main difference, and increaseth our *Non sumus* a great deal, above theirs. For, as that, the misery of all miseries, when a man is, and yet knoweth not himself to be miserable ; so, I say, that the delivery of all deliveries, when we know not our peril, till we be past it : and that was our case. Much trouble of fear, and care, much anguish of spirit is saved by it ; which the poor Jews were even worn, spent, and consumed withal : and which Jeremy, God wot, was in, a long time. We, not a moment. But without " heaviness for a night, we had joy in the morning." Sure, if this be a benefit, " So they cried unto the Lord, and He delivered them out of their distress ;" what call ye then this, They never " cried unto the Lord, yet He delivered them out of their distress ?" Then put these together : 1. we were not " consumed" at all : 2. there should have been fire ; there was not so much as smoke : 3. all should have gone ; not a man that perished : 4. all should have perished, and perished utterly, not a hair of any of their heads fell to the ground ;

5. we were not "consumed" at all; our consumers were consumed: 6. and we, without any care taken, were rid of our consumption : we were not; our enemies were. We, without consuming ourselves with thought, and anxiety of mind, delivered from our danger before ever we knew it. And remember withal, (not *Non taliter fecit omni populo*, but) *Non taliter fecit populo suo*, " He did not deal so," not ' with His own people,' as He did with us. Ps.147.20.

The effect we have; we were not what was it, that we were not? First, an *it* there was; a כי, a *quia* it had, that is, a cause certainly. It was not *forte fortuna*, by hap-hazard. No, it was no casualty (this fire) ; no more was the saving us from it : neither casual, but causal both. We will not then, with those in Esay, *libare fortunæ*, no healths to fortune; but seek out this It, even the cause that wrought it. In philosophy, they count him a happy man, that can find the cause: but sure, in divinity, miserable and unhappy we, if we find it not; but, with swine, feed and fill ourselves with the acorns, and never once look up to the tree, whence they came. A dangerous error, no less than the danger itself.

II.
The cause.
1.
It was
God.
Isa. 65. 11.
[Vulg.]

[Virg. G.2.
492.]

2. Our next caution must be, to take heed of *non causa pro causâ*. Where let me tell you this. There is a disease under the sun (and it is one of ours) : as to put all faults from ourselves, to others; so, good deeds, (as near as we can,) to pluck all to ourselves from others. Others, I say : not only men; but even God Himself. And that, two ways : 1. if any good be done, it was our own arm, or our own head did it : something in us; God is left out. But, if it be too evident, he had a hand in it; then it was God, 2. but not His mercy, not of Himself, but something from us there was, that moved Him to do it. So, either something in us, or something from us: whereof the one is against 'It was God;' the other, against 'It was His mercy :' not God, or not God's mercy; but we, or somewhat of ours. Ever our manner is, never to seek farther than ourselves : there we would fain find it. And there, if we can find any colour of a cause, in any wisdom or foresight of our own, it is as a mist, or cloud, to take God out of our sights, the first original true cause, the *causa causarum* of all such miraculous divine preservations as this was.

And yet, secondary causes there be, I know : and even in

this, man may seem to have a part. It was the letter that
was sent, it was the King's divination, which I reckon the
highest cause upon earth. This it was, and that it was; but
God it was, I am sure, above both. *He,* That did infatuate
him that sent the letter: That made them false among themselves; false to their oath, false to their ghostly Father, false
to their Maker. And God it was, That inspired that divination into His Majesty: logic or grammar could not reveal it.
God only could; could, and did, direct to that most true,
but, withal, most strange interpretation. Let God then
Ps. 115. 1. have that is His. *Non nobis Domine, non nobis, sed nomini
Tuo da gloriam,* "Not unto us, Lord, not unto us, but to Thy
Name be the glory of it given."

2.
It was
God's
mercy.

God it was: but, what in God? For (we see) it is not
enough to ascribe it to Him; but, for some reason, we must
go yet further. God may do it, and be bound to do it, and
did us wrong, if He do it not. What then in God? 1. His
power may seem to claim the chief place, in a deliverance.
But power and wisdom, and other six, that is, all the rest of
the Divine attributes, be but *communiter ad duo* (as the schoolmen term them): no prime causes themselves; but attendants only, and set on work by the two master-attributes,
1. justice, or 2. mercy. So that, justice it was; or mercy it
was. Mercy it was, saith Jeremy, and so may we all, in and
Ps. 145. 9. by his mouth that straight upon it pronounced, *Misericordia
Domini super omnia opera Ejus.* For if it had not been that
Jas. 2. 13. mercy, nay if, as St. James saith, it had not been *Misericordia superexaltat judicium,* mercy had not been "above all
His works," even justice and all, it had been evil with us.
Mercy it was; justice it was not. For then, our own good
deserts might procure it, as due to them; and so we come
about again, to find the first cause in ourselves, because we
were this or that. All cometh to one: if it were our own
foresight, it was not God; and if it were our own merit, it
was not He neither.

But, for this, I appeal to ourselves. For, I verily think, if
we would but call to mind (and here now, I would that every
man would call to mind), in what case he was for His soul to
God-ward, at that very time; whether in state of sin or of
grace; sure, if we did but return to our hearts, and there, as

Solomon speaketh, *cognoscere quisque plagam cordis sui,* every 1 Kings 8.
man feel how his heart beats ; that heart of ours would soon 38.
tell us.   Best claim not by justice: best, even confess, with
Jeremy, it was God, and God's mercy, without more ado.

We were in *consumpti,* if it were but our consuming sins :
1. if but of what then was, and, may I not say, still is consumed and wasted.   What huge sums in superfluity, riot, of
belly and back, and worse matters !   2. Our time : if but the
consuming of it in ease and idleness, and too well-known
fruits of them both.   3. Of the service of God, that is quite
consumed by most of us, now : fallen to but a sermon, if that;
and how little like a sermon, we hear it, and less (I fear)
after regard it !   4. Of God's name, that runs waste; and our
blessed Saviour, That is even piecemeal consumed in our
mouths, by all manner oaths and execrations, and that without any need at all.   These, with other sins, that fret like a
moth, and creep like a canker, to the consuming of our souls,
we should find, that, as it was our enemies' purpose we should
have been consumed; so it was our desert, to have been consumed : and that, it was His mercy only, we were not consumed.   This is the true cause, God's mercy.

In which, note these two : how fitly it answereth and meets
both with 1. our consuming, and 2. with us.

1. As the cruelty of man was the cause, we should have
been; so (full against it) the mercy of God, the cause we
were not.   The true cause of our safety, God's mercy; as
of our destruction, man's cruelty.

2. Again, to provide, that being out of our consumption, we
fall not into presumption, and so pluck a worse judgment
upon us.   The mercy of God, against our desert.   Our desert
it was, to have been ; His mercy it was, we were not.   His
justice, for our deserts, would have come upon us; it was His
mercy turned His justice from us, upon them.   His justice
would have subscribed the *sumus ;* His mercy it was that
gave the *Non,* and stayed it :   glory be to God, and to His
mercy for it.

Which mercy yieldeth us three things to be observed :
1. the number, 2. the nature, and 3. the property.

1. The number : that it is not *misericordia* but *misericor-*   His mer-
diæ ; not one, but many, even a plurality of them : a multi-   cies.
1. Their

SERM. tude of them, because a multitude of us; they many, because
IV.
——— we many : we many, and our sins many more; and where
sins are multiplied, there a multiplicity of mercies is needful,

Mat. 25. 9. *ne forte non sufficiant nobis et vobis,* lest there be not enough
for both Houses, and for all three estates in them : for so it
is to be wished, there may be a representation of all His
mercies, as that assembly is the representation of all the
realm : that so there may be enough for all.

2. Their   2. But then of mercy, the cause here is set down (another
nature.   cause): "because His compassions fail not." How hangs this
together? Thus.   The word, which here is turned "compassions," in very deed properly signifieth the "bowels."   It is
to shew, that not mercies, nor a number of them at large,
from any place or any kind, would serve for this work; but
a certain special kind of choice mercies was required; and
those are they, that issue from the bowels : *misericordiæ vis-
cerum,* or *viscera misericordiæ* (which you will).   You shall
find them together in some special works of God, such as
this was.

These are the choice : for, of all parts, the bowels melt,
relent, yield, yearn soonest.   Consequently, the mercies from
them, of all other, the most tender, and, as I may say, the
mercies most merciful.   The best, 1. both because they are
not dry, but full of affection, and come cheerfully (an easy
matter to discern between a dry mercy, and a mercy from
the bowels).   2. And because to mercy one may be inclined
by somewhat from without; when that fails, where are we
then?   But, the bowels are within Him, and when we have
brought the cause within Him, we are safe.   *Quando causam
sumit de Se et visceribus Suis,* that mercy is best, and yieldeth
the best comfort.

But, in this word of the Prophet's there is yet more than
"bowels." מעים were enough for them: רחמים are more; are
the bowels or vessels near the womb, near the loins : in
a word, not *viscera* only, but *parentum viscera,* the bowels of
a father or mother, those are רחמים, which adds more force

Lu. 15. 20. a great deal.   See them, in the parable of the father towards
his riotous lewd son : when he had consumed all viciously,
his fatherly bowels of compassion failed him not though.
See them, in the story, in David toward his ungracious imp

Absalom, that sought his crown, sought his life, abused his
concubines in the sight of all Israel ; yet hear the bowels of
a father, "Be good to the youth Absalom, hurt him not, use 2 Sam. 18.
him well for my sake." See them, in the better harlot of the $\frac{5}{1}$ Kings 3.
twain : out of her motherly bowels, rather give away her 26.
child quite, renounced it rather, than see it hurt. This is
mercy ; here is compassion indeed. *O paterna viscera miserationum!* when we have named them, a multitude of such
mercies, as come from a father's bowels, we have said as much,
as we can say, or can be said.

And mention of this word is not unfit, whether we regard
them (our enemies) *per quos itum est in viscera terræ* (in which
place, God's bowels turned against them and toward us), or
whether we think, that His bowels had pity on our so many
bowels, as should have flown about, all the air over, and
light, some in the streets, some in the river, some beyond it,
some I know not where.

Now, that which maketh up all is the property last put : 3.
quia non deficiunt, or (which is all one) *non consumuntur ;* Their property.
"fail not," or, as ye may read it, "consume not." And so,
as we begun, we end with *non consumpti*. There cannot be
a more kindly consequence than this : our not failing, from
their not failing ; we do not, because they do not. If they
did, we should ; but, *quia non consumptæ illæ non consumpti
nos*, 'for they are not consumed, no more are we.' And
why do they not fail? Because He Himself doth not. He
is the same still, He fails not : His bowels are as He is, so
they fail not, no more than He.

And in this, *quia non deficiunt*, is all the comfort we have.
For, since Jeremy's time, one would be amazed to consider
(the huge number of foul enormities that have been committed, and yet the parties that commit them not consumed),
where there should be mercy to serve for them all. One
would think, by this, they should have been drawn dry. So
they had, but for this לא כלו. It can never be said, Now,
there is all ; there is now no more left. No : an inexhaust
fountain there is of them : never dry, but floweth still fresh
and fresh. And look, even the next words, Jeremy tells us,
"they renew every morning :" no morning comes, but a
fresh supply of them. And even this morning, this fifth of

SERM.
IV.

November, we had a good proof of it. Yea, they are never perfect, the sum is never made up : there is still added every day; and they shall not be consummate, till the *consummatum est* of the world.

And but for these bowels, that still melt ; and for these compassions ever flowing and never failing, they (our enemies) had not failed of their purpose. But, because these failed not, they failed; because these consumed not, "we were not consumed." They are not only plentiful, as, in the plural; and choice, as, from the bowels, the bowels of a father : but perpetual : what talk we of perpetual? they are eternal. These three, their 1. multiplicity, their 2. speciality, their 3. eternity, these three we hold by.

III.
Our recognition.

And now to our recognition. To perform it to the full, as it deserveth, that (I know) we cannot. Worthily to celebrate, and set forth His mercies therein, according to their merit, what tongue of men or Angels can do it? But, shall we not therefore do it, as we can? "We were not consumed :" shall our thankfulness fall into a consumption? His compassion failed us not, shall our recognition fail then? Shall we not find our tongues as well to praise His mercies, as to pray for them? Can we pour out petitions in time of need, and can we not drop forth a few thanks when we have what we would? No, let this be the first : that we answer *Misericordiæ non consumptæ*, with *gratiæ inconsumptæ ;* that our thanks fall not into an hectic.

Then, that we imitate the three properties of this virtue that saved us, and to whom we owe ourselves : no other than those, that be expressed in the text.

1. That we keep the number, do it plurally. Not single thanks for plural mercies : that agrees not. Iterate them over and over, as much as we may. In the weight, we shall surely fall short ; let us make amends with the number. Do it oft, and many times ; in hope, that *sæpe cadendo*, they shall effect that, which *vi*, by any force in them, they are not able.

[Vid. not. in Ovid. ex Pont. 4. 10. 5. ed. Burm.]

This for every one, to give as many as we may, make them many. Now, as many as we are many. As we should have gone all together, as we should have gone ; so, and no otherwise, let us, together, here, all acknowledge His mer-

cies, this day shewed us, and praise Him, all of us, for Ps. 148.11.
them: Praise Him King and Queen, &c.

Yea, not only *Dicat nunc Israel,* but *Dicat nunc paries,* Ps. 118. 2.
Praise Him walls and windows, praise Him lime and stone,
praise Him roof and foundation, "let them praise the Name
of the Lord :" for "He said but a word," and they stood Ps. 148.
fast; He "commanded," *non,* and they were not stirred. 5, 6.
Jeremy speaks to a wall to weep: (Lam. 2. 18.) we may,
with as good reason, to rejoice and give thanks. All that
should have perished together, praise Him together.

2. Next, that we put Him not off with certain (I know
not what) hollow thanks, that have no bowels at all in them.
But do it, *de visceribus, de intimis fibris,* 'from the very
bowels, from the innermost veins, and the smallest threads
of them :' with Him, "Praise the Lord O my soul," וכל קרבי, Ps. 103. 1.
and "all my bowels, all that is within me, all my bones shall Ps. 35. 10.
say," &c. When the bones (the bones that should have been
shivered in sunder); when the bowels (the bowels that should
have been scattered abroad) speak, that is the right speaking.
If every one of us, to himself, would but say the very words
of this verse only, as they stand, "It was," &c. "It was,"
&c. Even this onward were worth the while; if it be not
for form, but feelingly spoken. *Dic, dic, sed intus dic,* 'say
it, but say it from within,' let the bowels speak it; though
our words fail us, they do not. And, indeed, the consumption should have been with fire; shall our recognition
be frozen? no spark, no *vigor igneus,* no fervour at all in it? [Virg. Æn.
How agree these, a fiery destruction and a frozen confession? 6. 730.]
It standeth us upon to be delivered, no less from cold thanks,
than from a hot fire.

3. And that we never fail to do it. No year to inter-
mit it, no week, and (I would I might add) no day neither.
Answer *Misericordia Ejus manet in æternum,* with *Misericor-* Ps. 136. 1.
dias Domini cantabo in æternum ; and not, mercies that never $\begin{smallmatrix}\text{Ps. 89.}\\1, 2.\end{smallmatrix}$
fail, with short thanks and soon done ; specially seeing their
not failing lieth upon our not failing them.

Now, it would do well to seal up all with a recognition
real; that is, the praise of mercy with some work of mercy.
What was done upon us this day? Our preserving. A work
of mercy it was. This work can no way so lively be ex-

S E R M.
IV.

Jas. 2. 16.
pressed, as by a work of like nature : nothing so well, saith St. James, by warm breath as by warm clothes. *Erga con- sumendos,* such as are in danger of it, not by fire, but by cold and nakedness.

This, as it is a most kindly way to resemble it ; so (withal) it is a most effectual means to procure the continuance and not-failing of it. *Magnes est misericordiæ Dei erga nos misericordia nostra in fratres;* 'of God's mercy to us, keeping us from consuming, our mercy toward our poor brethren is the loadstone, to keep them from the like.' So, under one, shall we both set it forth and procure it : procure that, we so much stand in need of, and set forth that virtue, to which we were so much this day beholden.

Now to God ; to Him, and to His mercy ; the bowels of His mercy, and the fresh fountain of them ; that suffered us not to be consumed, but delivered us ; and that from that fire, and that universal, utter, sudden, unnatural consuming by it, the decree whereof was so certainly gone forth against us, come so near us, and we not aware of it : that suffered us not to be consumed, but gave them to be consumed in our steads ; and hath this day presented us all alive to give Him praise for it : to Him, for the multitude of His mercies, for the *paterna viscera miserationum suarum,* that never fail, nor consume themselves, nor suffer us to fail, and be consumed : to Him I say, &c.

A SERMON

PREACHED BEFORE

THE KING'S MAJESTY AT WHITEHALL,

ON THE FIFTH OF NOVEMBER, A.D. MDCXIII.

PROVERBS viii. 15.

By Me Kings reign.

Per Me Reges regnant.

[*By Me Kings reign.* Eng. Trans.]

THESE words may well serve for a sermon, for they be a
piece of a sermon. For all the chapter is a sermon, preached
by one standing "in the top of the high places." "The high Prov. 8. 2.
places," that was then their Church; "the top" of them, that
was the pulpit.

It is the common question, Who preaches? Ever we must
know that: and though the whole book be Solomon's: and
though he be a "preacher" upon record; yet *major Salo-* Eccl. 1. 1.
mone hic, "a greater preacher than Solomon is here." He Mat. 12.42.
was but wise; it is Wisdom itself, made this sermon. And
we may be bold to preach what Wisdom preacheth: a sermon out of such a sermon cannot be amiss.

Specially, this Wisdom, the essential Wisdom of God:
which, upon the point, will prove to be none other but Christ:
and so, our text fall out to be *de verbis Domini,* that is, *de
verbis Domini secundum Salomonem;* for, so there be, no less
than *secundum Matthæum* or *Joannem.*

Which though they were uttered by Him, before He was
in the flesh, what of that? they be no whit the less; but full
out as good gospel, as if they had been recorded by any of
the four Evangelists: yea, and this we may add further;
even Gospel, before any Gospel of them all. Thus much
for the Author of the speech.

The speech itself seems, as if some question there were, *Per quem Reges ?* or some were about to bring the writ of *Quo Warranto,* to know how they claim to be Kings; how to hold their sovereign authority; by whose grant ?

And let not this seem strange : it is no new thing to bring this writ in like cases.

Exod. 2.14.
Mat. 21.23.
One was brought against Moses : "Who made thee a ruler ?" Nay higher; one against our Saviour Himself : "By what authority doest Thou these things, and who gave Thee that authority ?" Against Moses, against Christ; and why not then against Solomon and his fellow King ?

Exod. 3. 14.
Joh. 10. 36.
And this same *Per Me* here is an answer to all. "Who made you, Moses, a ruler ?" He, Whose name is I AM, sent me. Who gave Christ His authority ? He that "sanctified" Him, and sent Him to be the Messias of the world. And here now; Kings, by whom ? *Per Me,* by Him too. These words of His, *charta regia,* this their charter royal : and He That gave it them, will warrant it for good, and bear them out against all the *Per Me*s in the world. This for the nature of the speech.

Bellar.
contra
Barcl.
A point necessary, if ever, at this time to be weighed well, and looked into : wherein this question is put up, and so vexed, that it cannot rest : wherein they have set up an *Anti-Per,* and given him this sentence in his mouth, *Ego facio, ut Rex tuus Rex ne sit,* 'I will make your King no King,' this text *Per Me* notwithstanding. One, to sever *Reges* and *Regnant,* that they shall reign no longer, than He sees cause to suffer them. And is it not time then, to make good their tenures ?

And that do this text and this day. The text, in word; the day, in deed, *cum effectu,* really.

The text, the words indeed (as the words of Wisdom) are but few, and the sentence short; scarce any in Scripture so short : in our tongue, but four words, and they but four syllables. But it fareth with sentences as with coins. In coins, they that in smallest compass contain greatest value are best esteemed; and, in sentences, those that in fewest words comprise most matter are most praised. And such is this.

Exceeding compendious, that we must needs be without

all excuse, (it being but four monosyllables,) if we do not remember it.

And withal, of rich contents; for, upon these four sylla- bles, depend all Kings and kingdoms of the earth: of such force are they.

Of which four, the two latter, *Reges* and *Regnant*, be two as great matters as any be in the world. One, the persons themselves, as they be Kings. The other, the act of their reigning, or bearing rule over nations. These two latter de- pend on the two former, *Per, Me:* which are but one in effect; but He a great one. For it is here positively set down, *asserendo*, that these two latter are by this former; "By" and through Him, That says *Per Me.* "By" and through Him, Kings first settled in their reigns. "By" and through Him, ever since upholden in their reigns. "By" and through Him vouchsafed many miraculous preservations in their reigns. Thus far the text.

Then, "by the tender mercy of our God comes the day Lu. 1. 78. from on high," and giveth great light unto the text: this day, on which a very memorable memorial of a famous *Per Me.* One, in great capital letters: even of *Per Me Reges;* and not of *Per Me Reges* alone, but of *Per Me Leges* (and that too follows here in the verse); and of *Per Me Greges* too; all had gone up, but for this *Per Me.* This day, this *Per Me* soundeth in your ears, and this day this *Per Me* was sealed in your eyes, and this question actually decided.

For the order in treating whereof, our parts must be as The di- our words. Look how many words, so many parts: four of I. either. I. Of *Me* first, the cause: II. then of *Per*, the man- II. ner: III. after of *Per Me Reges*, the persons: IV. and last, IV. of *Per Me regnant*, the act.

Per Me. It is a general rule, *Per dicit causam:* the nature I. of this preposition *Per* is to note a cause certain. And a The cause, Me. certain cause excludeth chance. First then, Kings and king- I. doms have their *Per:* they be not *forte fortunâ,* 'at hap- Kings and king- hazard,' *ex concursu atomorum.* They be no casualties, the doms have wind blows no man to them, saith the Psalm. And *non* Ps. 75. 6. *temere*, saith the Apostle; where *non temere*, as it is "not in Rom. 13. 4. vain," so is it also not an adventure. Causal they are; casual they are not. A *Per* there is, a cause of Kings' reigning.

SERM.
V.
2.

What is that cause? *Per Me :* and *Me* is a Person; and a person is *naturæ rationalis individua substantia,* ' a single or determinate substance of a nature endued with reason.' It is not *res bruta vel muta,* ' no dumb thing or without understanding' is cause of them. He speaks (we hear) : saith, *Per Me.* And His very last words before these be, " I am understanding."

That cause
is a person.

Prov. 8. 14.

Isa. 65. 11.

Against those that do *Jovi mensam ponere,* ascribe it to the position of the stars, to this or that planet in the ascendant.

Jas. 1. 17.

No : it is not *de luminibus* (they be no persons); but *de Patre luminum* (He is). So a cause there is, and no impersonal cause, but *Per Me* a person.

3.
Another
person
beside
themselves.
1 Kings
1. 5.
Ps. 44. 6.
Habak. 1.
16.

What person? *Per Me regnant ;* and that is not *Per se regnant :* so, another person it is besides themselves; one different from them. That they reign is not by or from themselves, but by or from some other besides. *Regnabo,* saith Adonijah, but he failed : it would not be. To teach him, it is not *Per se,* by their " own bow or sword," nor *Marte* nor *Arte,* they reign ; and so to "sacrifice" to them. It is not their own place, they sit in ; nor their own power they execute : it is derived from another person ; *Ipse est Qui fecit nos, et non ipsi nos,* (may they also say,) " He it is That made us, and not we ourselves." A person, and another person.

Ps. 100. 3.

4.
But one
person,
not many.

And who is that other person? Let me tell you this first : it is but one person, not many : *Per Me* is the singular number. It is not *Per nos ;* so, it is not a plurality : no multitude, they hold by. That claim is gone by *Per Me :* one single person it is, *Per Quem.* The other, a philosophical conceit it came from, from those that never had heard this Wisdom preach. In this book, we find not any sovereign power ever seated in any body collective, or derived from them. This we find, that " God He is King ;" that " the kingdoms be His, and to whom He will, He giveth them." That ever they came out of God's hand by any *Per Me,* any grant into the people's hands to bestow, that we find not. One person it is.

Ps. 93. 97,
99.
Dan. 4. 17.

5.
That person neither
man nor
Angel.

I ask, then, this one person who He is? this I find at the twenty-fourth verse, that whosoever He is, He was, " when there were yet no *abyssi,* no depths, nor no mountains upon the earth, nor the earth itself;" He was before all these. I find again, at the twenty-seventh verse, "When the heavens were spread, a decree given to the sea, the foundations of the earth first laid, He was there a worker" together with God: was at the making of all, was Himself maker of all. So, neither man nor Angel; they were not so ancient, they created nothing, they were created themselves.

Then *sileat omnis caro*, "let all flesh keep silence," and *omnis spiritus* too, in this point of *Per Me*. Neither the spirit, that said of the kingdoms of the earth, "All these are mine;" nor he, that though he "have horns like the lamb, yet speaketh words like the dragon." These four syllables are a *supersedeas* to all books or book-makers for any man's *Per Me*, any man's claim. It is no man. And if no man, then no pope; for he also is "a man," as St. Peter saith he was; and *circumdatus*, "compassed with infirmities," St. Paul saith, "he is." Sure, he made not the earth; himself is made of earth. The *abyssus*, "the deep," was made, ere he ascended out of it: the seven hills, long before he sat on them. He is not this *Per Me*; they hold not of him: they hold of *Per Me*, That created Heaven and earth. _{Zech.2.13.}

And this *Per Me* will bear no *Per alium* besides. He that must say, *Per Me Reges*, must also say, *Per Me cœlum et terra*. None but He That can say the one, can say the other. Therefore none with Him in this *Per*. None to step forth and rejoin, *Etiam per me*, 'and by me too;' unless he can say *Etiam per me cœlum et terra*. *Per alium* then hath no place here.

But might not the High-Priest claim deputation under *Per Me*? For that, there is a ruled case of it here, in him that was the setter down of this (Solomon). Had the High-Priest, had Abiathar, ever a *Per me* for him? It is well known, his *Per me* went with Adonijah, against Solomon: his *Per me*, if it could, would have deposed Solomon. But so far was it from him to say *Per me* Solomon, that contrary, Solomon might say and did, *Per me* Abiathar. Depose Solomon he could not; deposed he was himself. *Non nobis Domine, non nobis*, would he have said: it was *Per Me* the wrong way with him.

Well then, being neither man nor Angel, (since they made not the world,) God it must be of force; there is, in the rea-

[Marginal references: Zech. 2. 13. Mat. 4. 9. Rev. 13. 11. Acts 10. 26. Heb. 5. 2. Rev. 13. 1; 17. 9. 1 Kings 1. 7. 1 Kings 2. 27. Ps. 115. 1. 6. But God.]

sonable nature, no other person left, but He : and He it is. He, the party that speaks : " By Me Kings," I am the cause that Kings reign. Then, *Reges quod sunt, per Deum sunt;* ' Kings, what they are, by God they are.' Πρῶτον ἀξίωμα, saith Chrysostom : and ' a special dignifying' of their states it is, so they are. It was, we find, wont to be the usual style, yea, even of popes themselves, writing to Kings, to wish them health *in Eo per Quem Reges regnant,* ' in Him by Whom Kings do reign.' And that was neither pope, nor people ; but God alone, Whose proper style that is.

In 13. ad Rom.

7. God, the Son.

By God then. I ask yet further, by what Person of the Godhead? so far we have warrant to go by this text. It is Wisdom, whose speech all this is : no created wisdom, but the Wisdom of God created all things, itself uncreate; that is, the Son of God. For, whom Solomon here calleth Wisdom, the same (in the thirtieth chapter after) he termeth the Son. " What is His name," (speaking of God,) or " What is His Son's name ?" By Him, by that Person do they reign : and now at the last, are we come to the right *Per Me.*

Prov.30. 4.

1. As the middle cause.

Per, the preposition, would teach us so much, if there were nothing else. *Per dicit causam mediam,* ' it designeth a middle cause.' And He is the middle Person of the great cause, *causa causarum : a Deo,* saith St. Paul ; *Per Me,* saith Solomon ; from God the Father, by God the Son. We may know it, it is Christ's preposition, this (ever) ; *Per Christum Dominum Nostrum.*

Rom.13.1.

2. As man.

And by Him, most properly : for in that He was to be man, all the benefits, which were to come from God to man, were to come by Him. He the *Per* of all: among which, this one of regal regimen is a principal one.

3. As Wisdom.

By Him again : because He is Wisdom (which I reckon worth a note) ; that the *Per* of kingdoms, whereby they consist, is not power so properly (the attribute of the first,) as wisdom (the attribute of the second Person): they stand rather by wisdom than force. Besides, *Sapientis est ordinare,* saith the great philosopher, ' the proper work of wisdom is to order.' And what is anarchy, but a disordered chaos of confusion ? Or what is rule, but an εὐταξία, ' a setting and holding of all in good order?' This being Wisdom's proper work, this *Per* is most properly His.

By Him, yet again : because on Him hath the Father con- 4. As a King.
ferred all the kingdoms of the earth : we read it in the second Ps. 2. 8.
Psalm. We see Him, Rev. 19, " with many crowns on His Rev.19.12.
head." Meet then it was, that the Kings of the several
quarters of the earth, should be by Him, That is *Rex uni-* Ps. 47. 7.
versæ terræ. That the Kings of the several ages of the
world should be by Him, Who is *Rex sæculorum,* Whose Ps.145. 13.
" dominion endureth throughout all ages." In a word: *ut*
utrobique regnetur per Christum ; and that all crowns, both
the crown of glory in Heaven, and the crowns of highest
dignity here on earth, should be holden of Him, all; as all
are. Thus by this time we see this *Per Me,* who He is.

Now return I to *Per :* there is much in the right taking II.
of this word. What *Per* is it? There is a *Per* of permission; The manner; *Per.*
as we say in the Latin, *Per me licet,* ' You may for all me,' 1.
good leave have you, I hinder you not. Or, as in English, Not by permission.
By Him, that is, besides Him they came, and He stopped
them not. Is this the *Per ?* Indeed some such thing is
blundered at, as if God only permitted them, and scarce
that.

Thus comes one of them forth with the matter, and makes
it the very first words of his book. The Priest, he is *a solo*
Deo ; but, the King, he is *ex importunitate populi:* the people
importuned God, and He yielded with much ado, *ægre,* (His
own word) ' against His will.' And so we must interpret
Per Me, that is, *Contra Me ;* " By Me," that is, all against
My mind it is, that Kings reign, but I bear them, or bear
with them. Upon the matter, this it is : they would have
Kings to be, by toleration only ; and so, by that *Per,* are all
the evils and mischiefs in the world. And are not Kings
much beholden to these men, think you ?

But, this *Per* we reject utterly : it cannot be. For, though
the Latin *Per* will bear this sense, the Greek διὰ, the Hebrew
בִּי will by no means; the phrase, the idiom of the tongue
will in no wise endure it. Διὰ will admit no permission;
nor בִּי neither. Away then with that.

How take we *Per* then? What need we stand long about 2.
it, having another *Per,* and of the same person to pattern it But by commis-
by ? *Omnia per Ipsum facta sunt,* saith St. John ; and the sion.
same saith Solomon by and by after, in this chapter. Then, John 1. 3.

SERM.
V.

as "by Him all things made" there; so, by Him Kings reign here. The world, and the government of the world, by the same *Per* both; one and the same cause institutive of both. That was not by bare permission, I trust; no more, these.

3.
By the Word.

Ps. 148. 5.

Ps. 82. 6.

Ps. 110. 1.

Joh. 10.35.

Rom. 13. 2.

Per Ipsum, they; and if *Per Ipsum, per Verbum, quia Ipse est Verbum.* For, how were they, the creatures, made? *Dixit et facta sunt;* by the Word, by Him. And how these (Kings)? By the same *Ego dixi.* Even by the same, that He Himself, *Dixit Dominus Domino meo.* As He then, they. And so doth Christ Himself interpret, *Ego dixi,* πρὸς οὓς ὁ λόγος ἐγένετο. A word came to them; and what manner was it? St. Paul telleth us it was διαταγὴ, "an ordinance," a word of high authority: the imperial decrees have no other name but Διαταγαὶ. This now then is more than a *Per* of permission. A *Per* of commission it is; a special warrant, an ordinance imperial, by which Kings reign.

4.
By His will.
1 Pet. 2.15.
Rom. 13.4.
1. Expressed by His word.

2 Chron. 9. 8.

By Him, then; by what of Him? by His will. *Hæc est voluntas Dei,* saith St. Peter, and *tibi in bonum,* saith St. Paul, "for thy good." His will then, His good-will toward men, expressed by His word: word of power (we have heard): and word of wisdom; for He is wisdom: and word of love; for even "because God loved Israel," did He set Solomon King over them.

2. By His deed.

1 Cor. 15. 10.
Job 36. 7.
Ps. 18. 39.
Ps. 89. 20.
Ps. 21. 3.

Expressed by His word. His word only? Nay, His deed too, His best deed, His gift; *Dedi vobis Regem;* gift of grace; as, even they acknowledge in their styles, that *Gratiâ Dei sunt quod sunt.* Given by Him, sent by Him, placed in their thrones by Him, vested with their robes by Him, girt with their swords by Him, anointed by Him, crowned by Him. All these 'by Hims' we have, toward the understanding of *Per Me:* so by Him, as none are, or can be by Him more.

3. By His Name.

Ps. 82. 6.

Expressed by His word and deed only? Nay (there is nothing but His Name besides) by His Name too; so by His Name, as His very chiefest Name, Christ, He imparteth to them. And, that is not without mystery: to shew their near alliance to Him. "I have said ye are gods:" which of the Persons, that are each of them God? It followeth, *Filii Altissimi,* "Sons of the Most High." Son, that is

Christ's Name; He the person then, to whom they are beholden: He by whom they are. To shew, they are sons,
and have their descent properly from Him, *Rex Regum* is Rev.19.16.
"upon His thigh;" and Melchisedek His first King and His
type, is brought in "without father and without mother," Heb. 7. 3.
to shew, that Kings are the generation of God.

"By" Him. Nay, more than "by" Him (if you look   5.
better upon the word). There is no "By" in the Hebrew; "By" Him,
and yet the word is בִּי. But that (in true and exact pro- Him.
priety rendered) is "In Me," not "By Me." The meaning is, that they are first in Him, and so come forth
from Him.

And yet, so from Him, as still they be in Him; both Isa. 62. 3.
corona Regis, saith Esay, and *cor Regis*, saith Solomon, Prov. 21.1.
their persons and estates both, *in manu Domini*.

And in Him, as He saith, "My Father in Me, and I in Joh. 17.21.
Him;" so, they in Him, and He in them. For, such is the
nature of the prepositions, the Holy Ghost hath made choice
of, as they may be inverted and verified both ways. For, as
it is true, they reign in and by Him; so is it likewise true,
He reigns in and by them. They in God, and God in them,
reciproce. He in them, as His deputies; they, in Him, as
their author and authorizer. He, by their persons; they,
by His power. And so having brought them to Him, even
into Him, and lodged them in Him, there let us leave them.

This while we have been in the two former; 1. *Per*,   III.
2. *Me*. Now to the two latter; 3. *Per Me Reges*, and The per-
4. *Per Me regnant*.   *Reges.*

Per Me Reges. And first, I am glad we have met with   1.
this word *Reges, in propriis terminis:* when we meet with *Reges in propriis*
some other, there is such pinching at them. The Apostle *terminis.*
speaks of Higher Powers. O, it is too general; it may be Rom.13.1.
powers Ecclesiastic, as well as civil; a mere shift. The
Psalmist saith, *Ego dixi Dii;* that is not home neither; Ps. 82. 6.
there is mention of Judges in the Psalm, as well as Princes.
But, here is a word, will hold them: Kings in express terms,
totidem literis. No evasion here, no shifting it. This is
home, I trust.

Per Me Reges. Why, what great matter is that? *Per
Illum omnia*, saith St. Paul, " All things are by Him." Rom. 11.
36.

SERM.
V.
Jas. 1. 17.
2.

Reges specially, above all other creatures.

Mat. 9. 8.

All things; but all good things specially, saith St. James. Why, by Him, there can nothing come, but good.

Thirdly then, special good things. By a special *Per*, they. And Kings are such, and for such reckoned up here, in this very chapter. Even for one of the principallest benefits vouchsafed mankind by God, this " By Me Kings :" for will ye but mark this, they have precedence, are reckoned up here, before the creation itself; for that cometh after, at the twenty-fourth verse. To shew, it is (as indeed it is) better for us, not to be at all, than not to be under rule. Better no creation, than no government. God is highly to be blessed for this *Per Me Reges :* that He hath given *potestatem talem hominibus,* " such power unto men."

3.

Reges, without qualification.
1. Of Religion.

Now, I weigh the word *Reges*. What? any by Him? any in gross without qualification? what, without any regard of religion at all? Sure, if none but true professors had been here meant, it must have been but *Per Me Rex ;* for none but one, but this Solomon, was then such, of all the Kings of the earth. But, in that it is *Reges,* the Holy Ghost's meaning is, to take in the rest, Hiram and Pharaoh and Hadad : they are in too, in this *Reges.* For, where the Scripture distinguishes not, no more do we. Be their religion what it will, by Him they are.

2. Of Tyranny.
Nu. 16. 3.
Hos.13.11.

But, what if they take too much upon them (Korah's exception)? Then it is *Dedi vobis Regem in irâ,* saith God by the Prophet. Angry I was, when I gave him; but I gave him though. *Per Me iratum,* it is ; but *Per Me* it is still ; *Per Me,* though with a difference.

4.
All by Him, made, and unmade.
Hos. 8. 10.
1 Sam. 8. 18.

Hos.13.11.

But this *onus principis,* (say they in the Prophet,) how may we be rid of it ? Is there any other *Per Me* to go unto, to deprive or depose them ? Sure, where the worst is reckoned that can be of them, *Clamabunt ad Dominum* is all I find. No *Per* to do it but He. By Him, and by none but by Him, they be ; by Him, and by none but Him, they cease to be. In nature, every thing is dissolved by the same means it came together. In law, institution and destitution belong both to one. In divinity, the Prophet in one and the same verse saith *Dedi vobis Regem,* in the fore-part ; and with one breath, *Abstuli eum,* in the latter. So, both pertain to Him ; *Dominus dedit, Dominus abstulit.* As for this new *Per me,* we argue from the text : he makes no kings (we know) ; and as he makes none, so he can unmake none. No right, to one *Per,* more than another.

All be Kings then by Him ; yet not all alike. God forbid, but there should be degrees, *magis* and *minus,* one more than another: but we should put a difference between Melchisedek and Nimrod ; between Solomon and Saul.

We say then, All Kings by Him; but, among all, and above all, such as he that set down this, such as Solomon ; for he, by the great capital *Per Me. Per Me iratum,* those other; *Per Me propitium,* he : and that is the *Per* indeed. Thus much he doth insinuate, by adding in the latter part of the verse, (which commonly is the *exegesis* of the former,) namely, if *justa decernunt* do come too. If he be a righteous King, as Melchisedek, " King of righteousness;" if he sow " the fruit of righteousness in peace," that is, be a peaceable King, as Solomon ; if he rule *Per Me,* that is, *per Sapientiam,* rule wisely. Those are *Per Me propitium ;* those are Kings *primæ intentionis,* Kings of special favour.

5.
All, but especially good Kings.

Heb. 7. 2.
Jas. 3. 18.

This for the person. Now to the act : *Per Me, Regnant.*

And I make these two, two diverse, because some are *Reges,* "Kings," and yet reign not (as true heirs defeated). And some reign, and are no Kings (as do all usurpers of the throne, *per fas nefasque).* Always, one thing it is to be a King; another to reign. Joash was the true King, all those six years he reigned not; Athaliah reigned all those six years, yet true Queen was she never any. Of such, God saith in Osee, *Regnaverunt, sed non a Me.* Why ? for, *Per Me Reges regnant,* " By Me Kings reign." Kings, of lawful and true descent, they reign by Me ; these were none such. So they reigned ; but, without any *Per* from *Me.* But, when these meet, and they that be *Reges de jure regnant de facto,* then it is as it should be : and *Per Me* it is, that they so meet.

IV.
The Act;
Regnant.

[2 Kings
11.]

Hos. 8. 4.

This *Regnant* I consider as an act, three ways : 1. as it hath a beginning; 2. as it hath continuance ; 3. as it hath rectitude or obliquity incident to every act. *Regnant,* that they reign at all ; *Regnant diu,* that they reign long ; *Regnant recte,* that they reign aright. And every one hath his *Per. Per, januæ,* ' By, the door:' by Him they enter their reign. *Per, lineæ,* ' By, the line,' which He stretcheth out over every government, longer or shorter : by Him they continue their reign.   *Per, regulæ,* ' By, the rule :' so reign, as they swerve not from Him, touch Him still ; continue with Him, and He with them, and so He will make them to continue long.

I am led to this, because you shall see these three duly set upon every King's head, throughout all the story of the Bible.

1. Such a King was so many years old, when he began his reign : there is his inchoation, his *Regnant,* his door of entrance.

2. And then, so many years he reigned in Jerusalem, or Samaria : there is his continuation, his *diu regnant,* his *Per* of line or continuance.

3. Then ever follows, if you mark it ; either, And he did well, and walked in the steps of his father David : there is the manner, his *bene regnant,* his rule or rectitude ; or, And he did evil in the sight of the Lord, and turned not from the ways of Jeroboam ; there is his obliquity, out of rule himself, and brought all out of rule with him.   This holds in all, and in all will hold, after they be once off of the stage.

I.
*Regnant,
Per,
januæ:*
The entrance.

As it is *actus inchoatus :* they reign, that is, they come to the crown, they begin their reigns.

It is generally true, that the main frame of government, the first raising of it, could be by none but this *Per Me.* But I insist on particulars rather ; wherein, any that shall but weigh what difficulties, what oppositions be raised, what plots and practices, to keep *Reges* from *Regnant,* those from it whose of right it is, shall be forced to confess, that even by Him they have their first entrance.   Take him that is next hand, Solomon : and he that shall mark Adonijah's plot, drawing the High-Priest, Abiathar, and the general of the field, Joab, into a strong faction against him, shall find, Solomon was bound to acknowledge that *Per Me* he came in.   Or if he will not, Adonijah himself will, he was forced to do it ; "That the kingdom was turned from him, and was his brother's, for it came unto him (even *Per Me*) by the Lord." This confession of his is upon record, 1 Kings, second chapter, fifteenth verse.   And your Majesty was *non ignara mali hujus,* was not altogether free from these : it is English I

speak. Possibly, from Joab you were; but not from Abiathar; his bulls, they were abroad: and some there were that
could not enter by the door, but were climbing up another
way. Yet for all these, you came to your reign, and you
came by the right *Per*, by the door: and, this I know; you
are one of the number of those Kings that ascribe their
Regnant to this *Per Me.* This, for *actus inchoatus:* now
they are in.

But when they are in, they may out again soon enough: **2.**
when begun, end quickly; if *Per Me*, as He was the cause *Regnant diu, Per,*
procreant, so He be not also the cause conservant, and make *lineæ:*
their reign *actus continuatus;* draw the line out along, keep *Their continuance.*
and continue them for many years in it. *Regnant* is true in
the first instant. One reigns, if it be but for a sevennight, as 1 Kings
Zimri reigned no longer: but what is that? Or what is it 16. 15.
to reign a month, as Shallum; or three, as Jehoahaz; or six, 2 Kings
as Zachariah did? Nothing: the continuance, *proprie lo-* 15. 13.
quendo, that is the reign; and *Regnant* without this *Per* is as 23. 31.
good as nothing. And the text is for this. The word in 15. 8.
Hebrew is not *Regnant* in the present, "do reign;" but *Reg-*
nabunt in the future, "shall reign, or continue reigning."
And so is the preposition *Per* for it too. For, *Per addit dura-*
tionem; ' adds ever a continuance,' where it is added; as is
evident, by per-sist, per-manent, per-durable, per-severance,
per-petuity.

And this now, questionless, depends upon God alone, even
their quick cutting off, or their long preserving in their reigns.
He can draw the line longer or shorter; draw it out still, or
snap it off. He can take them from their reign by the "hand-
writing on the wall," MENE, &c. He can take it from them Dan. 5. 25.
by *solvit baltheum Regum,* "taking off their collar," and "cast- Job 12. 18.
ing their throne down to the ground." He can call in a Ps. 89. 44.
foreign enemy, stir up a seditious subject, let loose the sea of
popularity in upon them; unlawfully to do it, but to do it
though. Many such things are with Him.

Now we are at the main. For, here comes all the danger:
there is such heaving and lifting at them after they be in;
such thrusting by force, such undermining by fraud: so
many *Per mes, Per me* Clement, Chastel, Catesby; and they
again so many *Pers, Per* knives, pistol, poison, powder, all

SERM. against this *Per* of continuance; as, be the former how it
V. will, they cannot but confess here, that *Per Me* it is that they
hold out their reigns.

And here, falls in kindly this day's design, and the visible
Per Me that happened on it: for by Him it was, and by His
Lament. 3. mercy, that King and all were not quite "consumed;" that
22. your reign and your life were not determined both together.
Ps. 30. 3. Not, that you "went not down," with David, "into the pit;"
but that you went not up, up into the air in (I know not how
many) pieces, and that now, after thus many years, it is *Regnant* with you still: and may it be *Per Me regnat* (so we all
pray); and not *Per Me regnat* only, but *Per Me regnabit,*
many times, many years more. I but put you in mind here
of what I told you right now: it is *In Me*, in Hebrew, not
Per Me; "in" Him, not "by" Him, though never so hard
by Him (for that is without Him); but even "in" Him, and
then they be safe.

And in Him you have reigned: for He hath enclosed you,
as it were, and compassed you on every side. As in a for-
tress, strong-hold, or place of defence; so have you reigned
in Him: that as David oft calleth God, so may you; your
Ps. 18. 2. "rock," your "refuge," your sanctuary of safeguard: so that
Ps. 89. 22. "the enemy" hath not been able to do you "violence," nor
"the son of wickedness" had power "to hurt" you.

Jas. 4. 6. And yet, there is more in this *Regnabunt*, "greater grace"
yet. For we may extend it yet further, to a continuance,
not in themselves, in their persons only; but, in their posterity too. That when it shall cease with them, and they in
their graves, yet shall it be *Regnabunt* still, and they reign in
their race and progeny, when they have done reigning themselves. This draws out the *Per* longer; for so reign they, many
ages; not their own only. Kings, in themselves; Kings, in
their seed; *Reges a sæculo in sæculum*, 'from one generation
to another.' By Saul, and by David, we may plainly see;
one thing it is, to bring one to be King, as Saul was; another, to establish the kingdom in his line, as with David it
was. And it is that he magnifieth so much, 2 Sam. 7. That
God had not only brought him thitherto, to the crown; that
[2 Sam. 7. was but a small thing: but that also He had spoken of His
18, 19.] servant's house, *in longinquum*, "for a long time;" for that is

the right *Regnabunt.* The right *Regnabunt* is not that in
Dan. 2. like an image, which when it is broken, nothing
comes of it; but the right is that, Daniel the fourth
chapter, where it is like a goodly tree that hath branches
come out of the stem, which will prove scions and be new
grafted again, and so successively derive itself down to many
generations. This also is *Per Me;* and altogether by him,
and in His hand, Who can establish succession, as to David;
and who can also bid Jeremy " Write this man destitute of Jer. 22. 30.
children, of him there shall none come more to sit upon the
throne of Israel."

This for the continuance, *diu regnant.* I will but touch   **3.**
the third : I would not have touched it, but that it is a *Regnant
recte; Per,*
special means for the second, of continuance. To *diu,* the *regulæ.*
way is by *recte;* to rule long, the way, to rule right : nay, it **The**
manner.
is the way to rule for ever : and without *recte,* the shorter
the better; better for them, and better for all parts.

Thus doth one *Per* still lead us to another : for as it is
true, *Per dicit causam,* so is it likewise true, *Per dicit regu-
lam.* By Him, as a cause ; by Him, as a rule : from which
rule not swerving, there is a direct promise, Deuteronomy,
the seventeenth chapter : " He shall prolong his reign, and Deu. 17.
not his alone, but even his children's too, in the midst of 20.
Israel." And by that rule, a long line shall be drawn, for
the drawing out of his reign many years.

And, this we need not seek for, anywhere else ; it is even
in the body of the word. For *rectitudo* and *rectus,* and *recte,*
substantive, adjective, and adverb, all come of *rego.* So doth
regula too itself : that they need be no strangers one to another ; there is an alliance, and there ought to be a reciprocal
reference between them and *regere,* and between *regere* and
them. *Erit apud rectissimum Rex,* saith Moses, Deuteronomy Deu. 33. 5.
the thirty-third chapter ; " He shall be as straight, as near [Vulg.]
the rule as may be."

Now, that rule is, here, *Me;* and *Me* is wisdom; and
wisdom is the rule which God Himself draweth His lines
by : and Kings, as in other points, so in this, to be as like,
and draw as near God as they may.

But then, care would be had, it be that wisdom which is
Me indeed. For Ahithophel's and Jeroboam's go for wis-

dom, in the world; but, indeed, such wisdom, as St. James termeth it, is "earthly, sensual," and hath somewhat of the devil in it. It is not that worldly wisdom, they be Kings by; but that which is from above, and that (I told you) is Christ. What they are, by Him they are; that they continue, by Him it is: Who is and will be *pro illis qui per Illum;* 'be for them, that be by Him;' and will not see or suffer the overthrow of His own ordinance.

And, may I not then commend Him (this *Per Me*) to them? That since they reign by that Wisdom which is Christ, they would reign by that, and by no other wisdom. And that reciprocation I touched before; that seeing they reign by Him, He may reign by them; *regnet per illos, qui regnant per Illum;* since they rule by Him, to be ruled by Him. There cannot be a more reasonable request than this; *Regnet per Reges, per Quem regnant Reges.*

Specially, since this *Per* of the rule will bring them to the *Per* of persistence; so long as they continue with Him, and He with them, He will continue them and their reigns, and nothing shall stir them. But, let go that, and take them to another *Per me.* And I dare not promise aught: if any have miscarried, he hath first let his *Per* go, and then after was put out of protection: and then the sons of perdition had power over him, and his continuance soon came to an end.

Take this then for the farewell of this point. Sever not *Reges* from *Per Me*, and you shall never sever *Reges* from *Regnant:* but if they have once lost their *Per Me*, marvel not, if they lose their *Regnant* not long after.

The application to the people.
But, this sermon was made for the people: to them then I turn. For as, if princes well weigh this *Per Me*, they will rule the better; so, if the people do the like, they will obey the sooner. This is sure: if *Per Me Reges regnant,* then *Per Me populi parent:* if from Him the power of sovereignty, by Him also the duty of allegiance; which we do bear them, even for this very *Per Me;* even therefore because they be of Him. *Δι' Αὐτοῦ,* saith Solomon here, *Per Ipsum,* "by Him:" *Δι' Αὐτὸν,* saith St. Peter, *propter Ipsum,* "for Him, for His sake."

1 Pet. 2. 13.

Two points I would commend to you, and so end. Christ

it is, That here speaketh: Wisdom it is that here speaketh. Since it is Christ here speaketh, it is against Christian religion; since it is Wisdom here speaketh, it is folly to hold, to say, or to do the contrary.

For Christ: if *Per Me Reges* be from Christ, from whom is the other *Per me?* *Per me rebelles, Per me regicidæ:* from whom they? If "By Me Kings reign" be Christ's; By me Kings slain, whose *Per* is that *Per?* That *Per* cannot be the *Per* of any, but of Christ's opposite: who is that? *Quæ conventio Christi et Belial?* "What agreement hath 2 Cor. 6. 15. Christ and Belial?" There he is: you see whose brood they be, that go that way, even Belial's brood. He, out of his enmity against *Per Me,* can neither endure *Reges* nor *Regnant;* but stirs up enemies against them both, both *Reges* and *Regnant.* Against *Reges, Regicidas,* to assault their persons; against *Regnant, Rebelles,* to subvert their estates.

And it is he that sets up this *anti-per,* who takes upon Joh. 10. 35. him to loose this Scripture; to sever *Reges* and *Regnant:* nay, (which is worse than this,) to make saints and martyrs of them, *qui vias dant ad delendos Reges,* "that set their ways Prov. 31. 3. to destroy Kings," against which there is a special caveat in the last chapter of this book. But, (which is worst of all; for though the rebel be evil, yet the rebel-maker is far worse:) he that raiseth up this new sect of rebel-makers, worse than rebels themselves: for if they be the brood of Belial, *qui vias dant,* what shall they be, *qui vias docent?* shall not they be *primogeniti Satanæ,* 'Belial's first-begotten?' that score out the way for destroying of Kings: tell, by whom, and in what sort it is to be proceeded; to make a very method or agend of it.

There is a short resolution in this text for all these. Seeing it is Christ, it must be unchristian, if not antichristian, to make any such course: Christ's disciples they are not; none of His sure, that either put their hand to practise it, or their pen, or tongue, to defend it.

And as, if this be Christ, it is unchristian; so, if this be Wisdom, then is this their course folly: and so it is, three ways.

1. Folly first, to seek to sever *Reges* and *Regnant* from *Per Me;* it will not be. To think, they can set themselves

S E R M.
V.
against Kings, and yet never have to do with God at all.
But, Kings, we said, are in God; so they must go through
Him, before they can come at them : they cannot deal with
Kings, but they must begin with God first. Gamaliel's po-

Acts 5. 39. sition is sound and good : all one to "fight with God," and
that which is of God : for they cannot be severed.

Acts 9. 5. 2. And if they cannot; to fight against God, to "kick
against the pricks," that is folly and madness, I am sure. Ye
may return them all for fools, that go about it : that think,

1 Cor.1.25. with their devices to outreach Him, "Whose folly is wiser
than their wisdom :" or by their practices to overbear Him,

1 Cor.1.25. "Whose weakness is stronger than their strength :" He will
be too hard for them, do what they can.

3. Specially, which is the third, having had so often, so
certain experience, that they which have gone about it still
come by the worse. For, extreme folly must it needs be, to
begin that, which none that ever yet began could bring to
good end; which all that ever yet began, ever came themselves to an evil end : as to an evil end have they come, all
the pack of them. These four words have put them all down.

And, as it falls out this day, of this folly we have *exemplum sine exemplo :* and in the success thereof, may all the
rest read their destiny ! For, by the light of this day, any
that is not blind may see, that by and through Him Kings
reign, in that, by and through Him, they that would have
blown them up are come to a shameful end. Blow them up,
they shall not; but blow themselves down they shall: down

Nu. 16.33. after Korah, the same way he went: even to their own

Acts 1. 25. place, with Korah and Judas, to the bottom of hell. That
so it may appear to all the world, since this *Per Me* is
Wisdom, if Wisdom set them up, folly it shall be, in them
that seek or set themselves to put them down ; to subvert
either *Reges* their persons, or *Regna* their states.

Lu. 7. 35. Let "Wisdom then be justified of her children :" and so
many as love *Per Me,* love and be friends and take part with
both their persons and states. If they be *Per Ipsum,* " by
Him," put our *Per* to His *Per,* that they may be by us too :
we cannot err, we are sure, if we keep the same *Per* that
Christ doth.

And, to conclude, let this be our last duty : since we know

whence they be, we know whither to go ; since by Whom
they be, to Whom to repair, if we have any business concerning them. If we have a good Prince, Whom to thank ; if
otherwise, Whom to appease.

But if a good, (for to that case I return,) never to look
upon Him, but to lift up our eyes withal to this *Per Quem.*
As, to thank Him, that He hath preserved him many other
times ; (but especially and above other this day ; him and
his, that is, him and us all :) so, duly to pray to Him, that
he which reigneth thus by Him, that is, by His appointment,
may safe, and well, and long reign by Him, that is, by His
protection. To thank Him, for *Per Me regnat,* and to be
suitors to Him, for *Per Me regnabit ;* that He would draw
out this *Per,* and make it a long *Per, Per multos annos.*
That it may ever be (as in the text it is) *regnabit* still ; still,
in the future, " shall reign."

" Shall reign" out his own age himself, in person : there
is one *regnabit.*

" Shall reign" in his issue and offspring, and that many
ages : there is another *regnabit.*

" Shall reign" in the life of memory, and a blessed remembrance of his time and reign, and that through all ages : there
is a third *regnabit.*

" Shall reign" all these. And, beyond all these, there is
another yet, as the last, so the best of all : " shall reign" all
these, *per Deum,* ' by God ;' and, after all these, shall reign
cum Deo, ' with God,' in the glory, joy, and bliss of His
heavenly kingdom, and that perpetually : which kingdom
shall have none end, be in *sæcula sæculorum.* To which
kingdom, I &c.

A SERMON

THE KING'S MAJESTY AT WHITEHALL,

ON THE FIFTH OF NOVEMBER, A.D. MDCXIV.

PROVERBS xxiv. 21—23.

*My son, fear thou the Lord, and the King; and meddle not
with them that are given to change.*

*For their destruction shall rise suddenly; and who knoweth the
destruction of them both?*

These things also belong to the wise.

[*Time Dominum, Fili mi, et Regem; et cum detractoribus non commiscearis.*

*Quoniam repente consurget perditio eorum; et ruinam utriusque quis
novit?*

Hæc quoque sapientibus. Latin Vulg.]

[*My son, fear thou the Lord and the King; and meddle not with them
that are given to change.*

*For their calamity shall rise suddenly; and who knoweth the ruin of
them both?*

These things also belong to the wise. Engl. Trans.]

S E R M.
VI.
Prov. 8. 15.
The text:
Anno 1613.
WE begin, this year, where we left the last. Then, " By
Me Kings reign;" now, by Me, *rerum novarum studiosi,*
'seditious persons' come to ruin and destruction. For, that
is the sum and substance of this text.

The sum
of the text.
It is a fatherly advice given by Solomon to his son, not to
meddle or make with them "that are given to changes."
And there was a change; such a change as never was seen
or heard in any age, meant and meddled in this day. So
the first verse interested in the day.

And, this is not a bare advice, and nothing else; but upon a penalty. And that penalty set down, by way of a prophecy. And that prophecy fulfilled, and that penalty extended, this day too. So, the second verse likewise. So that, this day, the first verse was justified; the wisdom of the counsel, that it is wise and good ; and, this day, the second verse was verified, the event of the prophecy, that it is certain and sure : for destruction followed them that followed not it.

The points in it are, as the verses are, two. 1. There The division. is an advice in the former: " My son, fear God and the King," &c. 2. with a penalty annexed in the latter: "For their destruction shall arise suddenly," &c.

There is in the advice, 1. first, a kind of commending of I. it, 2. then the advice itself.

1. The commendation stands first: for, *Fili mi*, I take to be a commendation. That it is a counsel a father would give to his son : and that is no evil one, we may be sure. Do but cast your eye over the counsels in this book, that are given with a *Fili mi*, you shall find they be *de meliore notâ*, special ones, all very well worth the giving.

2. The advice itself follows: the main drift whereof is a retentive against meddling with certain persons; persons such as this day brought forth. To fear, and to forbear. " Fear God and the King :" and forbear to have to do or deal with any such. It consists of two counterpoints, a *Fac* and a *Fuge*. ' Do' this, and ' eschew' that. The *Fac* is, " Fear God, and the King." The *Fuge* is, *Et ne commiscearis*, " Meddle not." Follow one, fly the other.

Now, it is punishment enough for a man, not to follow good II. counsel when it is given him ; yet hath God so ordered, as there goeth ever some further evil, with the contempt of good counsel. As, with the contempt of this, there goeth a penalty, no less than destruction and ruin; and that, a sudden destruction, and an unknown ruin. It shall surprise them on the sudden; and it shall be such withal, as *Quis scit*, saith Solomon, " Who knows ? " that is, no man knows, how fearful. Print well in your minds these four ; 1. destruction, 2. ruin, 3. *repente*, 4. *Quis scit ?* They be the *quatuor novissima* of the text. And, for fear of these, fear to meddle with these spirits.

SERM.
VI.

So Solomon sits here as a counsellor, and as a judge. A counsellor, to advise; a judge, to pronounce. Hear his counsel, then; if not, hear your sentence. And choose which verse you will be in. There is no escaping them both. In one of them we must be, all. Either in the verse of counsel, " Fear God and the King ;" &c. or in the verse of penalty, " For their destruction," &c.

III. The shutting up of all is, *Hæc quoque sapientibus :* so read it the Seventy with this verse, and so the Fathers all; and not, as now it standeth, with the verse following. The meaning is, that this is no counsel for fools : no man so wise, the wisest man that is, it may well become him to take it. Commonly, they that meddle in these matters want no wit ; are wise at least in their own conceits : therefore say the Seventy, Ταῦτα δὲ λέγω ὑμῖν τοῖς σοφοῖς ; " You, that think you are, and would be taken for wise, to you be this spoken."

I.
The advice.
1. The commendation thereof. From a Father.

I will speak a few words of the commendation. *Fili mi.* It is of a father, to his son. True and hearty is the counsel of a father to his child.

The very force of natural affection so whetting the wit, as oft, even a simple man will give his child no simple advice, but sound and good. But, if it happen not always to be of the best, it is the best he had, you may be sure. There might want brains; the good heart of a father was not wanting.

And he wise.

To supply that want, I ask secondly, who is this father? I find, that it is Solomon that speaketh : one famous for his wisdom among the sons of men: one able to give good counsel worth the following. And yet, I know not how, they that are holden for wise, otherwhile give not all the best. But it is because they bend not their minds; and they bend them not, because they respect not the parties much, they give it to. But, were it *Fili mi,* had they to him the hearty true zeal of a father, it would make them gather their wits together, and help it much. That is, if we could get these two to meet; the brains of a wise man, and the bowels of a father: if a father were Solomon, or if Solomon were a father : if a father were as wise as Solomon, or Solomon could be as kind as a father ; that were like to be good counsel indeed. For, as a wise man, he well could ; and, as a father, he sure would give his best. So none to that. Why, here they be both: this father is Solomon. The brains of Solomon, and the bowels of a father, both, in it.

What lack we yet? Somewhat: wise is not all. We find one wise, that would not have given this counsel, for he gave it not himself (as might be Ahithophel). None of his wisdom: away with it; it is devilish. No, this is Solomon: not only wise, but godly wise, with the "wisdom that is from above:" and that is the wisdom indeed. ^{Godly wise.} ^{Jas. 3. 17.}

In sign it is so; see, his counsel begins with "Fear God," the "beginning of" all true "wisdom," when all is done. And ever the counsel right, that is so grounded. If this come to the two former, I see not what can be required more. To the commendation of it then, all three meet in it. Here is 1. a father; the father is 2. wise; wise as 3. Solomon, his wisdom from the Spirit of God. There can be no more. To such a counsel, I trust, we will give ear. And so, I pray you, let us. ^{Prov. 9.10.}

The counsel hath in it a 1. *Fac,* and a 2. *Fuge.* The *Fac* is, "Fear God and the King." There is in it a single act, and a double object. The single act, 1. fear; the double object, 1. God, 2. the King. We begin with them, as in nature, first, *Deum et Regem.*

Where, at the first we see (and it is a good sight to see) God and the King, in conjunction. And no marvel, if *Rex quem,* and *Deus per Quem,* do join. But join they do, and join they may, and yet be in two several sentences, or in two several members of one sentence. *Et* would couple them, well enough. Joined nearer than so, in one and the same sentence; in one and the same member of one and the same sentence. And in one member they may be too; and yet some word between them, and not immediately. Here, so immediate, so hard one to other, as nothing in the world between them, but the *vau,* the *et,* the very solder, (as I may say,) that joins them thus together.

All this is but one; but I observe no less than five conjunctions of these two great lights, all within the compass of this text. 1. First with one *et.* 2. Then in one time (there is but one time between them both). 3. Thirdly, as with one *et;* so with one *et ne,* both: that is but one, neither.

Right margin annotations: 2. The advice itself. 1. The *Fac:* "Fear God and the King." 1. The object, "God and the King" in conjunction. 2. *Inter se.*

S E R M. 4. Fourthly, they have but one party in opposition to them
VI. both, *shonim.* 5. Fifthly, the trespassers against them both
שנים have but one end, *ruinam utriusque.*

All this, this joining, thus near, thus close, immediate thus
many ways; all this is God. God it is, That thus joineth
Himself to the King; and the King to Him. Not only here,
by Solomon, under the Law; but even in the Gospel also,
Mat.22.21. by Christ. He joins Cæsar and God too; and in a manner
as near: with the same *et,* and with but one *Reddite:* and
puts them and their duties, both, in one period. Here, God
before Cæsar; there, Cæsar before God.

Now, the nature of those that be joined by God is set
Mat. 19. 6. down by our Saviour thus. *Quod Deus conjunxit: quod* it is;
not, *quos* or *quæ:* no more plural, then: no, but *coalescunt
in unum,* "they grow together;" together into one, one
singular *quod.* God's conjunction is ever of the nature of
an union. One *et;* one *et ne:* one fear between them; one
opposite against them.

To these, thus joined by God, what is our duty? As we
find them close joined to our hands, so to keep them. First,
homo ne separet, not to sever them at any hand. Nay, *homo
ne solvat,* not to make the knot more slack or loose. Think,
it was not for nought, that our Saviour Christ said of this
Joh. 10. 35. Scripture in particular, *Non potest solvi Scriptura.* Not, *non
dissolvi;* but, *non solvi. Dissolvi,* the knot loosed quite; but
solvi, not made more loose, or slack, than He left it. One is
opposed to the joining; the other, to the near joining of
them. Not to do it ourselves: and not to endure them,
that are tampering about it. Not the Anabaptist, that
would put out *et Regem* clean. Not other, (little better,)
that put it out and put it in, at their pleasure; a King or no
King; to be feared or to fear; fast or loose; to join or to
stand aloof (as it were in opposition, the whole heaven in
sunder): *Timete Reges,* the accusative; or *Timete, Reges,*
the vocative, as falls fittest to their turn. Neither to endure
them, that would dissolve it clean; nor them that would
fain slacken it, to the end, to wring or wedge in a third between *Deum* and *Regem.* No; let them stand; and stand,
as they be left: unloosed, unloosened, *Deum et Regem.* They
that fall to be changers (after) in the text, begin their change

(ever) at this; at transposing, or interposing somewhat between *Deum et Regem.* Therefore, look to this well. This, for the first conjunction *inter se,* 'between themselves.'

Then are they joined again *in aliquo tertio,* in a third time. Why, in time? Indeed our Saviour Christ's *Quæ Cæsaris* is more ample a great deal: many things contained in it, besides. Of those many, this is but one; but this is one. And this one here is made choice of, because it falls fittest to the purpose in hand. Their conjunction in time.
2. The act.

The purpose is, to restrain from meddling. Now, fear is more restrictive than honour, or any of the rest. The philosopher calls it φίμος φύσεως, the passion that holds, as it were, the reins of our nature, to check us and keep us back from that which is hurtful; to which (otherwhile) we are but too inclinable. As, namely, there is a spirit in us: and that spirit, saith St. James, "lusts after envy:" and envy is at our superiors, toward whom, even the supremest of them, men stand not always in so good terms as were fit. Nay, so far forget themselves, sometimes, (witness this day,) as they fall to change; change with a witness, change them into ashes; put fire to them, and blow up King, and all. Here needs a retentive: fear is fit for that. Therefore it is fear, "Fear God and the King." Jas. 4. 5.

Of "Fear God" we shall soon agree, that He is to be feared. I would to God, we would, with as great accord, agree to do it, as we will easily agree, it is to be done: that so, it might be with us, as with holy Job it was, *ut timor noster spes nostra,* "from our fear might grow our hope;" the true hope, when all is done: even that, which riseth from fear, which makes us refrain to do evil, and so breeds in us the hope of all hopes, the hope of a good conscience. "Fear God."
Job 4. 6.

But "Fear God" is not all. *Et Regem,* "and the King:" him we must fear, too. "In water and blood," saith St. John; "not in water only, but in water and blood." So here: "God and the King:" not God alone; but "God and the King." *Non sufficit unum; oportet utrumque fieri in copulativis.* "God and the King."
1 Joh. 5. 6.

Hence riseth the second conjunction. As before of God, and the King; so here now, of the fear of God, and the fear of the King. And even the same benign aspect that is between God and the King, the same is there between the two fears: the very same, every way.

They be σύστατα, 'compatible' (as we say in Schools): they will stand together, go together, hold together well. They hinder not one the other. By the grace of God, we may do both: both be regal and religious too. We shall not fear the King a whit the less, for fearing God; nor, *vice versa*, God the less, for fearing the King.

Not the less? Nay the more. For, they be not only σύστατα, but συνίστανττα, not only a joint and mutual consistence between them, but a joint and mutual assistance, either of other. Not only, not hinder, but further; nor endure, but induce one the other. So that, that which is

1 Pet.2.13. here *et Deum*, is elsewhere *propter Deum*. And not only with God, but for God, we fear the King.

And though *Regem* stand last, be (as we say) *ultimum in executione*, yet is it, here in this place, *primum in intentione;* the sequel shews it. For, when he comes to the *et ne*, (mark it well,) the point of opposition, he saith not, Meddle not with irreligious persons, atheists, such as fear not God (so he should, if *Time Deum* had been principally meant): no, but "meddle not with the seditious." Now, they, we know, are, most properly, opposite to the King. The fear of God hath elsewhere his chief place, many times and oft. But, here, *Time Regem* is *primæ intentionis,* the very mark all this text levels at.

Then, why is it not *Time Regem,* and no more ado, and leave out *Time Deum* quite? for, what hath God to do here, in matter of this kind, of sedition? Not so: there is reason, *Time Deum* should be in, and fast in. In the point of allegiance, he that will lay his gronnd sure, it behoveth him, (as Gregory speaketh,) *arcessere rivum fidelitatis de fonte pietatis,* 'to draw down the stream of allegiance from the true conduit-head of it, the fear of God:' if thence it come not, it is *minus habens,* not as it should be. For, if it be right, *Time Regem* is to come out of *Time Deum.*

But "fear
God" first. Mark this method well. To have regal duties rightly settled, he goes up as high as God; begins with *Time Deum,* the fear of God. And thither we must, if we shall go soundly to work. It is not the common law, or any act of parliament,

that breeds *Time Regem*, kindly. If our fear to the King be taught us by the law of man, it is not yet upon his true base, his right corner-stone. To divinity we must; to this book, the book of the fear of God; if it be right, ground it there. And, if that might take place, there should need no law else, to sustain or preserve Kings or states.

Set this down then for a rule: that there is no surer friend, no surer stay to Kings, and their rights, than *Time Deum*, that is, true religion. And set down this with it: that it is a sure sign of a good religion, if it will join with *Time Regem* (the duty to the prince) well. For if it be a true *Time Deum*, it strengthens *Time Regem;* it weakens it not.

And on the other: that it is an infallible note of a bad one, if, either it shoulder the King from God, or shrink up the sinews of civil obedience.

But, if it make *Time Deum* to blow up *Time Regem;* make the Catholic faith to overthrow the Catholic fear of God (for both, I trust, be alike Catholic): if they persuade men, that the King, and the whole parliament must up, or the fear of God cannot stand; they are out of this text quite: they are clean beside *Time Deum*, as it was in Solomon's time: teach a new fear of God, falsely so called, without this book altogether.

But, what is become of *Time Regem*, with them? Sure, they that fear not to blow up the King, I will never say, they fear the King: they that put men in their *Amphitheatrum Honoris*, nay, in their Martyrology, or Calendar of Martyrs, for not fearing to attempt it, it is a strange fear they teach: indeed, rather *Time, Rex*, than *Time Regem.*

And another sort there is, not come so far; with whom yet *Time Deum et Regem* is not as it should be: that fear, I know not how, as if the fear of the King did abate somewhat from the fear of God; and there were no true fear of God, without some mixture of contempt of order and government. But, if one can grow somewhat bold, somewhat too bold with Kings, to teach them their duties; and fear not to " speak evil of such as are in authority," then, lo, he fears Jude ver. 8. God aright. And, none of the clergy fears God, but they that use it. Nor none of the laity, but such as bear them

SERM. in it.   And these two are the only fear-Gods in the land.
VI.
——— Others, that think, they may do both, and would gladly
do both, may not be allowed to fear God on the right
fashion; they fear the face of man.   And thus, with their
new fear of God, they put out of countenance the fear of the
King.   As if these fears cast out one another; and one
could not be in at the former, but of necessity, he must be
out at the latter.   What is this, but to make a disjunctive,
at the least, between them?

But you, beloved, never fear to do as St. Paul wills you:
Rom. 13. 7. *cui timorem, timorem,* "to give fear, to whom fear belongeth:" and, to the King it belongs, as here we see.
Ps. 82. 6. He that said *Ego dixi, Dii estis,* in so saying, said, *Et sicut
dii, timendi estis.*   Therefore, *Nemo timeat timere Regem,*
'let no man be afraid to fear the King,' and yet fear God
too.   You may do both; you must do both.   The text is
short, but full, in this point.   For, *Time Deum,* that is, Be
a good Christian; and *Time Regem,* that is, Be a good subject.   And, the better Christian, the better subject.

But indeed, I have not done well in speaking of them all
this while, as of two fears.   There is but one *Time,* in the
text.   If you strike it out from *Regem,* you strike it out
from *Deum* too: for there is but one in all, and they consequently to be feared, not with two, but with one and the
same fear, both.

This, for the conjunction : which I wish we may endeavour
by all means to maintain.   For, besides the offence to God
and His fear, it is a preparative to the change (which here
followeth) to sever God from the King, or the King from
the kingdom; to force them one from the other, that God
hath so straightly united together; hath Himself, and would
have us to do the like.   And now, after we have done with
the *Fac,* and the conjunction, let us come to the *Fuge* and
the opposition.

2. The
Fuge.
"And
meddle
not,"
&c.

"Fear God" then "and the King," wherein?   In many
other points; but, (to hold us to the text,) in this namely,
that you "meddle not" with these following.   And, even by
this, ye may take measure, whether ye fear them or no, by
your fearing to join with such, as this day brought forth.
For if ye join with them, ye oppose straight to both those :

not to the King alone, but to God; to His fear, as well as the King's. Indeed, to the fear of them both. For to both are these here set in opposition. It is not "Fear the King" alone, and "meddle not with them;" but, God is in too, as well as the King.

Nor, it is not, "Fear God and the King," and then over again, with two for two: "and meddle not," either with irreligious, or seditious persons; but with seditious only. Sedition is jointly opposed to both; and no less to God, than the King. To either, in equal opposition.

I note here no less than four oppositions besides the *et ne;* as before, four conjunctions besides the *et:* against the King; 2. against God; 3. against both; 4. against the fear of both. 1. The King: for it is (this meddling) a trespass at common law against him, his crown and dignity. 2. God: for it is a sin also against God's law, against Heaven and Him: not only these on earth, *læsæ majestatis;* to God's Majesty no less than the King's. 3. Both *Deum et Regem:* for it is directly against both tables, and against the two first Mat.22.38 and great commandments of both tables. 4. And, being a sin against fear, it will prick fast toward presumption; and, that is a high sin: if that once "get the dominion" over Ps. 19. 13. any, he shall not be "innocent from the great offence." So, against the 1. King, 2. God, 3. both, the 4. fear of both.

But, by this, clear it is, whoever they be that "meddle" with these, *eo ipso* they fear not God. Directly: for, if the commandment be, "Fear God, and meddle not," one cannot do both; both be a meddler, and yet fear God though. He cannot say (with the meddlers of this day), Yes, yes; meddle with the powder plot, and yet be a good Catholic, and fear God well enough for all that. Nay, fear God the better; and be the better reputed of, you know where, for this very meddling.

But, that in this point we may proceed to purpose, we are to see first, 1. who be these *shonim,* שׁנִים; 2. and then, what it is to meddle with them.

The word, in the original, is very pregnant, and plenteous What in signification; which hath made divers turn it diversely. these changers The Vulgar turns it *cum detractoribus,* "such as detract be. from" princes: and well. Ours, before, was, "with the seditious :" and it was well so.　Now, we read, " with them that are given to change :" and that is well too.　For, all are in it : and well may so be.　For detractors, changers, seditious, all come to one.

Detractors.　For they that in the end prove to be seditious, (mark them well,) they be first detractors : or, as the nature of the Hebrew word is, biters.　It is of *shen*, a tooth ; they have teeth in their tongues.　Ever, the first thing that

moves to a sedition is Shimei's tongue.　As at first it did (sedition), so doth it still, begin "in the gainsaying," in the contradiction "of Korah."　So began he : This Moses,

and this Aaron, they take too much upon them, do more than they may by law ; they would have somewhat taken

from them.　So Absalom : Here is no body to do any justice in the land.　So Jeroboam : Lord, what a heavy yoke is this on the people's necks !　"Meddle not" with these detractors.

Then secondly, when they have made the state present naught, no remedy, we must have a better for it ; and so, a change needs.　What change?　Why, religion, or the Church-government, or somewhat, they know not well what, stands awry.　Ye shall change your religion, said they of this day, and have one for it, wherein, for your comfort, you shall not understand a word, (not you of the people,) what you either sing or pray ; and for variety, you shall change a whole communion, for a half.　Now a blessed exchange, were it not?

What say some other?　You shall change for a fine new Church-government : a presbytery would do much better for you than a hierarchy ; and, perhaps, not long after, a government of states than a monarchy.　"Meddle not" with these changers.

Now thirdly, whom you find thus magnifying of changes, and projecting new plots for the people, be sure, they are in the way to sedition.　For, mark it, they do *sedire*, that is, *seorsim ire*, ' go aside ;' they have their meetings apart, about their new alteration.　Now of *sedire* comes sedition, side-going.　For, if that be not looked to in time, the next news

is the blowing of a trumpet, and Sheba's proclamation, " We have no part in David."　It begins in Shimei, it ends in Sheba.　But so, at last, all (ye see) comes to one ; *shonim* all.

And now to the meddlers. But first will you observe, here What, the meddlers. are two sorts in the text; 1. they that meddle, and 2. they, with whom they meddle. The seditious, that is, the contriver of the treason; and the meddlers, that is, his complices. And that it is not, Be not yourself seditious; but, "Meddle not" with such as be. Be not the author, or ringleader; but, Be no fautor of them, have no part or fellowship in the business. *Ne commiscearis,* Be not a mixed traitor; for, mixed and pure, both are naught.

As for them, that are in it at the main, as they say, he doth not so much as once speak of them : of them, there is no question. Only, directs his speech to them, that are brought in on the by. Tells them, in so being, they are as deep in as the others. No accessory here : as is the seditious, so is the meddler: author, and fautor, all alike. Alike, first : for both without the fear of God and all religion, alike. Alike, again : for liable to the same penalty after, *ruinam utriusque.*

Well now, what is it to meddle, this *commisceri?* I would note two things to you out of it; 1. the nature of the word, 2. and the extent.

The nature I take to be worth a note. *Commiscearis* is a 1. The nature of *Ne commiscearis.* mixture : what manner of mixture is it? Out of the Hebrew word, it properly betokens that mixture or medley, that is, of the light with the darkness after the sunset, *in crepusculo,* in the owl-light, as we call it. That is Ereb properly (thence cometh the poets' Erebus; ye know what that is). Now this, in very deed, is rather a confusion than a mixture : and might well have been turned *Ne confundaris,* " Be not confounded" together, they and you ; or, as St. Peter speaks, "Run not together with them to the same confusion." So, a confused 1 Pet. 4. 4. mixture it is, or a mixture to confusion.

You shall see, it is a word well chosen. Take it of the persons, and a confused mixture it is. For, even the children of light, (not always so wise in their generation,) that is, some plain-meaning men, are sometimes drawn in too, by some illusion or other, to meddle and to join with these sons of darkness. As, some went with Absalom to the paying of his 2 Sam. 15. 11. vow, in simplicity, and were in before they were aware. For, being there with him, they must do as he did. Just the medley of the Pharisees, and John's disciples.

Or take it, of the plot itself. In it also, such a mixture there is; for they want not some glistering pretences, as it were a false light, cast on the plot. But go to the bottom of it, and there it is *caligo tenebrarum,* the very dungeon of darkness: and well, so; as being wrought in a dark cellar under ground by the sons of Erebus in the skirts of Erebus itself.

3.
1 Tim. 3.
16.
Rev. 17. 5.

Or, look to the carriage of it : there shall you plainly discover a very blending of light with darkness, of the oath of God, with the work of the devil ; the sacrament of godliness, with the "mystery" in the whore's forehead, of all abomination ; of the loosing from lesser sins, with the binding to a greater ; mashing together holy duties with lewd practices ; and not mingling, but confounding oaths, sacraments, absolutions, with the works of Ereb, or Erebus, of the blackness, and of the darkness of hell itself.

2. The extent of it.

1 Kings
1. 7.
1 Kings
12. 3.

2 Sam.
20. 1.
2 Sam. 16.
21.
1 Kings
1. 7.
2 Sam.
16. 7.
2 Sam. 20.
14.

Judges 9.
4.
Prov. 11.
21.

1 Sam. 26.
9.
Esther 2.
22.

Now of the extent: "Meddle not." How many ways may one be, or be said to be a meddler? That may he many ways ; as many, as one may be partaker of another man's sins. 1. By being a champion or leader for them ; as Joab to Adonijah. 2. By being spokesman, or orator for them ; as Jeroboam to his crew. 3. By blowing the trumpet, animating them, setting them on; as Sheba to his. 4. By giving them shrewd advice, how to manage their matters ; as did Ahithophel to Absalom. 5. By saying mass, praying for their success; that was all Abiathar could do. 6. By bruiting infamous speeches or libels of David ; that was all that Shimei. 7. By harbouring or receiving them ; as the city Abel did Sheba, and should have been sacked for it. 8. By furnishing them with money or supplies otherwise (as it might be, contributing to the powder) ; as the men of Shechem, to Abimelech. 9. By that which Solomon calleth "hand in hand," that is, digging with the pickaxe, co-operating with them, in the vault. 10. By being (if not party, yet) privy to it, and not opposing ; as David had been to Saul's death, if he had not hindered Abishai: *non obstans.* 11. Or, at the least, privy and not disclosing it ; which had been Mordecai's case, if he had concealed the eunuch's treason : *non manifestans.* 12. And last, (which I take to be full out as bad, if not much worse than any of the rest,) by speaking or writing, in praise or defence, either of the deed or the doers: their case, Numb. 16. 41. calling Korah and his company "the people of the Lord:" for sure, if the consenter be in, the commender much more.

All these make up this medley. To these, or any of these, well may it be said, *Ne commiscearis.* Now I know, degrees there be, in mixture; more or less: but here is no degree. Only, *Ne commiscearis*, simply. Not, in no great quantity; but, not in the least scruple, not at all. It is rank poison; the least drop of it is deadly. Never so little is too much.

Therefore, absolutely, *Ne commiscearis*, "meddle not" with them at all: not with absolving them, not with giving them the oath, not with praying for them; above all, not with offering the unbloody sacrifice, for so bloody a treason. Jacob's counsel is best: *In consilium eorum ne veniat anima* Gen. 49. *tua*, not to come once among them. To separate yourselves [6.] from the tents of Korah, touching whom, you know what God gave in charge, and what Moses proclaimed: "Away Nu. 16. 26. from them, come not near them, touch not any thing that is theirs." It is infected; they have the plague: if you meddle with it, it will bring you to destruction.

So are we come to the second verse, to the penalty. And, II. it is not more than needs. 1. For sure, even good counsel The penalty. enters but slowly into us, we are so dull, if it have not an edge given it: be not seconded with some forcible reason, to help it forward. 2. Now, no reason more forcible, or of better edge to enter us, than that which is taken from the fear of some great mischief or main inconvenience, which will surely take hold of us, if we take not hold of the counsel. 3. And, as none more forcible, so none more fit for the present counsel: it is, to fear. Now, to induce fear, what way more fit, than to set before us some matter of terror, some fearful object or consequent, it will bring us to. And what more fearful, than of all the five fearful things set down by [Vid. Arist. the philosopher, the most fearful, that is, the fear of death? Eth. 3. 6. This? why it works with beasts, and even with the dullest of 3.] them, Balaam's beast: spur him, strike him, lay on him with Nu. 22. 23. a staff, ye shall never get him to run upon the Angel's sword, upon his own death; that shall ye never. Sure, we are to think: His first commandment God headed with the best head He had; and that was, *Morte morieris.* He thought it the surest, and most likely to prevail. And, if any thing hold us, this will. If ye fear neither God nor King; yet fear this.

1.
Destruc-
tion.

1. But yet, if we weigh the word, (destruction,) there is more in it than death. To death we must all come; but this, it will bring you to an untimely end. Not fall of yourself; but destroyed: even plucked down a great while before you would fall.

2. Nay, nor it is not untimely death, neither; there is more in it than so (in destruction). All that die before their time are not destroyed. God forbid. No: there goeth some evil touch, some shame, some foul uncouth end ever with it; that is it, that makes it destruction.

2.
Nay, ruin.

3. But what manner destruction? Some may be restored, and built again: this is *ad ruinam,* (that is added in the latter part of the verse,) 'to ruin:' so that, never built again; never repaired more: that is, to utter destruction.

4. And yet, there is more still. For, these two, 1. ruin and 2. destruction, they be not used of a person, properly; but, as the word gives, of a house or structure. Add this then, that it will be the ruin and plucking down, not of yourself alone, but of your house too. And, indeed, how many great houses have been ruined by it!

Then, if this will not hold you from meddling; that it is a sin, a double sin, against both tables; that it is a sin of presumption: if this will not; let this, that it is destructory, a destroying sin; one of those sins, that follows them that meddle with it, hard at the heels, and never leaves them, till it have brought them to destruction and utter ruin: them, and their whole house, it eradicates; it pulls all up by the roots. Sin itself is a *nimium;* yet, is there a *nimium,* in sin

[Eccl. 7.
17.]

too. "O be not over-wicked," saith the Preacher; "be not too foolish," so very wicked, so over foolish, as to shorten your own days, to make you die *tempore non suo,* before your time come: yea, to be destroyed utterly, you, your house and all. Sure, if this come of it, he bade you not fear, for nought.

Nay, this is not all: he goes further. Of all retentives, fear; of all fears, the fear of death; death and destruction. Now, of all destructions, this (for all destructions are not of one size neither; some more fearful than other). But this, this is no common one: it hath two attendants, to make it more fearful than the ordinary destructions or visitations of other men. The former two, as it were manacles for the hands; not to have a hand in it: these latter, as fetters to the feet; not to go about it. But still it runs upon two; as it were, one for the King, another for God, still.

This is the first: "Their destruction, it shall rise sud- denly." Every word hath his weight, if you mark them. "It shall rise:" fitly. For, sedition, we call it a rising: one rising he punisheth with another. "Rise," it is; not *surget*, but *consurget*: as early up, rise as soon, as the sin itself. From the first moment of sin, their destruction : rises with it, followeth it at the heels, is still hard behind it; if they could look back, and see it, it is not an inch from them.

3.
And that
"sudden-
ly."

2. "Rise," and "rise suddenly." "Let death come sud- denly at unawares" (it is David's prayer): and so shall it come (it is Solomon's prophecy): come *ab improviso*, break forth, and surprise them in a very sudden. Fitly, this too: their meaning was, to have dispatched all of a sudden: as soon as the paper burn, the powder go off. Quick and sud- den surprising, therefore, doth best befit them: the punish- ment, in every point, comes home to the sin.

Ps. 55. 15.

3. Sudden things confound, and are therefore the more fearful. Fit this again: these would have brought all to confusion. (What a confusion had there been this day!) Meet therefore they should be amazed with the suddenness of the breaking out; and the confusion they meant, fall upon their own souls.

4. But, what manner of confusion? The word he uses in Hebrew sheweth that: it is properly the confusion they are in, that are in a thick mist or fog; that after they have been a while in it, are they know not where; and when they come out of it, find themselves where they never meant to have come.

4.
And
eternally,
*Et ruinam
eorum quis
scit?*

This fits likewise: in a mist they walked, carried their matters mistily; and at last, lost themselves in it. In dark- ness they delighted, (dark vaults, dark cellars,) and darkness fell upon them for it. And when they were out of their dark vault, found themselves in a dark prison; which they little thought ever to have come in.

It doth very well, this suddenness, set out to us the course and carriage of this sin. It will flatter one, and draw him on, a great while. All things will seem so subtilely contrived, so cunningly carried, so secretly kept, and so long; commonly, till the very time it should be done in : and then, even on a sudden, all breaks out; and that, strangely : and all the goodly cobweb, that was so many months in spinning and weaving, comes me a broom, and in a minute snaps it down and destroys it quite : the cobweb, and the spider; the plot itself, and the author and all. To have their treason kept in, so many proroguings of the parliament; their cellar, so fitly chosen; their powder, so safely laid in, and so well couched; and all in a readiness : and then, ἐξαίφνης, in a night, suddenly to have all come forth, so strangely; and all their long consultations and often deliberations quashed all in a moment! "Their destruction shall rise suddenly," this is the first.

But this is nothing to the other, *Et ruinam eorum quis scit?* That, that is the fearful one indeed. For nothing so fearful, as that, a man cannot tell what to make of it. Who knows their ruin? Who knows? that is, no man knows. Good Lord! what might that ruin be, that no man knows? No man knows? Why, do we not all know, what it is they suffer, that come to this destruction? they are drawn, hanged, &c. We all know it. It is rather *Quis nescit?* than *Quis scit?* (this), one would think.

No : *Quis scit?* saith Solomon, and he knew well what he said. It is unknown, their ruin : what then shall we make of it? Sure, no destruction, here. All here, the worst is known of them. It must be some otherwhere, in some other world than this. And so it is. And that is *Quis scit?* indeed. That, no man knows. For, it is, as truly said of the pains of hell, as of the joys of Heaven, *Quis scit?* "Eye hath not seen, nor ear heard, nor hath it entered into the heart of man," what, or how great they be; the one, not so joyful, but the other as dreadful : unknown, both. *Quis scit?* equally true of both. For, *nemo scit, nisi qui accepit*, no man knows them, but they that be in them.

1 Cor. 2. 9.

Rev. 2. 17.

And it were well, when they meddle first with it, they would bethink them of this. If a man might know beforehand, it were this, or it were that, or it were we know what; then it were not so fearful. But *Quis scit?* goeth beyond all conceit. But they do, they know not what; and so, they suffer they know not what. The meaning is: they perish here, they perish everlastingly; that this destruction is eternal destruction, and no other.

And indeed, the latter word sheweth as much: which is not every ruin, but properly the ruin, or fall into a fire: it is taken from לפיד, that is, a burning firebrand. This also is fit: fire they meant, and they end in fire; even in hell fire. For, so is the nature of the word; and so is the Hebrew proverb upon it, לפיד לא פדיון; it is a ruin, from which there is no redemption. It is a fall, or ruin, from whence no rising. A fall, into the bottomless pit, into the furnace there: if they once come there, they never come thence. So, it comes suddenly; but, it lights heavily. They know not, when it comes; but, when it comes, it pays home. When the mist breaks up, they find themselves among the firebrands there. And if nothing else will, let this move them.

And *utriusque* we may not leave out. It is added, to make sure work. For if it had not, it might have been imagined, that these four *novissima* had been to come upon them only, that fear not God. That there be no mistaking, in the reference to whom, it is expressly set down, *utriusque horum:* it is, upon both of them; one, as well as the other: as well of those, that fault in their duty toward the King; as those, that are void of the fear of God. And again, as well those, that meddle or make; as those, with whom they meddle or make, the plotters themselves. Both of them, in the same condemnation: both come to the same destruction. So, as we find God and the King joined in one fear, at the first; so, here find we again the trespassers against either, wrapped up in one destruction at the last. *Ruinam* one end, *utriusque* " of them both." And, such end may ever come of such beginnings.

And thus, now, he knits up all, Ταῦτα δὲ λέγω ὑμῖν τοῖς σοφοῖς, " Be this spoken even to you that be wise." For, III. The conclusion.

S E R M.
VI.
―――
" These
things
belong to
the wise."

Solomon's own son, indeed, was no very wise man. So, it might seem perhaps to be given to him, (this counsel,) and such as he was, none of the wisest: fools may not meddle; wise men may. Now, commonly, they be no fools, want no wit; they think, they bear a brain, that meddle in these matters. Therefore, is this addition; to shew, that how wise soever they take themselves, or be they never so wise, it may well become them to take this advice here. *Hæc quoque sapientibus;* it concerns them too.

There was one, as wise as ever they will be, whose counsel, in his time, was holden as the oracle of God: yet, this great wise man, for meddling in this, contrary to it, proved but a fool, and made up the number of those that came to this untimely and unknown ruin and destruction. And now where he is we know; what he suffers, we know not. It was Ahithophel, I mean.

And strange it is, that is observed of his name. For *thophel* is a fool; and *achi* is a cousin german, at the least, if it be not nearer. So, as wise as he was, his name was ominous, and gave him to be (as he proved) *germanus stulti;* a wise man, but of whom a fool might have claimed kindred: as of him, he might; and of all, he may, that meddle as he did. This Ahithophel, as wise as he takes himself, he shall be the wiser, if he take this counsel.

We have done with the text now: the day will hold us yet a little. For the day subscribes *Probatum est* to this text, and sets a seal to it.

Thus it shall be, saith Solomon. But was it thus? Ask the day, and it will ask you, Was it not thus? was not " this Scripture this day fulfilled," not in our " ears," but in our eyes (indeed in both)? Was there not an execution of this sentence upon it? Did not Solomon shew himself to be, not only a wise man, but a prophet, and that a true one?

This day was delivered, and brought forth certain sons. You have heard what the father hath said to his sons; will ye stay a little, and hear, what the sons will say to their father? take his counsel or no? No: these sons were wiser than their father, saw deeper, as they thought, into the matter, than Solomon; thought not him wise enough to advise them. Not him; but got them a heap of new fathers, that gave them other manner counsel; even to try a conclusion with Solomon, upon this text.

Will ye hear some new divinity, how some fathers here with us counselled their ghostly children? the fathers of the society, their sons of the society, the wicked society of this day? You shall see the text turned round about, clean contrary.

My sons, fear God and the Pope (so is the new edition): and as for those that would fain change things here, do meddle with them, say Solomon what he list. *Ecce major* Mat. 12.42. *Salomone*, "Lo a greater than Solomon" (you know where). He (as yet it stands in the gloss to be seen) made this book of Proverbs authentical by citing it: and, as He made it, can unmake it again at His pleasure. Nothing in it shall bind you. Here is the counsel crossed.

But then, how shall we do with the latter verse? For that take no thought. Where he tells you, this Solomon, of destruction, it is nothing so: on with your powder-plot notwithstanding. You shall be so far from this, he tells you, that if ought come to the plot or you, otherwise than we wish, it shall be no destruction; no, but a holy martyrdom, and *Quis scit?* Who knows the blessed estate you shall come to by these means? but martyrs you shall be straight upon it, in print: and who knows, whether there may not be wrought a straw miracle, to confirm as much, if need be?

But to put you clean out of doubt, for your meddling: you shall have of us the fathers of the society to meddle in it, as well as you; to make up this holy medley with you: to confess you, to absolve you, to swear you, to housel you, to say mass for you, and to keep your counsel in all holy equivocation. You see, what work was made; how the matter was used with this Scripture, when time was; how the fathers of the society took this father by the beard, and affronted him and his counsel, in every part of it.

What shall we say of these sons and these fathers? Sure, their Catholic faith we will not meddle with; but, what Solomon saith, we may be bold to say, and pronounce: fear of God there was none in them; neither in the father nor in the son. Neither in them, that gave the counsel; nor in them, that took it. None of them, God's servants; Him they feared not: none of them Solomon's sons; him they heard not.

But, of the twain, the fathers, that gave the counsel, far the worse: who, what Solomon terms destruction, that turned they into edification: and what he ruin, that changed they into exaltation; *et gloriam utriusque quis scit?* A strange change: that, now become glorious, that, before these days, was ever damned as detestable! Changers right: change States, and change Churches, so long, till they change divinity and all; set up a new fear of God, a fearful one to Kings and to Kingdoms; and that had like, this day, to have cost many a thousand men's lives.

And needs there not a retentive, when these coin such motives? when that, which by father Solomon here is so straightly forbidden, is justified, nay, is sanctified, and glorified by these? anti-paters, anti-Solomons, anti-greater-than Solomon, they.

Well, look to the end. See, what became of this sanctified sedition. Sure, here Solomon was in the right, read their destiny truly. For surprised they were, and blanked all of a sudden; and that, strangely; and carried away straight to their utter ruin: and their ruin who knoweth? Not their ruin here, or fall from the ladder; but a greater ruin, and into a deeper place: how low, into what torments, *Quis scit?* saith Solomon, and so say I. Their end here we saw. Their end who knows? or how they hang in hell for it? And all, for not following this advice.

To draw to an end: their ruin we know not; that is, *Quis scit?* But, by their ruin, who knows not? that is, *Quis nescit?* For all men see and know, how highly these meddlings displease God, Who hath so many ways, so strangely, both of old and of late, and still doth testify to the world plainly His deep dislike of them: that a wonder it is, that still there are, that dare adventure upon them; save that, God, for want of His true fear in their hearts, suffers this efficacy of error, this strange delusion to besot them.

But, let them take this from Solomon; that, *toties quoties,* Mic. 3. 10. so oft as they seek to "build Sion in blood," so oft shall their building end in destruction: and so oft as they rise to that end, they shall rise to their ruin: fathers and sons, and sons' sons, to the end of the world.

But we, beloved, who have better learned to fear God, I

trust, if Solomon shall acknowledge us for his sons, or God for His servants; if we will be the children of Wisdom, let " Wisdom be justified of her children." Let us do Solomon Mat. 11. the honour, to think him wise enough to give us counsel. [19.] And since we see, he is proved a prophet, and not a word of all this text is fallen to the ground; that strange examples there have been of it, and that, many; and this day, one *exemplum sine exemplo*, an example *per se*, a matchless one, in this kind : having these before our eyes, and having in remembrance the four *novissima* in the text, 1. destruction, 2. ruin, 3. *repente*, and 4. *Quis scit ?* let us fear those four ; and fearing them, persist as we have done hitherto, in the fear of God and the King; and ever fear, to have to do or to deal with them that fear neither. So I pray God, we may; and that this may be the fruit, even our fruit; and His blessing upon that, hath been spoken, that we may live and die *timentes Deum et Regem*, ever pure from this mixture. And so God make us all.

A SERMON

THE KING'S MAJESTY AT WHITEHALL,

ON THE FIFTH OF NOVEMBER, A.D. MDCXV.

PSALM cxlv. 9.

*The Lord is good to all, and His mercies are over all His
works.*

*Suavis Dominus universis, et miserationes Ejus super omnia opera
Ejus.*

[*The Lord is good to all, and His tender mercies are over all His
works.* Eng. Trans.]

SERM.
VII.

TEN years it is now since our memorable delivery as upon
this day: and we here to celebrate, not the anniversary only,
but the *decennalia* of it. Now, in numbering, it is well
known, that at ten we begin anew at the figure of one; we
return again ever to the first. So do we now. For, this was
the first, *Misericordiæ Domini super opera Ejus.*

We shall never forget it, so many of us as then heard it,
that it was the first, that it was thought (and that, *authore
magno*) to be the fittest theme of all, wherewith to begin the
first solemn thanksgiving of all, for the great mercy of God,
and for the great work of that mercy this day shewed upon
us all.

To this then the first, (every way the first,) may I crave
pardon to put to my poor cipher, and make it ten, this tenth
year? So, as it was the first fruits, it may be the tenth. So,
they may be, as they should be, *primitiæ et decimæ de eodem,*
both out of one and the same.

It led us at the very first, whither first and last we must come; to the true cause of that our delivery: of that, and of all other we have had, or ever shall have, the *super omnia* of His mercies.

That deliverance when it came, it came not *temere*, it had a cause. That cause was God, and, in God, His mercy. "It was the mercy of God, we were not consumed:" so said we then (out of Jeremy) at the seventh year. That mercy of His, that is *super omnia*: so say we now (out of David) at the tenth. For, this is King David; and, that way, not unfit neither: as, written first by a King; applied since by a King; in the case of saving a King and a kingdom: or rather, one King, but more kingdoms than one. Lament. 3. 22.

It was then spoken, to the praise. And it is a praise; and it is out of a praise. For so is this Psalm entitled: David's praise. For howsoever the prayers and the praises all in this book are (for the most part) of David's penning; yet, two there are, he hath singled out from the rest, and set his own mark on them, as proper to himself. The eighty-sixth Psalm, his *tephilla;* David's own prayer: and this here his *tehilla,* his own praise or thanksgiving. As if he had made the rest, for all in common; but reserved these peculiarly for himself.

With *Exaltabo Te Deus,* it begins: he will exalt God, every day, and for ever: so he vows, in the two first verses. For what, will he exalt Him? For many high perfections in Him. For the greatness of His nature, which is infinite, at the third; for the greatness of His wondrous works, the fourth; for His glorious majesty, the fifth; for His mighty power, the sixth; for His goodness, subdivided into His justice and mercy; for His justice, the seventh; and for His mercy, the eighth. And here now, in the ninth, in this verse, and these very words, He sets the *super omnia,* the crown and garland (as it were) on mercy's head; gives it the sovereignty over all. *Exaltabo Te,* God he will exalt: and *exaltabo in Te,* in God he will exalt His mercy, above all the rest.

Upon the matter then; all is, as we said, but a praise of mercy. And a praise, not *positive* (that is not so effectually); but by way of comparison (held ever the better). The sum.

In a comparison, ever, three points we look to: 1. with

S E R M. whom it is made, with the works of God. 2. How large it is
VII.
laid: not with some one or more, but with them all; all
comers (as they say). 3. And, in what? In the point of
super (in that there is so much ado about), the point of supremacy; whether above, whether superior to other.

Two things of God there are set down; 1. His mercies,
and 2. His works; these two compared: compared in the
point of *super*, and mercy found to carry it. Hers the supremacy. All His works, high all, great all, all excellent;
but *major horum misericordia*, the highest, greatest, most
excellent of them all, mercy: that, the *super omnia* of them
all. Of these then.

The di   First of the words as they stand in order.
vision.
I.   Then, of mercies *super*, and that three ways: 1. *super*,
II.   "above;" so we read it; 2. *super*, "over;" so the Seventy,
ἐπὶ πάντα· 3. *super*, "upon;" so we pray, *Fiat misericordia
super nos*, "let Thy mercy be upon us." 1. *Super*, "above,"
it may be, (as a spire is,) and not reflect down, and be "over;"
2. *super*, "over" it may be, and hover aloft; not descend, or
come down upon us. 3. But *super*, "upon," is it, when it
lights upon us; that is, *Fiat misericordia super nos*.

And of these, 1. as well for mercy's honour, that is over
them, 2. as for the good of the works, that are under it.

III.   Then come we to a *super* in this *super*. Upon some of
God's works, more than other some: and so to ourselves;
and so to this day.

For sure this Scripture, if it be well looked unto, doth
competere, 'agree to' no case, so, as it doth to ours; nor to
ours, as this day. We are His works once, and those mercies
of His, here said to be "over all His works," have been over
and upon us. "Upon us," in Psalm the eighty-eighth, and
many other times; but, above all other, most sensibly this
day; this day, of all days. And that with such a *super*, in
so high a degree, in such, so great a mercy; so great a work
of mercy, as great as ever was any. In saving so great
a number, from so strange and unheard-of a cruelty; by
a mercy, *super omnia*, I may say; from a cruelty, *super
omnia*, I am sure.

IV.   Then lastly, what we are in *super* to God, for this *super*.
Where 1. of the *super* "upon" the head of all God's works,

for these His mercies thus over them. 2. And, of all His works, and above them all, of the *super* remaining upon our heads, for divers besides, but for this ʳday and this work *super omnia;* above all the days, we ever saw; above all the works, He ever wrought for us.

And, it is the tenth year, this; and naturally, *decumana sunt grandiora.* A *fluctus decumanus,* a deep flood it was, had like to have "gone over our souls;" and a *misericordia decumana,* a mercy of a large size it was, that made, it went not then. That we perform then *laudes decumanas,* great praise and large thanks, now, this *anno decimo,* some way answerable to the greatness of our peril, and to the greatness of the mercy, that made us so well pass it. The numbers of seven and ten are not without their weight. The seventh, the Sabbath; the tenth, God's part. Both ways, as the Sabbath day, as the tenth year, sacred to God is this day, and our duty upon it. ^{Ps. 38. 4; 124. 4.}

Misericordiæ Domini. Misericordiæ. To look into the nature of the word mercy; it is best conceived, by the object, and by the act. Mercy hath for her object *circa quod,* her matter and metal to work upon, misery: the best virtue, the worst object of all. It is not so plain, this, in our English word mercy, as in the Latin *misericordia,* for, there, is misery full out at the length. ^{I. Of the words in order. *Misericordiæ,* "the mercies."}

Upon this object, the proper act of mercy, *miseratio,* as the Fathers read this text. *Misericordia* is the habit; *miseratio,* the act, which is nothing else but *misericordia eliquata,* that which runs from mercy at the melting; the act that relieves us of misery, and all the degrees that lead to it, necessities, impotencies, defects, distresses, dangers, and whatsoever would make our case miserable, more or less.

To relieve these, is the act; and, (this you must take with you,) without merit to relieve them. The opposition, the Church makes, in divers her collects: *Non nostris meritis, sed Tuâ solâ misericordiâ,* with an express *obstante* of all merit. For, the eye of justice will relieve all them that deserve it. Goodness *in merentes,* that is justice. Goodness *in immerentes,* yea, and sometimes a degree farther, *in male merentes,* that is mercy properly. "Nevertheless," saith the one hundred and sixth Psalm, for all they deserved it, ^{Ps. 106. 44.}

(to be miserable,) "when He saw their misery," (saw that, and nothing else to move Him,) that moved Him, and "He heard their complaint," and gave order for their relief. This is mercy.

Miseri-cordiæ Ejus: "mercies" in God.

This mercy is in God; *misericordiæ Ejus.* Indeed, such is the immutable constancy of the Divine nature, as we should hardly conceive it to be in this wise flexible, but that great care is taken of this point (of no one so great); that there is mercy in God, there be *misericordiæ Ejus.*

[Vid. p. 272.]
[Luke 1. 78.]

But what mercy? From the nature and force of the word רחמים, which (I am not now to tell you, I have done it heretofore) is properly the bowels; that is, there are "tender mercies in God" (so we turn it in the *Benedictus*). Not of the ordinary sort, slight, and such as pierce not deep, come not far; but, such as come *de profundis,* from the very bowels themselves; that affect that part, make the bowels relent.

And what bowels? Not the bowels of the common man (for then מעים had been the right word); but רחמים are the bowels of a parent, (so we said the word signifies,) and this adds much: adds to mercy στοργὴν, ' natural love.' To one strong affection, another as strong, or stronger than it.

And what parent? the more pitiful of the twain, the mother. For רחם (the singular of this word) is Hebrew for the womb; so as this, to the two former, addeth the sex; the sex holden to be the more passionate, and compassionate of both. 1. Of all mercies, those from the bowels; 2. and of all bowels, the bowels of a parent; 3. and of the two parents, those of the mother, those from the womb: such pity as the mother takes of the child of her womb; such, as the womb, of the child that lay in it. Mercies are in God; such mercies are in God.

And God, willing to set forth unto us the exceeding great tenderness of His mercy, to have it throughly apprehended by us, *humanum dicit,* speaks to us in our own *puerilis.* And, to express the efficacy of His action, takes to Him the affection; and to express the affection, takes to Him the part of the body, the seat of it, the bowels; and the bowels of a parent; of that parent, whose bowels, in our nature, are the pitifulest of all, the mother. And, if you will, you may add this: that one mother hath but one womb for all her children; but He speaks here of God in the plural; as if He had the compassion of more wombs than one, the pity of many mothers put together.

It is good news for us, these mercies are in God; but, better yet, that they are in Him, with a *super*. But, best of all, that that *super*, a *super*, not *super quædam*, but *super omnia*.

In God with a super.

Much is said in few words, to mercy's praise, when this is said, *super omnia*. *Nihil supra* were much, 'none above it;' but *super omnia*, it "above all:" he that saith that, leaves no more to say: there is no higher degree; *super omnia* is the superlative.

And that super, super omnia.

Super omnia, "above all." For, *opera Ejus*, "His works," these two might well be spared. All, are "works;" and all are "His works." *Super omnia opera Ejus*, that is, absolutely *super omnia*. For, "works" is no term diminuent here; "all His works," that is, all simply. Beside God, and "His works," there is in the wide world, nothing at all.

But yet, with His works, with them it is laid; and well: not, with God's other attributes, absolutely; but with them, in the point of works. His attributes are all alike; all, as Himself is; infinite, all; and one infinite is not more than another. But take the works, and (*Virtus in actione*, we know) lay it there: compare the works of any of them, nay, of all of them, with the works of mercy, and mercy carries it clear. More works; more, in number: if they their thousand, mercy her ten thousand; more great, more glorious works, of it, than of any of them all; nay than of all of them: *super omnia opera*, that it is. And now to our *super*. And first, *super*, "above."

1 Sam. 18. 7.

Super, "above," is said here by way of figure. Properly, *super* is of height: height is a dimension that pertains to quantity; and quantity, to bodies, whereof mercy is none. The meaning is, it is the chiefest. So, Heaven in the greater world; so, the head, in the less: both of them the highest, both of them the chiefest; chiefest of all, and rule all. As, indeed, of whom is *super* said, so rightly, as of the sovereign? So doth mercy: namely, His power, which may serve for all. *Deus*, saith the Church, the eleventh Sunday after Trinity, *Qui Omnipotentiam Tuam parcendo maxime et miserando mani-*

II. Of their super. 1. Super, "above."

SERM. *festas;* "God, Which shewest Thine Almighty power, most
VII. chiefly, in shewing mercy."

1 Sam. 9. 2.

But, to keep us to the letter. *Super,* "above," is either
1. real, or 2. local. 1. Real, as Saul above the people, "higher

Lu. 19. 4. by the head and shoulders" than any of them. 2. Local,
as Zaccheus; though of low stature, yet above, in the top of
a sycamore tree.

1. Above really.

Mercy is itself highest. We will soon end this point, by
the heavens, the uppermost of all His works. "His mercy,"

Ps. 108. 4. saith the one hundred and eighth Psalm, is ἐπάνω, "above;"
and that, with a μέγα, " a great way above the heavens;" and,
if above them, above all under them. It is itself highest.

2. Above, locally. 1. In place.

And it hath the highest place of all, above all, the precedence before all. The highest place. The ark was, on earth,
the figure of the spiritual Heaven : over it were the Cherubims; above, upon the top of their wings, was the mercy-
seat ; there sits mercy, in the highest place of all.

2. In pre-cedence.

As the highest place, above all; so the precedence, before
all. In God's own style framed and proclaimed by Himself,

Ex. 34. 6. Exodus, the thirty-fourth chapter, consisting of thirteen titles,
(מרום, measures or degrees,) next after "The Lord God," the
very first is this word here. And take this withal; that, of
the thirteen, nine of them belong to mercy : that proportion
it hath, that so, it may have the *super* every way.

From this place it hath, " over all," (and by God's appointment; it took it not itself;) we gather the place it hath in
God's esteem. That, which one most sets by, he sets by himself, and next himself : ever, the dearest, the nearest still.
God, by thus setting it next to Him (none between God and
it in His style) shews plainly, what virtue it is, He loves above
all; and what virtue He commends to us above all. To us all;
but specially, to them that are above all: to be *super omnia,*
in them that be *super omnes.* As the nobler the nature, and
the nearer to God, the more easy ever to take the impression
of it. To hold you no longer in this first. It is one of God's

Gen. 14. 19.

titles, Melchisedek first gave to Him, *Altissimus.* As He,
Altissimus ; so mercy, *altissima* ever : *altissima, in Altissimo,*
'the highest virtue in Him that is Most High,' "Which is

Rom. 9. 5. God, above all to be blessed," and to be blessed for this
above all. And this, for *super,* "above."

But, there is more than so, in it. *Super* is "over;" ἐπὶ

2.
Super,
"over."

πάντα, is "over all." All that are above are not over. It is not above only, as an obelisk or maypole, higher than all about them, but have neither shadow nor shelter; no good they do. Mercy hath a broad top, spreading itself over all. It is so above all, as it is over them, too. As the vault of this chapel is over us, and the great vault of the firmament over that. The *super* of latitude and expansion, no less than of altitude and elevation.

And this, to the end that all may retire to it, and take covert: it, over them; and they, under it. Under it, under the "shadow" of it, as of Esay's great "rock" in the wilder- Isa. 32. 2. ness, from the heat. Under it, under the shelter of it, as of Dan. 4. 12. Daniel's great tree, from the tempest.

"Over all His works," now. "O Lord," saith the one *Super*
omnia,
over all.
Ps. 104.
24. hundred and fourth Psalm, "how manifold are Thy works!" We shall never get through half of them, God knows; *Non est pertransire infinitum.* We will contract them, thus: take the two extremes, so shall we take in all betwixt them. "Over 1. All His
works,
His *opera.* all," that is, none of them all so high, but as high as they be, they need come under it. Nor none of them all so mean, but as mean as they be, they are not left out: one way or other, within it, under it, all. So we divide His works into His *opera,* and His *opuscula;* and over both it is.

None so high: none on earth, not His saints (who, of all on earth, have the *super,* are of highest perfection). In them Job 15. 15. He found no stedfastness, they be *vasa misericordiæ* all. If Rom. 9. 23. you will take it with Jacob's staff, he saith, *Minor sum cunctis,* "he is under them, under them all." Gen. 32. 10.

Not in earth then: no, nor in Heaven. Neither Heaven itself, nor the brightest part of Heaven, the stars; they are not "clean in His sight," they also need it. Nay, not the Job 15. 15. Angels, the very brightest of them all; in them He found *pravitatem,* σκολιόν τι, somewhat amiss, even in them. So, Job 4. 18. over them too; they need it. The very Seraphin have some- Isa. 6. 2. thing to cover. As for the Cherubin, they will set mercy Ex. 37. 9. a seat upon the top of their wings; so glad and fain are they to have it over them. All the tongues of saints and Angels must say this verse with us, *Misericordiæ Domini super omnia*

SERM.
VII.

opera Ejus. Both say it, for both need it : and if both they, I would fain know, who needs it not.

2. All His
opuscula.

Now, as none so high ; none of His *opera*, His folio works : so, none so mean, none of His *opuscula*, but over them too. As His art no less wonderful, in making the ant, than the elephant; so, His care no less over the one, than over the other. *Naturas rerum minimarum non destituit Deus ;* the very *minims* of the world, His mercy leaves them not destitute.

Ps. 104. 11.

Not "the wild asses," without a place to "quench their thirst."

Ps. 147. 9.

Not "the young ravens" crying on Him. Not the sparrow of

Mat. 10. 29.

half a farthing, lets not them light on the ground without His providence. Even these, even such His mercy is over also. It is not *pallium breve ;* the mantle is wide enough, it leaves none out.

None out ? What say you to hell, and those there ? Not them ? Nazianzen (that had the honour to be called the divine of his time) thinks it may be maintained, not them : and so do the schoolmen all, inasmuch as even there, mercy moderates too. That it is not, with them there, as it might and should be ; but *tolerabilius*, 'easier' than they do deserve

Lu. 12. 47.

by much. None, no not in that place, though "beaten with many stripes;" not yet with so many, as the quality of his offence, in rigour of justice, would require. This is sure : *Deus præmiat ultra, punit citra ;* 'God ever rewards beyond, but punishes on this side ; short still, of that we deserve : that

Hab. 3. 2.

His very punishment is tempered with mercy, that, "even in His wrath, He remembereth mercy."

But we will not stand upon this ; we need not : we shall find another *super* for these, anon. For many are the *super*s of mercy. Not in any one, possibly ; but in one sense or other, "over all." Then, (if it go by *Quo communius eo melius*,) none so good, for none so common, I am sure.

The reason is *Ejus*, referred to mercy. Mercy the maker of them all.

And reason, why mercy should spread the wing of her mantle thus over all. All are *opera Ejus. Opera Ejus : Ejus* may be referred indifferently, to mercy, as well as to God. Mercy hath the name from רחם, 'the womb.' For, she was the womb, indeed, in which all were conceived at first, and she delivered of them all. Plain, by the one hundred

Ps. 136. 5, 6, 7.

and thirty-sixth Psalm : "Who by His excellent wisdom made the Heavens, Who laid out the earth above the waters,

Who made great lights, &c." And the cause of every one, at the end of every one, and of twenty more, "For, His mercy endureth for ever." That set all on work: His wisdom, to contrive; His power, to execute; appointed all, did all.

It was mercy, and nothing but mercy, set the creation in hand. For, it is well known, *in non ente* there could be no moving cause at all. Nothing we were; we, and all His works: in nothing, there can be nothing to induce, why it should be brought out of the state of being nothing. So that, His mercy it was, that removed that universal defect of nonentity at the first.

And having then made them, it is kindly that *viscera misericordiæ* should be over those *opera* that came *de visceri-bus;* whom it brought from nothing, to be over them, and not see them cast away, and brought to nothing again. The eagle, saith Moses, the poor hen, saith our Saviour, will do it for their young ones: stretch their wings over them, to preserve them, what they can. <small>Mercy the preserver of all.</small> <small>Ex. 19. 4.</small> <small>Mat. 23. 37.</small>

So that, these very two words, *opera Ejus,* contain in them a reason, why mercy should do no less. A reason? Nay two. 1. One, for that they be *Ejus,* "His." "I am Thine, O save me;" a good reason. His they be, a part of His possession. That alone is enough with us, to preserve that is ours; only because it is ours, though we never made it. 2. But besides that they be His, they be His handy-work. Another good inducement, "Despise not, O Lord, the works of Thine own hands." We see then, why "over all;" *quia Ejus, quia opera;* 'because His,' all; 'because His works,' all. And it is well for us, the reason is laid so large. For, whatever we be or do, or whatever become of us, His we are, and His works we are still. So, still "His mercy is over" us, and we under it. <small>The reason. 1. In *Ejus,* His pos-session. Ps. 119. 94.</small> <small>2. In *opera,* His handy works. Ps. 138. 8.</small>

It made me say at first, this *super,* as it is highly to the praise of mercy, that it is "over His works;" so it is every way as highly to the good of all His works, which are under mercy. The vanity Solomon saw ("one set over others for their hurt") hath no place here. That mercy is over all, is for the general good of all, and that is ever a blessed *super.* We shall not need to fear any heart-burning, any emulation, for this *super;* or to ask what the works say to it: they all <small>*Super omnia.* 1. For mercy's praise. 2. For the good of His works. Eccl. 8. 9.</small>

say, Amen, Hallelujah: glad are they, that mercy is in that place; they would have none other, if they might. It fol-
Ps. 145. 10. loweth next, *Confiteantur Tibi opera,* His works are ready all to confess, to acknowledge this supremacy without any scruple; to take the oath to it.

For *super,* "over," there is no doubt, that it is as the Cherubims' wings, stretched from one side of the temple to the other: over all, for all to fly under, and find succour there. *Tutissimum est,* (say they that can say least by it;) when all is done, nothing whereto we may so safely commit ourselves. And therefore *super omnia,* that *super omnia* we

1. For if above all His works, above His judgment. might trust in it. But I say, that even *super,* "above," it is not, as a bare pole upright; there is a brazen serpent upon the top of it, for us to look up to and receive comfort by. I will touch two or three; for thus we deduce. First, if it be "above all His works," it follows, then, above every one of them: and one will serve the turn. Of all the works of God there is no work we are afraid of, but one; that is, His judgment, the work of His justice. Above that, it is; for, "above all" it is. And that is to our comfort greatly. For which, (besides this general "above all," therefore above it,) we owe to St. James, that we have it expressed in particular, even in terms terminant: *Misericordia superexaltat judi-*

Jas. 2. 13. *cium,* "Mercy is exalted" (more than exalted, super-ex-alted) "above judgment," *nominatim.* That work of His, we most stand in awe of, over that work by name mercy

Ex. 20. 5, 6. triumpheth. And, in the very Decalogue, there may you see the *super* of a thousand to four, in mercy over justice. Even there, even in the roll of His justice, the law; there, would God have it extant upon record, that mercy is above it.

And if mercy be above it, thither (to mercy) we may remove our cause, as to the higher court. There lieth an appeal thither, *A solio justitiæ ad thronum gratiæ,* 'from

Heb. 4. 16. the bench of justice, to "the throne of grace" and mercy.' There, we may be relieved. Now, if it be above that *opus,* that work of God's, for God's works we seek no more.

2. Above all our works, our sinful works. A second we deduce thus. If it be "above all His works," shall it not much more be above all ours? What are we to Him; ours to His? No work of ours then, or to be done by

us, but the "mercy of God is above" it; no sinful work, I
mean; that we err not Cain's error, his sin was above God's Gen. 4. 13.
mercy. No; mercy above it. *Grande est barathrum pecca-*
torum meorum (it is Chrysostom); *sed major est abyssus mise-*
ricordiæ Dei; 'Great is the whirlpool of my wicked works,
but greater is the Bethesda, the wide and deep gulf of the
mercy of God that hath no bottom.' And indeed, it were
not truly said, It is "above all His works," (all His, and
much more then above all ours;) if any of all our works
were above it; no more than, There is a "Lamb that taketh Joh. 1. 29.
away the sins of the world," if there were any sins in the
world, He takes not away. And this is the *super* indeed,
that would be looked into by us, by reason of another *super :*
Iniquitates nostræ supergressæ sunt capita nostra, "Our sins Ps. 38. 4.
are gone up, over, above our heads ;" over head and ears in
sin. And another *super* yet, above them; even "the phials Rev. 16. 1.
of God's wrath" hanging over our heads, ready to be poured
on us and them, were it not, that mercy is above them,
and stays them. Were it not that over whom misery, over
them mercy: else were we in danger to be overwhelmed
with them every hour. We see then, the comparison was
well laid in *super.* Our sins, over us: judgments, over them;
but mercy over all, *super omnia.* Always, where there is
super, there is *satis ; satis superque* shews, *super* is more than
satis. Enough then there is, and to spare, for them all.

One more. Not only above all ours, but if it be "above 3. Above
all His works," then is it above all the works of them that the works
be His works : and so (not to hold you,) above the devil and works.
all his works. For he also is one of them : of God's making,
as an Angel; of his own marring, as a devil. Above his
works, I say, and above the works and practices of his limbs,
and all they can do or devise against them, over whom His
mercy is. The Son of God, saith St. John, in mercy therefore appeared, *ut solveret opera diaboli,* that "He might 1 Joh. 3. 8.
loose, undo, quite dissolve the works of the devil." No work
shall he contrive, never so deep under ground, never so near
the borders of his own region, but God's mercy will bring it
to light; it, and the workers of it. His mercy will have
a *super,* for their *subter.* There shall be more in mercy, to
save; than in Satan, to destroy : more, *Dicat nunc Israel;* Ps. 124. 1.

SERM.   more, may this realm now say.   A notorious work of his, as
VII.   ever any ; nay, *super omnia*, as never was any, this day by
————   His mercy brought to light, and dissolved, quite dissolved.

Ps. 44. 1.   We heard it not with our ears, our fathers told it us not; our
eyes beheld this *super*.

3.   So we are come to our own case, ere we were aware, that
Super,   is, *super*, " upon."   Over all it is; yet, not over all alike; at
" upon :"   leastwise, not upon all alike; upon some, more than over
1. " upon"
some more   other some.   *Æqualiter est Illi cura de omnibus*, but, not
than other
of His   *æqualis;* ' equally, a care of all, but not an equal care,
works.   though.'   No, His mercy over all in general is no bar, but
upon some there may be a special *super ;* and so, some have
a *super* in this *super* too.

For, if the reason, why " mercy is over all His works," be
because they be His works; then, the more they be His
works, the more workmanship He bestows upon them, the
more is His mercy over them.   Whereby it falls out, that as
there is an unequality of His works, and one work above
another; so is there a diverse graduation of His mercy, and
one mercy above another; or rather, one and the same
mercy, as the same planet in auge, in the top of his epicycle,
higher than itself, at other times.

2. Upon   To shew this, we divide His works, (as we have warrant,)
man more   into His works of *Fiat* (as the rest of His creatures) ; and
than other
creatures. the work of *Faciamus*, as man, the masterpiece of His works;
Gen. 1. 26. upon whom He did more cost, shewed more workmanship,
than on the rest: the very word *Faciamus* sets him above all.
1. God's προβουλία, that He did deliberate, enter into consultation as it were about his making, and about none else.

Gen. 2. 7. 2. God's αὐτουργία, that Himself framed his body of the
mould, as the potter the clay.   3. Then, that He breathed
into him a two-lived soul, which made the Psalmist break
Ps. 8. 4.   out *Domine quid est homo, &c.*, " Lord, what is man, that
Thou shouldst so regard him," as to pass by the heavens,
and all the glorious bodies there, and passing by them,
breathe an immortal soul, put Thine own image upon a
Ps. 8. 6.   piece of clay?   4. But last, God's setting him *super omnia
opera manuum Suarum*, " over all the works of His hands."
His making him, as I may say, Count Palatine of the world;
this shews plainly, His setting by man more than all of them.

As he then, over them; so, God's mercy over him. Over all His works; but, of all His works, over this work. Over His chief work, chiefly: in a higher degree. And not without great cause. Man is capable of eternal, either felicity or misery; so are not the rest: he sins; so do not they. So, his case requires a *super* in this *super*, requires mercy more than all theirs.

Upon men then, chiefly. They, the first *super* in this *super*. But of men, (though it be true in general, "He hath shut up all under sin, that He might have mercy upon all,") yet, even among them a *super* too, a second. Another workmanship He hath yet: "His workmanship in Christ Jesu," the Apostle calls it, "His new creature," which His mercy is more directly upon, than upon the rest of mankind. *Servator omnium hominum,* "the Saviour of all men," saith the Apostle; marry, *autem,* "most of all, of the faithful Christian men." Of all men, above all men, upon them: they are His work wrought on both sides; creation on one side, redemption on the other. For now we are at the work of redemption. Rom. 11. 32. Eph. 2. 10. Gal. 6. 15. 1 Tim. 4. 10.

And here now is mercy right, in kind, רחמה רחמי, *rahame rahama,* the mercy of the bird of mercy, that is the pelican's mercy (for כהמת is the pelican, which hath her name of mercy, as the truly merciful bird). For, here now is not the womb to hatch them, nor the wings to cloke them, but the pelican's bill of mercy, striking itself to the heart, drawing blood thence, even the very heartblood, to revive her young ones, when they were dead in sin, and to make them live anew the life of grace. This is *misericordia super omnes misericordias.* Shall I say it? (I may truly;) mercy in all else, above His works; but in this, above Himself. For when it brought Him down from Heaven to earth, to such a birth in the "manger," such a life in "contradiction of sinners," such a " death on the cross," it might truly be said then, *Misericordia etiam triumphat de Deo.* You shall mark therefore, at the very next words, when he comes to his thanks, it is *Confiteantur Tibi opera Deus;* but *Sancti Tui benedicant Tibi:* "Thy works, let them say *Confiteor;* Thy redeemed, Thy saints, let them sing *Benedictus.*" Thy works, let them tell truth and confess; but Thy saints, let them speak all Lu. 2. 12. Heb. 12. 3. Phil. 2. 8. Ps. 145.10.

good and bless Thee; highly bless Thee, for this Thy high
mercy of all other upon them, as of all other, they have most
cause to do.

To elevate it one degree, one *super* more. For (I know
not how, but) you shall observe, that even among the faithful,
even among them, God singles out some one people still, from
the rest, that He makes of above the rest, and vouchsafes His
special favour upon, more than the rest, though Christian
men, as well as they; and no reason in the world to be given
of it, but the *super* of His mercy. It was ever so: some
nation, of whom it might be said, *Non taliter fecit omni*
Ps. 147.20. *nationi,* "He hath not dealt so with every nation." Nay,
non omni is *nulli,* "He hath not dealt so with any nation."
Some, of whom it might be said, Of all the people in the
earth I have chosen you, to come nearest you, to vouchsafe
you My chiefest, My choicest mercies, *super omnes.* Not in
matters only pertaining to the soul, in which all Christians
are interested alike; but even in the things pertaining to the
course of this life, secular, (as we call them,) and temporal:
Ps. 21. 1. in them too. And, in both, is better than one alone. In
saving that way with the salvation the King rejoiceth in;
saving them from plots and practices, even against their
worldly prosperity; from Ahithophel's plots, from Absalom's
vow, and such like.

III.
Our *super*
in this
super.
And now to our *super.* For, may not we, think you,
reckon ourselves in all, in this last "above all?" His works
first: so are all His creatures. His chief workmanship: so
are other men. His workmanship in Christ: so are other
Christians. But above all these, His *non taliter.* For, if we
be not very dim-sighted, without any perspective glass, we
may see such mercies and favours of His, *super,* upon ourselves, as (sure) the nations round about us have not seen:
and, I think I may say, not any nation on the earth seen
the like.

Many ways might this be made appear, and many days
brought to give us light to it; but, let all else pass in silence:
this day, this fifth of November, is *instar omnium.* Nay, is
super omnes, 'before, beyond, above them all:' to elevate to
Luke 1.78. us this point of "the tender mercies of our God, whereby
this day sprung from on high did visit us." This day, I say,

enough and enough, to bring from all our mouths that it brought from his Majesty's, and that with admiration, *Misericordiæ Dei super omnia opera Ejus !* And the *Confiteantur,* and the *Benedicant* of right belonging to it.

We, right now, divided His works: we will now divide His mercies. That do we, according to their object, which is misery: and that is double. 1. For, either it is already upon us, and we in it; 2. or but over us, yet so over us, as we are within the shadow of death, at the very pit's brink (as they say), and even now ready to be tumbled in. To quit us of these two, there is a double mercy (they follow at the fourteenth verse). 1. *Erigit lapsos,* 2. *sustinet labentes,* "lifts up them that be down, and stays them that be going down." There is a *super* in these too. 1. One of them the better (which our *Pater-noster* will teach us); *Ne inducas* first, and then *Libera.* Better, "Lead us not" in, than "Deliver us out." If we are in, "Deliver us;" but, better never come in at all. Jonas was delivered, so was Nineveh. Nineveh's was better (they came not in) than Jonas': he was in, but got out. That of *Libera,* God send us too, if ever we shall need it; and send it all them, that at this present do. But yet, give me the mercy of *Ne inducas,* let it not light, let it pass over : the Passover, that is the memorable deliverance; that, the high feast.

And that was the *super* "upon" us. And it behoved so to be. We were not in: it came not to that; thank mercy for it. If it had, it had been past with us, past *Libera :* that other mercy could have done us no good. If it had not been *Prævenisti, Post venisti* had come too late. For, if in, never out more. This, our first *super.*

But, being not in, we were as near it, as near might be, and scape it. Over, it was; nay, it was rather under us, then : but all is one, *super* or *subter,* either will serve here : that *subter* would have ended in a *super,* sent us up high enough, I wot well; therefore we will keep the word of the text ; *super,* let it go.

First, when it was contrived, over us it was. Then, when it was set in hand, over us yet more. But, when it came to *parata sunt omnia,* all ready for the match, and the match for it (for so near it came) then it was over us; I trow, hard over

Marginal notes:
1. The mercy of *Ne inducas.*
[Ps. 145. 14.]
2. The mercy of *Libera,* from a cruelty close to us.

SERM.
VII.

us; and then to scape it, when it was even in a manner ready to seize on us, that is another *super:* for, then to scape it, that doth us the more good, ever; and that is ever praised, for the superior deliverance. The second *super.*

3.
And close, from us.

Specially, if you add the third: that when it was so near us, and we to it, it was not so close by us, as close from us, we knew it not. And none so miserable as they that are so, and know not they are so; nay, think it clean otherwise. The Laodicean misery, that (we say) is of all other the most

Rev. 3. 17.

woful. *Tu dicis quod,* "Thou sayest" thou art this, and thou art that; safe, and sure, and happy; and behold thou art none of all these; but, even then, when thou sayest it, mise-

Jer. 6. 24.

rable, and even in the jaws of death. That is the misery, that comes as the "throws of a woman in travail:" as the flood, upon the old world; as the fire, upon the five cities.

Mat. 24.
37.
Luke 17.
26, 28.

And that was our case right: they in "the days of Noah," they "in the days of Lot," never reckoned less of the flood or the fire, over them; than we, of the powder, under us. And I blame us not. Who would not have thought himself safe in that place? who, that he might not have trodden on that threshold, that floor, without danger? If safe at all, if any where, there. It is the asylum, the surest place, one would think, in all the land. Ἐφ' ᾧ φρονεῖς μέγιστα, ἀπολεῖ τοῦτό σε· 'where our greatest trust, there our danger most deadly:' and that is, ever, the *super* of all miseries.

Being then so over us, or under us; under us, and near us; near us, and we not aware of it; so near, that they made full

Ps. 124. 3.

account (I say not, as the Psalm, "to have swallowed us up quick," but) to have blown us up quick, and in a moment sent us up, shivered all to pieces: it was a third, and a principal *super,* this, more than ordinary, that made us *superesse,* 'to remain still alive' after so great, so present, so secret a danger.

4.
The *super omnia* of this cruelty.

And yet another *super* more, against this last: which will serve, as black work (I mean their cruelty) to make this white work of God's mercy shew the better to us. It is a *super omnia* too. As our deliverance, a work of mercy, *super omnia;* so, our intended destruction, a work of cruelty *super omnia.*

Super omnia, 'above all examples,' to begin with. For,

the like never seen, nor heard of. Nay, not to be raked out
of any story, in any age, of any country, civil or savage, of
the like. And *super omnes,* " over all" it would have gone,
not spared any, no degree, high or low : no estate, nobles or
commons; no calling, sacred or civil; no sex, King or Queen;
no age, King or Prince ; no religion, their own or others.
This is but *super omnes;* nay, *super omnia* it was too. *Super,*
Up with lime, and stone, and timber, iron, glass, and lead ;
up with floor, windows, and walls, roof and all. Yet another
super omnia : all bands of birth, country, allegiance, nature,
blood, humanity and Christianity ; tread upon them, trample
upon them all, tear them all in pieces. Never such a *super
omnia,* in all senses. So, indeed, a cruelty for the devil himself: to make the opposition perfect, of God's mercy and
Satan's cruelty. Of whom, to give each their due, it may be
said, and no less truly said, *Crudelitates ejus super omnia
opera ejus,* ' His cruelties are above all his works ;' than of
God, that " His mercies are above all His."

Super omnia opera ejus it is ; and *contra omnia opera Dei ;*
' above all his own, and against all God's works.' The enemy
of God he is, and so of all God's works ; and of those His
works most, that God most sets by, that is, mankind; and of
that part of mankind most, God hath done most for, and so
may be thought most to favour, that is, Christian men ; and
then of them, if there be a *Non taliter* in His mercy, a *Non
taliter* too, in his malice, straight. If a *super omnes,* with
God ; a *super omnes* with him, *in sensu contrario.*

To any creature (only because it is a creature) is he cruel;
he will into the hog-sty to shew it, rather than not to shew Mat. 8. 31.
it at all.

But to man ; to one man, rather than to a whole herd of
swine.

And among men, his malice is most at Christian men :
they are nearer to the kingdom of God. To keep them from
that, himself hath irrecoverably lost, that is, Heaven; and
to plunge them into eternal misery, whereinto himself is
fallen, without all redemption.

And among Christian men, to the best sort; to public
persons, rather than to private mean men.

But, if he could get a whole parliament together : a King,

SERM.
VII.

his nobles, his commons; that is, a King, kingdom and all; and up with them all at once, all together: there were none to that: that, lo, he would over sea and land to compass. For, that were indeed, with him, a *super omnia :* he never had done the like.

Of this their father, were those ungodly men of this day. Ungodly, I say; for Solomon sets us this sign, to know un-

Prov.12.10. godly men by : *Viscera impiorum crudelia,* if " the bowels be cruel," then ungodly, certainly. No pity, no piety, with him. And we find, that mercy is a plant of our nature; so incident to the nature of man, as they are holden inhuman, that are without it. No pity, no humanity. Why then, Satanity it must be, if God and man disclaim it; even of him, *cujus crudelitas super omnia opera ejus.*

Now God cannot abide cruelty at any hand. By what He placeth highest, may we know what He loves best (mercy); and by that, may we know, what He can worst away with

Mat.18.28. (cruelty). Nay, if once he take his fellow by the throat, deal cruelly with him, never hear him more. No cruelty can He endure, at all : specially, no such cruel cruelty, as this, that passed all.

And in this case of ours, I make no doubt, God was moved both ways.

Ps. 141. 7. One way, by mercy; for us, that "our bones might not be scattered" in every corner; as, "when one heweth wood," chips fly about. And again; for them, we should have left behind, that *Videns Jesus turbas misertus est eis,* He looked

Mat. 9. 36. upon them too, and saw they should have been ἐκλελυμένοι and ἐῤῥιμμένοι, "scattered all," and "hurried up and down," like a sort of poor masterless sheep. His mercy wrought with Him, in both these respects.

But, on the other side, their cruelty moved Him also. And, I am persuaded, God looking upon those merciless-bowelled men, when in their hearts they hatched that monster of cruelty, even at the sight of that barbarous resolution, (yea more than barbarous,) His heart even turned against them, His very soul abhorred that devilish intention of theirs. They had thought to have had the day; but, to the high praise of His mercy, and to the confusion of Satan and all his cruelty, He gave order, mercy should have the

day : and she had it, that there might be a mercy *super omnia,* above this cruelty *super omnia :* as there was. Their counsel brought to light, brought to nought, brought upon their own heads ; and both counsel and counsellors brought to a shameful end.

Nay, would they make men's bowels fly up and down the air ? Out with those bowels ; what should they do in, that have not in them that, that bowels should have. Would they do it by fire ? Into the fire with their bowels, before their faces. Would they make men's bones fly about like chips ? Hew their bones in sunder. Just is David's prayer : " Their delight was in cruelty, let it happen to them ; they loved not mercy, therefore let it be far from them." ^{Ps. 109. 17.}

But, how now ? We are gone now from mercy quite. No, no : there is mercy even in this severity. In the Psalm of mercy, slaying is made a work of mercy : slew the first-born of Egypt, cruel Pharaoh, cruel Og, " for His mercy endureth for ever :" mercy, in ridding the world of such. For they are not worthy to be *inter opera Dei,* ' among God's works,' that renounce that virtue, that is *super opera Dei,* " over all God's works." ^{Ps. 136. 10, 15, 20.}

And so now ye see that *super,* I told you, we should come to at last : over hell, and them there. The *super superantis,* ' the over of an overcomer,' of mercy a conqueror. Above His other works, with the *super* of a sovereign, to protect them : upon the devil and devilish men and their works, with *super aspidem et basiliscum,* to tread upon them, to " make His enemies His footstool," and so a *super,* " over" them too. ^{Ps. 91. 13.} ^{Ps. 110. 1.}

And now, we have set mercy in her chariot of triumph ; in which, if ever she sat, she sat in the *super omnia* of this day. Let us now come to the last *super,* the *super* of duty remaining upon the head of all God's works, for His mercy over them all : but, among them all, and above them all, upon our heads, (if it were but for the sovereign mercy of this day,) what we were in *super,* to God, for it. ^{IV. The *super* of our duty.}

The *super* upon all God's works follows in the words next ensuing, *Confiteantur.* Are " His mercies over all His works?" Why then, O all ye works of the Lord, all flesh, " every thing that hath breath ;" but chiefly His chief work, ^{From His works. Ps. 145. 9. Ps. 150. 6. Ps. 145. 12.}

"the sons of men," the nations and the kindreds of the earth, come all to confession; all owe this, to confess, at least. Confess? what? Nothing but mercy, and the *super* of the mercy. Nothing, but that it is, as it is: do but as God doth, exalt it, place it where He sets it. Let the deep say, It is over me; and the dry land say, It is over me: and so, of the rest, every one: so many works, so many confessions.

There is a further *super*, "upon" His "saints:" they owe more to Him than His ordinary works. His works, but to confess; His saints, to confess and "bless," both. They are double works, "needle-work on both sides;" more becomes them. *Te decet hymnus in Sion:* both, to confess it is above all; and to bless and praise it, above all. For, if it be above all, it follows, more praise is to come to Him for it, than for all. If mercy, above all; the praise of His mercy, above the praises of all.

There is a further *super* yet, upon us that have found and felt the *super* of it; the *Non taliter*, say I, above works and saints both. All are bound; but we that are here, *super omnes*, more than all, we. We that should have been martyrs of Satan's cruelty, it stands us in hand to be confessors of God's mercy, as, to which we owe even ourselves; ourselves, and our safety; safety of souls and bodies, every one of us.

Then, let the King, Queen, and Prince; let all the three estates; let the whole land delivered by it from a chaos of confusion; let our souls, which He hath held in life; let our bodies, which He hath kept together from flying in pieces; let all think on it; think how to thank Him for it; say, and sing, and celebrate it above all. We, above all; for it, above all.

For, if ever mercy were over work of His; if ever work of His, under it directly; it was so over us, and we so under it, this day. If ever, of any it might be avowed; or to any applied; if ever, any might rightly and truly, upon good and just cause, say or sing this verse; we of this land may do both: it will fit our mouths best, best become us.

For, such a work did He shew on us this day, as, if mercy have a *super omnia* of other, this may claim a *super omnia* of it, of mercy itself. His mercy is not so high above the rest of His works, as this day's work, high above the works of it. That, supreme to all; this, supreme to it. Mercy, in it, even above itself.

We then, that have had such a *super* in this *super ;* we, of all others, nay more than all others, to have it yet more specially recommended. A bare confession will not serve; but the highest confession of all, to take the oath of the supremacy of it. We, if ever any, to say it and swear it: if it had not been in sovereign manner over some of His works, (that is, ourselves,) we had been full low ere this, *infra infimos,* beneath, under all His works; not now above ground, to speak and to hear of this theme.

Let it then claim the supremacy in our *Confiteantur,* and in our *Benedicant,* both ; above works, saints, and all. And that, not mentally or verbally alone ; in heart so to hold, and in tongue so to report it ; but, which is worth all, really in work so to express it. I mean, as our thanks for His mercy above all our thanks; so our works of mercy, above all our works. But, be they so? His are so; are ours? I would to God, I could say they were; but sure they are not. "His mercy above all His works." With us, in this point, it is clean contrary; all our works above our mercy. The least, the last, the lowest part of our works, are our works of mercy : the fewest in number, the poorest in value, the slightest in regard. Indeed, *infra omnia,* with us, they.

But sure, God, in thus setting it "above all His works," sheweth, He would have it, with us so too. That which is *super omnia Ejus,* to be *super omnia nostra ;* as "above all His," so 'above all ours' likewise. And Christ our Saviour would have it so: His *Estote,* is *Estote misericordes ;* and Lu. 6. 36. how? Not barely, *Estote ;* but *Estote, sicut Pater vester cœlestis ;* "merciful as He." And how is He? So as, with Him, it is "above all." To imitate Him then in this, let it be highest with us ; as, with Him, it is highest. Sure, we are not right, till it be with us so too: as in God's, so in ours: above ours, above them all. That so, it may have the supremacy, in *Confiteantur,* in *Benedicant,* in praise and thanks, in words, and works, and all.

To set off the *super* of this day then, and to conclude. If the generality of His works confess Him for theirs ; and the speciality of His saints bless Him for theirs; what are we to do, how to confess, how to bless for the singular mercy of this day (and let all others go)? Sure, our "mouths to be filled with praise" as the sea, and our voice in sounding it out, as the noise of His waves, and we to cover the heavens with praise, as with clouds for it.

But we are not able to praise Thee, O Lord, or to extol Thy Name, for one of a thousand. Nay, not for one of the many millions of the great mercies, which Thou hast shewed upon us and upon our children. How often hast Thou rid us from plague, freed us from famine, saved us from the sword, from our enemies compassing us round, from the fleet, that came to make us no more a people!

Even, before this day, we now hold; before it, and since it, have not Thy compassions withdrawn themselves from us. But, this day, this day above all days, have they shewed it *super omnia ;* and, not over, but upon us.

Wherefore, the powers Thou hast distributed in our souls, the breath of life Thou hast breathed into our nostrils, the tongues Thou hast put into our mouths, behold, all these shall break forth, and confess, and bless, and thank, and praise, and magnify, and exalt Thee and Thy mercy, for ever. Yea, every mouth shall acknowledge Thee, every tongue be a trumpet of Thy praise; every eye look up, every knee bow, every stature stoop to Thee, and all hearts shall fear Thee. And all that within us, even our bowels: those our bowels, that, but for Thee, had flown we know not whither: even our bones; those bones that, but for it, had been shivered bone from bone, one from another, all shall say, "Who is like unto Thee, O Lord," in mercy? "Who is like unto Thee, glorious in holiness, fearful in praise; doing wonders," wonders of mercy, as this day, upon us all, to be held by us and our posterity in an everlasting remembrance?

[Exod. 15. 11.]

Glory be to Thee, O Lord, glory be to Thee: glory be to Thee, and glory be to Thy mercy, the *super omnia,* the most glorious of all Thy great and high perfections. Glory be to Thee, and glory be to it: to it, in Thee; and to Thee, for it: and that by all Thy works, in all places and at all times. And, of all Thy works, and above them all, by us here; by the hearts and lungs of us all, in this place, this day, for this day, for the mercy of this day; for the mercy of it, above all mercies; and for the work of this day, above all the works of it. And, not this day only, but all the days of our life; even as long as Thy mercy endureth, and that "endureth for ever:" for ever, in this world; for ever, in Ps. 136. 1. the world to come; *per*, 'through' the cistern and conduit of all Thy mercies, Jesus Christ.

A SERMON

THE KING'S MAJESTY AT WHITEHALL,

ON THE FIFTH OF NOVEMBER, A.D. MDCXVI.

ISAIAH xxxvii. 3.

The children are come to the birth, and there is not strength to bring forth.

Venerunt filii usque ad partum, et virtus non est pariendi.

[*The children are come to the birth, and there is not strength to bring forth.* Engl. Trans.]

S E R M. VIII.

I HAVE taken this piece, and no more. More I could not, you see. It will not fit our turn, or this day, the fore-end of the verse : " This is a day of trouble, rebuke, blasphemy," cannot we say. We must say, This is a day, not of trouble, but of joy; not of rebuke, but of praise; not of blasphemy, but of thanksgiving, with us. And so may we say too, and yet keep these words for our ground, still. Nothing lets, but that one and the same day may be, both a day of joy, and of sorrow. They that have the day, and they that lose the day, the day is but one; but, to the winner, a joyful day; to the loser, not so; but, a day of sorrow and of blasphemy, otherwhile. And so was this day a day of sorrow, to some : they might have taken up the whole verse, as it stands : those (I mean) that, do what they can, must be fain to father the children, that this day were coming, but came not forth. That they came not forth, the want of strength to be delivered, made it to them a day of sorrow (some say of blasphemy too) : not so, to us. To us, a day of praise and thanks, that they lost their so looked for and longed for children; that they were not born, who, if they had been born, would have been the bane of us all. To us then, as this day, a day; so this, a verse of joy.

The words are in Hebrew of the nature of a proverb; and The sum. used by them, as a by-word, upon the defeating of any plot. Not, every defeating; but then, when a plot is cunningly contrived, and closely followed, and is near brought to the very point to be done, yet not done though; but defeated, even then: then, take they up this proverb and say, *Venerunt, &c.*

And, two ways take they it up, thereafter as the design is. If it be bad, yet well laid, and well seconded, and for all that, in the end disappointed; then utter they it cheerfully, " Aha, the children," &c. but as God would, &c. by way of gratulation. But, if good, and for a while come fairly forward, but in the end prove to nothing; then take they it up, with a sigh, " Alas, the children," &c.

It cannot be denied, but good King Hezekiah, whose the words are, spake them here in some grief. Grief, two ways; for 1. first, grieved he was to hear how Rabshakeh had raged and raved, and spewed out most horrible blasphemies. Fain would he, he and his men, rather than their lives, have been at him for it. They were even great with this, as it were, and the children come to the birth; but their strength served them not, they durst not give him a word, for fear of a further mischief, if they should provoke him. Now there is no more hard and grievous case in the world, than when a man shall be forced to hear blaspheming, and not be in case to answer it home.

2. But, the King of Ashur, his master, was not far off, with his forces; but at the siege of Libnah, not past a dozen miles off. That town, not like to hold out long, and then have at Jerusalem, and they, God wot, but meanly provided to welcome him. But a poor remnant, to so huge a host; so huge, as with their very feet they " dried up rivers," as Isa. 37. 25. they went. *Non erant vires,* was their case right; and this was here a second grief.

For the words, though they sound as if the queen or some great lady were in child-birth, yet no such matter. All is

SERM.
VIII.
— spoken by allegory: and no woman, but the state of the kingdom, here meant.

And it is no new thing to set forth states by women. The Prophets do it oft: Esay's Hephzi-bah, Ezekiel's Aholah and Aholibah, Osee's Lo-ruhamah, all shew it. Nothing more common with them, than "the daughter of Babel" for the state of the Chaldeans; "the daughter of Sion" for the state of the Jews.

Isa. 62. 4.
Ezek. 23.
36.
Hos. 1. 6.
Isa. 47. 1.
Isa. 37. 22.

And not to women only, but to women with child; then specially, when there comes any shrewd plunges upon an estate. *Filia Sion quasi parturiens,* "Sion is ready to cry out," in the Old; and in the New, the Church then hard bested, is represented by a woman ready to fall in labour. And states, when they would be delivered of aught, (would and cannot,) as it were the throes of child-birth seem to be upon them; and this proverb, then not unfitly applied to them, *Venerunt, &c.*

Jer. 4. 31.

Rev. 12. 2.

A woman, her time is come, and strives to bring forth, and cannot, not having strength for it; this we know is a case of great extremity: we know it by Rachel, by Hophni's wife, both which were in the case here; at the point to be delivered, and wanted strength, and it cost them both their lives.

Gen. 35.
16, 17.
1 Sam. 4.
19.

Now, as when a woman is so, all about her are at their wits' end, know not what to do, or whither to turn themselves: no more did Hezekiah (but even turns to the Prophet Esay; as at such times prophets shall have their turns, not oft besides). To him they send for *Leva orationem,* "Lift up thy prayer;" prayer, now: for, but in prayer, no help is left; if that relieve us not, we are gone. This spake then Hezekiah in grief.

Isa. 37. 2,4.

It grieves me, on a day of joy, to hold you so long in a point of sorrow; but the turning all into present joy will make amends. To that, I come.

This, for the present, was their case; but this was not their case, long. For, within a while after, before the end of the chapter, the very same words, by the very same persons, were (or might have been) taken up in a far other, more joyful key. Then, when the King of Ashur, he that cast them into this agony, as he was upon removing to come to-

wards them (and so, the children, as it were, come to the
very birth indeed); God put a "ring in his nose," turned
him about home again, as fast as ever he could, upon news Isa. 37.29.
of invasion of his country by the Ethiopian. When, being
so near come to the birth, he came not, had not the power Isa. 37. 9.
to come one foot toward them; then, I hope, the case was
altered; then might they have said this text as an *Io pæan*
with joy, *Venerunt, &c.*

And this, lo, is our very case, this day. For, why are we
here met, but that (as the text is) a birth there should this
day (the fifth of November, this very Tuesday) have been
with us? should have been, but was not: that was not:
this day should have been a dismal day; that it was not so.
A birth was in bearing, and *Venerunt ad partum* (I promise
you): that it was not born, that it was *partus non partus,* 'a
birthless birth,' it is with us a day of joy: and as this, a day;
so this, a text of joy: and thanks be to God, it is so. And we
say these very words of Hezekiah, not as here he did, but, as
after, he might have, and as we, this day, may speak them,
with a cheerful accent, *Venerunt ad partum, &c.*

There be in the text two parties, which make us two parts: And di-
I. the children, and II. the mother. The children, in the vision.
I. II.
very first word; the mother in the last: *pariendi* it is here;
parienti it is 2 Kings 19. If there be no strength *pariendi,* 2 Kings
it is because there is none *parienti.* Of these two, two things 19. 3.
are here said; one affirmed, the other denied.

Affirmed; the children were ready: denied; the mother
not, *Non erant.* The children not unwilling; for they were
come: the mother unable; for, by that time they were come,
her strength was gone. The end is left for us to gather; for
if no strength to bear, no birth there will be. No more there
was. And, that there was not, it is holiday with us, to-day.

Applying all to our case, I am to tell you first: 1. these
children, who they were; 2. and secondly, how near to the
birth they came; 3. thirdly, of the strength to bring them
forth, the failing of it, and how it came to fail. Upon these,
two questions: 1. one, why they were not suffered to come
forth? 2. Why they were suffered to come so far? 4. And
last of all, of the *Tu ergo,* or inference upon all this: which
is not that, which Hezekiah infers, the next verse, *Tu ergo*

leva orationem; but another *ergo,* as it were a new birth of ours, *Tu ergo leva gratiarum actionem.* Yes, yes: that, and *leva orationem* too: and so let us lift up our prayer, and for nothing more, than that we may raise a good levy of thanks indeed, to send up to God, that there was no strength to bring it forth, when it was so near brought.

The children are the first word, and so offer themselves to be begun with. And with them, we must begin; for, on them all depends, whether the day shall be kept, or the text uttered with joy or not. For indeed, *primâ facie*, it may seem to be somewhat an unkindly joy, to take pleasure in the perishing of children, when they be come to the birth. Yet such may the children be, that are to come, as it makes no matter; nay, as we well may wish, they may; and well rejoice, if they do miscarry there, and come no further.

To begin, from the beginning. There read we of the "seed of the woman," and the " seed of the serpent:" we are back at our text straight. If it be the woman's seed, save it alive in any wise, let it come, not only to the birth, but from the birth, well; and if by any mischance it do not, say the words of the text, but say them with grief, *Venerunt, &c.* On the other side, if it be the " seed of the serpent," away with it, let it not come to the birth; if it do, let it not be born, stifle it in the womb, and be glad when you have done, and say with joy, and spare not, *Venerunt, &c.*

And yet I cannot tell neither, whether we make the rule so general, as to extend to all the woman's seed. But, if the
children be, as of Moses it is said, ἀστεῖοι, " proper sweet children:" nay, if they be but according to kind, regular births; when they be come so far, it is grief, if they come no further. But, otherwhiles there fall out these same παρεκβάσεις φύσεως, *naturæ errores,* ' misshapen, monstrous births;' and then, in that case, and for such, it skills not when they be thither come, if farther they come not. Yea, I dare say, it will not discontent the unhappy parents that begat and bare them, though this verse be verified of them, that when they come to the birth, they might not be born, but have the womb for their grave, and no strength to deliver them.

Since then, upon the matter, all is thereafter as the children be, our first enquiry is to be, what these children were? Where, let me tell you this, you shall not look for such children as women go with (the verse is proverbially, not verbally to be understood). Not of any woman's birth; none there was, at the speaking it. Hezekiah meant it of Sennacherib's intent to sack Jerusalem; and we of their attempt or enterprise, this day, to have made a massacre of us all : of them, that went big with this monster.

To begin with the soul, then, of these children. For, there is not only *fructus ventris,* there is *partus mentis :* the mind conceives, as well as the womb : the word *conceiving* is alike proper to both. Men have their womb, but it lieth higher in them; as high as their hearts; and that which is there conceived and bred is a birth. So I find the Holy Ghost in the Psalm calleth it; " Behold, he travaileth with mischief, Ps. 7. 14. he hath conceived sorrow and brought forth ungodliness." And that is, when an evil man, in the evil womb of his heart, shall hatch or conceive some devilish device, and go with it as big as any woman goes with her child, and be even in pain, till he have brought it. This is the birth here meant : and there in the heart, is the *matrix* or conceptory place of all mischief. Thence, saith our Saviour, *de corde exeunt,* Mat. 15. " from the heart they come" all. 18, 19.

Usually they say in schools, *Conceptus, conceptio ; partus, opus :* ' The conceipt is a kind of conception ; and the work, a kind of birth ;' the imagination of the heart is an embryo conceived within; the work now brought to pass is a child born into the world. Nay, they go further, to more particularities, and carry it along through all the degrees of childbearing. 1. When a device is intended, then is, say they, the child conceived, as it were. 2. When projected and plotted handsomely, then, the child articulate. 3. When once actuated, and set in hand, then is it quick. 4. When so far brought, as all is ready, then the child is come to the birth. 5. And when, *actum est,* all is done, and dispatched, the child is born. 6. But, if it fall out otherwise than was looked for, no strength to bring it forth, then have you a dead-born child. 7. And look, with the natural mother what "joy" there is, when " there is a man-child born into Joh. 16. 21. the world ;" the same, for all the world, is there, with these bad men, when their imaginations prosper. And what grief the poor woman hath, at the perishing of the fruit of her body, the like, in a manner, is there with them, when their powder will take no fire. So have you the soul, or spiritual part to begin with.

Will ye see the body also, in the birth of this day? You may, even *ad oculum*, have it laid out before you. In imitation of the natural womb wherein we lay, and whence we come all, there is, by analogy, another artificial, as art doth frame it. Such, I mean, as was the Trojan horse, of which the poet—*Uterumque armato milite complent,* the belly or womb, when it was full of armed men: and so many armed men as there were, so many children, after a sort, might be said to be in it. And, if that; may we not affirm as much of the vault or cellar, with as good reason? The verse will hold of it too—*Uterumque nitrato pulvere complent.* The *uterus,* or womb of it, crammed as full with barrels of powder, as was the Trojan horse, with men of arms. This odds only : every one of these children, every barrel of powder, as much, nay more force in it to do mischief, than twenty of those in the Trojan horse's belly.

[Virg. Æn.
2. 20.]

The more I think of it, the more points of correspondence do offer themselves to me, of a birth and coming to a birth, and that in every degree : 1. The vessels first give forth themselves, as so many embryos ; 2. the vault, as the womb, wherein they lay so long ; 3. they that conceived this device were the mothers, clear ; 4. the fathers were the fathers, (as they delight to be called,) though oft little more than boys ; but here, right fathers, in that they persuaded it might be, why not? might be lawful, nay meritorious then : so, it was they, that did animate, give a soul, as it were, to the treason ; 5. the conception was, when the powder as the seed was conveyed in ; 6. the articulation, the couching of them in order, just as they should stand; 7. the covering of them with wood and faggots, as the drawing a skin over them ; 8. the *Venerunt ad partum,* when all was now ready, train and all; 9. the midwife, he that was found with the match about him, for the purpose ; 10. and *partus,* the birth should have been upon the giving fire. If the fire had come to the powder, the children had come to the birth, *inclusive,* had been born.

But *Non erant vires,* which I turn, there was no fire given: and so, *partus* they wanted, as God would.

And, that only wanted; for all the rest held to a hair. Nothing, that could be in a birth, was wanting; all, to be pointed at, from point to point; that the text is fitly enough applied to it. By this time, ye see the children, both body and soul. Now, when looks the mother; when reckons she, her time will come.

Will ye now (which is the second point) weigh a little better, what is in these three words, *Venerunt ad partum.* **2. How near the birth.** 1. First, they were not upon their way, coming; but *Venerunt,* "they were even come." 2. And come; not *versus,* 'toward,' but even *ad,* "to." 3. *Ad,* "to;" not *loca partui vicina,* 'some parts near or next to it;' but *ad partum,* "to the very birthplace," the neck or orifice of the matrix. Or, if you will take *partum* for the time; not *ad tempora partui propinqua,* 'within some few days of their reckoning;' but *ad partum,* "to the very time," the day, and within a very little, to the hour itself; it missed not much: that is, as near as near might be. If ever there were a *Venerunt ad partum,* and no *partus* upon it, here it was.

And, if you marvel, it was *ad partum,* and not *ad parturitionem* first: marvel not at that; why it would have been a very short travail that. That of the Prophet, (in the sixty-sixth chapter), *Antequam parturiat, peperit,* would have been **Isa. 66. 7.** fulfilled in it: "she would have been delivered before ever she had fallen in labour." To the birth they came, then. And you will remember, how far they came, how many degrees they passed, before they got thither. They came 1. to generation; they came 2. to conception; they came 3. to articulation; 4. to vivification; 5. to full maturity; and yet none of all these our *Venerunt* here. Passed all and every one of these, never stayed, till they came 6. even *ad partum,* could come no further, unless they had come forth: which God forbid! and so He will, you shall see. For, thus have we done now with the first part, the children.

Now to the mother's part. The children came to the birth, and the right and the kindly copulative were. To the **II. The mother.** birth they came, and born they were: in a kind consequence, who would look for other? It is here, *Venerunt, et non :*

thither they came, and no farther; there stopped. *Ad* in
(*ad partum*) is but *usque ad, exclusive;* that is, to it they
came; through it, they came not.

And, why came they not? By means (as is here set down)
of a *Non erant.* Somewhat there was not, that would have
been; somewhat missing; a *Non erant* there was, whatsoever it was.

What *Non erant* was that? It was not, *Non erat ingenium,*
I am sure: pestilent wit they lacked none, as deep, as dangerous an invention, as ever came into the brain of man.
Neither came it thither, or was bred there, without the seed
of the serpent. Nor can it be said, *Non erat,* that they
wanted will; for, so maliciously were they bent in that
wretched will of theirs, as they resolved to know neither
friend nor foe, but up with all together. Nor did they want
opportunity, of a place: got the vault first, and the cellar
after. No, nor means: had their iron tools; had powder
enough, and good stowage for it. These they had, all; yet
Non erant, saith the text. What *Non erant* might that be?
Non erant vires, " they had no strength."

To a birth there go two things: 1. the children must be
come thither, to the birth-place; 2. when the children be
come thither, there must be strength, at least as much to
deliver them. *Ad partum, opus est nixu; ad nixum, opus est
viribus:* 'to a birth there goes a kind of stress; to a stress
there is required some strength.' *Nixus inanis sine viribus;*
and *nixu inani nihil paritur;* 'to no purpose is the stress;
if there be no strength, but all in vain: and if that be in
vain, there will no birth be (no more there was); but the
child perish: and if the mother escape, it is well; but oft
they go both. And so fell it out here; the children dead
born, and the mother died for it too. To speak without
allegory. To the producing of any effect two things there
go; 1. counsel and 2. strength: not counsel alone; but

counsel and strength. For as strength without counsel will
produce but a *mola;* so counsel without strength will prove
but an aborcement. We see daily, many excellent devices
come to nought; all because they be not strongly followed
to execution. Strength then there would be.

And, strength they had not. Not strength? Yes, sure,

that had they. To follow them in the allegory : the mother was strong, else would the children never have come so far as they did, to be so ripe and ready for the delivery. And the children were strong children ; strong enough, but with one small spark, to have sent us all up aloft, if we had been twice as many more. To leave the allegory : strength they had enough, to handle the pickaxe, to dig deep into stone walls; strength enough, to lay in great barrels, and those all full, and a great many of them. Strength enough, to remove them up and down, as they might stand best for the purpose; and to clap on iron and stones, and wood enough, upon them. And, how then was there no strength?

You will easily mark, *vires* is the plural number; and so, many strengths there be : and that he saith not *vires* simply, any strength at all; but, *vires pariendi,* " strength to bring forth." *Vires* is one thing ; *vires pariendi* another. *Vires* they had ; *vires veniendi ad partum :* else had they never come so far ; but *vires pariendi,* that they had not.

For *partus* is *opus,* we said ; and nothing was done. All the while, till they came *ad partum,* their strength served them well. At the instant, they should have been brought forth, it failed them : strength there was to carry it along, to bring it so far ; but not *pariendi,* to bring it to issue.

To bring a thing to issue, that passes the devil's power. He could give them the counsel (as no doubt he did ; it was too devilish, to grow in any man's head). But the strength to issue, that lieth not in his hand. Ye may be sure, if it had, they had had that too. He longed, as much as they, to hear the blow, and see the sight. He that helped them to lay in the powder, would have helped to have put to the fire, had it been in his power. But it was more than they could do : the strength to issue is God's ever, and He took it from them.

Domini sunt exitus : " the issues of all attempts are in the hands of God," them He reserves to Himself, as His own peculiar ; yea, even of evil attempts. For, howsoever He be not at the beginning of them ; at the end, He must be, or no end will be : *Domini sunt exitus.* The " horse" may be " prepared to the battle;" the "lots cast in the lap;" the cellar made ready for the powder ; and the powder for the

Ps. 68. 20.

Prov. 21. 31.
Prov. 16. 33.

S E R M.
VIII.

2 Sam. 17. 14.
Esther 7. 7, &c.
2 Chron. 20. 37.
Isa. 37. 36.

cellar : and, when all is done, that the wit or malice of the devil or man can do or devise, comes God and dashes all in a moment. The counsel of Ahithophel ; Haman's high favour ; the great fleet at Ezion-geber ; Sennacherib's huge host ; defeats them all. For counsels may be in the heart of man, and words at his tongue's end, and acts at his fingers' end ; yet nothing shall be said or done, unless God will so have it. He gives or denies success, as Him pleases. That when the children are upon the point to be delivered, there shall be strength or no strength to do it, as pleases Him. And here it pleased Him not ; so, no birth there was ; but *quando filii venerunt, vires abierunt,* 'when the children were come, all the strength was gone.'

It seems, it was somewhat doubted, lest when it came to the pinch, this strength should fail : therefore was there strength sought, even the strength of prayers : to *Leva orationem* they gat them ; but they sent to the wrong party : not

Nu. 23. 8.

to Esay, but to Balaam, to "curse, where God did bless ;" and to bless that cursed birth of theirs, which His very soul abhorred. So many prayers were said, they might have a good heir. They say, there were so, for Queen Mary's child : but she had no child to come ; these had. But all in vain : when the time came, for all their masses, and processions, and rosaries, and Jesus' psalters, it would not be. No children came, strength there was not.

And will you know, how it came to fail them, this strength ? Ye may, and never go out of the text, or the terms of child-bearing. Or ever the birth was fully come, one of the complices fell to be with child : and no remedy, but he must needs be delivered before his time ; had not the power to keep his hand from the paper, and so disclosed it. And, disclose a treason, and the neck of it is broken, the strength of it is

Judges 16. 18.

gone ; as Samson's strength soon was, when the Philistines knew once, where it lay. And this was the strength, and none but this, that failed them. An easy strength, (one would think,) to hold one's tongue, or to hold the fingers still. That, had he not ; but for lack of that, must needs be scribbling ; and that marred the fashion of the birth quite. His not having the strength, not to bring forth his, made, they had not the strength, to bring theirs forth. His putting his hand to the paper, made, there could be no fire put to the powder; made, the mid-wife was intercepted; and so, the birth, though near the delivery, yet never delivered.

And yet, I cannot tell you neither: for when this work of darkness was brought to light, the light was so dim, and the riddle so dark, even then; that, for all that bringing to light, the children were coming forward to the birth, still; till strength was given to deliver us from this birth, by another travail. For, a travail I will call it, the studying, and the bringing forth of the hidden mystery, of the burning of the paper, the riddling of that riddle. For, so came out, who the children were, and of what element they were made; what, and whereabout the womb was, they lay in. So by a birth; and by that birth, we were delivered from this. That birth smote all dead. For, it was found, even so: and then came *prostratio virium* indeed. Then, all strength, indeed, was quite and clean taken from them. That being taken from them, they were not delivered; and by their not being delivered, we were all delivered.

To the joy now. Divide the text: *Venerunt ad partum,* is their joy; *Non erant vires* is ours. That, theirs, for a time; this, ours for ever. To make their grief the greater, when it came, they were for awhile put in joy. Glad were they, I dare say, to see it go current, kept close so long. They even itched for joy at it, and fell into a foolish paradise: provided a protector and all. Comes me *Non sunt vires,* all their joy was at an end, and with that began their sorrow. We, by their grief, shall best conceive our own joy, taking the whole verse entirely together.

1. The joy *of Non erant vires.*

A grief it was, and it went to their hearts, these children, that they came not. A double grief, that when they held well so long, and were so likely to come, yet they came not; had strength all the while, had it not, then. *Venerunt ad partum,* and *Venerunt ad portum,* are much alike. Any wrack is a grief; but no grief to the grief of that wrack, that is made, even in the very haven's mouth. To go the voyage well, and arrive well, and then, before the very port to sink, and be cast away! To bring the game to the upshot, and then to lose it! It trebled their grief, that so many Lady's psalters, and Jesus' Psalters were said for it; and that neither

Jesus nor our Lady blessed the birth no better. And last, that the children perished; and perished not alone, but the mothers went too, and some of the fathers, for company. It should have been, *Parientes pepererunt;* it was, *Parentes,* or *parientes* (if you will) *perierunt.*

Now look, how many ways they were grieved, and said, Alas, for *Venerunt ad partum,* alas for *non erant vires;* so many ways do we rejoice, and say, It is well, that *Venerunt ad partum;* thanks be to God, that *Non erant vires.* 1. First, for *Non erant vires,* by itself: that, defeated it was. 2. Then, for *Venerunt ad partum, et non erant vires,* together: that it prospered so long, and yet defeated it was; this was *Gaudete* with an *Iterum dico.* 3. Then, that without any *Leva orationem* on our parts; without any on ours, and against so great a levy of theirs, of I know not how many prayers and processions, and all for the prosperous success of a business known to none but the superiors. 4. And, to make it *terque quaterque,* that we saw them come tumbling down, that made full account to have seen us fly up.

That we were delivered from a danger so near; brought to so narrow a point: we not praying, nor so much as once Ps. 126. 1. thinking on the matter, but delivered as it were in a dream: ourselves not only delivered from, but they that so sought ours, delivered to their own destruction; brought not forth, but were themselves brought forth to Judas' end, the end of all traitors : and their children, not brought out, but as ἐκτρώματα, pulled out of the womb of the cellar, piece and piece, and never saw the sun alive, or the sun them; pity it should.

2. The reasons of *Non erant vires.* Shall I now tell you a reason or two, why *Non erant vires pariendi?* 1. one out of *pariendi,* 2. the other from *Non erant vires.*

1. Why they not suffered to come forth. 1. This *pariendi* was indeed *pereundi;* the bringing forth a quantity of powder, the perishing of a whole parliament. They were not; but, put case they had come forth, (it is well we are in case to put this case:) certainly they had been Gen. 35. 18. 1 Sam. 4. 21. Benonis, "Sons of sorrow," to this whole land: Ichabods right, our glory had been gone clean. For, what a face of a commonwealth had here been left? *Exclusive* they came *ad partum;* if, *inclusive* they had, their *inclusive* had been our

exclusive. We had been shot off, and that out of this life
and this world, every one. *Venerunt,* if they had come *ad
partum;* if they, *ad partum,* we *ad perniciem. Non erant
vires:* if there had, these *vires* had been *virus* to us, and their
pariendi our *pereundi.* If those children had not been lost,
many fathers had been lost; many children had lost their
fathers, and many wives their husbands. There had been
a great birth of orphans and widows, brought forth at once.
What manner of birth should this have been; first in itself,
then to us? In itself: we said, for vipers, there should be no
strength to deliver them. Were not these vipers? the womb
they lay in must have been rent, for them to come forth.
Were they not the brood of vipers? What talk you of a
viper, that sometime (it may be) stings a child to death; or
an elder body, if it be not looked to in time? What are
vipers, to them, that at once, would not have stung, but have
sent up and torn in pieces a King, a Queen, a Prince, and I
know not how many of the nobles, clergy, commons; all the
estates of a realm, a whole country, their own country, all at
one blast? We said, for monsters, there should be no strength
to deliver them. These were such monsters, as not in Christendom alone, but even in Afric, (that mother of monsters,)
the Turks and Moors, and all that heard of it, were amazed,
that ever the earth should bear such a brood of miscreants.
For, they should not (as children) have cried at their birth,
but roared as devils; or, as if all the infernal furies had broke
out of hell together. Let this serve; it was so out of measure
bad, as it was too bad, ever to be brought. What marvel
then, if nature shrunk in, and would give no strength for
such a birth as that.

2. Shall I tell you another, why *Non erant vires?* I will:
it is somewhat a strange one, but it is raised out of the words
of the text, and it is a birth born of late, and christened by
the name of a *Non erant vires,* that you may know, they be
akin, this and that: and so I hope it comes not out of season,
since for that child's sake, this I hope fared never a whit the
better.

You cannot but remember a clause not long since printed,
and so (as it were) a child but lately born, a cardinal's child
it is (I mean the tenet late taken up at Rome): that all is

now to go, all Christianity to stand or fall, by *Sunt*, or *Non sunt vires*.

The old Christians never knew of any such birth as this:
Id fuit, quia deerant vires, saith the Cardinal. As much to say as, If they now in these days be so as they were, carry themselves quietly, it is *quia non sunt vires :* and to hold no longer than *donec erunt ;* and then you are like to hear of them, to have them go again with such another birth. (You shall have them as mild as Gregory the First, when they have no strength ; but as fierce as Gregory the Seventh, when they have.)

Nay, and they would bear the world in hand, this child may claim kindred of the Fathers : that this was the mind of the blessed saints and martyrs, in the persecutions of the Primitive Church. That, with them, all went by *si adessent vires ;* and if then they had had strength, never an emperor should have kept his crown upon his head. For, it was neither allegiance, conscience, Christian duty, nor respect, that held them in. *Id fuit, quia deerant vires :* as (if they had not been wanting) full well they should have understood. That they were gentle and meek, gramercy, *non erant vires ;* that and nothing else. O write a book for God's sake, *de gloriâ martyrum* (Turonensis so hath) of the glorious martyrs that suffered then ; but it was because they had no strength : else, the emperors should have suffered, not they.

But, they mightily wrong the Fathers, to father this opinion on them. Two hundred years after Christ, in the midst of the fervour of persecutions, Tertullian tells us another tale ; that they had strength then, more than enough ; and so, suffered then, upon a better *quia,* than *quia non erant vires.* Well, near two hundred years after that, the ecclesiastical story sheweth, under Julian the Apostate, and under Valens the Arian, they wanted no strength then (the greater part of the Apostate's army being Christians ; and the chief leaders and bravest companies under the Arian, being orthodox). And two hundred years yet after that, against the Lombards, Gregory saith, there was then strength enough, to have left them neither King nor Duke, if all had gone by *vires,* then. But he, good man, might not *miscere se,* ' meddle with aught' that might be the death, *cujusquam,* ' of any one man.' And these would have been the death of I know not how many, but that *non erant vires.* No such children then, as those, this day brought forth. It is not the divinity of the old Christians, but of the new Jesuits, this. They must take the child to themselves : it is no babe of the Fathers, it is a brat of their own breed ; hatched in these days of ours, never heard of before. And such a one it is, as if it be let go, we shall have a generation of monsters come of it soon.

He began with *vires :* another since him saith, If ye have not *vires, virus* will serve as well. And since that, another : If *vires* and *virus* fail too, go to it with firework : *pulvis serpentis,* which is worse than *virus serpentis ;* ' serpentine powder' worse than ' serpentine poison.' Poison kills one by one ; powder, with one puff, dispatcheth all. For poison, ye may have a counterpoison ; no antidote for powder, if it once take fire. Poison gives men leave yet to die with some leisure ; powder, that it doth, it doth at once, in a moment.

To the utter confusion of this error, that all is to go by *Sunt vires,* was it, that *Non erant vires,* this day. And do but mark it, that God pays them with their own money. They put all upon this very point : in this point, God this day foiled them. They go all, by strength ; and that strength then failed them. All, upon *si essent vires :* God took order, *quod non essent vires.* And God never let them have strength, that so resolve to put it ; that, can they once gather strength, no King, no state shall stand before them ; but blow them up, sink them, poison them ; one way or other, away with them all.

You see the reason, with God ; but see you not withal, next under God, whereto we are to ascribe our safety ? Even to *Non erant vires.* There is a point hangs by that. For, while that lasts, while ye keep them there, ye shall have the Primitive Church of them ; have them lie as quiet, as still, as ever did the barrels in the vault, till *vires* (like fire) come to them ; and then, off go they : then, nothing but depose Kings, dispose of kingdoms, assoil subjects, arm them against their sovereigns : then, do they care not what.

SERM.
VIII.

2. Why
they were
suffered
to come
so far.

1. Reason
on God's
part.

Isa. 37.
8, 9.

2. On our
parts.

But, if the powder take not fire, then shall you straight have books tending to mitigation; then, all quiet again. Certainly, thus standing, it were best to hold them *in defectu virium,* to provide *ut ne sint;* to keep them at *Non sunt vires,* till time, they be better minded in this point, and we have good assurance of it. For, minded as they are, they want no will, no *virus:* they tell us what the matter is; strength they want, they write it, they print it; and *si ad-essent vires,* they would act it in earnest.

But yet, why was it suffered to come so far? Why not taken sooner? Evil, we all know, is best nipped in the bud; best ever destroyed in the spawn. Being then so evil, as it was, why was it let go all the while?

I will give you two reasons: 1. one on God's part, 2. the other on ours. 1. On God's part. I know not how, but ye shall observe that He loves, that He takes delight thus to do. It is His play with leviathan. To suffer his whelps and him to have their course for a time, and for a long time; and then suddenly give them a twitch, and down they come. Let them go even till they come to the birth, and then come in the neck of them with a *Non sunt vires,* and all is marred.

Here in the text, how many countries won Sennacherib! How near was he let come to Jerusalem, even to Libnah, within less than a dozen miles! News came suddenly, of the blackamoors invading his country; back he goes, had not the power to stir one foot farther. How far was the Invincible Navy suffered to come sailing in 1588, to cast anchor even before the Thames' mouth, every hour ready to deliver her children ashore. In an instant, a fatal faintness fell upon them; their strength and courage taken from them; about they turned, like a wheel; fled, and had not the power to look behind them. But, *non erant vires pariendi,* we all know. God loves thus to do: and then to do it, *cum venerunt ad partum.* His glory is the greater, He can let it come so nigh, and then put it by: let it alone till then, and then do it.

2. There is another on our parts. For, easy account, and but easy, would have been made, if they had been taken at first: no great matter that. That we might make no easy

account, we escaped not easily, but hard and scant : so to
make our escape the stranger, and our joy the more, that
it went so far, and came so near, and yet missed us.

Of itself, it is best, *ut malum ubi primum contingit, ibi mo-
riatur,* 'evil be crushed at first,' the serpent's head trodden,
at his first peeping in, or putting it out. But God doth not
always that, which in itself is best to do ; but that, which
will best affect us, and we take in best part. And so did He
this : thereby to beget in us, and bring forth of us, a new
birth of praise and thanks according.

For, now we have done with this degenerate birth of 3. The
theirs, we are to stay a little, and see if we can get another, inference.
a more kindly birth, come from ourselves. For, barren we
may not be : this delivery from theirs, is to make us delivered of another ; we to bring forth somewhat, for their
not bringing forth.

What is that ? The text will lead us to it, if we look but
over to the next verse. For there, when any evil travail
threatens us, we find by Hezekiah, the kindly birth then, Isa. 37. 4.
on our parts, is *Tu ergo leva orationem,* " a levy of prayers."
Now, that being turned away, and turned away in a manner
so miraculous, the natural kind issue then is another *Tu
ergo, Tu ergo leva gratiarum actionem,* a new levy of thanks :
a new *Leva quia levatus,* for His easing of us of so heavy
a chance, like to light so heavy on us.

At the present, sure, while it was fresh, we were ravished
with it : for the time, we seemed to be even with child, as
if we would bring forth somewhat ; and somewhat we did
bring forth, even an Act, that we would from year to year,
as upon this day, bring forth and be delivered of thanks and
praise, for this delivery, for ever. And here we are now, to
act that, we then enacted ; even to travail with this new
birth. God send us strength, well to be delivered of it !

For, so shall we double our joy : 1. one joy, for the turning away of that miscreant birth of theirs ; 2. another, for
the welcoming this of our own.

This birth, we now travail with, is a good and a blessed
birth. Blessing and glory, and praise and thanks, are *in
bonis,* all : all, good in us (if any thing be good in us) ; the
best fruits of our nature, when it is at the very best. And

if they be brought forth, it is as it should be, and as God would have it.

But if (which God forbid) they should either not come, or when they be come, our strength fail, and they not brought forth, then are we at an after-deal again; then would not this day be so joyful for the misgoing of the other, as sorrowful, for the abortion of this. Our joy (at least) not so entire, but mixed with sorrow: for, there is sorrow even to death, if we go with so good a fruit, and it come to the birth, and there perish; if we shall but make an Act, and do no act upon it.

We seem to sorrow at nothing more, than that many a good purpose there is, and many a vow made in time of need, sickness, or adversity (so many, as it is by divines held, there be more good purposes, and that by odds, in hell, than there be in Heaven); but abortive purposes and vows all. For, O that we were but the one half of that we then promise to be, when we want and would have somewhat? O then, how thankful we would be! How never forget! How fast the children come to the birth, then! And when we have what we would, our vigour quails presently, our strength is gone from us; *et non sunt vires pariendi.* For, all the world seeth, nothing we bring forth. Alas, how many aborcements are there daily of these children! Nowhere may this verse be taken up, nowhere so oft, so fitly applied; nowhere so used upon better cause than this, upon the failing of good desires and intents.

That this we may do, to take us to *Leva orationem:* let this be our last. To lift up our prayer first, against such un- Hos. 9. 14. natural births as that was, the Prophet Osee's prayer: " Give them, O Lord: what wilt Thou give them? a barren womb and dry breasts." There was no strength for that birth of theirs; it was well there was not: thanks be to God, there was not: thanks be to God for *Non erant vires.* And, *ne sint vires,* say I, 'never let there be strength' for any like this birth; never strength, but weak hands and feeble knees, for any such enterprise. *Ne vires pariendi;* nay, *ne veniant ad partum;* not neither, not so far: nay, *ne ad conceptionem;* nay then, *ne ad generationem,* if it may be. If it may not, but they escape thither, to the birth; then lift up your last

prayer, and let this be it, and let it come up to Heaven, into
God's presence, and enter in even to His ears, for the equity
of it; in all such designs that *pariens* may be *sine viribus,*
and *partus, sine vita :* the mothers, no strength; and the
children, no life : but child and mother perish both, as this
day, they did. And, better so they perish, than such a
number, than a whole country perish, by their means. This,
a *Ne veniant* and a *Ne sint vires,* against theirs.

But, for ours, for our praise and thanks, *veniant,* 'let them
come;' and *sint, O sint vires,* 'and let there be strength'
when they come, for such, so good a birth. Ever be
there strength, to kindness, to thankfulness, to the accomplishment thereof, whereto we are in duty so deeply bound.
Strength ever to all honest and good resolutions. Pity,
but they would be so; pity, there should want strength
for them. Well may they be conceived; come well to the
birth; when they be come thither, vigour enough to deliver
them; and never, when they be come so far, to miscarry.

We may take our light from that. It is *Venerunt filii :*
and *filii* is the plural number. So, more than one; many
there would be. And *filii* falls well with the word *gratiæ,*
which lacks the singular. No such phrase as *agere gratiam.*
A single thank was never heard of. And both falls well
likewise, to quit the birth, we were quit of: for, the barrels
were many and full, and so would our thanks be.

Again, they would be *filii;* that is, such as children be;
and children be flesh, blood, and bone; I mean, some real,
some substantial thanks. Not to travail (as it were) with
wind, with a few words only, which are but air, and into
the air they vanish again. *Partus opus,* ye remember, we
said before: some work there would be, *actio gratiarum,*
somewhat actually done, leave some reality behind it, as in
a child there is.

Thus far, like; but then, a difference. Come it would,
not as did theirs, *ad partum exclusive,* thither and no farther;
but *inclusive,* to the birth, and from the birth; have the
blessing of the womb and of the breasts : of the womb, to
bring it forth; of the breasts, to bring it up, till it proved
somewhat worth the while.

That so we may rejoice as much in the affirmative of

this birth of ours, *Venerunt et sunt vires ;* as we did in the negative of that of theirs, *Venerunt et non erant vires.* So doing, God shall again and again turn away those births, if any be in breeding: take away all strength from them being bred, as to-day He did: and give us new occasions daily to bring Him forth praise and thanks, for His daily continued mercies, in delivering our King, our land, us and ours all.

A SERMON

PREACHED BEFORE

THE KING'S MAJESTY AT WHITEHALL,

ON THE FIFTH OF NOVEMBER, A.D. MDCXVII.

LUKE i. 74, 75.—7th and 8th verses of BENEDICTUS.

That we being delivered from the hands of our enemies might serve Him without fear.

In holiness and righteousness before Him, all the days of our life.

Ut sine timore, de manu inimicorum nostrorum liberati, serviamus Illi,

In sanctitate, et justitiâ coram Ipso, omnibus diebus nostris.

[*That we being delivered out of the hand of our enemies might serve Him without fear,*

In holiness and righteousness before Him, all the days of our life. Engl. Trans.]

"THE children were come to the birth, and there was no strength to deliver them." There we left last. Their not being delivered was the cause of our being delivered. And now I go on. ^{Isa. 37. 3.}

Isa. 37. 3. The text the year before.

And our being delivered was to this end, "that we being delivered from the hands of our enemies, might serve Him," &c. For I demand: Delivered we were, as this day; why was it? Was it that we might stand, and cry out of the foulness of the fact? or stand, and inveigh against those monsters that were the actors in it? Was it, that we might bless ourselves for so fair an escape? or bestow a piece of a holyday on God for it? And all these may we do: and all these we have done; and upon good ground, all. Yet none

The end, or *ut*, of this day's deliver-ance.

of these the very *ut ;* nor we delivered, that we might do these. But when all is said, that can be said, hither we must come: to this *ut* here, and pitch upon it; for this is indeed the *ut finalis;* the right, the true, the proper "that:" "that," for our deliverance, we bethink ourselves, how to do Him service.

Take the whole tract along, from the first word *Benedictus:* there is "visited and redeemed" in the first verse; "a horn," or a mighty salvation, in the next: after, we " saved from them that did hate us:" but you shall see, that all these suspend still, no perfect period, till you come to this. But at this, there is. " Visited," redeemed," "saved," mightily saved: why all? For no other end, but that being so " visited," " redeemed" and " saved," we might wholly addict, and give over ourselves, to the service of Him, Who was author of them all.

Our delivery from, the grand delivery by Christ.

I wot well, that principally and properly, the whole song referreth to the deliverance of deliverances, our final deliverance, from our ghostly enemies, and from their fire, (the fire of hell,) by our blessed Saviour; which was so great, as it was able to open the mouth, and loose the tongue of a dumb man, and make him break forth into a *Benedictus.*

But, inasmuch as in every kind, the chief giveth the rule, or as we say here, the *ut,* to all that are from and under it; and that ours and all other deliverances, that have been or shall be, are from or under that of His: our enemies, set on by those enemies; ours lighted their match at their fire, (the fire of hell,) and so do all others whatsoever : therefore is it, that this text aptly may be, and usually hath been, ever applied to any deliverance, from any enemies whatsoever: those

The same *ut.*

of 1588, these of this day : the same *ut* in all; as coming all from the same *principium a quo;* and tending all, to the same *finis ad quem*, that here is set down.

I.
The same cause from whence.

For the *principium a quo ;* we have formerly endeavoured to set that straight, from whence our deliverance came: even from the goodness of God; yet not expressed under that term goodness, but under the term of mercy, as elsewhere. As

Lu. 1. 72.

here, (but a verse before,) " to perform the mercy." And

Lu. 1. 78.

a little after, " through the tender mercies of our God."

" Mercy."

Which term is made choice of, for two causes: one, it in-

cludes misery; the other, it excludes merit: and so, fittest
for our turn.

1. Goodness may be performed to one, though in good
case; not mercy, but to such only as are in misery. In
misericordia there is misery, ever. And this, to put us in
mind of our case, the extreme misery we had come to, but
for His merciful deliverance.

2. Again, goodness may be shewed to such as may seem
some way to deserve it: so cannot mercy. For, but where
merit is wanting, mercy is not pleaded properly. These set
us right, in the *principium a quo*, that we ascribe it not to
a wrong cause. Out of Jeremy: "It was the mercy of the
Lord, that we were not consumed." Out of the Psalm:
"That mercy of His, that is over all His works."
And now, to the *finis ad quem*. For, we are as easily, and
no less dangerously mistaken in that. By mercy's means,
without all merit of ours, we were not consumed, but delivered from so great a misery, so near us: why were we so?
Were we *liberati* to become libertines, to set us down, and
to eat, and to drink healths, and rise up, and see a play?
was there no *ut* in it? Yes: what was that? *ut serviamus Illi.*

So, there grows an obligation out of it. For *ut* is a con-
ditional, and implies ever a kind of contract, at least that
which is not named, but is much used: *Do ut des, facio ut
facias.* So that, the text is of the nature of a bond or covenant. And I give it not that denomination of mine own
head: I find it so called in express terms, but a verse before,
"to remember His holy covenant."

A "covenant" then names it. And a "covenant" divides
it: for a "covenant" is ever between two; the two here,
God and us.

The "covenant," on God's part, is at the fourth verse:
"That we should be saved from our enemies." Which
"covenant" is here pleaded, as performed by Him, under
liberati.

The "covenant," on our parts, rests; that then "we should
serve Him" for it. His part is kept, *liberati* shews that:
then may we put in suit, for ours, that is, for *serviamus.*

On God's part, I set forth these:

Lam. 3. 22.
The text
An. 1612.
Ps. 145. 9.
The text
An. 1615.
2.
The same
end where-
to.
[See 1 Cor.
10. 7.]

The sum
or sub-
stance of
the text.
*Contrac-
tus inno-
minatus.*
Lu. 1. 72.

The di-
vision.

I.
[Lu. 1.71.]

II.

God's
part, the
covenant.

Our part.
The con-
dition.
The mat-
ter.

The man-
ner.

1. That we were "delivered;" 2. that "from our enemies;" 3. that "from the hands of our enemies;" 4. "that
without fear," (for so it stands in the verse,) *ut sine timore
liberati;* "that without fear being delivered." So it may be
taken; and so it is taken, by sundry of the Fathers.

On ours, I reckon these. Our service; the matter, and
the manner of it. The matter wherein: "serve Him in
holiness," "serve Him in righteousness;" not "holiness" or
"righteousness" alone, but serve Him in both.

The manner how (often no less acceptable than the service
1. itself). 1. *Ut sine timore;* that our service be freely and
2. cheerfully done (now we are out of fear). 2. *Ut coram Ipso,*
that unfeignedly, as "before Him," not before men (before
3. whom we may and do often halt). 3. And for the time of
it, *ut omnibus diebus,* that we faint not, or give over, but
continue in it "all our life long." Three qualities of ours,
and indeed of every true and faithful service. That these be
done; and that they may be done; and that, that which shall
be spoken may tend to this, that they may be done, &c.

1.
The equity
of God's
covenant.

Ut liberati, "That we being delivered." To shew the great
equity on God's part of the covenant, we say first: that we
were to serve Him, though *liberati* were left out; being, or
not being "delivered." This to be our first point.

1. *Ut,*
without
liberati.

The noble army of martyrs, it was all their case, they
served out their service, without any *ut liberati,* any bond of
temporal deliverance. Far from any *liberati,* were they three,

Dan. 3. 17,
18.

that were upon casting into the fire, and even then said:
"Our God, Whom we serve, He can deliver us out of thy
hands, and from the fiery furnace. But, if He will not,"
(not deliver us,) "Be it known unto thee, O King, we will
not serve thy gods, nor worship the golden image which thou
hast set up." That is, serve Him we will, whether He deliver
us or no. Will ye hear an heroical spirit indeed? Not, *etsi
me non liberarit,* 'though He should not deliver me;' but,

Job 13. 15.

etsi me occiderit, "yea, though He should kill me," to die
for it, I will do my duty, and serve Him, though. It is Job.
These stood not upon *liberati;* but, deliverance, no deliverance, come of it what would, they were at a point, would

1 Cor. 6. 5.

and were resolved to serve Him. And, (πρὸς ἐντροπὴν, *ad
erubescentiam nostram dico,* I speak it not to our commend-

ation;) if there were in us any remnant of their generous
spirit, God should not need to come in indentures with us.
It savours somewhat of a mercenary, that. *Serviamus* should
hold, and let *liberati* go whither it would. And we, live and
die, His servants, though He had not, or should not deliver
us. This is *ut*, without *liberati*.

But then *ut*, with *liberati*. If God take us, as He finds
us, and say with the Apostle, *Parco autem vobis,* "Go to, I
bear with you;" and κατὰ συγγνώμην, "by way of indul-
gence," condescend to condition with us, if He come to *ut
liberati*, shall not that hold us? Our duty being absolute,
depending upon no *ut*, if upon special favour, God will come
in bonds, and let it run in this tenor, That being delivered
we shall serve Him; else not, shall we not then do it? This
being done, I marvel what we can allege, to decline our
duty; unless we mean, it should be fast with God, and loose
with us; He bound to do all for us; and we free, to do
nothing for Him.

And yet a third (to magnify His mercy yet more, and to
tie us the harder to our covenant) *ut* is not only with *liberati*,
but with *liberati*, first. God is bound, and first bound, to do
for us, before we do aught for Him. It is not, that we should
serve Him first, and then He deliver us, after; but that He
should first deliver us, and after, when we are delivered,
then, and not before, we should do our service. It is not
liberandi, shall be, or may be hereafter; it is *liberati*, are
already. So we are aforehand with Him. He hath done
His, before we begin ours. *Liberati*, you see, precedes *serviamus: liberati* the tense past; *serviamus*, but the present
(and I would it were the present) I doubt, for a great part
it is yet to come.

And the reason, why He will have it so to precede, is, He
would have our service grow out of His favours; our duty,
out of His bounty. That is the right, and, indeed, the evan-
gelical service. If He have us at the advantage, on the hip,
as we say, it is no great matter, then, to get service at our
hands. None more servile than we, then. But that, is the
legal, for fear. And that sometimes He hath, but likes it
not; He would have it, out of love, out of the sense of His
goodness, have our hearts broken with that. That is the

only acceptable service to Him, that grows out of that root : the *serviamus* that grows out of *liberati ;* delivered and serve : first delivered, and then serve. This for the equity of the covenant on God's part.

The performance of God's covenant.
Now come I to plead, that on God's part this covenant was performed, that *liberati* we were. Heaven and earth would rise against us and condemn us, if we should not confess *liberati,* this day. Heaven saw it, and was astonished ; and it is gone over all the earth, the fame of it. But that, we do. The keeping of this day, the meeting of this assembly, are both to acknowledge and profess, that a *liberati* there hath been.

1.
That " delivered."

Twice " delivered."
Nay, not one alone : two there have been ; and two such, as our eyes have seen, but our ears have not heard, neither could our fathers tell us of the like. Two such, as no age ever saw, nor can be found in any story : that of 1588, this of 1605 (both within the compass of seventeen years). One by strand, the other by land, as they say. From a fleet by sea, from a vault by land, *de abyssis terræ,* (as saith the Psalm,) as well as *de abyssis maris ;* a summer and a winter deliverance : either of them, like this of Zachary's, able to bring *Benedictus* from a dumb man.

Ps. 71. 20.

2.
" From our enemies."
So, " delivered" we were. But a delivery is a thing at large : though it be from a mischance, from some heavy accident, it is a delivery. But, if it be "from our enemies," it is so much the more : as, in that, there is nothing but casualty ; in these, there is rancour and malice, they hate us : so this the greater danger by far.

Mortal enemies.
And there is much in the enemies : of them, some reach but at our states, lands or livelihoods ; other some, nothing will satisfy, but our lives. Every enemy is not mortal : where he is, the danger is deadly. Ours were such, sought to bring utter destruction on us ; and not on us alone, but on ours ; nor on us and ours only, but on the whole land in general.

Secret enemies.
Ps. 74. 4.
Again, of such as be deadly, some are roaring enemies, (the Psalm so calls them,) such as threaten and proclaim their enmity, like those in 1588. Others lurk, like vipers, that sting to death, without any hissing at all ; as were ours this day : which are the more dangerous a great deal.

More than *liberati,*
This made it indeed to be more than *liberati,* ours. *Libe-*

rati is properly " set free," and freeing is but from servitude. which is,
This was more. Our death was sought, and we " delivered" " set free."
from death, and that a fearful death ; unprepared, suddenly,
in a moment, to be shattered to pieces. And yet it was Yet *libe-*
liberati too, in the proper sense ; for upon the matter, it was *rati* too.
from both. The Prophet's division would have taken place
in it : *Qui ad mortem, ad mortem ; qui ad servitutem, ad ser-* Jer. 43. 11.
vitutem ; " They that had been blown up, to death ; they
that had been left, to servitude" (to a state more miserable
than death itself). So, in one *liberati*, we had two. Both
from that of Haman's lots, which were to death (one that
was פוּר in Hebrew, this was *Πῦρ* in Greek) ; and from that Esther 3. 7.
of Babylon besides, which was thraldom and confusion. Thus
were we " delivered from our enemies."

But " from the hands of our enemies" is more than " from 3.
our enemies." For let the malice of an enemy be what it " The
hands
will, if his " hands" be weak or short, or we far enough from of our
them, the matter is so much the less. But if we come within enemies,"
not " our
his reach, if he get us within his " hands," then God have enemies."
mercy on us.

Specially, if there be in his " hands" a knife thus engraven:
To cut the throats of the English heretics, as in 1588 divers,
so engraven in Spanish, were brought from the fleet, and
shewed. Or if there be in his " hands," a match, ready to
give fire to thirty barrels of powder (not so few). If the
" hands" be such, that is then a delivery, not from our enemies only, but from their " hands," or, as we say, from their
very clutches. Ye will mark, that through all the Psalms,
ever the part is still enforced : not from the lions, but from Ps. 22. 21;
the lions' paws ; from " the horns of the unicorns," from 124. 6.
the teeth of the dog; so here, " from the hands," from the
bloody " hands of our enemies."

Further I say, it is more, to be delivered " from" their 4.
" hands," than out of them. For if out, then in, first. They " From"
their
must first be, in the " hands," that are delivered out of them. " hands,"
But " from" them, that may be from coming in them at all. not out of
them.
The better deliverance of the twain. And that was ours; and
that was Christ's : He is said to have " loosed the sorrows of
hell," *non quibus nexus est, sed ne necteretur*, saith Augustine : In Act. 2.
' not, wherewith He was bound; but that He might not be 24.

at all bound with them.' So we, not by taking us out, but keeping us from, from their "hands," "from the hands of our enemies."

"Deliver-ed," the manner of it. *Eruti.*
Let me yet stay a little. For methinks we may find in this word not only our deliverance, but even the very manner, and the means of it. Not in *liberati*, the Latin; but in St. Luke's own words, ῥυσθέντες: that will come home to both.

Ρυσθέντες, that is properly *eruti*. *Eruti*, that fits us, for the manner, two ways.

From a dark hole. Ps. 7. 13.
Eruere is *de tenebris in lucem educere*, 'out of some dark deep hole, (as it might be the cellar,) to bring forth something to light' (as it might be those same *vasa mortis*, vessels there couched, and destined to the blowing us all up). It must be some dark vault or pit, *unde*, 'from whence;' well there-fore said of us *eruti*, that were delivered from a pit danger,

[Ps. 71. 20.]
a danger under ground, *in abyssis terræ*, "in the deep of the earth."

From a ruin or fall.
Secondly, *eruere*, the compound, is from *ruere*, the simple, that is, from a ruin. Not as if we should have fallen into the pit, but that there was there bestowed within it, that which would have sent us up, that down we should have come, have fallen down, all to pieces. *Ruina* it would have been, and therefore *eruti*, right. And they talk of helping *incen-dium ruinâ ;* here, there had been *incendium* and *ruina* both, and neither helped other, but both been past all help.

With the ruin of our enemies.
Delivered from a ruin; but *eruere* is then in kind, when we are so delivered from a ruin, as with their ruin, that sought ours. So it was, we parted not of even hands, we from them, and they from us, neither of both, a fall. No: we fell not:

Ps. 20. 8.
(no fall with us:) they fell, and had a foul fall. We were so "delivered from their hands," as they delivered into ours. We *eruti;* they *ruti* and *cæsi* both, 'fell and were slain.'

Ps. 9. 15.
" The pit they digged, they fell into themselves; in the snare they laid, was their own foot taken." The highest deliver-ance of all (so much made of in the Psalms).

Implied in *cornu salutis.* Lu. 1. 69.
And thus much was before implied, when it was called *cornu salutis*, " a horn of salvation." The salvation that so comes, comes ever with the perdition of the adverse party. So is the horn expounded in Deuteronomy the thirty-third

Deu.33.17.
chapter : With these shalt thou strike thine enemies, and

push them, as any wild beast. *Ventilare* is the word, toss them up into the wind, upon the top of their horns, till they have gored them, and brought them to their end. Such was our " horn of salvation," or, as we turn it, " a mighty salvation." God shewing His might no less against them, than for us : " visited and redeemed" us mightily, in His mercy ; " visited and" ruined them as mightily, in His wrath.

And again, in this, not only the manner how, but the means whereby : for " He hath raised up a horn of salvation." Now to raise up must needs be interpreted of a person, the means of the delivery. Who was that ? In Daniel and the Revelation I find it *totidem verbis : Decem cornua, decem Reges sunt ;* alluding therein, as to their great power, so somewhat to the anointing thence poured on their heads : that it should be *salus Regia,* and *per Regem,* ' a delivery wrought by a King;' the King of Heaven to work it, *mediante Rege terreno, in cujus labiis divinatio,* if ever it were in any's, who did thereby *eruere* that, out of the dark phrase, by which we all were *eruti.* And so, not the manner alone, but the means in it too, that we were *eruendo eruti.*

marginal notes: " Delivered." The means of it. By a king. Dan. 7. 24. Rev. 17. 12. *Eruendo.* By picking out. Prov. 16. 10.

And last, that all this was *sine timore.* For in the verse so it stands, first, *ut sine timore liberati.* And stands so first, that we might take special notice, and note of it. And though divers writers draw *sine timore* to *serviamus,* as if there were an hyperbaton, to " serve Him without fear;" yet what should let us so to take it as it stands ? Specially, since divers of the ancients take it so. (I name Origen, Titus Bostrensis, Chrysostom, Theodoret, and Theophylact.) But we may well reconcile them both, if we say, (which truly we may say,) " that without fear we were delivered, to serve Him in a state without, or void of, fear."

marginal notes: 5. " That delivered without fear."

It is a great favour, when we are " delivered," to be " delivered" *absque hoc,* that we be [not] at all put in any " fear." Some are sometimes saved from their enemies, but it is, with some fright first. It was the Jews' case, when from Haman ; it was ours, *in anno* 1588. <i>(margin: Esther 4. 3.)</i>

They that are so, it cannot be denied, but " delivered" they are, but not *sine timore liberati,* not " delivered without fear." This was " without fear." Our case, just. We had no sense, and so, no " fear" at all of the danger, till it was past. I cannot better express it, than in Theodoret's own words: *Sed si sic dicendum est,* saith he, *veluti non sentientes, ita nos de periculo transtulit in securitatem;* 'If it may so be said, without any sense or feeling at all, did He translate us from the depth of danger, into the state of security.' In which point, ours did come near to the great delivery of the world by Christ, what time the world little thought either of their own peril, or of His pains aud passion, That delivered

" Without fear" or any other passion.
it. Yet, in this, ours had more than was in Christ's own delivery. That there, though it were " without fear," yet not without somewhat as evil as " fear." For Christ's was wrought by His innocent death (a matter of sorrow and grief). But in ours there was none, neither fear nor grief, nor any other unpleasant passion. No innocent suffered here; none but they, that had their heads in the contriving, or their hands in the digging about it. " Without fear" it was, without any thing else, that might taint our delivery with the least matter of grievance.

The recapitulation of all the former.
So then, 1. " delivered" we were: 2. and not from the casualty of any mischance, but from the malice of "enemies;" " enemies," and those 3. capital; and those 4. close hidden "enemies:" "from" them, yea 5. "from" their very "hands;" and 6. "*from*" their "hands," not *out of* them. And our delivery was *eruti,* 7. "from" something *in abyssis terræ;* and 8. " from" a ruin too; 9. and that, with their ruin, that sought ours. 10. Our salvation, *cornu salutis,* a royal deliverance; 11. and yet *eruendo* it was. 12. And all *absque timore,* 13. or *absque* anything else, that might blemish our joy with matter of sorrow in the least degree.

And this for God's part, Who hath remembered " His holy covenant," I trust, and performed it in every clause; nay in every word, to us, to the uttermost.

II.
Our covenant or condition.
" Delivered, that we should."
Now to our part, which we may be put in suit for. *Liberati* then is clear. But how? absolutely? at large? *absque aliquo inde?* No condition annexed? No *ut?* Yes: take the *ut* with you. *Liberati ut,* " Delivered, that we should;" should do somewhat; for *naturaliter obligamur ad dantem.* This *ut* is natural: there groweth a natural obligation between him that doth, and them that receive a good turn (and a deliverance, specially such an one, is a good turn). The fields we

till, the trees we plant, shew it. They return their fruit to them that bestow labour or cost upon them. That, I know not how, but so it falls out, in matter of benefits, we be not so soon loosed, but we be tied again; nor eased, but loaden afresh; nor freed, but bound anew. It is the law, the bond of nature this, *Liberati ut.*

And that *ut* is *ut serviamus.* And this particular *ut* groweth out of the law of nations. There the law is, *ut victus sit in potestate victoris,* ' the conquered, ever, in the power of the conqueror,' to take his life, or to save it, at his pleasure. But if he will save it, then comes the voluntary *ut,* or covenant. He that hath his life saved, to vow to bestow it, in his service, that did save it. *Servi* (the very name) came of *servati.* They that should have died, and were saved, did willingly covenant, *Serva et serviam,* to serve him, by whom their lives were preserved. This being the law of nature, and nations, why should not the God of nature, and King of nations, be allowed it? that if our lives have been by Him saved, we should, from thenceforth, come to this *ut, ut serviamus Illi.* " Should serve Him."

Well, well, it is past now; if it were to come: it is, " that we being delivered;" if it were, ' that we being to be delivered,' we would tell another tale then: we would be glad and fain so to covenant, O deliver us (then) but for this once, and we would serve Him, that we would, and be holy and righteous, and what He would besides. Put any *ut* to *liberati,* then. We would then seek it of Him, that now is offered by Him, to be delivered, if being so delivered, we will covenant, but to do that, which we were bound to do, delivered or no. We would have covenanted to serve Him.

And why should we think much of this *serviamus?* All the world knows, if the plot had gone on, and the powder gone off, the whole land should not have scaped *ut serviamus;* but should have served *duram servitutem,* been not in service, but in servitude. Their servitude is changed into this service. A blessed exchange for us. Great odds between those two: nay, no comparison at all, between God's service, and their servitude; their bondage, thraldom, slavery, tyranny: I cannot heap too many names. God's service is freedom in respect of that; nay, without any respect at all, We should have served, if not delivered. And served a worse. For the service, *serviamus.*

SERM.
IX.

His service is perfect freedom : we say it, we pray it, every day.

For the party, *Illi.*

And if no comparison in *serviamus;* none in *Illi,* I am sure. Nay, if there were any thing to mislike in *serviamus,* amends is made for it, in *Illi.* For the service is much thereafter, as the *Illi,* the party is, Whom we serve. *Dignitate Domini honorata fit conditio servi;* 'He may be so great a state, we serve, as it is an honour to serve Him.' Now, how great a Lord the Lord of lords is, what shall I need tell you ? "There is no end of His greatness." How great, and how good withal, *res ipsa loquitur :* that appears by our delivery, in part ; and more shall, by His eternal reward, laid up for them that serve Him. There is, in all the world, no more honourable, nor beneficial service, than this *serviamus Illi.*

For His greatness.
Ps. 145. 3.
For His goodness.

If we serve not Him, some other we must, and worse.

Rom. 6.
18, 20.

But say, we have no mind to serve Him ; if we serve not Him, yet serve we must, and serve we will, if not Him, some other. It is the condition of our life, one or other serve we do. We must hold of some lord : if free from one, another we serve ; and who is that other ? When we are "free" from God, "from righteousness," we serve sin and Satan, a worse service I dare say ; better then be free from them, and "serve God in righteousness."

Those worse be His enemies.

But, if we will not serve Him, I ask, what will we do then ? will we serve His enemies ? for so are these. We were not "delivered from our enemies," to serve His enemies, I am sure. That were a foul shame for us : that were against all reason. But if we serve not Him, we serve them. Resolve then to serve Him, That hath saved us : not His enemies, in a profane and unrighteous ; but Him, in a holy and righteous course of life. And so, am I now come to that, wherein our service lieth.

The matter of our service, wherein.

"In holiness and righteousness." In which two, in a sort, are recapitulate the two tables of the law : holy to God, righteous to men. *Quod quis reverentur se habeat ad divina, quod quis laudabiliter cum hominibus conversetur,* saith Chrysostom ; 'reverently to perform holy duties, laudably to have our conversation among men.'

"Holiness and righteousness" both.

Both these, first ; not either of them. To spend our service but in one, is but to serve Him by halves : in both then

to serve Him. Neither in an unrighteous holiness; nor in
a holy kind of unrighteousness. Neither with the Pharisee,
to have all our holiness in our "phylacteries" and fringes, and Mat. 23. 5.
frequenting the lectures of the law, no matter how we live;
nor with the Sadducee, live indifferent honestly, but neither
believe "spirit," nor look for "resurrection:" be Christians, Acts 23. 8.
like Agrippa, *in modico*, a little religion, upon a knife's point, Acts 26. 28.
will serve us. Neither in "holiness" then only, nor in "righteousness" only, but in both.

In both; but in their order though, as they stand; and "Holiness"
"holiness" stands first. So, to reckon of that as our prime first.
service. For if there had not been some meaning in it, it is
sure, "righteousness" might have served for both: religion,
"holiness," all virtues are συλλήβδην in it. *Suum quique,* Matt. 22.
saith "righteousness;" and in that, is *quæ Dei Deo ;* 'every 21.
one his due,' and so God His.

Yet are they ever thus parted, here, and elsewhere: partly,
to set out God's part by itself, (as "the fat from the sacri- Ecclus. 47.
fice,") for the dignity of His person: partly, to keep up the 2.
distinction, which ever hath, and ever must be maintained,
of severing things sacred from common; and holy, from
human duties. And partly also, to check the conceit that
runs in the world abroad, O he is a good man, lives quietly
with his neighbours, pays every man his due. Every man
his due? and how then? shall God lack His due? I trow
not, but have His too, and His first. Reason is, He be first
served.

And "holiness" is His due: you may read it, in the
plate of gold in the High-Priest's forehead, "Holiness to Exod. 28.
the Lord:" you may hear it from the mouth of the Sera- 36.
phim, they mention none of all His attributes, but that: Isa. 6. 3.
that they do, and do it thrice over. Pointing us thereby,
what is chief in Him, and should be chief with us, and
whereto we should chiefly direct our service. "Holiness"
is His due; and (hear you) so His due, as the Apostle is
direct, *totidem verbis*, without this due paid, "without holi- Heb. 12. 14.
ness, shall no man ever see God."

But then, you will mark, it is to "serve Him in holiness." To "serve
"Holiness" is one thing; to "serve" God "in holiness," is Him in
another: "holiness" we have, (at least think ourselves to holiness."

SERM.
IX.

have,) but a stately, surly kind of "holiness" it is, so as in our "holiness," we "serve Him" not. But it is not enough to be holy: a service "in holiness" is required at our hands: that we acknowledge a service "in holiness," and as servants, carry ourselves, and serve Him in it.

Our service "in holiness" "in the congregation." Ps. 111. 1.

Our service "in holiness" I divide, as the Psalm doth, either *in secreto sanctorum*, when we are alone by ourselves (as there "in secret" good folks fail not to serve Him) ; or *in synagogâ*, in the open assembly, "with the congregation."

Deu. 29. 29.

Our secret "holiness" I meddle not with. *Abscondita Deo nostro*, I leave it to God. I hope, it is better, and more service-like, than our outward is. As *abscondita Deo*, so *revelata nobis*. Our Church-service, our service *in synagogâ*, the outside of it so, that is no secret; all men see what it is, that full homely it is, nay full rude it is (and lightly the meaner the persons, the more faulty in it). Our "holiness" is grown too familiar and fellow-like; our carriage there can hardly be termed service, there is so very little of a servant in it.

When we do not only serve Him, but do our service before Him, (both are in the text, *Illi* and *coram Illo*,) as that we do when we come hither, it is to profess our service,

Ps. 97. 5.

that we come. When we come "before the presence of the Lord, the presence of the Lord of the whole earth," (so the Psalm doubles it, to make us think on it the better,)

Ps. 96. 9.

then, saith he, "worship Him *in decore sancto*, in a holy kind of decency," or, as we read it, "in the beauty of holi-

1 Thes. 4. 4.

ness." Our "holiness" should have a kind of beauty with

1 Tim. 2. 2.

it. "Holiness and honour," the Apostle joineth them together ; "godliness and gravity," εὐσέβεια καὶ σεμνότης, and them too. Now this is that, the world complains of; there is not that *decor*, that "beauty," not that honour, not that σεμνότης, that "venerable grave behaviour," in our "holiness ;" we carry not ourselves in His holy sanctuary, where our "holiness" should be at the holiest, nor at His service there, as servants should, and use to do.

Our service in adoration or worship of Himself. Ex. 20. 5. Ps. 95. 6.

We stumble at the very threshold. Our very first service, or rather the introduction to our service, in the first table, the table of "holiness," is there set down to be *Adorabis*. We turn it, "shalt worship." How that is, we are told every day in the Psalm, "Let us worship, and fall down, and kneel before the Lord our Maker." It was ever in the Primitive Church, the first voice was heard, the first thing they did, *Ante omnia adoremus Dominum Qui fecit nos,* "Before we do any thing, let us fall down and worship the Lord That made us." And it shall never be found, that they came in without it. But this shall, that men came to the temple, purposely to adore, and that, that they did, though their time or occasions would suffer them to do nothing else. That, they held a service, of itself. Now, adoration is laid aside, and with the most, neglected quite. Most come and go without it; nay, they scarce know what it is. And, with how little reverence, how evil beseeming us, we use ourselves in the church, coming in thither, staying there, departing thence, let the world judge.

Why? What are we to the glorious Saints in Heaven? Do not they worship thus? Off go their "crowns," down "before the throne they cast them," and "fall down" themselves after, when they worship. Are we better than they? Nay, are we better than His saints on earth, that have ever seemed to go too far, rather than to come too short, in this point? There was one of them, and he was a King, (no less person,) when it was thought, he had done too much. What? uncovered? yea, uncovered, saith he, and if that be too vile, *Vilior adhuc fiam plusquam,* "I will be yet more vile." Why, it is "before the Lord," before Whom we cannot be too low. To humble ourselves before Him, it is our honour, in all eyes, save such as Michal. And I read of none, but of Rabshakeh, that upbraided King Hezekiah, for saying to his people, "You shall worship before this altar." No more then is sought from us, than Kings on earth, than crowned Saints in Heaven, in their holy service, do before Him.

In Malachi's time, things were grown much to this pass, that now they are, to this want of regard: to think any service, though never so slight, would serve God well enough. When they were come to this, God is fain to take state upon Him, and to tell them plainly, He would have them know, He is a King, and "a great King." 1. Great: for "He is King of the whole earth;" others, but of some part of it. 2. Great: for "He is King for ever

The worship of the saints in Heaven. Rev. 4. 10.

Of the saints in earth.

2 Sam. 6. 22.

Isa. 36. 7.

God's disdain of our worship.

Mal. 1. 14. Ps. 47. 7. Ps. 10. 16.

SERM.
IX.

Rev. 1. 5.

Mal. 1. 13, 8.

and ever;" others, but for a term of years. 3. Great: for "He is King of Kings," and they His lieges too, whose lieges we all are. And so falls to terms with them, that He held scorn to be so slighted over, even to these very words: "Shall I take it at your hands?" And then, bids them go, and do but "offer" such service as this to their Prince, do but come before him on that fashion: see, if he will be content with it, or "accept his person," that is, give him a good look, if any should so appear in his presence. No more will God: He knoweth no reason, why any King or creature on earth should be used with more respect, or served with more reverence, than He.

Our service in His holy things. In the Sacrament. Mal. 1. 7.

Thus serve we Him, in His holy worship: how serve we Him, in His holy things? how serve we Him, in our "holiness" there? I will begin, and take up the same complaint that the Prophet Malachi doth. First, *Mensa Domini despecta est,* "The table of the Lord is not regarded." That Sacrament, that ever hath been counted of all holies the most holy, the highest and most solemn service of God; (where are delivered to us the holy symbols, the precious memorials of our greatest delivery of all;) why, of all others they speed worst. How are they, in many places, denied any reverence at all, even that which prayer, which other parts have? No service then, no servants there; but bidden guests, hail fellows, homely and familiar, as one neighbour with another. And not only, *de facto,* none they have; but *de jure,* it is holden, none they ought to have. And that, so holden, as rather than they shall have any, some will suffer for it, or rather for their own proud folly, in refusing it.

Ps. 116. 13.

1 Cor. 10. 16.

What time they "take the cup of salvation," they will not invocate, at least not be *in specie invocantis;* as the King, the Prophet, would. What time they receive the "cup of blessing," they will not receive it as a blessing, as children receive it from their parents, and their children from them. Both which, invocation and receiving a blessing, were never done, but *de geniculis.* What shall the rest look for, if thus we serve Him, when we are at the holiest?

Our service of God in the service, that is, in prayer.

Shall we now come to the service indeed? λατρεῦσαι, the word here in my text. It is no new thing, for one *species* to carry away the name of the *genus* from the rest, as in this:

for, though there be other parts of God's service, yet prayer
hath borne away the name of service from them all.   עבידה
the Hebrews call their Common Prayer, and that is service.
And the Greeks, theirs, Λειτουργίαν, and that is so too. And
we, when we say, At service time, and the Service book, and
refuse to be present at divine service, mean so likewise. And
God Himself seems to go before us, and direct us so to do;
for His house He hath named "the house of prayer" (ob- Isa. 56. 7.
serving the rule, to give it the denomination, from that
which is the chiefest service in it). As indeed, when all is
done, devotion is the proper and most kindly word of "holiness;" and in that serve we God, if ever we serve Him.
Now, in what honour this part of "holiness" is; what account we make of this service, do but tell the number of
them that be here at it, and ye shall need no other cer-
tificate, that in His service we serve Him but slenderly.

"Thou hast magnified Thy Name and Thy word above Ps. 138. 2.
all things," saith the Psalm. After invocation then of His Our service of
Name, let us see how we serve His word; that part of His God in
the word.
service, which in this age (I might say in the error of this
age) carries away all. For what is it to "serve God in holiness?" Why, to go to a sermon: all our holiday "holiness,"
yea and our working-day too, both are come to this, to hear
(nay, I dare not say that, I cannot prove it, but) to be at
a sermon.

The word is holy, I know, and I wish it all the honour
that may be; but God forbid, we should think, that *in hoc
uno sunt omnia.* All our "holiness" is in hearing; all our
service, ear-service: that were in effect, as much as to say, 1 Cor. 12.
17.
all the body were an ear.

An error it is, to shut up His service into any one part,
which is diffused through all; another, so to do, into this
one. It is well known, that, all the time of the Primitive
Church, the sermon was ever done, before the service begun.
And that, to the sermon, heathen men, infidels, and Jews,
heretics, schismatics, *energumeni, catechumeni, pœnitentes,
competentes, audientes,* all these, all sorts of people were
admitted: but, when they went to service, when the liturgy
began, all these were voided; not one of them suffered to
stay. It were strange, that that should be the only or the

SERM.
IX.
chief service of God, whereat, they which were held no servants of God, no part of the Church, might and did remain
no less freely, than they that were.

But even this holy word, (wherein all our "holiness" is,)
how serve we Him in it? Nay we serve Him not, we take
the greatest liberty there, of all other. We come to it, if we
will; we go our ways, when we will; stay no longer than we
will, and listen to it, while we will; and sleep out, or turn
us and talk out, or sit still, and let our minds rove (the rest)
whither they will; take stitch at a phrase or word, and censure it, how we will. So, the word serves us to make us
sport; we serve not it. At this part of our service in "holiness," we demean ourselves with such liberty (nay licentious-
ness rather), that holy it may be, but sure, service it is not,
nothing like. And truly, it is a notable stratagem of Satan,
to shrink up all our "holiness" into one part; and into that
one, where we may be, or not be: being, hear or not hear;
hearing, mind or not mind; minding, either remember or
forget: give no account to any, what we do or not do; only
stay out the hour, if that, and then go our way; many of us,
Ezek. 33.
32.
as wise as we came; but all (in a manner) hearing, as Ezekiel complaineth, a sermon preached, no otherwise than we
do, a ballad sung: and do even no more of the one, than we
do of the other. Eye-service God likes not, I am sure;
1 Sam.3.9.
no more, should I think, doth He ear-service. "Speak on,
Lord, for Thy servant heareth" (and well if that, but scarce
that otherwhile); but "Speak on, Lord," whether Thy servant hear or no: would any of us be content with such service? Yet this is all: to this, it is come. Thus we "serve
Him in holiness:" this service must serve Him (as the world
goes); for, if this way we serve Him not, we serve Him not
at all.

Our service
"in holi-
ness" out of
the congre-
gation.
But all God's service in "holiness" is not in the church.
Some is abroad. And, when we are forth of the church,
neither word, nor Sacraments, nor Common Prayer, there:
only there, we serve Him in His name.

To His
name.
Ps. 111. 9.
Ps. 99. 3.
And "holy and reverend is His name," saith one Psalm;
and "great and fearful is His name," saith another. Now,
how unholily, this "holy;" how unreverently, this "reverend
name" is used; upon how small cause, this great; how with-

out all fear, this "fearful name" is taken up in our mouths,
I must say it again and again, which St. Augustine saith :
Aures omnium pulso, conscientias singulorum convenio ; 'I
speak to the ears of all in general, I convent the conscience
of every one in particular, that heareth it.' That, which by
Him is "magnified above all things," is by us vilified beneath Ps. 138. 2.
all things. We pray for it first ; we regard it last, certainly. Mat. 6. 9.
For if it be indeed " holy," let no man count it " common." Acts 10.15.
If not count it so, not use it so : for what we use as common,
eo ipso we make it unholy, *quantum in nobis est ;* for, " common" and " holy" are *contra-dividentia.*

1. And to make it so common, that is, to profane it ; evil
enough that. 2. But in the eagerness of our spirits, to use
it to grievous execrations, that is more, even to " pollute" it : Ezek.39.7.
a worse matter far. 3. But beyond both these, to let it
come to this, that we grow unsensible of both, and both pass
from us, and we have no feeling of either, this is worst of all.
Call we this to " serve Him in holiness," for this day's delivery, when we so serve His name ?

But neither is all God's service "in holiness" alone ; some Our service
is in honest dealing with men, " in righteousness :" God is to God "in
righteous-
served in that too. He that hath done a good piece of jus- ness."
tice, downward ; that hath done his duty to his superior
upward ; that hath dealt equally with his even Christian :
in so doing, hath not only dealt well with men, but done
God good service also. That a man may go from church,
and yet say truly, he goes to serve God, if he go about
these.

Well, how goes our " righteousness ?" how serve we God
there ? divers errors are committed in that too.

One is, of them, that think " holiness" a discharge from "Holiness"
" righteousness" quite. So they serve God, and hear lec- held a discharge
tures, as the term is, they take themselves liberty to pay no from
debts, to put their money out to usury, to grind their tenants ; " righteousness."
yea, and so they miss not such a lecture, in such a place, they
may do any thing then. Nay, God is served in righteous
doing, as well, nay, better, than in holy hearing.

A second kind, (which I like not neither,) that when men " Righteousness"
deal honestly, keep touch, pay their debts, they are so brave, held no
so imperious upon it, so like great lords, as if " righteous- service.

S E R M.
IX.

ness" were no service, all were mere liberality they did, men were bound to them for doing it, they were not bound to do it. Nay, we serve "in righteousness," too; that also is a service sure.

"Righte-
ousness"
measured
by the com-
mon law.
Isa. 29. 13.
Mic. 6. 16.

A third, and that very common, of them that make the law of man a scantling of their "righteousness;" and, further than that will compel them, they will not go, not an inch; nor so far neither, *sine timore*, but for fear. Yea, not only our "righteousness" to men, but even our fear to God is taught us by man's precepts; and in both, so "the statutes of Omri be observed," all is well. But, whatsoever a man else may make sure, he cannot make sure his soul, by the law of the land. This "righteousness" here, goes up to God and His law; and pierces deeper beyond the outward act, even to the inward man: whence, if ours come not, or whither, if it reach not; man we may perhaps, but God, "in righteousness," serve we not.

Our"right-
eousness"
too much
work.

But even according to man's law, our "righteousness" goes not well so, neither. The philosopher gives a rule, when a people is just or righteous, according to man's law (God's he knew not): and that is, when justice wants work, hath little to do. By which rule, ours is in no very good case: men are so full of suits, so many causes depending before every seat of justice, so much to do; and all to repair the wrongs of our unrighteous courses, while each one seeks rather, to overrule men by wrong, than to serve God by right.

The seats
of righte-
ousness
faulty.
Hos. 5. 10.

[Or mear-
stones,
stones set
up for
boundaries
in open
fields.]

And, this were not so evil, if all the injustice were below: if the seats which are set to do justice and righteousness were themselves right. For, fares it not even with them, as the Prophet Osee saith, "The princes of Israel are as they that remove the landmark?" Each seat seeking to enlarge their own border, and to set their meer-stones within the others' ground? A full unnatural thing in a body, that one arm should never think itself strong enough, until it had clean shrunk up the sinews of the other. But I stay. These things being amended, we shall be so much the more in a forwardness, to serve God both "in holiness and righteousness:" and so, for the matter of our service, keep our covenant.

The man-
ner of our

For the manner, now. To serve Him, 1. *sine timore*, "with-

out fear;" 2. *coram Ipso,* " before Him ;" 3. *omnibus diebus* service,
nostris, " all the days of our life."   how.

1. *Sine timore,* " without fear." And so, in a sense we do. That
So " without fear" at all, as if men were afraid, to seem to " without
fear God. But this is no part of his meaning. " Without
fear" here, is not " without" fear of Him, of God ; but, that
being now " without fear" of our enemies, we should do it,
the rather. For, who being in a bodily fear ; who having Exod. 14.
Pharaoh and his host hard at their backs, could quietly 10, &c.
think of serving God ? That even God Himself did rid His Exod. 20.
people of that fear, before ever He gave them His law, to 20.
serve Him by. But when men's minds are quiet from the
agony and terror of it, when they are settled *in tranquillo ;*
they should, in all reason, then better intend His service.

And will we, think you, if we be so out of fear, intend it
the better ? without doubt, in experience, we find it contrary.
For, except we be held in fear, we scarce serve Him at all :
how soon we are out of fear, we forget ourselves, and our service, yea, God and all. True ; yet, for all that, the service,
so done in fear, is but a dull heavy service. It likes Him not.
God loves *lætus lubens,* when, being at liberty, with a liberal
mind, we do what we do. *Læti serviemus Regi,* say they in Gen.47.25.
Genesis, and it pleased the King : and it pleaseth God as [Vulg.]
well, if the service we do, we do it cheerfully, without mixture of fear, or any servile affection.

Without this fear to serve Him ; but not without His fear.
Nam si Dominus, " if He be a Lord," (as if we be His ser- Mal. 1. 6.
vants, a Lord He is,) *ubi timor ?* " where is My fear," saith
He in Malachi? As love, to a father ; so fear, to a lord,
doth belong most properly. And, this is not Old Testament
only : the Apostle is as direct in the New ; if we will serve
Him to please Him (and as good not serve, as serving not
please) ; if we will so serve Him, we must do it " with reverence and fear ;" λατρεῦσαι εὐαρέστως μετ᾽ αἰδοῦς καὶ εὐλα- Heb. 12.
βείας. Neither rudely then, without fear ; nor basely, with 28.
fear ; but reverently, with fear ; and cheerfully without fear
(that is the meaning).

2. To serve Him, *coram Ipso,* " before Him." *Coram Ipso ;* " That be-
for *coram Me* is the term of the law ; as if He were present, fore Him."
and looked on. And it helps much to our service, so to 17.

do it: helps our reverence, not to do it rudely (we do it before Him): helps our sincereness, without hypocrisy, to do it, as before Him: for these two words, *coram Ipso*, are the bane of hypocrisy.

All things are before Him: in nothing can we get behind Him, or where He cannot see us. But, some things are before Him and men, both: those we call not "before Him," properly. Properly, that is "before Him," that is before none but Him. That is, the heart. *Coram homine,* the service of the eye; *coram Ipso,* the service of the heart. Men love no eye-service neither, if they could discover it; but they are fain to take it: the heart is not *coram ipsis ; coram Ipso* it is. Upon that, is His eye: and nothing pleases Him, if the heart be away; for that, of all other, is His peculiar *coram Ipso.*

It is a broken service, if any part; chiefly, if the chief part, (the heart,) be away. It would be entire, and with all parts, since all are "before Him."

It is a mock service, as if what serves man, would serve Him; as if we could compliment it with God, with faces and phrases, as with men we do.

"That all the days of our life."
Mat. 23. 25.
Judith 7. 30.
3. The last is, *omnibus diebus nostris.* As sincere, without feigning; so, constant without fainting. *Coram Me* excludes the Pharisaical service of "the outside of the platter;" *omnibus diebus,* the Bethulian service, for certain days, and no longer.

You shall have few, but will serve God at a brunt: have certain pangs of godliness come upon them at times: be affected for the present, with a delivery, grow a little holy upon it. That little is little worth. God complains in Malachi, that in their holiness, they puffed, and blew, as men short-winded, quickly weary of it, and soon out of breath. And in Osee, that their righteousness was "as the morning cloud," scattered and gone, before the sun was an hour high.

Mal. 1. 13.

Hos. 6. 4.

To "serve" Him then, not with *usurâ exigui temporis,* 'some small time:' *primis diebus,* two or three days at the first, and then *defuncti,* we have quit ourselves well; but from day to day, as long as there is a day left to serve Him in; so long to serve Him. To serve Him to the very last.

"The merciful and gracious Lord hath so done His mar- Some
vellous acts, that they ought to be had in everlasting remem- days more
brance;" all of them.   But some more especially: for some than some
are more than marvellous, as was this of ours.   That if *qui-* though.
busdam diebus would serve for them; *omnibus diebus* is little Ps. 111. 4.
enough for this: so more than gracious, so more than marvellous, so more than both, in this, as the memory of it
never to die, never to decay, but our days and it to deter-
mine together.

And for all that, though *omnibus diebus*, "all our days," More,
and in them all; yet, not in them all alike.   So in all, as in the days since.
some, more than other some; *Suscipiunt magis et minus.*   So
then to serve: as in our days after the delivery, we do it,
more, and better, than before: and upon the day itself, that And this
is, as this day, we do it most of all. day most.

Thus, we have laid forth our covenant, both for matter and It will be
manner.   Wherein, if we deal as just men, we must keep it; wisely done to
and if we deal as wise men, we will keep it.   For, who knows, keep our
but we may, perhaps, stand in need of a delivery again?   If covenant.
we behave ourselves frowardly in His covenant, what shall
become of us then?   How shall we hope for such another
at His hands?   And if He do not, who can deliver us from
such another?

But, such another, we hope, shall never come: and I wish, We shall
and hope so too.   But should hope so the rather, if I could be "with-out fear"
see, we did but set ourselves to serve Him, as hath been said. of such
Otherwise, the devil, he is our enemy (that is once).   And if another.
we had no other, he is enough: an unquiet spirit he is; I
trust him not, though ever since he sleeps the fox' sleep.   For
the breach of our covenant, if he be let loose, he is able to
do mischief enough.   And we have the amends in our hands.
Liberati we had, *Serviamus* we returned not.   Return it then,
and then we shall be "without fear" of any more.

And not only "without fear," but we shall be in hope We shall
also; and that, not of a new deliverance only, if need be, but be in hope of a reward.
of a further matter.   For though our service be due, without
any; but much more due, upon a delivery, especially such as
ours this day was, though no more ever should be done for
us; yet that we may know, we serve a Lord of great bounty,
this shall not be all: over and above our assurance to be

S E R M.
IX.

Reward is
in the
body of
the word
λατρεύειν
to serve.

The re-
ward of
our ser-
vice.

"Without
fear."

Rev. 14. 11.

"Before
Him."
Ps. 16. 11.

"All the
days of
our life."

delivered, *toties quoties*, we shall not be unconsidered for our service, besides. Let our delivery go, *transeat :* He desires no service, but for a reward.

And so I return now to the word of our service, the word of our text, λατρεῦσαι. In λατρεῦσαι there is λάτρον; and λάτρον is a recompense or reward. God's service is λατρεία. "Delivered" we were, by covenant; of His great bounty, rewarded we shall be beside. It is in the very body of the word, this.

So here is λύτρον and λάτρον· λύτρον in our delivery, and λάτρον in our recompense. Let one of them, λύτρον or λά-τρον; or, if not one of them, both of them prevail with us, to see Him served.

And what shall the reward be? I will tell you that, and so end. It shall be the grand deliverance in the *Benedictus* here. As ours of the day was a riddance of us, from our bodily enemies, for the time; and we set in a state of temporal peace, which we have enjoyed ever since; so, the final reward of our service shall be a riddance from our ghostly enemies, for ever, that come not with a puff or blast of powder, but with a lake of fire and brimstone, "the smoke whereof shall ascend for evermore." To be rid of them, and so being rid, to enjoy a state of perfect, of eternal peace and security, without ever fearing more, *sine timore* indeed.

And to make it every way correspondent : for *coram Ipso*, here; it shall be, *coram Ipso*, there. "Even in His presence, in Whose presence is the fulness of joy."

And for *omnibus diebus*, here; all the days of this transitory short life : we shall enjoy it all the days of Heaven. *Omnibus diebus?* nay *omnibus seculis*, 'all the ages of eternity.' And so, for that, which in law is held but as a lease of seven years, have an everlasting freehold in His heavenly kingdom, there to reap the reward of our service, world without end.

A SERMON

PREACHED BEFORE

THE KING'S MAJESTY AT WHITEHALL,

ON THE FIFTH OF NOVEMBER, A.D. MDCXVIII.

ESTHER ix. 31.

*To confirm these days of Purim according to their seasons, as
Mordecai the Jew, and Esther the Queen had appointed
them, and as they had promised for themselves, and for their
seed, with fasting and prayer.*

*Observantes dies Sortium, et suo tempore cum gaudio celebrarent,
sicut constituerant Mardochæus et Esther, et illi observanda sus-
ceperunt a se, et semine suo, jejunia et clamores et Sortium dies.*

[*To confirm these days of Purim in their times appointed, according
as Mordecai the Jew and Esther the Queen had enjoined them,
and as they had decreed for themselves and for their seed, the matters
of the fastings and their cry.* Eng. Trans.]

HERE have we the making of a new holyday (over and
above those of God's in the Law). And the making it, by
royal authority, and the people's assent; and so, of the nature of an act or statute; a good precedent for us that have
made the like. Here is a joint concurrence, of Mordecai's
advising, Queen Esther authorizing, they (that is the people)
undertaking for them and "their seed" to confirm, what?
"Purim:" there is the day. When? at the appointed times:
that makes it a set day. How? with "fasting" and crying,
that is, "prayer:" that makes it a holyday. Upon what
ground all this? That is in the word Purim, the name of
the day. It is called Purim: Purim, that is, lots, as much
to say as, The lot-holyday.

This name it came to have, for that there was a dismal day coming toward them, by means of a lot cast; which yet it was their lot to escape. In the remembrance of which escape, this day was thus ordained: and the like may so be upon like occasion.

The sum.
Thus it was. Haman, one in highest favour with King Ahasuerus, had taken a displeasure at Mordecai: and a feud it was, the strangest feud that hath been heard of: not with all of his kin, or all of the name; but with all of the nation, all the Jews, because Mordecai forsooth was a Jew.

His quarrel was at Mordecai alone, none had offended him, but he; yet such was his pride or malice, or both, as I know not how many thousands, men, women, and children, must die all, for no other cause, but that it happened, Mordecai to be their countryman. For, other trespass had they made him none.

Well, in the height of his favour with the King, and by a wrong suggestion, he obtained the lives and goods of all the Jews in the land. And, when he had them now in his hand, and might have dispatched them out of hand; that, he would not: (see how men shall be transported and forget themselves!) in a strange kind of insolency, (they call it a bravery,) fell to make a lottery of their lives. And Pur, "the lot," was cast; what month first; then, what day of the month, they should have all their throats cut. It fell to be the thirteenth of Adar, that is, February: and then he got a proclamation, that upon that day all the Jews should be put to the sword.

[Esth. 3. 12, 13.]

But, before that day came, by the goodness of God, it was the poor Jews' lot, to escape for all that: and in the mean time, the lot turned upon the lot-caster; and he that intended this great massacre, it fell to his lot, to be hanged himself. And, this was the ground of their holyday. That, in remembrance of this lottery-day that should have been, the fourteenth of Adar, as the eve or vigil, and the fifteenth, as the feast or holyday itself, should religiously be kept for ever; as, to this day, it is.

Esther 7. 10.

[Esth. 9. 21.]

This comes somewhat to our case. For, as they were in danger then, by a lot; so were we, this day, by a plot, in as great danger as they, and as strangely delivered: we, from our

plot, as they from their lot; and so, as deeply bound, and
by this text, as perfectly enabled, to make a day of Purim,
as ever were they.

A plot and a lot, though they sound alike, yet with us
they differ much. A lot seems merely casual; a plot is
laid with great circumspection; but, with God, they are in
effect all one. The best-laid plots, with Him, prove no
better, but even as uncertain lots, but even hap-hazard, if
He list to disappoint them. So as upon the matter, *quoad
Deum,* lot or plot, no great odds; both come to one. Seeing
then, there is no more odds, and that there is in every text
a predominant word, and in this text the word Purim is it,
we will insist upon that word, and account them "lots"
both; ours, as well as theirs.

To make a like day, with a like observation, there are re- The di-
quired I. a like ground, II. and like authority. vision.

To shew the ground like, we are to shew the lots to be
like; theirs, and ours: like 1. in the casting in, the intent
or danger; 2. like in the drawing out, the event or escape.

In the casting the lots or intent, these four: 1. The lots I.
that were cast; their peril and ours. 2. The parties on
whom they were cast; the Jews and ourselves. 3. The
parties by whom they were cast; their Haman and ours.
4. And the cause or colour, for which they were cast.

In the drawing or event, four more: 1. the means of their
and our escape, 2. the manner, 3. the time, and 4. the issue.

In all these, to match theirs and ours. And, in all these,
I make no doubt, this of ours will more than match that of
theirs; the lot of our danger more fearful, the lot of our
deliverance more wonderful.

And if so, then have we as good ground as they; nay
better, than they any.

This for the ground. But that alone is not enough: yet II.
lack we authority. Here it is: the Queen, by advice, enjoining it; the people submitting to observe the day, at the
appointed time.

We conclude then: the ground being all one on which
(a famous deliverance); the authority the same by which
(the Queen there, the king here, enjoining it); these being
alike, a like bond to us, *super animas nostras,* for a like day

SERM.
X.

of ours, even the day on which it was our lot to escape; at a like time, that is, once a-year; and in like manner, to be holden as theirs, with prayer and crying, though of another nature.

And this record here, in the roll of Esther, shall be our warrant for so doing, against all opposers.

I.
The ground.

"The lot is cast in the lap, but God giveth the hap :" it is Solomon, in Proverbs chapter sixteen, verse the thirty-third. We begin with the "lot in the lap," Haman's lap, the danger; and come after, to the hap God gave, the

1.
The danger.

happy deliverance. The danger. 1. They and we had but one lot both; to be destroyed quite, utterly. And we agree in two more: 2. to be destroyed all; 3. to be destroyed at a set day; these three.

But in all three, our lot the worse, every way. And the worse it is, in the lap, (the lot,) the better it is in the hap, if we scape it.

1.
Utter destruction.

Utter destruction to both. But their lot was a sword, to be slain; our Pur was πῦρ πυρὸς, our lot, fire and powder, to be blown up. Of the twain, this the worse.

The sword is in a hand, and that hand is guided by the heart, and that heart may relent at the sight of a silly innocent babe, a poor old man, a woman great with child; so, some hope, for some to escape there. But, fire, no hope for any: fire cannot relent, that spares none.

Jude ver. 23.

Yet St. Jude speaks of saving some by "plucking them out of the fire;" but not this fire; no plucking out here, no scaping for any; all dispatched in a moment, past saving all.

Rom.9.29.

Facti essemus sicut Sodoma; nay worse. That came from Heaven; this, from hell: from hell-ward, at least. There,

Gen.19.22.
Gen.14.16.

three; here, not one should have escaped. Lot's case, his lot will end this; his lot, to all intents, better, when he escaped the fire of Sodom, than when the sword of the four Kings in battle. This, the most destructive destruction of all; if any more than other, this is it. Might we draw lots for our death, we would never draw this. And this was our lot.

2.
General destruction.

A general lottery was intended in both. Truly might His Majesty have said, as ever did Queen Esther, chap. 7. 4: *Traditi sumus, ego et populus meus,* "Betrayed we are, I and my people."

And will ye mark, how like of Haman it is said, *Pro nihilo* Esther 3. 6.
duxit in unum Mardochæum manus mittere, " He thought it
nothing to lay hands on Mordecai alone," *magisque voluit
omnem nationem perdere,* " no less would serve him, but the
havoc of the whole nation ;" third chapter, sixth verse. Said
not our Haman the same ? What, lay hands on the King ?
(as one of them offered :) Tush, that is not worth the while,
magisque voluit omnem nationem, nay, if we shall do it indeed,
be right Hamans, up with King and Parliament and all ;
make a general lottery of it in any wise. Haman right, this,
in his own terms.

But, though in this, they seem to be even (both our lots) ;
yet draw them, ours is the longer, sensibly. For, though
Haman presumed very near, when he came to the King's
side, touched the Queen's life; yet well fare Haman, say I,
in this, the King he touched not; no harm to him ; the
King was out of Haman's lottery. Here, the King was in
too ; ours went to Queen, and Prince, Peers, and Prelates,
and Commons, yea King and all. *Omnem nationem,* but not
Regem, there. *Omnem nationem, et Regem,* here. This was
universal indeed; and we, in this, beyond them.

Theirs was *in diem,* " against a day." Ours was so too.   3.
So, the lots even.   On a set
                                                           day.
With Haman, *Missa est sors in urnam, quo die deberet gens* Esther 3. 7.
interfici: exiit Adar. Die they must, that was resolved ;
that was not enough. (See whither pride will carry men !)
He would cast the dice, as it were, draw cuts, make a lottery,
of no less matter than men's lives. And that, not of a dozen
or a score, but of a whole nation, which day and which month
they should die all. And, in this casting, they went from
month to month, and from day to day, till at last, there,
(with Haman,) " the lot fell on the fourteenth of Adar ;"
and with ours, on the fifth of November.

And, take this with you too: Haman's lottery was in
Nisan, that is, March, the first month, but it fell not till
Adar, that is, February, the last month; so, a twelvemonth
between. And, was it not so with us ? A year before, nay
more than a year, was our day set. And first, it was in the
month Adar, in February (as theirs was, just) ; but, by pro-
roguing the Parliament we scaped, and were reprieved once

SER M. and again.　But, to it again they went, and so at last the
　X.　lot fell on this very day, to be the day of our Purim.　Thus
far, the lots even.

1.　　But then here again there fell odds on our parts, two
But their
day known, ways : 1. one, the Jews had notice of their day; it was
ours not. proclaimed : so, they that could, might have slipped away
secretly, and so scaped.　And they that were watched, that
they could not, well; yet they might make their souls
ready, and die prepared.　And even that, when there is no
remedy, but die we must, it is good not to be surprised on
the sudden, but to have some warning, that so we may
make us ready for God.　But see our case now : we knew
not of our day, we.　The day was kept as close as the
powder : we had gone off suddenly, to the great hazard
(as it may be feared) of many a soul, that for default of
this, had perished indeed : perished here and perished eternally.　Against a lingering death we pray not; *ab impro-
visâ morte*, we do : and *mors improvisa* had been our lot
then.　Here is then the first odds.　Both were *in diem;* but
theirs *in diem certum*, certainly known to them all.　Ours,
as I may say, *in diem certum*, and yet *incertum :* certain
to Haman, to them (they knew it perfectly); uncertain to
us; we knew not whether any such day, or no : we had
gone to it, we had drawn our lot blindfold.　So, ours worse
than theirs.

2.　　Another odds there is, (worse yet than this,) in the days.
Theirs an
ordinary, For, what was the fourteenth of Adar, but an ordinary
ours a par- common day ?　But, the fifth of November (as it fell out) was
liament-
day. the first day of a Parliament; a famous day, as comes in
many years.　That, not only when we should have said, *Pax
et securitas;* but when we should have been in all our glory,
1 Thess. then even at the time, *Repentinus veniet super eos interitus,*
5. 3. the most unseasonable time of all had been our lot; a heavy
lot if it had light.

When men go to their death they would go mourning, all
in black, as the manner is; but, when they are going in all
pomp and magnificence, then to be shot off, and fly all in
pieces ! no man would draw that lot, if he could scape it.
Yet that was our lot, and at that very time.

For a King to be made away, is a thing not unheard of;

but, in this manner, a King to be made away, in his robes royal, the imperial crown on his head, the sceptre in his hand, sitting on the throne of his kingdom, in the midst of all his states, then, and there, and in that manner; that passes all: that, the lot, that never yet hath been heard of. And let it never be heard of: let never King have the lot so to perish: pity any ever should. Yet this was yours, Sir, like to have been. Too much odds this. And this for the lot, that was cast.

Now for the parties, on whom this lot cast. There, sure I am, we have the vantage. The parties, in the text, who were they, but a sort of poor scattered Jews of the captivity, in a strange country far from their own, and in their enemies' hands? Far otherwise was it with us, here. No captives we, but a flourishing kingdom, as any under heaven. Not in any foreign part, ours; but, at home in our own native soil. _{2. The parties, on whom.}

It had been somewhat, for Ahasuerus to take away so many lives at once; but his captives they were, he might do with them what he would, in rigour of law: so, their end had been by lawful authority. But, in ours, no colour, no shadow of any law; but a most barbarous treachery against all law, both of God and man. Alas, the Jews they had neither prince nor peers, they were no state. What talk I of them? I should wrong ourselves much, to stand on this any longer.

This, for 'upon whom.' Now, by whom, the lots were cast. For, it was our lot to have our Haman, too. The lot-master, and the plot-master, I hold them Hamans both. But first, where they had but one, we had many. And then, theirs nothing to ours. Haman was, to the Jews, a stranger in nation, for he was an "Agagite:" a stranger in religion, for he was a heathen man. Ours were no strangers in nation; the same nation, that we. No Turks or infidels, but professing the same Christ that we; and better than we (they say); for, right Catholics, they; and not Christians, but (which is more than Christians) Jesuits, some of them. Better, for an Israelite to suffer at the hands of an Egyptian, than of an Israelite his brother, as Moses told them. Better, at the hands of the uncircumcised, than of the people of God. The _{3. The parties, by whom.} _{Esther 3.1.} _{Ex. 2.13.}

SERM.
X.

Jews, they had perished by the hand of an alien and a pagan; if our lot had been so, it had been the less unhappy. But, our lot it was, to be shot through with our own ordnance; Jesus to have blown up Christ; and one Christian man to have committed such a butcherly barbarous act upon another, nay, many others, such an act, as never was heard of among the heathen, to the eternal stain of all that profess Christ.

Esther 7. 6.
" Wicked Haman" is his epithet: too good for those, that not only as a brood of vipers, sought to gnaw out the bowels of their own dam (which Haman never did); but, in such sort did it, as all the malice of man, calling to it the malice of the devil, could never invent the like. But a degenerate Christian is the worst man; and the worst man is the worst creature, of all others.

4. The
cause, or
colour.
Esther 3. 5.
[Virg. Æn.
i. 8, 9.]

And what might be the cause of all this? It seems, the same in both. Haman's was, because that he was not worshipped by Mordecai. And, in ours too, if we ask, *quo numine læso, quidve dolens,* we shall find, it was much to that, even the not worshipping of one no whit less proud than Haman. And here, they will fall short too. For, in our, Mordecai must fall down, and kiss his feet; which Haman in all his pride never required.

But, it were hard to destroy a whole nation, for no other cause, but that one man of them would not make him a leg. We must have some other than this, some better pretence must be had, sure. So have all evil things, one thing for the cause, another for the colour. In good, one serves for both. Sure, in effect, the same was that of ours, that here was sug-

Esther 3. 8.
gested by Haman. These same Jews, saith he, they are a people with a religion by themselves: as much to say, with us, as a sort of heretics they be, the world were well rid of them; it makes no matter, up with them all.

But then, here comes a difference again, to make ours the

Esther 3. 8.
worse. Haman made it but a matter of policy, " It is not for the King's profit to suffer them." Ours made it no less than a matter of religion. Religion was at the stake. A case of mere conscience: not to do any thing, but the oracle consulted first, the father provincial, who *ex tripode* resolved it for such. And, as if he had had all our lives in his hand, answered in no other style than did Ahasuerus: *De populo*

fac quod libet, " As for this people, do with them what ye list:" with them and with the King too (which was more than here did Haman) : blow them up and spare not. And though there be of our own Catholics among them, no force : blow them up for all that : it is for religion, this.

I conclude all with the very sight, if this lot of theirs had fallen to our lot.

It had been a heavy sight, (as in the massacre of Paris,) to have seen men tumbling in their own blood here and there in the streets ; nothing to this, to see men torn in sunder, heads from shoulders, arms from legs, both from the body; quarters and half quarters flying about ; the brains fly one way, the bowels another; blood spilt, like water in the river, in the fields, in every corner of the streets ; never the like sight, and so never the like lot to this.

Now then : since in our lot 1. the destruction more de-structive (for by powder) ; 2. more general (for King and all with us) ; 3. upon a less certain, and upon a more famous day; (our nation more noble, our Haman more wicked, their cause and colour more to be abhorred ;) I conclude, our lot was the worse, and the worse the lot, the better the escape : the better it, and the better deserving a holyday for it. And this for the lot in the lap.

Now to God That giveth the hap.

Where first I note, that the word Pur, it is no Hebrew, but a Persian word; yet it was thought meet to retain it. They give this reason, for that the same word Pur, in He-brew, signifieth to disappoint : shewing plainly, that the Hebrews' God should give a Hebrew Pur to the Persian Pur, disappoint the Persian lot ; and though it were cast, yet not suffer it to light, though.

We find at the twenty-fourth verse, Haman did cast but Pur in the singular, but one single lot (he needed cast but one, since all were to go one way, none to escape) ; yet the day is called Purim, that is the plural, as if there were more than one, some other, beside that of Haman's. And so it was fit there should, that there might be as well a good lot as an evil. The truth is, there can be no lottery of one; there behove to be two at least : two diverse. The law is so. The first lots we read of, that ever were cast, were between the

2.
The event.

"two goats," whose lot it should be to die, and whose to escape, to be the scape-goat. Here was never a scape-goat in Haman's; slain goats, all: so, beside the law quite. God took Haman casting lots beside the law, and He took the matter into His own hand; and He did it regularly, made two lots, to two ends, and for two parties. One for Mordecai and the Jews, them one; for Haman another: God put in one, for him too, by his leave. Mordecai saith it plainly in the Greek Supplement, in the first chapter and the tenth verse, that God made two lots and gave them forth, one for His own people, and one for the wicked (meaning "wicked Haman"). So have ye Haman's Pur (he cast but one, which was disappointed and never drawn); and God's Purim (two of His putting in, and both drawn). And it is well we have removed it out of Haman's, into a better

hand, that we may say, *In manibus tuis sortes meæ*, as saith the Psalm, Not in Haman's hands are our lots, but in Thine.

Two good hopes we have thereby. 1. One, that though it was nothing with Haman, to lay hands on Mordecai, nor with ours, on the King; yet with God it will be somewhat, nay, much: that God will be otherwise minded, than Haman or they. Not, *Magisque voluit omnem nationem perdere;* but, *Magisque voluit omnem nationem servare;* rather see Haman hanged, and a dozen such as he, than that a whole nation should perish in this manner.

2. And then secondly, seeing they be now in God's hands, be the lot what it will, or in what lap it will, in Haman's own lap, (to be sure,) yet when it comes to the drawing, God will give it forth, which way, and with what success He pleaseth. And when all is done, what Haman, nay, what Ahasuerus himself doth purpose, God will dispose; and there shall be neither lot nor plot against the Lord. And so we come to God's Purim, to His lottery.

1.
The
means.
Wherein we are again before them as many ways; in the 1. means, the 2. manner, the 3. time, and the 4. issue, all four. 1. The fewer means, the more like a lot: and we had no means. They had; and used means, both to God and man. To God, by fasting and fervent prayer, which prevails with Him much. To man, to King Ahasuerus; they had the Queen's mediation, which prevailed with him too. We used

none, either to God or man; fasted not, prayed not, suspected no evil to be toward, and so used neither. There is no cause, no means in a lot. It is St. Augustine's note, that it is therefore termed the "lot of the righteous," in the Ps. 125. 3. Psalm, and in the Apostle *sors sanctorum*, for that, merit or Col. 1. 12. means there is none at all; God only allots it to us. And such was ours: not by means, as they; but delivered, as I may say, from a lot, by a lot, a mere lot. So our Purim, we may say, was more pure than theirs.

But though no means we had to God, yet a means from   2. God we had; they, and we both. For, from a King it came, The manin both. But far otherwise, in the manner, with us, than ner. with them, two ways. 1. First, with them, the delivery came from the King, and well might; for, from him came their danger, from his proclamation under his hand and seal; without which Haman could have made no lottery of himself. With us, in a better manner; and so, our lot better. For, from the King came our escape; but no danger from him. He, as deep in the danger as we. Nothing that was evil, nothing that pertained to any peril, from him: but, our safety solely and wholly from him, next to God.

Another yet. For in theirs, the King, that had been misinformed by Haman, was set right by the Queen's more true information; and this, is a regular, common way. But ours, by no information of Esther or of any; only, by mere inspiration, immediately from God, by making that come into the King's head, which neither did, nor would have come into any man's head else: the more sure, that it came from God, since so great a salvation was wrought by it. For, the burning of the paper, if he had taken it in the sense that others did, or any would have done, we had all been burnt indeed, as soon as the paper. But, God drew from him a sense beside all sense, even as it were by a lot, since (to all men's seeing) it was rather a casual than a rational interpretation. The drawing of that sense was even like the drawing of a lot; so that, *sorte merâ servati sumus;* and never any more true Purim, than this of ours. And though men, when they escape, stand not much on the means or the manner (it is well they are well): yet, it cannot choose but do us much good, to see ourselves saved by so royal a means, and in so

SERM. miraculous a manner. It is a sign *quod respicit nos Deus,*
X.   ' God respects us,' in the manner of whose saving, He would
shew so divine a miracle.

3.   But beside the means and the manner, thirdly the circum-
The time. stance of time is worth the considering; for in both, all came
about in a night. Haman had made all sure: so sure, as he
had set up the gallows and all, and meant to move the King,
Esther 5. and made no doubt but to have Mordecai hanged the next
14.   morning. This was over-night. And that very night, did
Esther 6. 1. God take order, the King could not sleep. And, by that
means, was Mordecai's good service read to him. Sure, for
saving the King's life, he deserved not to lose his own.
Now, it comes to the drawing. A good lot, a prize: honour
for Mordecai. And this good lot, for Mordecai's honour,
God drew even out of Haman's own mouth; he was, by the
King, made to be the proclaimer of it.

It stayed not there: but, the day following, the King
being rightly informed by the Queen, her people were no
such people, as Haman made them; one of them had saved
Esther 8. the King's life: with this, forth came there a good lot for
9, 10.   the Jews: the former proclamation called in, the posts sent
with all speed to publish another for their deliverance.

Now comes Haman's lot. God took him casting lots upon
His people, and He cast one upon him too. For, when the
Esther 7. Queen fell on her knees, and begged her own life of the
3, 4.   King, he was justly displeased with Haman's presumption,
that durst come so near him, as touch her life; and straight
Esther 7. allotted him the same death, he had hight Mordecai. And
9, 10.   the same day, in the same place, and even upon the very
same gallows, he had purposely set up for him, the night
before, it came to his lot, to be fairly hanged himself. This
is God able to do: to make Haman, in the lot he cast for
the Jews, unwittingly to draw his own destiny; and make
the day, by him set for them, the fatal day of his own destruction. To do this, and upon so short warning to do it;
for all this was done in the space of four and twenty hours.
Prov. 21. 1. Wherein, we see it verified, that Solomon saith: that "the
King's heart is in God's hand, and He turns it as a water-
course," to run which way He will have it; and otherwhile
makes a dam in it, and diverts the current a quite contrary

way, clean back upon Haman, to overflow him, and to drown him. Thus did He with them.

And so did He with us, and more also; and that, in less time. For, ours was nearer than so; and the nearer it came, the fairer our lot, to escape it.

For, with them, the fourteenth of Adar was not yet come: the posts had time to go and come, before it; but with us, it stayed till the very day itself was come. In a night, both: but ours, the night, the next night before; so was not theirs. Ever, the Scripture doth press this point: not "till the day, Mat. 24. Noah entered into the ark;" not "till that morning, that Lot went out of Sodom." So ours, not till the very night immediately preceding the dismal day itself. And then, when powder, and train, and match and all were in a readiness, then comes me God with His, *Stulte, hâc nocte,* and dashes all. They were delivered, before the day came: the Lu. 12. 20. day itself came, before we were delivered; it was *hâc nocte,* indeed, literally. So, we escaped more narrowly; our lot more near the drawing. So, ours was *potior tempore.*

And *potior jure* too. For, though the same issue, to both; 4. yet in that also, have we the better. A delivery there is mentioned, in the one hundred and twenty-fourth Psalm: "Our Ps. 124. 7. soul is scaped even as the bird out of the snare of the fowler; the snare is broke, and we are delivered." And this is worth the drawing. But, this is but Pur, a single lot: for, if that be all, the bird is escaped, and that is well for the bird; but, the fowler, (save that he is a little deluded,) he is not hurt; and so, he can soon set another snare again. This is but Pur.

But Purim is better; when the fowl scapes, and the fowler escapes not, but comes himself to a foul end. "The snare is broken:" no, the snare is whole, and they taken in the snare. It sprung only, and away went the fowl; but with the spring, the knot was knit anew, and Haman, and his fellow-fowlers caught and strangled in it.

And this, lo, is Purim: Purim, after the Hebrew idiom, is the great lot. To scape a snare; and in the same snare to have (not their foot, but) their neck taken that set it: there is no greater. The Passover is no greater: there they scaped, and Pharaoh drowned; here, they scaped, and Haman hanged.

Mat. 24. 38.
Lu. 17. 29.

The issue.

SERM.
  X.

[Esth. 9.
25.]

Esther 7.3.

Ps. 21. 11.

Job 20. 29.

Ps. 16. 6.

Will ye look back to the King's sentence at the five and
twentieth verse? This it is: *Malum, quod cogitavit contra
vos, avertatur in caput ipsius ;* not, *Avertatur a capitibus ves-
tris :* Esther's first petition was no more: "Let my life be
given me," turn away my destruction: that it is too; but
that is not it. This is it: *Convertatur in caput ipsius,* the
evil he devised, be it turned away from your heads (that is
well): not a hair fall from any of our heads; but the same
evil they devised, be it turned upon their own heads that
were the devisers, this is it: and this is as much as the King
could grant, or the Queen could desire.

And this same is the lot of this day. "They imagined
such a device as they" were near the performing, yet "were
not able to perform." The non-performance was well, the
scattering of their imaginations; we scaped by the means.
But further, they were taken in their own turn, and the evil
they devised against us, returned upon their own heads;
their heads, and quarters both. To Haman's end they came :
nay, to a worse than Haman's, and justly; for, their device,
worse than his. The place, they meant to have done execution upon us in, under the same place, they themselves executed. Before their eyes, on whom their cruel bowels had
no compassion, were their cruel bowels burnt. The heads,
from which it came, to have blown up the house; the house
hath blown up their heads, and so they be Agagites right.
Their bodies plucked in pieces, their quarters rent in sunder:
so their meaning was to have dealt with ours: "This is the
lot of the ungodly from the Lord." Their evil lot, and (under
one) the same, the happy lot of our deliverance.

And so we have done with Purim now. For, by this it is
plain, 1. ours was altogether without means, and so more lot-
like; 2. ours was more miraculous in the manner, and (for all
the world) like a lot; 3. ours was more near brought in time,
and, like a lot, drawn at the instant; 4. ours was beyond
theirs, in the *avertatur ;* for, ours without sackcloth or ashes,
fasting or crying at all; and in the *convertatur ;* for, our
fowlers came to a fouler end than theirs; and what would
we more? Never might David more truly say, than we,
"The lot is fallen to us in a fair ground, the Lord hath
maintained our lot."

This, God hath drawn for us: shall we now draw for Him again ; and for this so fair a lot, allot Him somewhat of our part? *Memento* is set before the great, and so before all holy-days. All He would draw from us is, but that the lot of this day, or the day of this lot, may never be forgotten. A benefit would not be forgotten; not man's : God's much less. Such a benefit especially. For, even in God's there is a difference : God hath His daily benefits, and those to be remembered of course. But, some other He hath so rare, as the like never seen: those would have a more than ordinary regard. For, where God is extraordinary, we to be so too. If He make it a memorable day, by some strange delivery, we to make it memorable, by some rare acknowledgment. They seem willing so to do, here. *Illi sunt dies quos,* say they. *Ille est dies quem,* may we say, *nulla unquam delebit oblivio;* and so let us say: and so said, and so done, is as much as God re-quireth. But our thankfulness is not to fly away, like a flash of powder. To fix it then, *fiat volatile fixum;* that would be done. And, fix it, in any thing else but time, time will eat it out. Best then fix it in time itself: and, that hath been ever thought a wise way ; so shall it roll about with the time, and renew as it doth. And so, time, which defaceth all things and bringeth them to forgetfulness, shall be made to preserve the memory of it, whether it will or no. Fix it in time: what part of time ? A day : *Memento diem,* saith God in His law, and so points us to the proportion of it. Set some day ; and let there, then on that day, be some special commemoration of it.

1. This lot to have a time of remem-brance.

But, that day, or time, is to be a set day. Fix it in time; but fix the time too. The word of the text, וְיֹם, is an ap-pointed day, that comes once a year ; as *solenne* is *quod solum in anno.* Now this, some will not hear of: no set days, no appointed times, they ; but keep them in memory, all the year long. I like not that. For so, when time was, it was said by some, they would not have this day nor that day to fast on, but keep a continual fast, they : and it seemed a pretty speculation at first, but proved nothing but a specu-lation : what their fast is come to, by this time we see. It is to be doubted, if other set times were likewise taken away, their continual feast would prove to no better pass, than

2. A set time, or day.

SERM.
X.
their fast is: better be as it is, and we do, as God and good
people have done before us.

Provided that it shall be lawful for them to keep the
memory of this day, every day, if they be so disposed. So
yet, as they be content to allow some such day, as this, for
them that are not of so happy memories; for fear, lest if it
be left at large to every man's daily devotion, it may fall to
be forgotten; and where it now hath one day, then to have
none at all.

3.
The day it
fell on.
And if a set time, what day can we set so fit, as the day
itself it fell on? With them, the fourteenth of Adar; with
us, the fifth of November. It cannot but be the best way
(this) that God took Himself: and God took this. The same

Lev. 23. 5. days, He did His noble acts upon, those very days did He
order once a-year solemnly to be kept. The fourteenth of
Nisan, did the destroyer pass over them; that day, from year

Lev. 23. 16. to year, did He ordain the Passover to be holden. Fifty
days after, He granted them His law: in memory of this
gift, they to keep yearly the day of Pentecost. Can we go
by a better example than this of God's own?

These two were not all; but God did as great acts after,
as these were, for the same people. They then, setting
before them this way scored them out by God (for every
famous benefit, a solemn day); for those other benefits after
vouchsafed them, they did appoint like solemn days, of
themselves.

We instance in this of Purim, which Moses and the Prophets never knew. We instance in another after this, which
Esther or Mordecai never knew, the *encænia*, or feast of new
dedicating the temple, after it had been polluted by Antio-
chus, recorded in the tenth chapter, twenty-second verse of
John. And I would fain know, why it should not be like
acceptable to God, to keep the fourteenth of the last month
Adar, for their deliverance from Haman by Esther in Persia;
as it was, to keep the fourteenth of the first month Nisan,
for their deliverance from Pharaoh by Moses in Egypt: *Quid
interest?*

The ground being moral, or rather natural, as reducible
to thankfulness, which is a virtue of the law of nature: the
prime example being God's own: by warrant of it, the former

Church having institute others, the Christian Church knew
nothing to bar it from doing the like: so holydays she appointed too. It is St. Augustine (*de Civitate* x. 4): *Memo-* [X. 3.
riam beneficiorum Dei, &c. 'The memory of God's benefits Ben. ed.]
we Christians keep sacred and holy, by holding solemn feasts
for them, lest else, by revolution of time, forgetfulness might
creep upon us, and we prove unthankful.' And do we any
other thing in appointing this day, than all these did? I
conclude, with the style of the Councils: *Sequentes igitur et
nos per omnia Sanctorum Patrum vestigia;* 'We, herein, do
but tread in the steps of our holy Fathers,' and follow them
who were followers therein of God Himself.

If it be said, All this while we hear no precept alleged,
we have nothing but example: no more had Esther here;
precept had she none. Only God's example she had: picked
the fourteenth of Adar out of the fourteenth of Nisan: from
Pharaoh, that; from Haman, this. It is true, *Dirigimur
præceptis,* 'By precepts we take our direction;' but it is no
less true, *Instruimur exemplis,* 'We receive instruction, in
a great part, from examples also.' One serves for our rule, the
other for our pattern; and we, as to obey the one, so to imitate the other; for, *Perfectio inferiorum assimilatio superio-
rum,* 'The inferior hath no greater perfection, than to become
like to them that are his superiors.' 'Superiors,' I say, and
that, in time, no less than in place; that is, such as have in
former times laudably gone before us. The Bible sheweth
this plain: there, beside the books of the law, that serve for
precepts to direction, God hath caused to be written the story
of the Bible, to yield us examples, for imitation. And those
books of story are in Hebrew called, The former Prophets;
to shew, before there came any predictions into the world,
there was a prophetical force in them, to guide God's people
by. "To the law, and to the testimony;" for the practice [Isai. 8. 20.]
of the saints runneth along with the law, under the name of
"testimony;" their lives having ever borne testimony to God
and His truth. And as the Hebrews say, A barren divine
shall he be, *qui nescit facere legem de prophetis,* 'that out of
the saints' practice, cannot frame a law.'

The ground then being laid: if this be agreed of, that
a day, that a set day, and that this very day may be ap-

SERM. pointed; we have two points more to touch; 1. the authority
X. by which it is to be enjoined; and the 2. manner, according
to which it is to be observed.

II.
The au-
thority by
which it
was en-
joined.

1. The authority first. For, be the ground never so good,
yet are not we to take up days, of our own heads, but by
order of authority; they are to be enjoined us. Whose authority here? There be in a law but three things, 1. advice,
2. authority, 3. and submission; they be all here. It should
seem, at the first, Mordecai did only by a letter advise them,
ut susciperent et revertente semper anno celebrarent honore,
verse the twentieth, before; and this, before he was in place.
That letter of his, either not taking place, or not place
enough; and they being either laid down, or so like to be,
here cometh now שינית, a second, to confirm that, as the word
is, and this no advice now, but בכל תוקף, with all authority;
of the nature of a law, to establish them for ever.

Now, this could not Mordecai, nor Esther, nay nor both
of them do, of themselves, in Persia; not without the regal
authority there, or without commission from it. Not send
over the hundred twenty-seven provinces; nay, not over any
one province of them, but by vigour of Ahasuerus' warrant.
His warrant they had at the twenty-fifth verse, and by it
proceeded they, to do all this. What Esther did, she did
in the power of Ahasuerus.

Now Ahasuerus, it is well known, was a heathen King;
yet have we here a feast established by his authority. So
Jonah 3 7. was the King of Nineveh a heathen too; yet have we a fast
Dan. 3. 29. enjoined by his. So was the King of Babel a heathen King;
yet a law by him made, upon pain of death not to blaspheme
Ezra 5. 13; the true God. So were Cyrus and Darius; yet the temple
6. 12. built by their authority. Things pertaining to religion, all.
So that there is, in the regal power, of all, yea, even of
heathen Princes, to confirm and to enjoin what may tend
to the worship and service of God.

Power against the truth, or for falsehood, I know none: no
2 Cor. 13. " power to destruction;" to " edification," all. And " prayer
10.
1 Tim. 2. 2. is to be made," without ceasing, " for Kings," that they may
apply their power to these, to edify in the truth. So they
will, if Mordecai may be in place to advise them, not Haman.
But if they misapply it, and not to the end God gave it them

(for He that gave it them is to take account of them for it, and He will require it at their hands); to Him they be respondent.

But, be this, here, and ever remembered: if by a heathen Prince's power this was done, shall it be denied to a Christian Prince, to one in whom Ahasuerus' power and Esther's religion both meet, to take order for days, or rather rites of that nature? Well then, having both our ground, and our authority, לקים, (which word is three several times repeated in this one verse): 1. once for Mordecai that advised; 2. once for Esther that enjoined; and 3. once for the people that undertook to observe it; it is the Jews' operative word whereby they enact all their statutes: Be it then enacted. What? *Ut nulli liceat dies hos absque* [Esther 9. *solennitate transigere*, verse the twenty-seventh; "That it 27.] be lawful for no man to pass these days without solemnizing."

To a law there go two כאשר, two *caashers*, two "accordings." Both twain are here: 1. "according" as Esther, with Mordecai's advice, enjoined it; 2. and "according" as they (that is, the people) took upon them, decreed to observe it.

Which observing is the life of every law: even the public approbation, or giving allowance of it, by the constant keeping it. The second "according" is added for the people's commendation: that what was prudently advised, and lawfully enjoined, was by them as dutifully observed.

And this they not only did, but bound themselves moreover, and their seed, so to continue. Themselves, and that with the highest bond, *super animas suas;* (which is more than upon themselves, and would not have been put in the margin, but stood in the text;) upon theirs, and upon their seeds, never to let them fall. The word is קבל at the twenty-seventh verse; that is, to make a *kabala*, or tradition of it. And that is the true tradition indeed: when a thing orderly taken up (there is קים) is carefully and out of conscience kept up, (there is קבל) and delivered over from the father to the son, and from the son to the nephew, to all succeeding ages;

SERM. none daring to transgress it, on the charge of their souls.
  X.   This *kabala* made it a perfect law.

2.   Now, a word of the manner of the keeping them, and so
The man- an end. They enacted to keep the Purim-days. How to
ner of
keeping it. keep them? It will lead us, this, to the nature of them,
whether as holydays or no. For, at this, there be that
stick too. A *feria* they will allow them, a play-day, or
ceasing from work; or a *festus dies*, if you will, a day of
feasting, or increase of fare; but not *dies sanctus*, no holyday, not at any hand; for, then may Esther make holydays
(they see) it follows. What should one say to such men as
these?

For 1. first, it is plain by this verse, they took it *in animas*,
"upon their souls;" a soul-matter they made of it. There
needs no soul for *feria* or *festum*, play or feasting. 2. Secondly,
the bond of it reacheth to all, that *religioni eorum voluerunt
copulari* (verse the twenty-seventh), "to all that should join
themselves to their religion." Then, a matter of religion it
was, had reference to that: what need any joining in religion,
for a matter of good-fellowship? 3. Thirdly, it is expressly
termed a rite and a ceremony, at the twenty-third and
twenty-eighth verses, as the Fathers read them: rites, I
trust, and ceremonies (as holydays are no more:) pertain to
the Church, and to the service of God; not to merry meetings; that is not their place. 4. Fourthly, they fast and
pray here, in this verse; fast the eve, the fourteenth, and so
then the day following to be holyday, of course. 5. Fifthly,
with fasting and prayer here, alms also is enjoined, at the
twenty-second verse. These three will make it past a day
of revels or mirth. 6. Lastly, as a holyday the Jews ever
kept it, have a peculiar set service for it, in their seders; set
psalms to sing, set lessons to read, set prayers to say (and
that at four several times as, out of Nehemiah the ninth
chapter, and the third verse, their manner is on holydays),
good and godly, all. None, but as they have used, from all
antiquity. 1. Being then taken on their souls; 2. restrained
to the same religion; 3. directly termed a ceremony; 4.
being to be held with fasting, prayers, and 5. alms, works
of piety all; 6. the practice of the Church concurring;

theirs was a holyday clear, and so ought ours to be. Thus have we a precedent upon record, to draw up ours by; the superiors to enjoin such a day; the inferiors to observe it.

And as a warrant to do it; so, a rule how to do it : with fasting and with crying, that is, prayer, earnest prayer (the last word). What, and must we fast then? That were no good lot in the end of a text. No: if we will pray, well : I dare take upon me, to excuse us from fasting. Their fasting was, to put them in mind of the fast, their fathers used, by means whereof they turned God, and God turned the King's heart, and so all turned to their good. But, for us, we have no such means to remember in ours; we used not any, and so hold ours without any. They had two days; their holyday had a fasting day. Our lot is to have but one; and that, no fasting day; an immunity from that. So much the better is our lot; a feast, without any fast at all. _{Esther 4. 3}

But though without fasting, not without earnest prayer (meant here by crying); nor without earnest thanks and praise, neither. For joy also hath her cry, as well as affliction : "The voice of joy and health is in the dwellings of the righteous." But, prayer (sure) will do well at all hands, that a worse thing happen not to us. But, prayer is but one wing : with alms it will do better, make a pair of wings; which is before prescribed, at the two-and-twentieth verse. "So to eat the fat and drink the sweet ourselves, as we send a part to them for whom nothing is provided : *Dies enim sanctus est,*" saith Nehemiah; for, by his rule, that makes it a right holyday. _{Ps. 118. 15} _{Neh. 8. 10.}

But, prayer is the last word here, ends the verse; and with that, let us end. Even that all, that shall ever attempt the like, let Haman's lot be their lot, and let never any other light on them but, *sors funiculus.* Let Queen Esther's prayer, and King Ahasuerus' sentence ever take place : *Malum quod cogitavit, convertatur in caput ipsius : ipsius,* or *ipsorum,* one, or many. "Let not the rod of the ungodly light on the lot of the righteous. Let God, in Whose hand our lots are, ever maintain this day's lot to us; never give _{Ps. 125. 3.}

SERM. forth other, but as in this text, and as on this day, on the
X. fourteenth of Adar, and on the fifth of November. And
praised be God, this day, and all our days, That this day
Ps. 35. 27. shewed, that He taketh "pleasure in the prosperity of His
servants," and from all lots and plots doth ever deliver
them.

END OF VOL. IV.

Made in the USA
Columbia, SC
20 October 2022

69776762R00233